THE INVINCIBLE IRON MAN

WORLD'S MOST WANTED

INVINCIBLE IRON MAN VOL. 2: WORLD'S MOST WANTED ... BLE IRON MAN #8-13. First printing 2009. Hardcover ISBN# 978-0-7851-3828-0. Softcover ISBN# 978-0-7851-3413-8. P... ICE OF PUBLICATION: 417, 5th Avenue, New York, NY 10016. Copyright © 2008 and 2009 Marvel Characters, Inc. All rights r... copy in the U.S. (GST #R127032852). Canadian Agreement #40668537. All characters featured in this issue and the distin... acters, Inc. No similarity between any of the names, characters, persons, and/or institutions in this magazine with those of... rist is purely coincidental. Printed in the U.S.A. ALAN FINE, EVP - Office Of The Chief Executive Marvel Entertainment, Inc... edia; JIM SOKOLOWSKI, Chief Operating Officer; DAVID GABRIEL, SVP of Publishing Sales & Circulation; DAVID BOGART, S... ommunications; JIM O'KEEFE, VP of Operations & Logistics; DAN CARR, Executive Director of Publishing Technology; JUS... rations Manager; ALEX MORALES, Publishing Operations Manager; STAN

THE INVINCIBLE IRON MAN

WORLD'S MOST WANTED

WRITER: **MATT FRACTION**
ARTIST: **SALVADOR LARROCA**
COLORS: **FRANK D'ARMATA**
LETTERS: **VC'S JOE CARAMAGNA**
ASSISTANT EDITOR: **ALEJANDRO ARBONA**
EDITOR: **WARREN SIMONS**

COLLECTION EDITOR: **JENNIFER GRÜNWALD**
EDITORIAL ASSISTANT: **ALEX STARBUCK**
ASSISTANT EDITORS: **CORY LEVINE & JOHN DENNING**
EDITOR, SPECIAL PROJECTS: **MARK D. BEAZLEY**
SENIOR EDITOR, SPECIAL PROJECTS: **JEFF YOUNGQUIST**
SENIOR VICE PRESIDENT OF SALES: **DAVID GABRIEL**
BOOK DESIGNER: **RODOLFO MURAGUCHI**

EDITOR IN CHIEF: **JOE QUESADA**
PUBLISHER: **DAN BUCKLEY**
EXECUTIVE PRODUCER: **ALAN FINE**

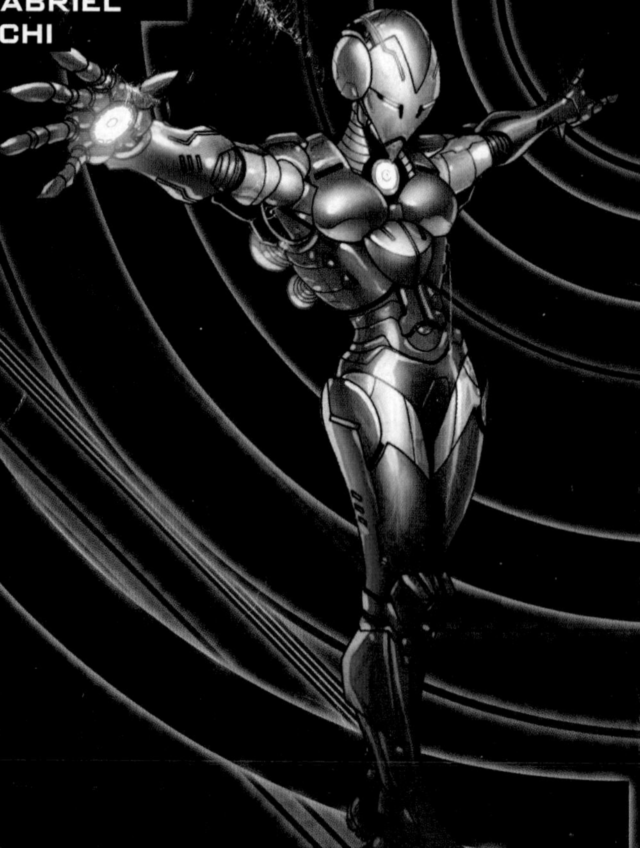

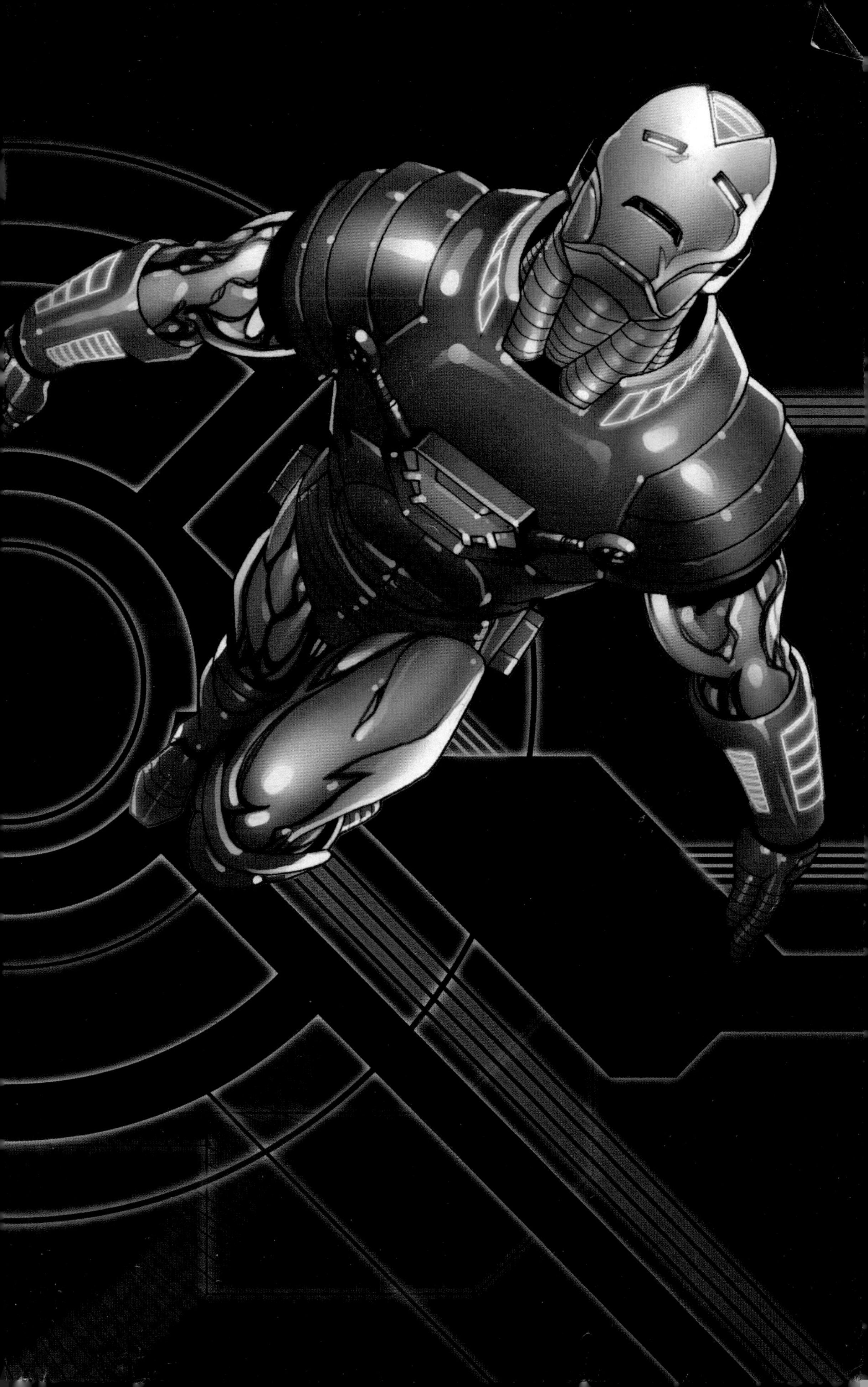

PREVIOUSLY:

Tony Stark has faced and defeated his worst nightmare — a maniac super-terrorist aping Tony's own technology and selling it on the black market. Attacking multiple targets around the globe, Ezekiel Stane and his suicide armies murdered innocent people, attacked other heroes, and targeted Stark Industries facilities worldwide.

One such attack nearly killed Pepper Potts, Tony's right-hand woman. Her life has been saved by the implantation of electromagnetic repulsor technology, like the technology that set Tony on the path to becoming Iron Man.

And then the Skrull invasion came.

Shape-shifting aliens infiltrated all aspects of human life, and planted a destructive virus in Stark technology, causing it to fail around the world — from cell phones to toasters to the Extremis armor that made Tony Stark into Iron Man. In the ashes of the invasion, Stark technology is synonymous with failure.

Tony Stark held himself accountable for his failure to prevent the invasion. For his troubles, he was stripped of his roles as leader of the Avengers and director of a now defunct S.H.I.E.L.D.

Norman Osborn, the man behind the government-sponsored super-villain team, the Thunderbolts, has risen to power in Tony's place. With Stark and S.H.I.E.L.D. out, Osborn now sits at the head of the newly formed peacekeeping agency, H.A.M.M.E.R.

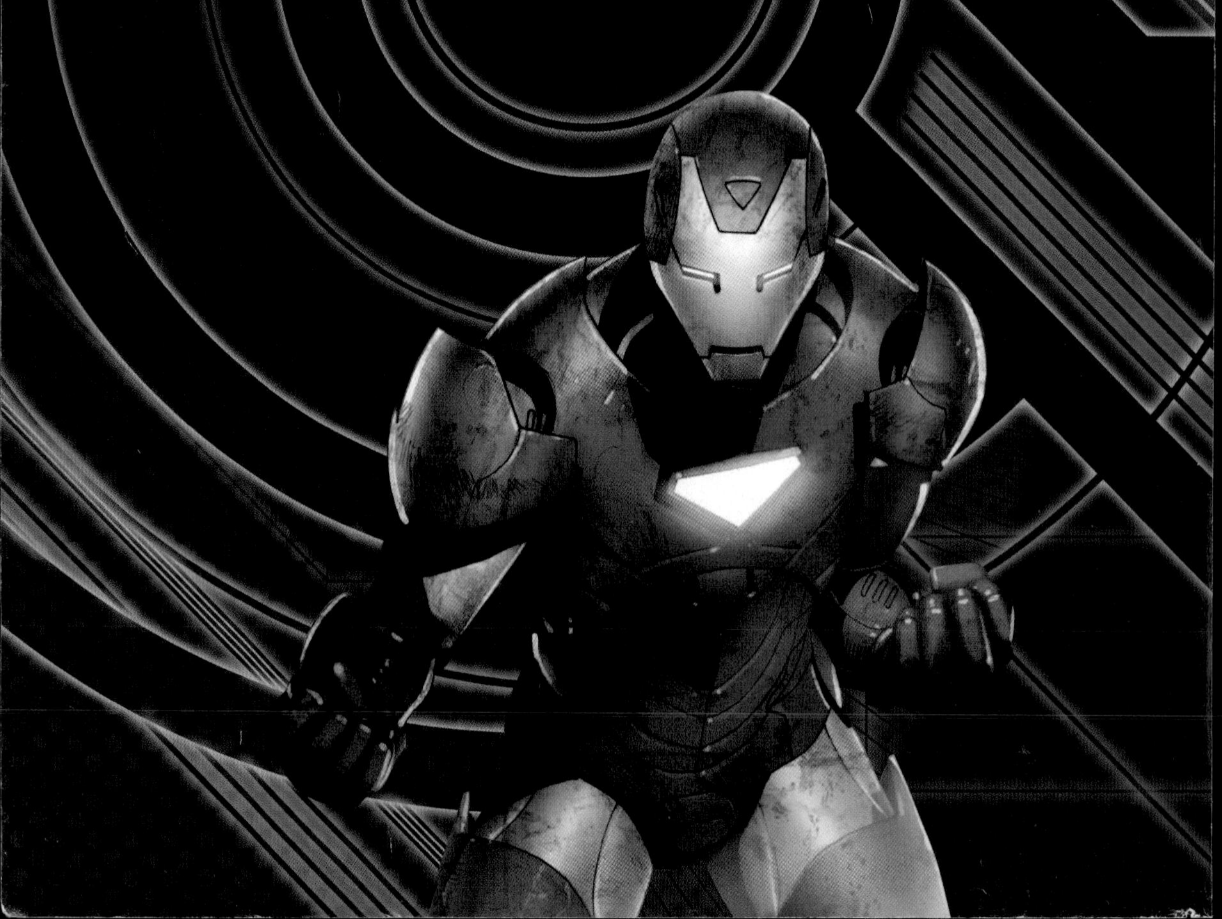

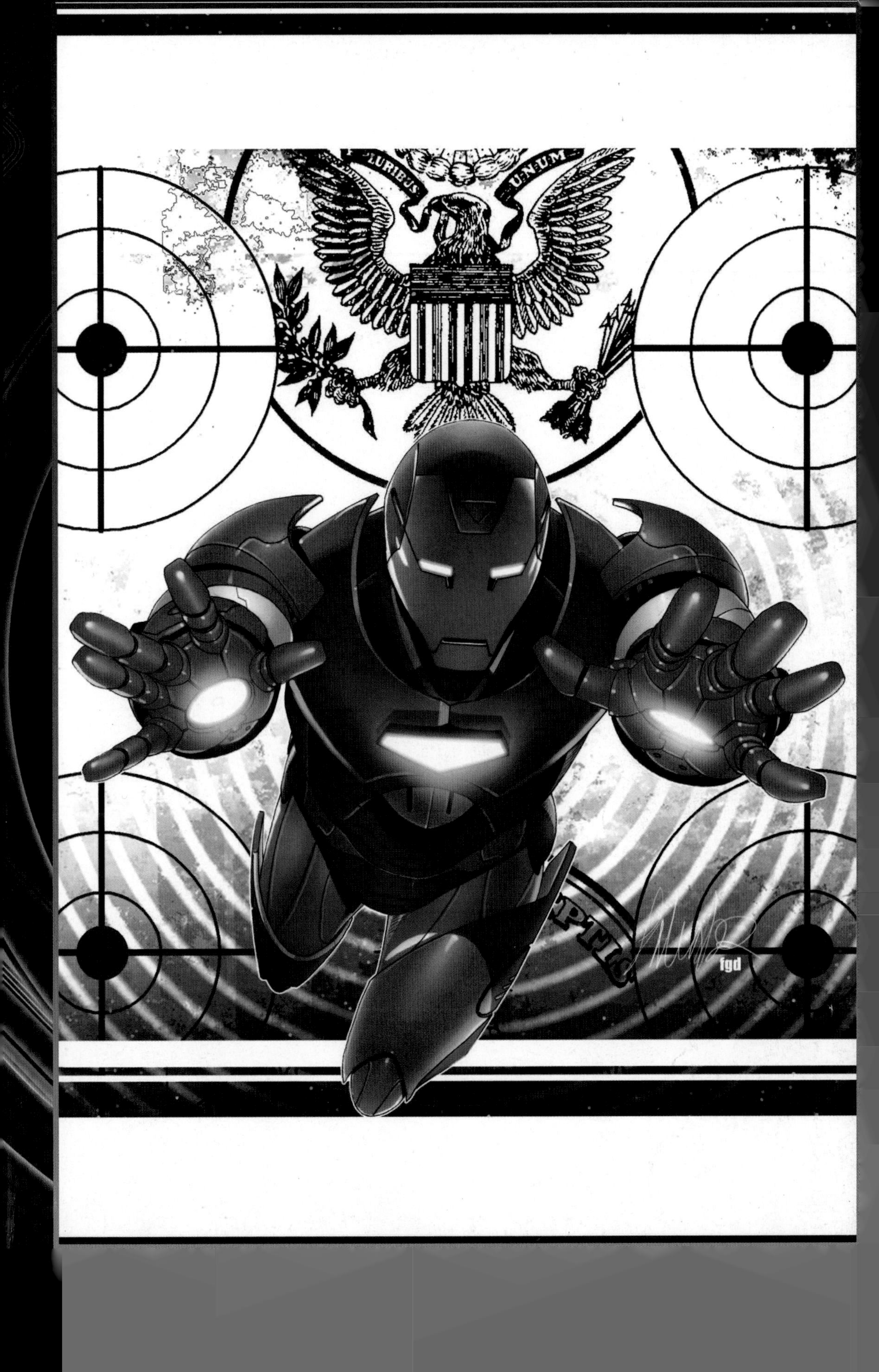
fgd

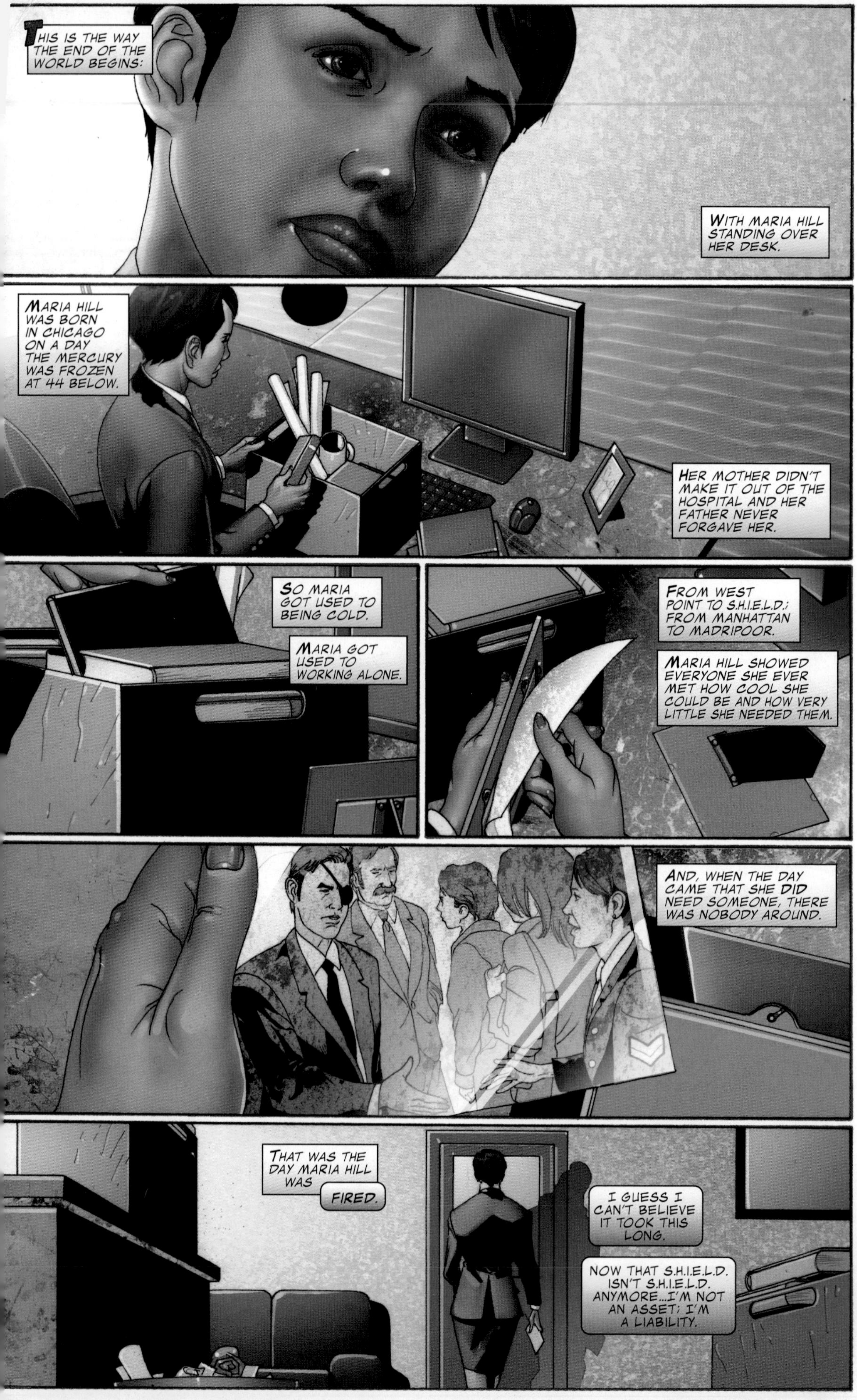
THIS IS THE WAY THE END OF THE WORLD BEGINS:
WITH MARIA HILL STANDING OVER HER DESK.
MARIA HILL WAS BORN IN CHICAGO ON A DAY THE MERCURY WAS FROZEN AT 44 BELOW.
HER MOTHER DIDN'T MAKE IT OUT OF THE HOSPITAL AND HER FATHER NEVER FORGAVE HER.
SO MARIA GOT USED TO BEING COLD.
MARIA GOT USED TO WORKING ALONE.
FROM WEST POINT TO S.H.I.E.L.D.; FROM MANHATTAN TO MADRIPOOR.
MARIA HILL SHOWED EVERYONE SHE EVER MET HOW COOL SHE COULD BE AND HOW VERY LITTLE SHE NEEDED THEM.
AND, WHEN THE DAY CAME THAT SHE DID NEED SOMEONE, THERE WAS NOBODY AROUND.
THAT WAS THE DAY MARIA HILL WAS
FIRED.
I GUESS I CAN'T BELIEVE IT TOOK THIS LONG.
NOW THAT S.H.I.E.L.D. ISN'T S.H.I.E.L.D. ANYMORE...I'M NOT AN ASSET; I'M A LIABILITY.

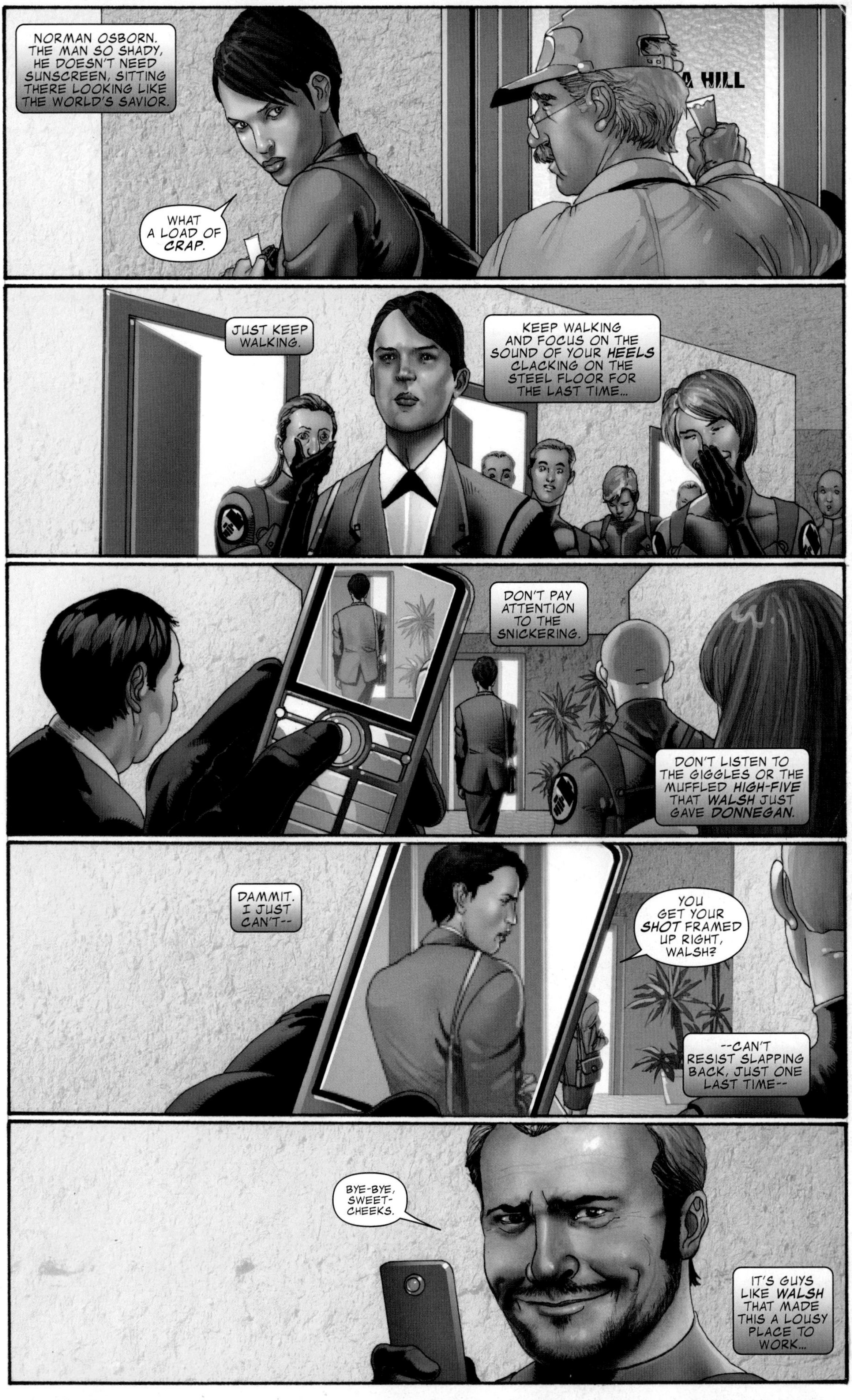
NORMAN OSBORN. THE MAN SO SHADY, HE DOESN'T NEED SUNSCREEN, SITTING THERE LOOKING LIKE THE WORLD'S SAVIOR.
WHAT A LOAD OF *CRAP*.
JUST KEEP WALKING.
KEEP WALKING AND FOCUS ON THE SOUND OF YOUR *HEELS* CLACKING ON THE STEEL FLOOR FOR THE LAST TIME...
DON'T PAY ATTENTION TO THE SNICKERING.
DON'T LISTEN TO THE GIGGLES OR THE MUFFLED *HIGH-FIVE* THAT *WALSH* JUST GAVE *DONNEGAN*.
DAMMIT. I JUST CAN'T--
YOU GET YOUR *SHOT* FRAMED UP RIGHT, WALSH?
--CAN'T RESIST SLAPPING BACK, JUST ONE LAST TIME--
BYE-BYE, SWEET-CHEEKS.
IT'S GUYS LIKE *WALSH* THAT MADE THIS A LOUSY PLACE TO WORK...

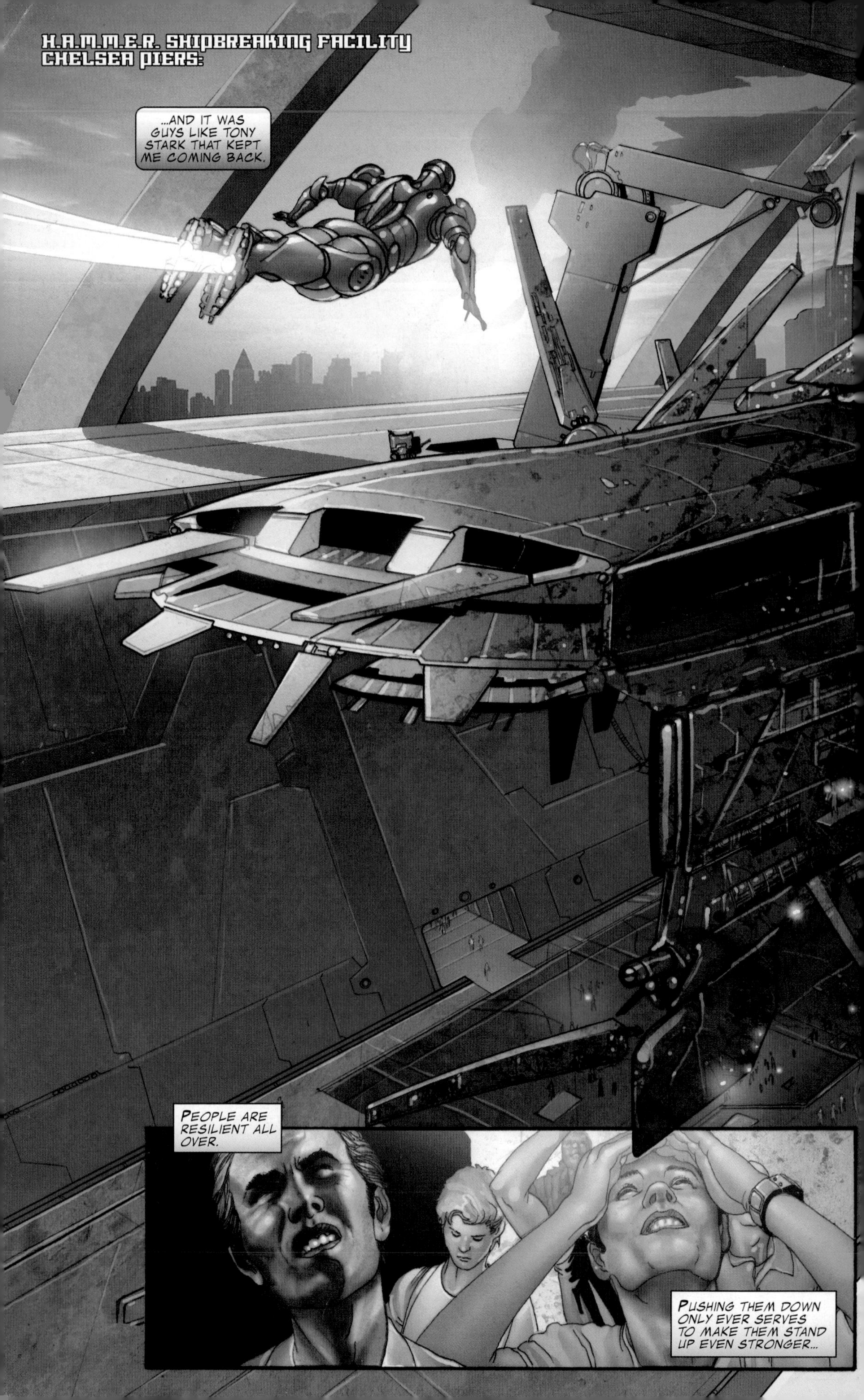
H.A.M.M.E.R. SHIPBREAKING FACILITY
CHELSEA PIERS:
...AND IT WAS GUYS LIKE TONY STARK THAT KEPT ME COMING BACK.
PEOPLE ARE RESILIENT ALL OVER.
PUSHING THEM DOWN ONLY EVER SERVES TO MAKE THEM STAND UP EVEN STRONGER...

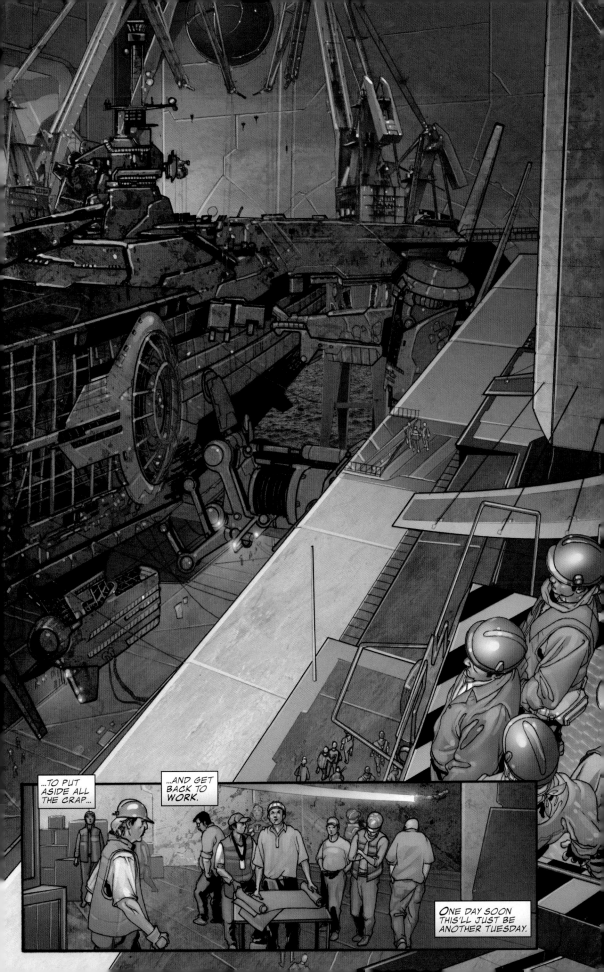

...TO PUT ASIDE ALL THE CRAP...

...AND GET BACK TO WORK.

ONE DAY SOON THIS'LL JUST BE ANOTHER TUESDAY.

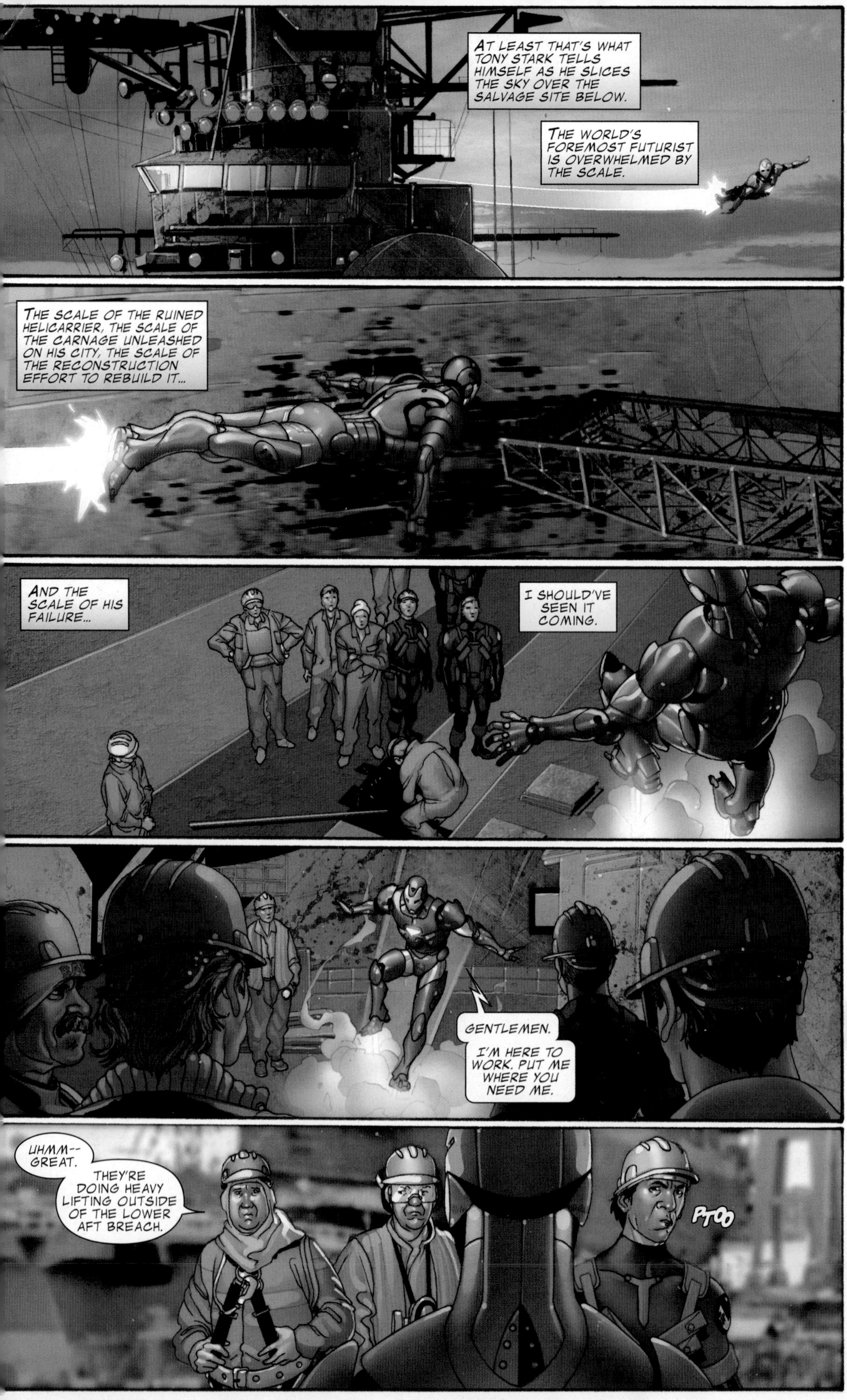
AT LEAST THAT'S WHAT TONY STARK TELLS HIMSELF AS HE SLICES THE SKY OVER THE SALVAGE SITE BELOW.
THE WORLD'S FOREMOST FUTURIST IS OVERWHELMED BY THE SCALE.
THE SCALE OF THE RUINED HELICARRIER, THE SCALE OF THE CARNAGE UNLEASHED ON HIS CITY, THE SCALE OF THE RECONSTRUCTION EFFORT TO REBUILD IT...
AND THE SCALE OF HIS FAILURE...
I SHOULD'VE SEEN IT COMING.
GENTLEMEN.
I'M HERE TO WORK. PUT ME WHERE YOU NEED ME.
UHMM-- GREAT.
THEY'RE DOING HEAVY LIFTING OUTSIDE OF THE LOWER AFT BREACH.
PTOO

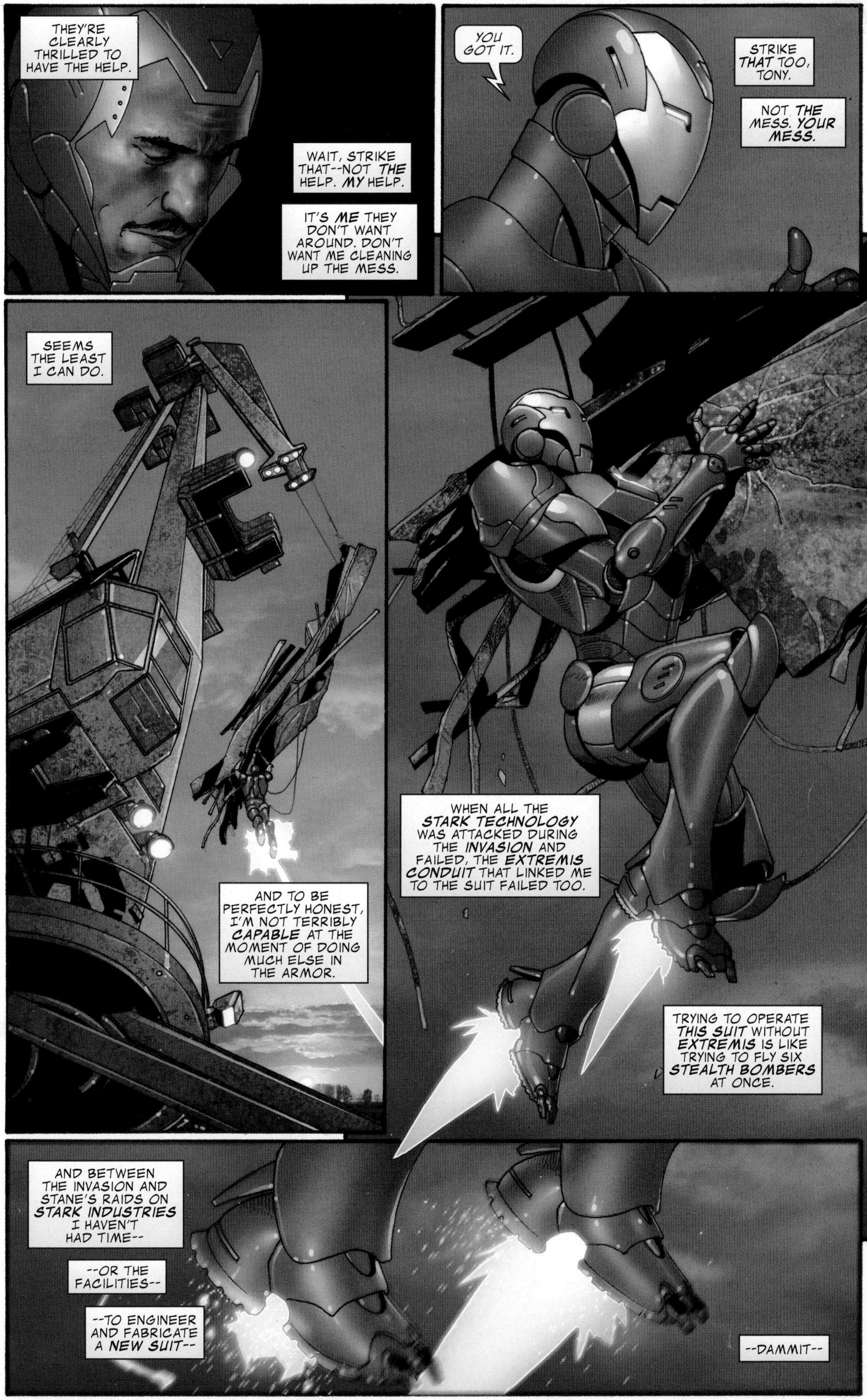

THEY'RE CLEARLY THRILLED TO HAVE THE HELP.
WAIT, STRIKE THAT--NOT THE HELP. MY HELP.
IT'S ME THEY DON'T WANT AROUND. DON'T WANT ME CLEANING UP THE MESS.
YOU GOT IT.
STRIKE THAT TOO, TONY.
NOT THE MESS. YOUR MESS.
SEEMS THE LEAST I CAN DO.
AND TO BE PERFECTLY HONEST, I'M NOT TERRIBLY CAPABLE AT THE MOMENT OF DOING MUCH ELSE IN THE ARMOR.
WHEN ALL THE STARK TECHNOLOGY WAS ATTACKED DURING THE INVASION AND FAILED, THE EXTREMIS CONDUIT THAT LINKED ME TO THE SUIT FAILED TOO.
TRYING TO OPERATE THIS SUIT WITHOUT EXTREMIS IS LIKE TRYING TO FLY SIX STEALTH BOMBERS AT ONCE.
AND BETWEEN THE INVASION AND STANE'S RAIDS ON STARK INDUSTRIES I HAVEN'T HAD TIME--
--OR THE FACILITIES--
--TO ENGINEER AND FABRICATE A NEW SUIT--
--DAMMIT--

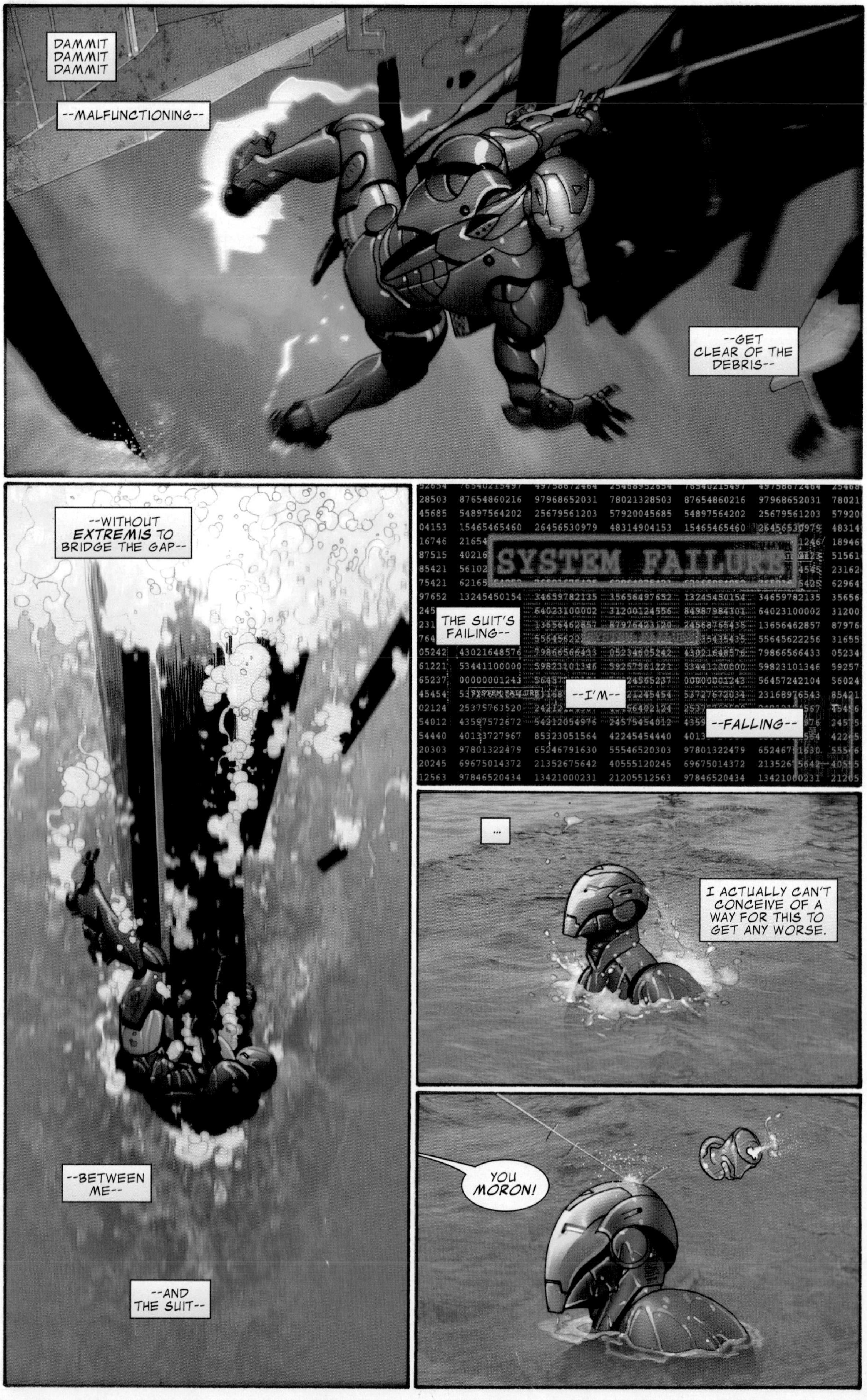
DAMMIT DAMMIT DAMMIT
--MALFUNCTIONING--
--GET CLEAR OF THE DEBRIS--
--WITHOUT EXTREMIS TO BRIDGE THE GAP--
--BETWEEN ME--
--AND THE SUIT--
SYSTEM FAILURE
THE SUIT'S FAILING--
SYSTEM FAILURE
--I'M--
--FALLING--
...
I ACTUALLY CAN'T CONCEIVE OF A WAY FOR THIS TO GET ANY WORSE.
YOU MORON!

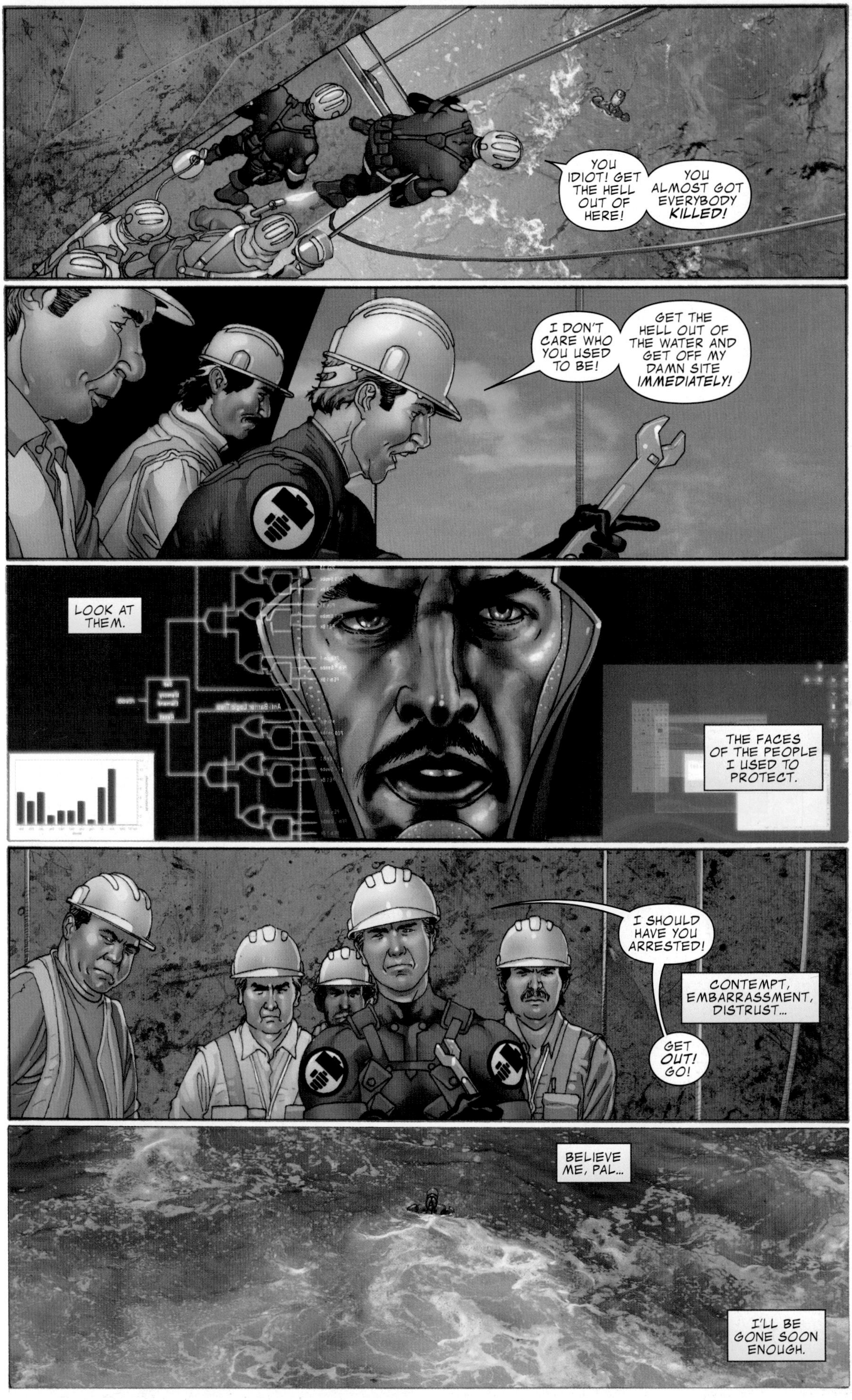
YOU IDIOT! GET THE HELL OUT OF HERE!
YOU ALMOST GOT EVERYBODY KILLED!
I DON'T CARE WHO YOU USED TO BE!
GET THE HELL OUT OF THE WATER AND GET OFF MY DAMN SITE IMMEDIATELY!
LOOK AT THEM.
THE FACES OF THE PEOPLE I USED TO PROTECT.
I SHOULD HAVE YOU ARRESTED!
CONTEMPT, EMBARRASSMENT, DISTRUST...
GET OUT! GO!
BELIEVE ME, PAL...
I'LL BE GONE SOON ENOUGH.

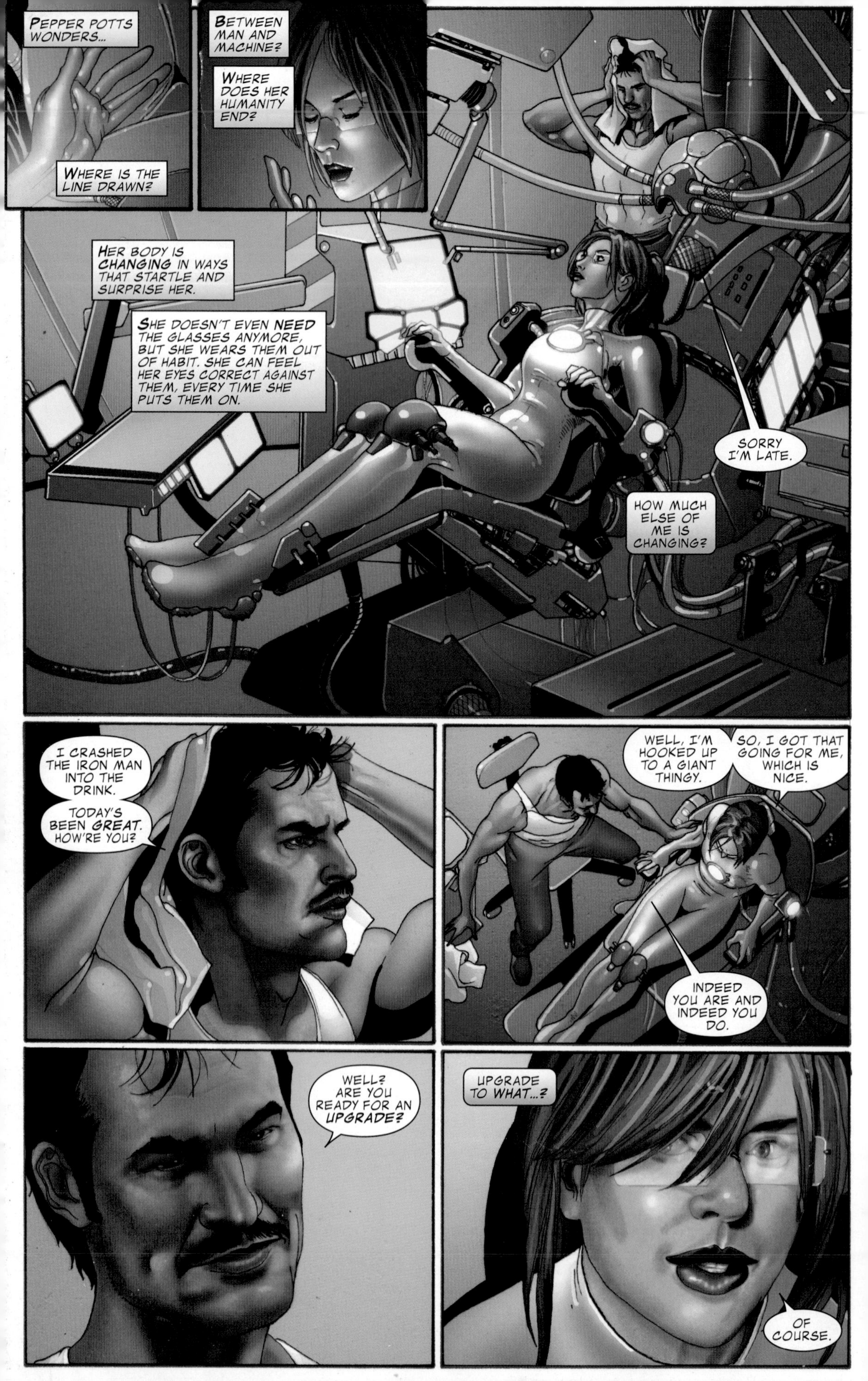
PEPPER POTTS WONDERS...
WHERE IS THE LINE DRAWN?
BETWEEN MAN AND MACHINE?
WHERE DOES HER HUMANITY END?
HER BODY IS CHANGING IN WAYS THAT STARTLE AND SURPRISE HER.
SHE DOESN'T EVEN NEED THE GLASSES ANYMORE, BUT SHE WEARS THEM OUT OF HABIT. SHE CAN FEEL HER EYES CORRECT AGAINST THEM, EVERY TIME SHE PUTS THEM ON.
SORRY I'M LATE.
HOW MUCH ELSE OF ME IS CHANGING?
I CRASHED THE IRON MAN INTO THE DRINK.
TODAY'S BEEN GREAT. HOW'RE YOU?
WELL, I'M HOOKED UP TO A GIANT THINGY.
SO, I GOT THAT GOING FOR ME, WHICH IS NICE.
INDEED YOU ARE AND INDEED YOU DO.
WELL? ARE YOU READY FOR AN UPGRADE?
UPGRADE TO WHAT...?
OF COURSE.

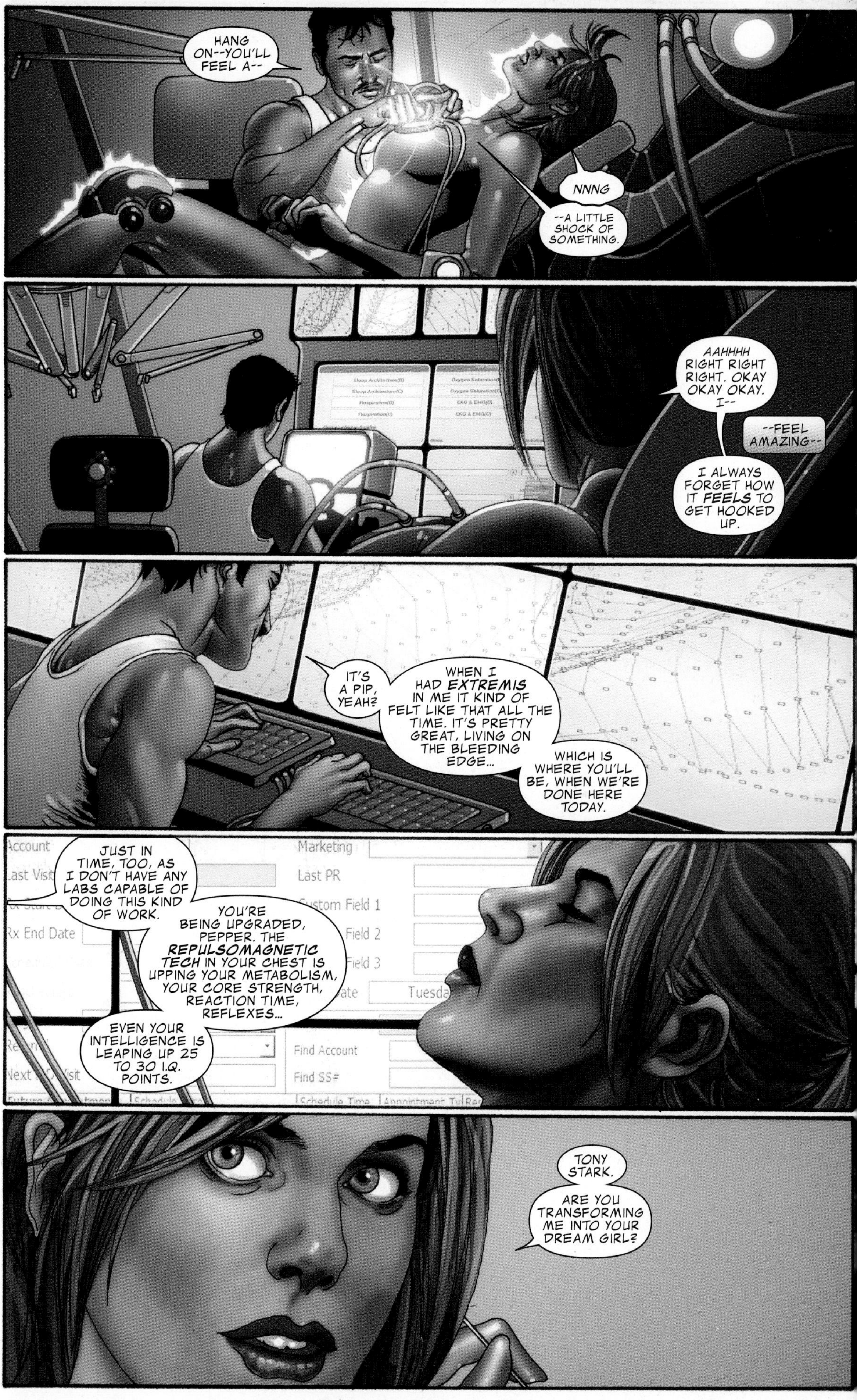
HANG ON--YOU'LL FEEL A--
NNNG
--A LITTLE SHOCK OF SOMETHING.
AAHHHH RIGHT RIGHT RIGHT. OKAY OKAY OKAY. I--
--FEEL AMAZING--
I ALWAYS FORGET HOW IT FEELS TO GET HOOKED UP.
IT'S A PIP, YEAH?
WHEN I HAD EXTREMIS IN ME IT KIND OF FELT LIKE THAT ALL THE TIME. IT'S PRETTY GREAT, LIVING ON THE BLEEDING EDGE...
WHICH IS WHERE YOU'LL BE, WHEN WE'RE DONE HERE TODAY.
JUST IN TIME, TOO, AS I DON'T HAVE ANY LABS CAPABLE OF DOING THIS KIND OF WORK.
YOU'RE BEING UPGRADED, PEPPER. THE REPULSOMAGNETIC TECH IN YOUR CHEST IS UPPING YOUR METABOLISM, YOUR CORE STRENGTH, REACTION TIME, REFLEXES...
EVEN YOUR INTELLIGENCE IS LEAPING UP 25 TO 30 I.Q. POINTS.
TONY STARK.
ARE YOU TRANSFORMING ME INTO YOUR DREAM GIRL?

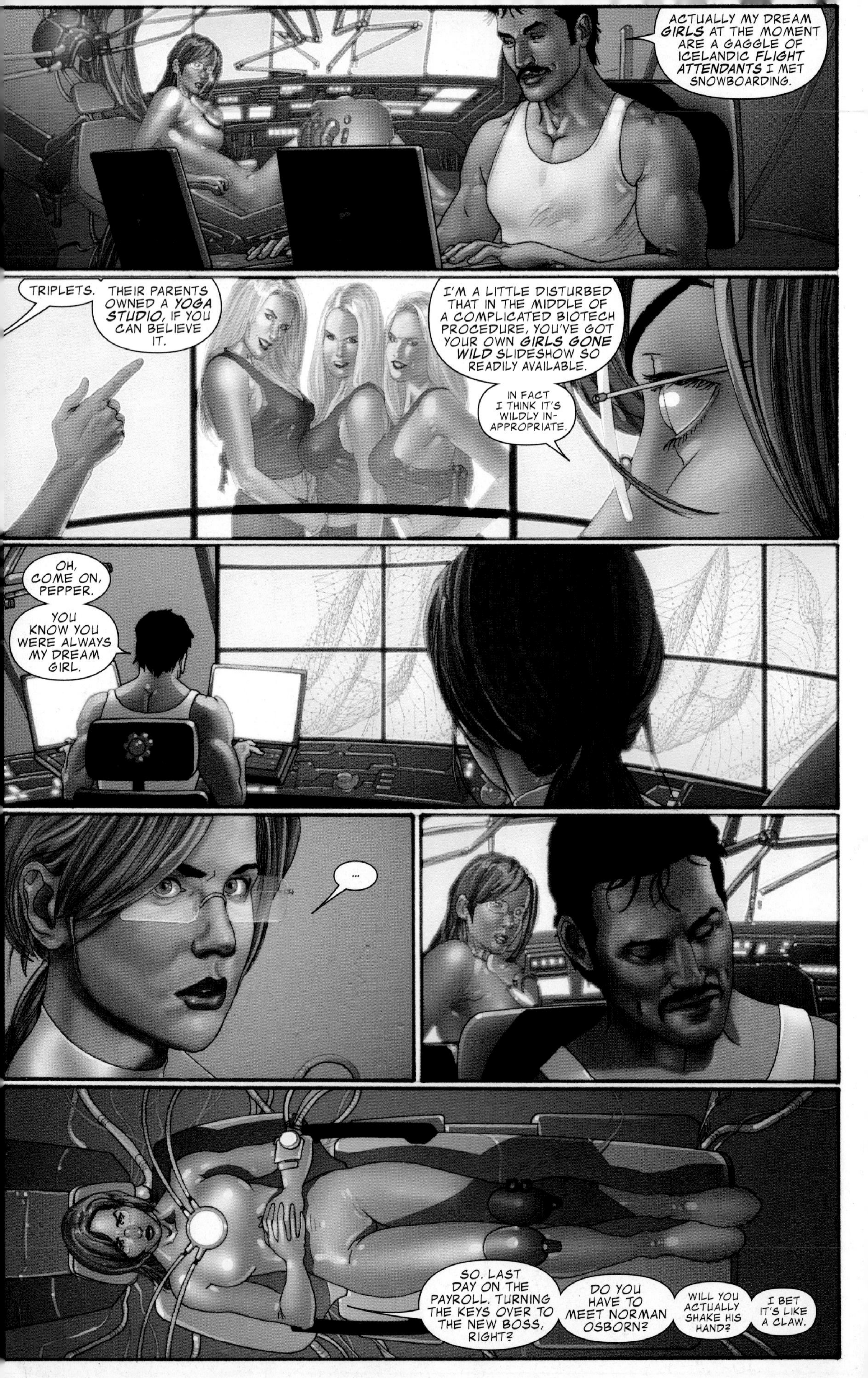
ACTUALLY MY DREAM GIRLS AT THE MOMENT ARE A GAGGLE OF ICELANDIC FLIGHT ATTENDANTS I MET SNOWBOARDING.
TRIPLETS.
THEIR PARENTS OWNED A YOGA STUDIO, IF YOU CAN BELIEVE IT.
I'M A LITTLE DISTURBED THAT IN THE MIDDLE OF A COMPLICATED BIOTECH PROCEDURE, YOU'VE GOT YOUR OWN GIRLS GONE WILD SLIDESHOW SO READILY AVAILABLE.
IN FACT I THINK IT'S WILDLY IN-APPROPRIATE.
OH, COME ON, PEPPER.
YOU KNOW YOU WERE ALWAYS MY DREAM GIRL.
...
SO. LAST DAY ON THE PAYROLL. TURNING THE KEYS OVER TO THE NEW BOSS, RIGHT?
DO YOU HAVE TO MEET NORMAN OSBORN?
WILL YOU ACTUALLY SHAKE HIS HAND?
I BET IT'S LIKE A CLAW.

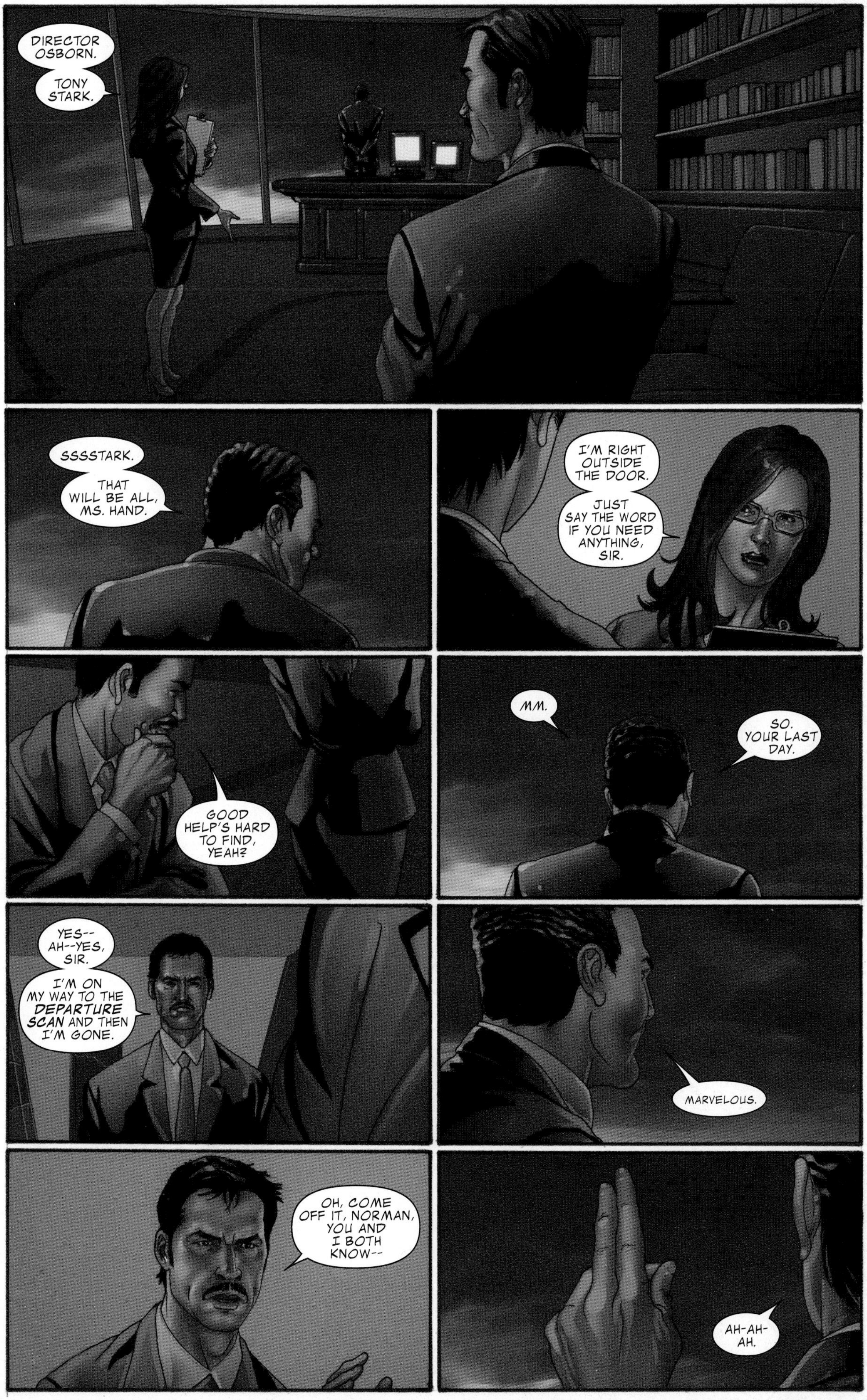
DIRECTOR OSBORN.
TONY STARK.
SSSSTARK.
THAT WILL BE ALL, MS. HAND.
I'M RIGHT OUTSIDE THE DOOR.
JUST SAY THE WORD IF YOU NEED ANYTHING, SIR.
GOOD HELP'S HARD TO FIND, YEAH?
MM.
SO. YOUR LAST DAY.
YES--AH--YES, SIR.
I'M ON MY WAY TO THE DEPARTURE SCAN AND THEN I'M GONE.
MARVELOUS.
OH, COME OFF IT, NORMAN, YOU AND I BOTH KNOW--
AH-AH-AH.

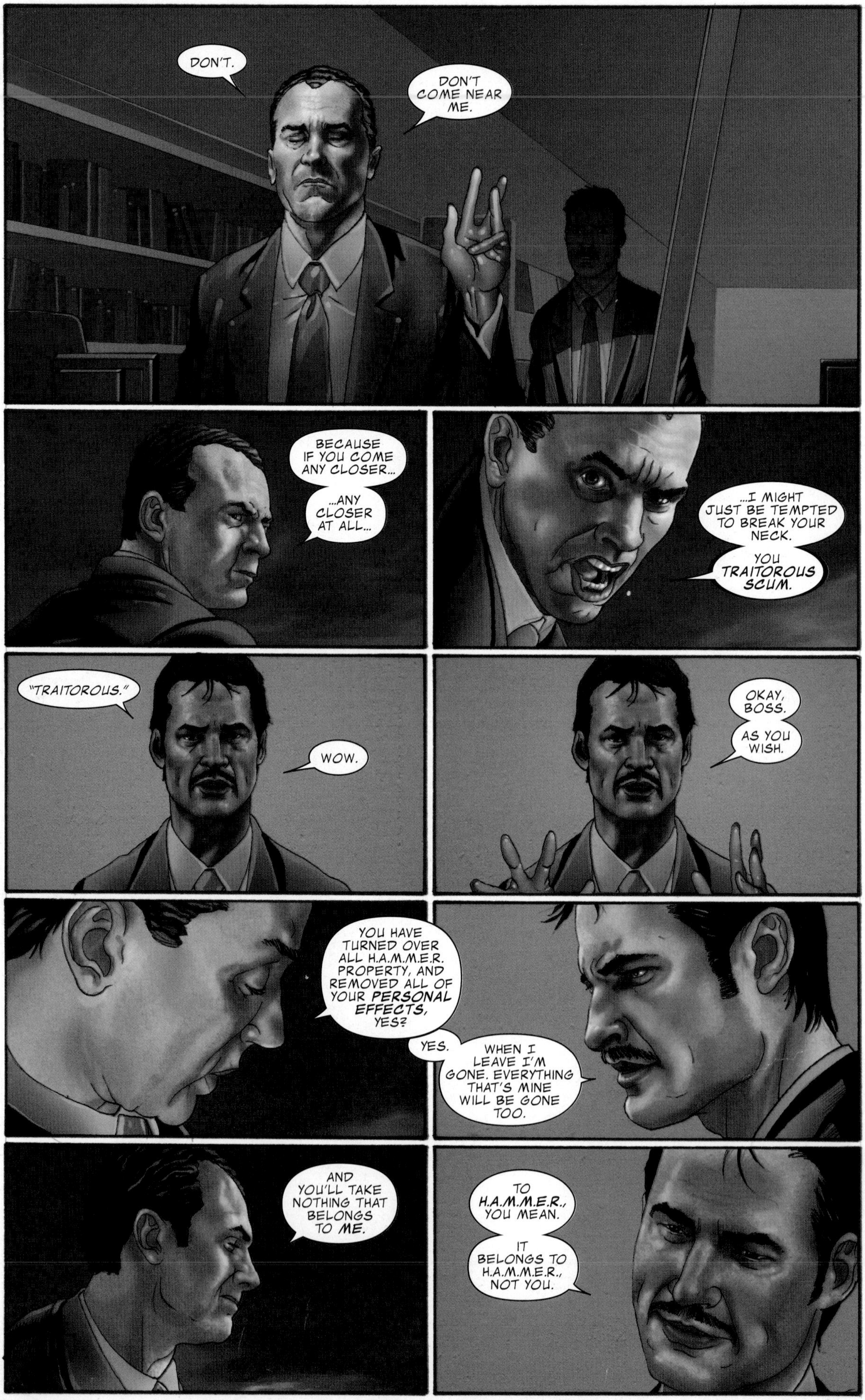
DON'T.
DON'T COME NEAR ME.
BECAUSE IF YOU COME ANY CLOSER...
...ANY CLOSER AT ALL...
...I MIGHT JUST BE TEMPTED TO BREAK YOUR NECK.
YOU *TRAITOROUS SCUM.*
"TRAITOROUS."
WOW.
OKAY, BOSS.
AS YOU WISH.
YOU HAVE TURNED OVER ALL H.A.M.M.E.R. PROPERTY, AND REMOVED ALL OF YOUR *PERSONAL EFFECTS,* YES?
YES.
WHEN I LEAVE I'M GONE. EVERYTHING THAT'S MINE WILL BE GONE TOO.
AND YOU'LL TAKE NOTHING THAT BELONGS TO *ME.*
TO *H.A.M.M.E.R.,* YOU MEAN.
IT BELONGS TO H.A.M.M.E.R., NOT YOU.

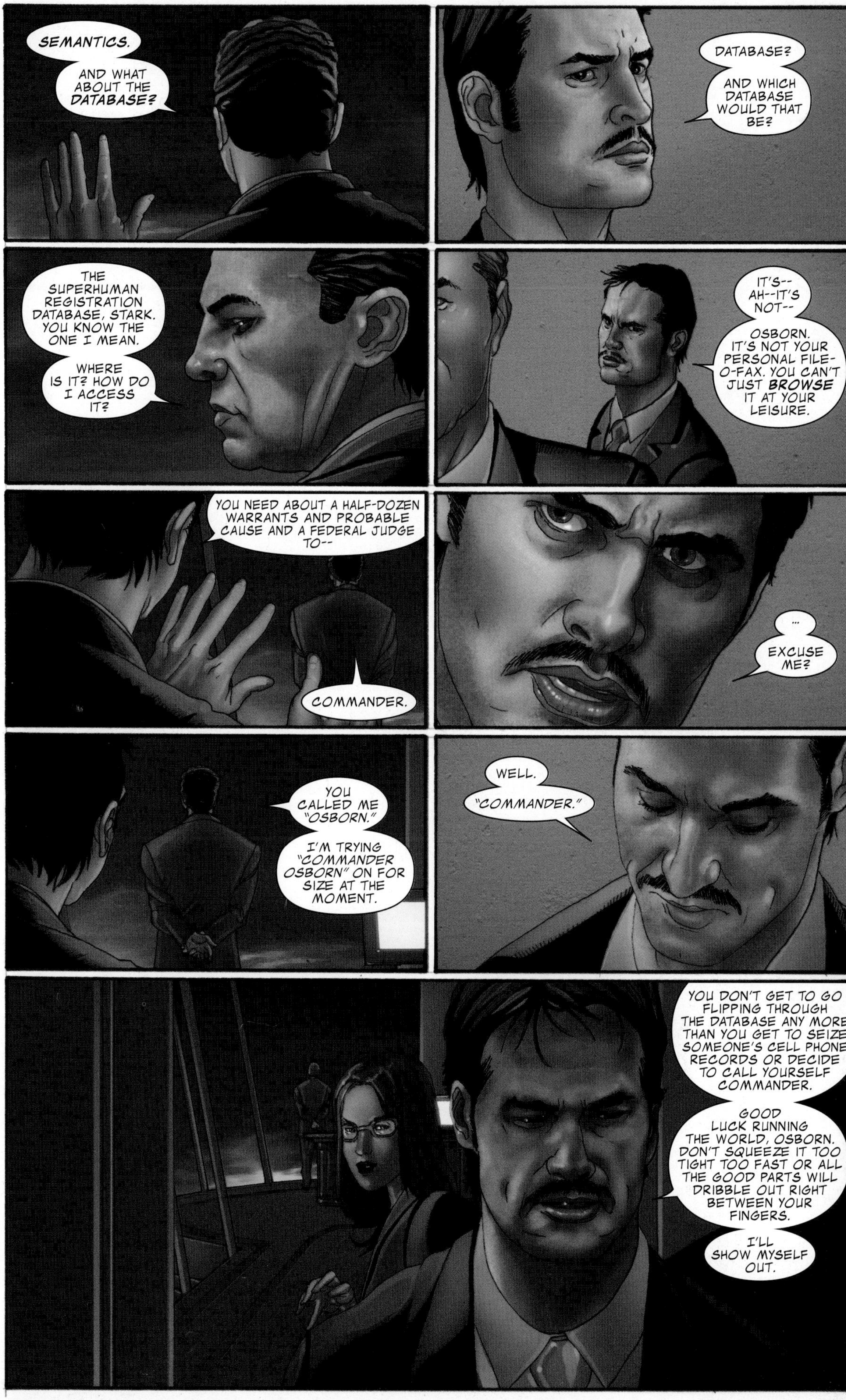
SEMANTICS.
AND WHAT ABOUT THE DATABASE?
DATABASE?
AND WHICH DATABASE WOULD THAT BE?
THE SUPERHUMAN REGISTRATION DATABASE, STARK. YOU KNOW THE ONE I MEAN.
WHERE IS IT? HOW DO I ACCESS IT?
IT'S-- AH--IT'S NOT--
OSBORN. IT'S NOT YOUR PERSONAL FILE-O-FAX. YOU CAN'T JUST BROWSE IT AT YOUR LEISURE.
YOU NEED ABOUT A HALF-DOZEN WARRANTS AND PROBABLE CAUSE AND A FEDERAL JUDGE TO--
COMMANDER.
...
EXCUSE ME?
YOU CALLED ME "OSBORN."
I'M TRYING "COMMANDER OSBORN" ON FOR SIZE AT THE MOMENT.
WELL.
"COMMANDER."
YOU DON'T GET TO GO FLIPPING THROUGH THE DATABASE ANY MORE THAN YOU GET TO SEIZE SOMEONE'S CELL PHONE RECORDS OR DECIDE TO CALL YOURSELF COMMANDER.
GOOD LUCK RUNNING THE WORLD, OSBORN. DON'T SQUEEZE IT TOO TIGHT TOO FAST OR ALL THE GOOD PARTS WILL DRIBBLE OUT RIGHT BETWEEN YOUR FINGERS.
I'LL SHOW MYSELF OUT.

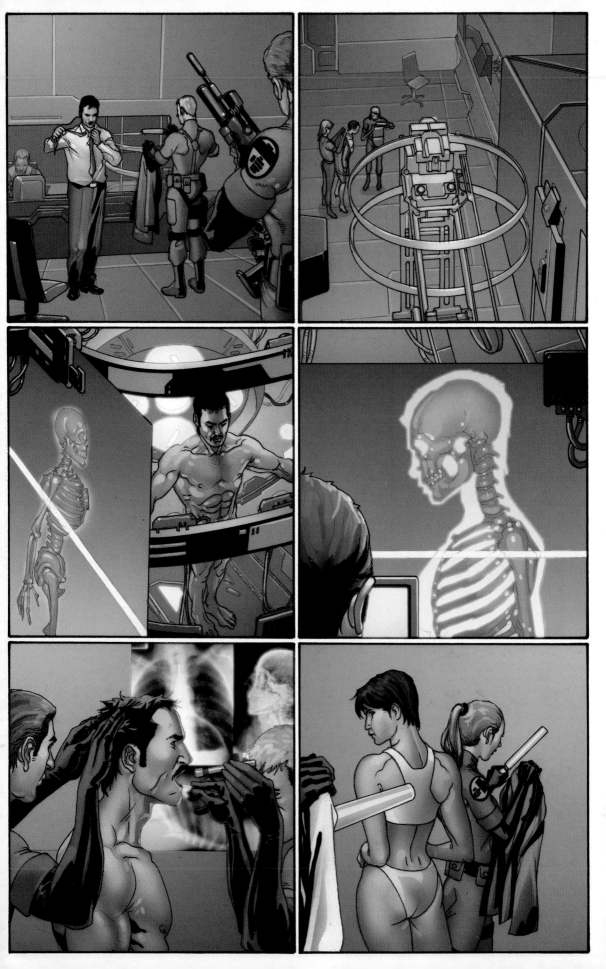

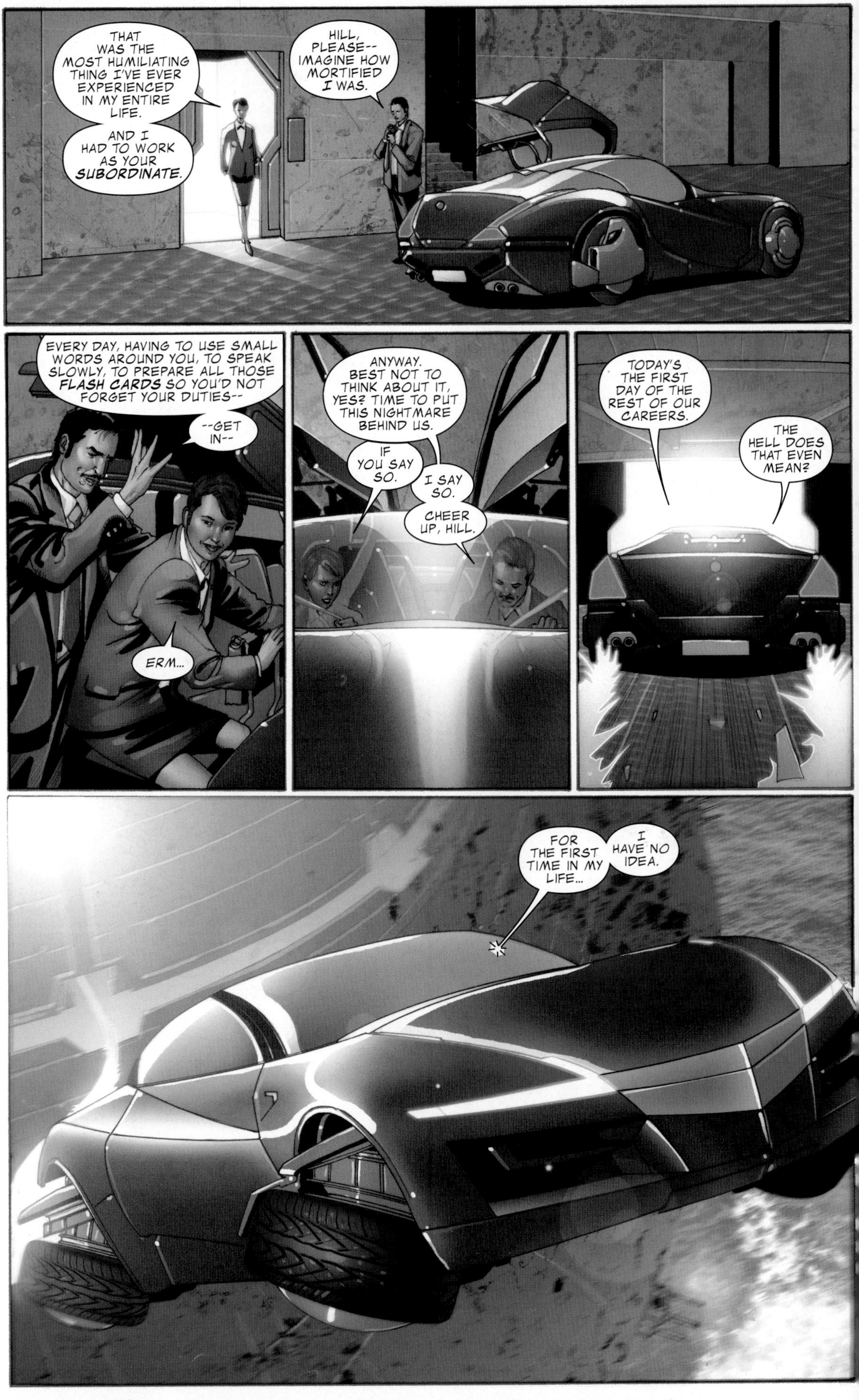
THAT WAS THE MOST HUMILIATING THING I'VE EVER EXPERIENCED IN MY ENTIRE LIFE.
AND I HAD TO WORK AS YOUR SUBORDINATE.
HILL, PLEASE-- IMAGINE HOW MORTIFIED I WAS.
EVERY DAY, HAVING TO USE SMALL WORDS AROUND YOU, TO SPEAK SLOWLY, TO PREPARE ALL THOSE FLASH CARDS SO YOU'D NOT FORGET YOUR DUTIES--
--GET IN--
ERM...
ANYWAY. BEST NOT TO THINK ABOUT IT, YES? TIME TO PUT THIS NIGHTMARE BEHIND US.
IF YOU SAY SO.
I SAY SO.
CHEER UP, HILL.
TODAY'S THE FIRST DAY OF THE REST OF OUR CAREERS.
THE HELL DOES THAT EVEN MEAN?
FOR THE FIRST TIME IN MY LIFE...
I HAVE NO IDEA.

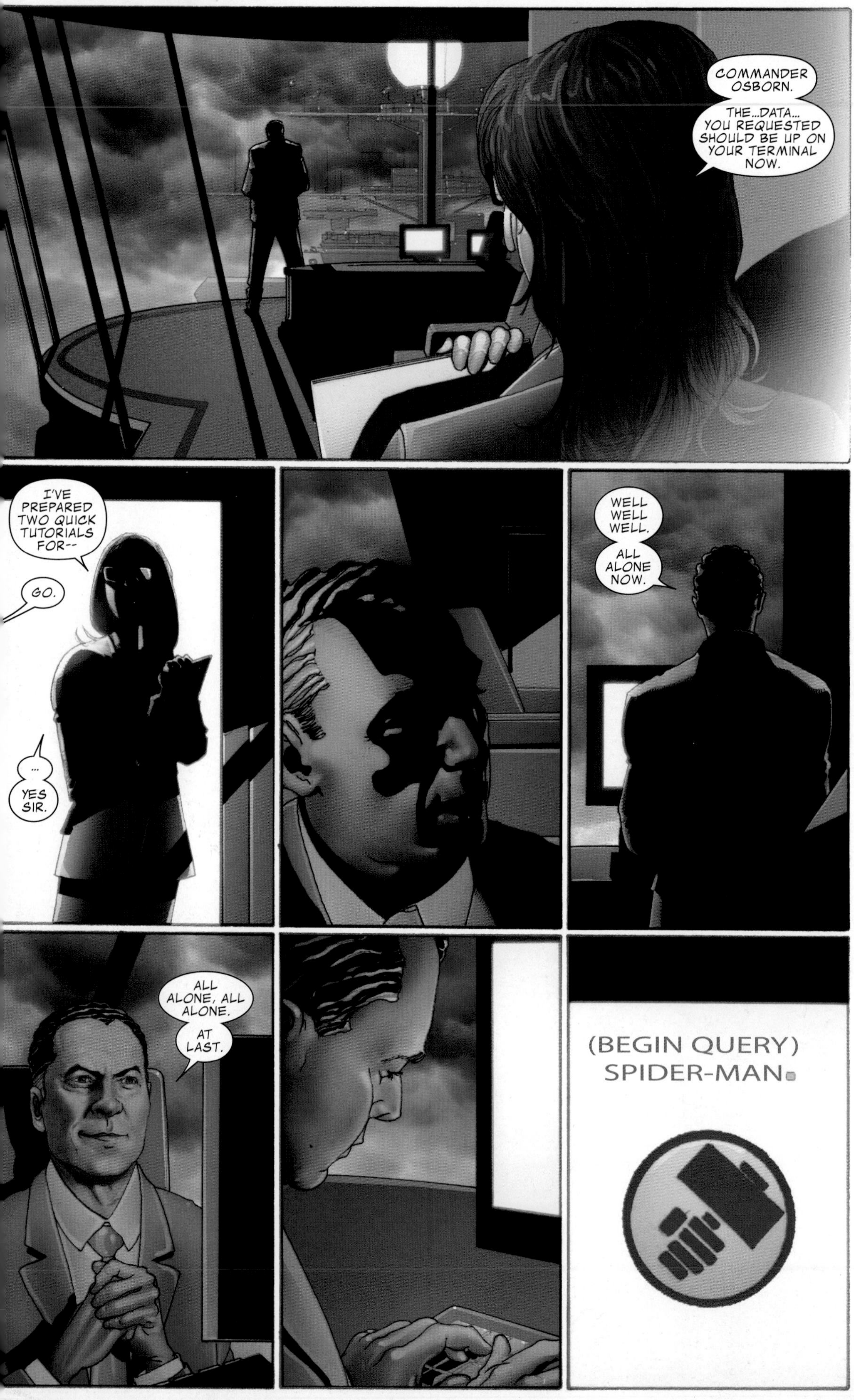

COMMANDER OSBORN.
THE...DATA... YOU REQUESTED SHOULD BE UP ON YOUR TERMINAL NOW.
I'VE PREPARED TWO QUICK TUTORIALS FOR--
GO.
...
YES SIR.
WELL WELL WELL.
ALL ALONE NOW.
ALL ALONE, ALL ALONE.
AT LAST.
(BEGIN QUERY)
SPIDER-MAN

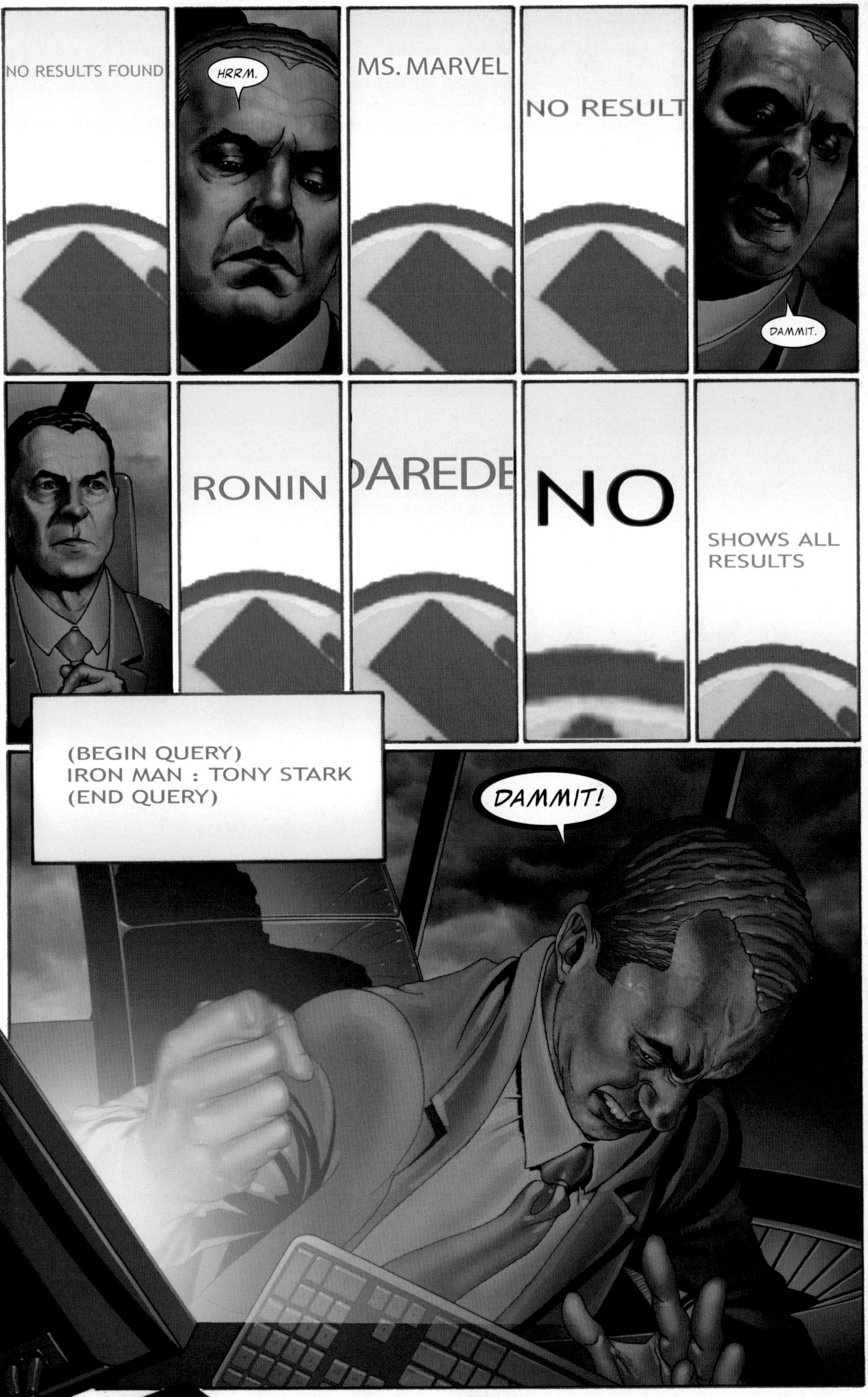
NO RESULTS FOUND
HRRM.
MS. MARVEL
NO RESULT
DAMMIT.
RONIN
DAREDE
NO
SHOWS ALL RESULTS
(BEGIN QUERY)
IRON MAN : TONY STARK
(END QUERY)
DAMMIT!

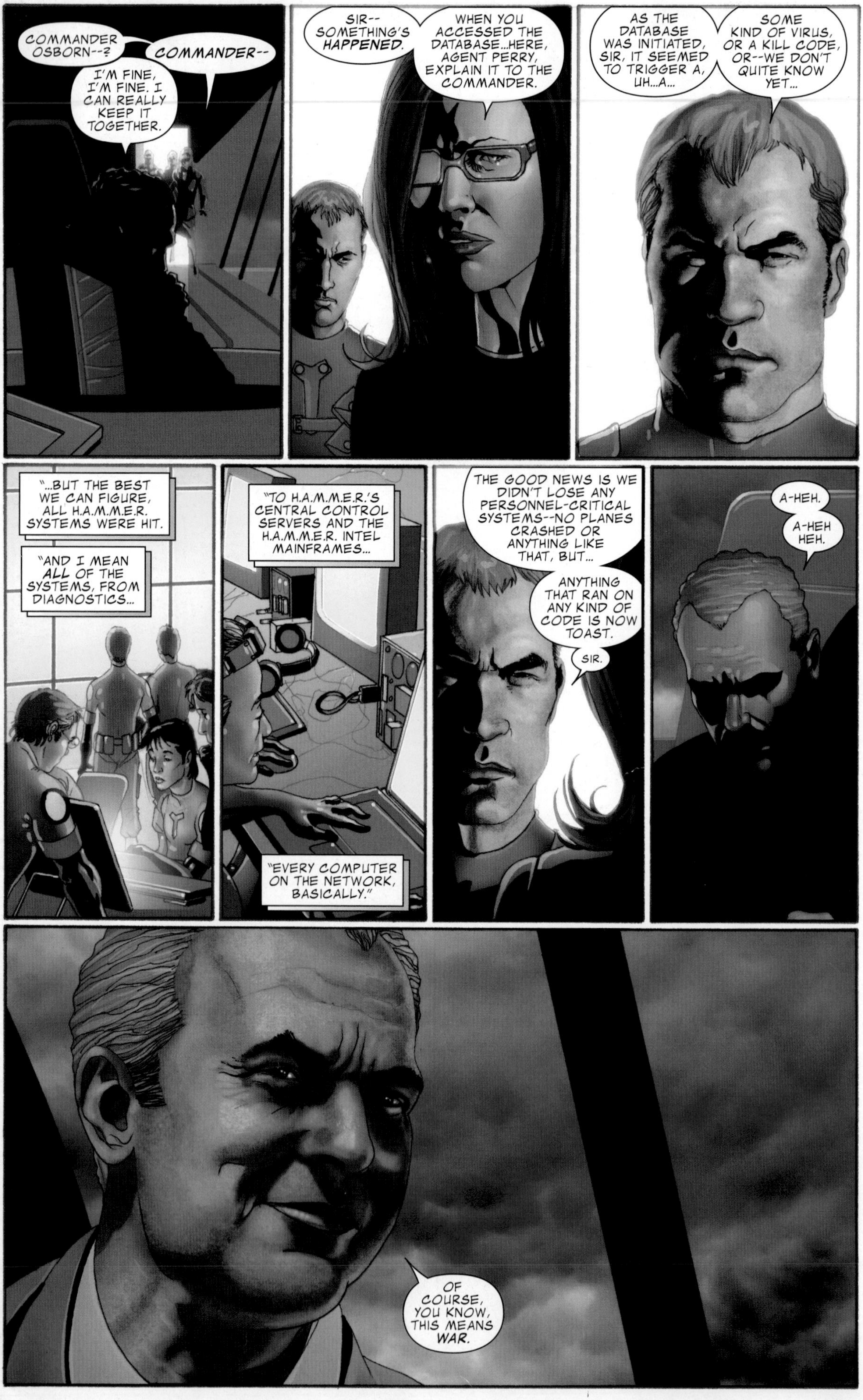
COMMANDER OSBORN--?
COMMANDER--
I'M FINE, I'M FINE. I CAN REALLY KEEP IT TOGETHER.
SIR-- SOMETHING'S HAPPENED.
WHEN YOU ACCESSED THE DATABASE...HERE, AGENT PERRY, EXPLAIN IT TO THE COMMANDER.
AS THE DATABASE WAS INITIATED, SIR, IT SEEMED TO TRIGGER A, UH...A...
SOME KIND OF VIRUS, OR A KILL CODE, OR--WE DON'T QUITE KNOW YET...
"...BUT THE BEST WE CAN FIGURE, ALL H.A.M.M.E.R. SYSTEMS WERE HIT.
"AND I MEAN ALL OF THE SYSTEMS, FROM DIAGNOSTICS...
"TO H.A.M.M.E.R.'S CENTRAL CONTROL SERVERS AND THE H.A.M.M.E.R. INTEL MAINFRAMES...
"EVERY COMPUTER ON THE NETWORK, BASICALLY."
THE GOOD NEWS IS WE DIDN'T LOSE ANY PERSONNEL-CRITICAL SYSTEMS--NO PLANES CRASHED OR ANYTHING LIKE THAT, BUT...
ANYTHING THAT RAN ON ANY KIND OF CODE IS NOW TOAST.
SIR.
A-HEH.
A-HEH HEH.
OF COURSE, YOU KNOW, THIS MEANS WAR.

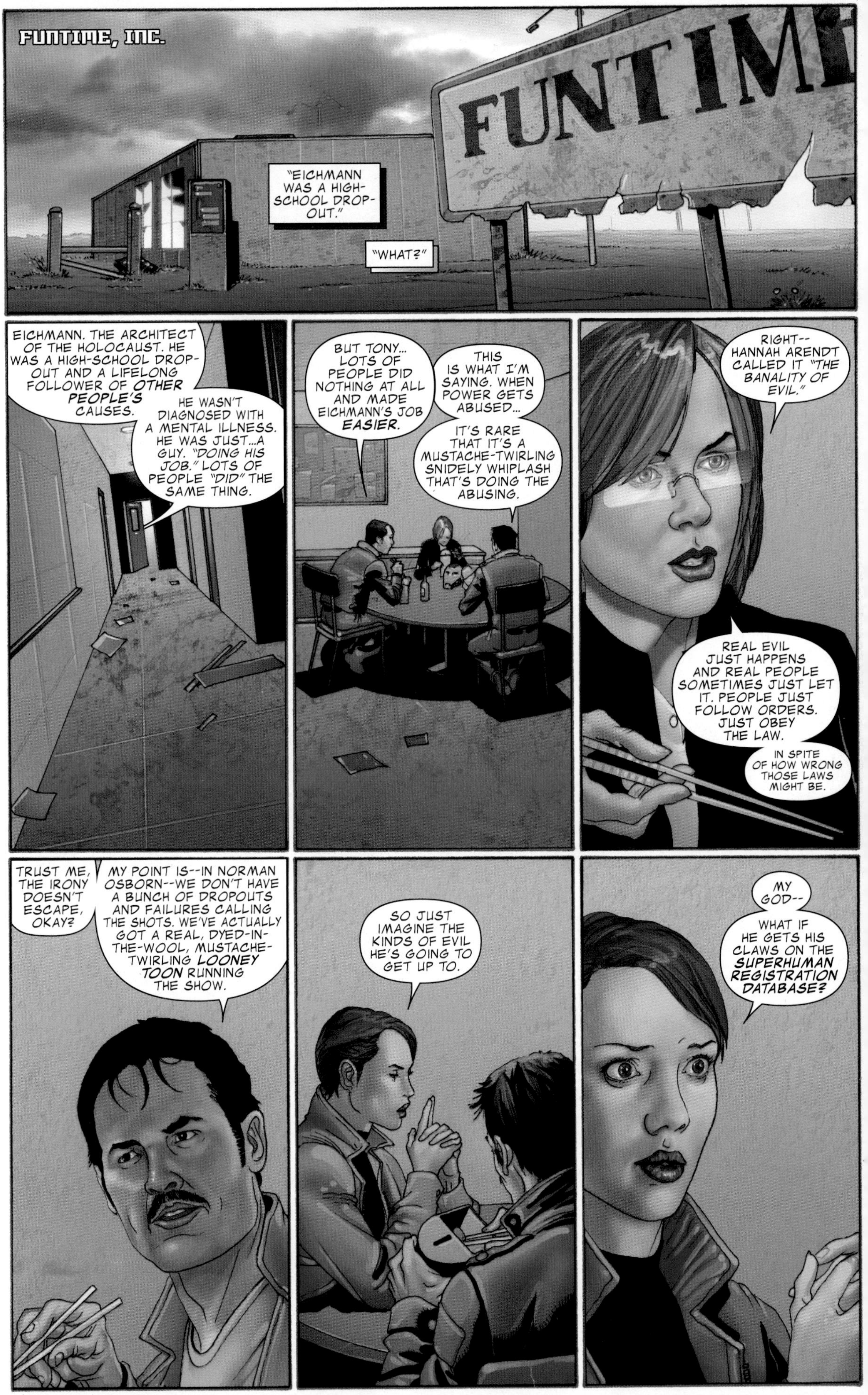
FUNTIME, INC.
FUNTIME
"EICHMANN WAS A HIGH-SCHOOL DROP-OUT."
"WHAT?"
EICHMANN. THE ARCHITECT OF THE HOLOCAUST. HE WAS A HIGH-SCHOOL DROP-OUT AND A LIFELONG FOLLOWER OF OTHER PEOPLE'S CAUSES.
HE WASN'T DIAGNOSED WITH A MENTAL ILLNESS. HE WAS JUST...A GUY. "DOING HIS JOB." LOTS OF PEOPLE "DID" THE SAME THING.
BUT TONY... LOTS OF PEOPLE DID NOTHING AT ALL AND MADE EICHMANN'S JOB EASIER.
THIS IS WHAT I'M SAYING. WHEN POWER GETS ABUSED...
IT'S RARE THAT IT'S A MUSTACHE-TWIRLING SNIDELY WHIPLASH THAT'S DOING THE ABUSING.
RIGHT-- HANNAH ARENDT CALLED IT "THE BANALITY OF EVIL."
REAL EVIL JUST HAPPENS AND REAL PEOPLE SOMETIMES JUST LET IT. PEOPLE JUST FOLLOW ORDERS. JUST OBEY THE LAW.
IN SPITE OF HOW WRONG THOSE LAWS MIGHT BE.
TRUST ME, THE IRONY DOESN'T ESCAPE, OKAY?
MY POINT IS--IN NORMAN OSBORN--WE DON'T HAVE A BUNCH OF DROPOUTS AND FAILURES CALLING THE SHOTS. WE'VE ACTUALLY GOT A REAL, DYED-IN-THE-WOOL, MUSTACHE-TWIRLING LOONEY TOON RUNNING THE SHOW.
SO JUST IMAGINE THE KINDS OF EVIL HE'S GOING TO GET UP TO.
MY GOD--
WHAT IF HE GETS HIS CLAWS ON THE SUPERHUMAN REGISTRATION DATABASE?

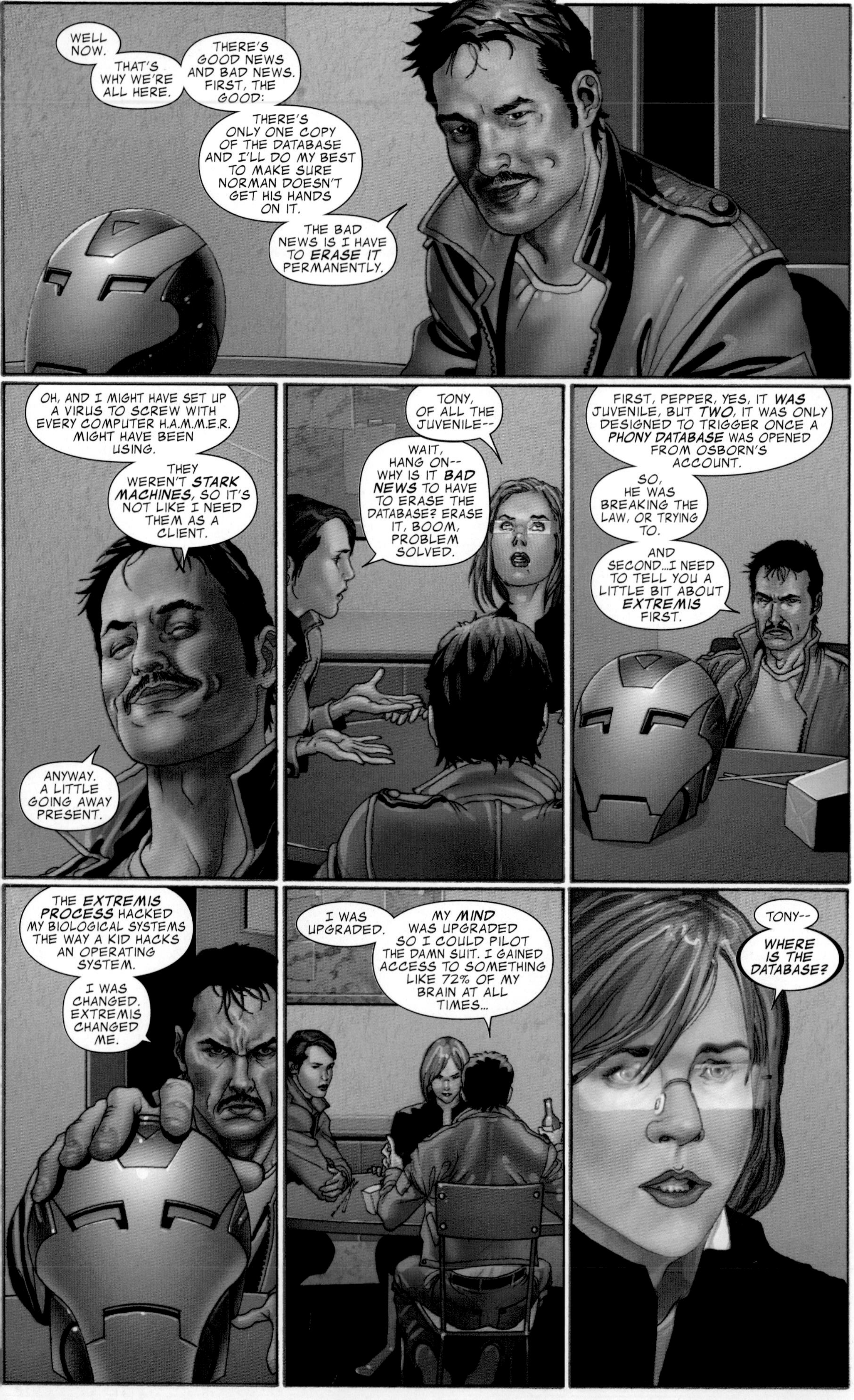
WELL NOW.
THAT'S WHY WE'RE ALL HERE.
THERE'S GOOD NEWS AND BAD NEWS. FIRST, THE GOOD:
THERE'S ONLY ONE COPY OF THE DATABASE AND I'LL DO MY BEST TO MAKE SURE NORMAN DOESN'T GET HIS HANDS ON IT.
THE BAD NEWS IS I HAVE TO ERASE IT PERMANENTLY.
OH, AND I MIGHT HAVE SET UP A VIRUS TO SCREW WITH EVERY COMPUTER H.A.M.M.E.R. MIGHT HAVE BEEN USING.
THEY WEREN'T STARK MACHINES, SO IT'S NOT LIKE I NEED THEM AS A CLIENT.
ANYWAY. A LITTLE GOING AWAY PRESENT.
TONY, OF ALL THE JUVENILE--
WAIT, HANG ON-- WHY IS IT BAD NEWS TO HAVE TO ERASE THE DATABASE? ERASE IT, BOOM, PROBLEM SOLVED.
FIRST, PEPPER, YES, IT WAS JUVENILE, BUT TWO, IT WAS ONLY DESIGNED TO TRIGGER ONCE A PHONY DATABASE WAS OPENED FROM OSBORN'S ACCOUNT.
SO, HE WAS BREAKING THE LAW, OR TRYING TO.
AND SECOND...I NEED TO TELL YOU A LITTLE BIT ABOUT EXTREMIS FIRST.
THE EXTREMIS PROCESS HACKED MY BIOLOGICAL SYSTEMS THE WAY A KID HACKS AN OPERATING SYSTEM.
I WAS CHANGED. EXTREMIS CHANGED ME.
I WAS UPGRADED.
MY MIND WAS UPGRADED SO I COULD PILOT THE DAMN SUIT. I GAINED ACCESS TO SOMETHING LIKE 72% OF MY BRAIN AT ALL TIMES...
TONY--
WHERE IS THE DATABASE?

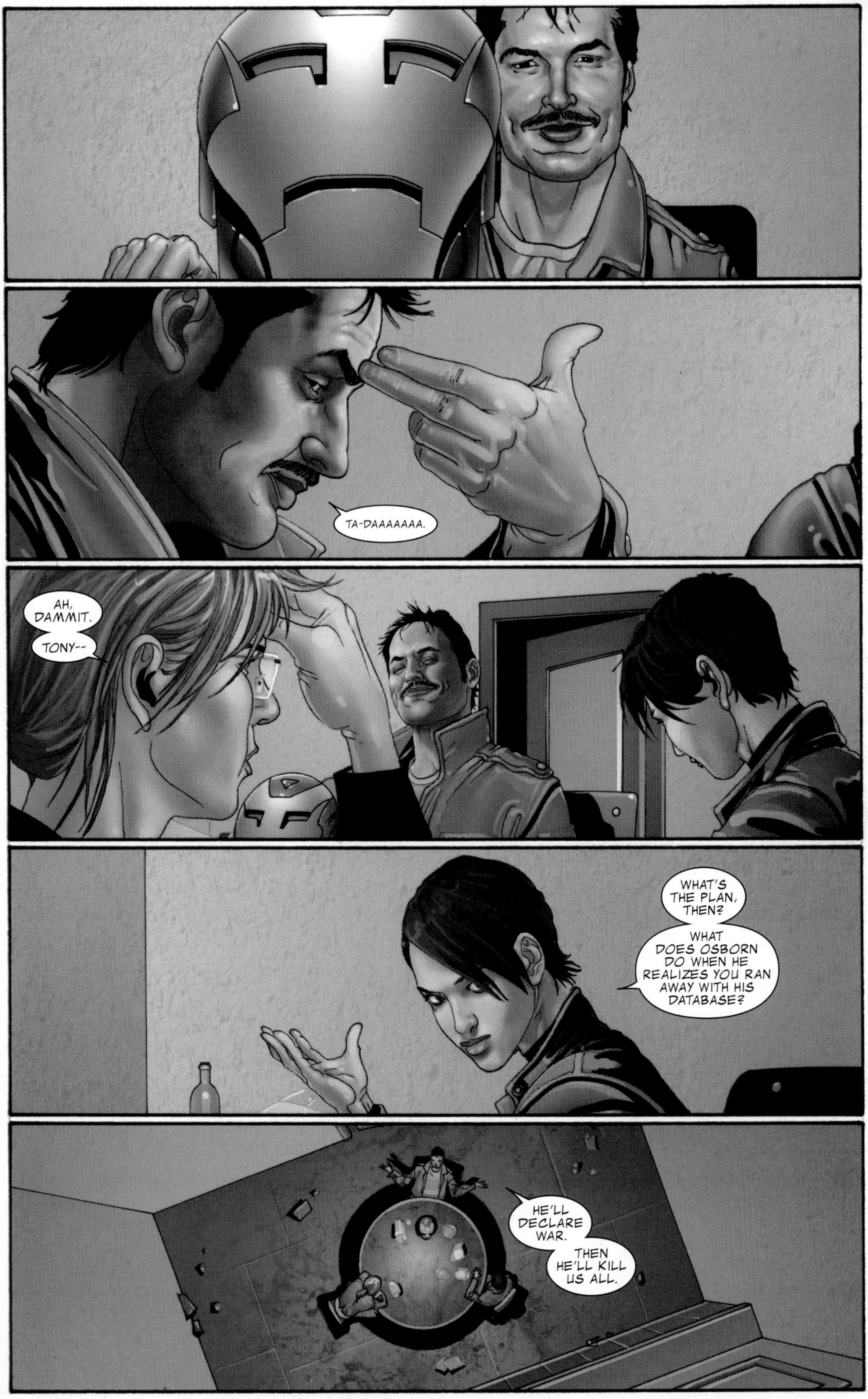
TA-DAAAAAAA.
AH, DAMMIT.
TONY--
WHAT'S THE PLAN, THEN?
WHAT DOES OSBORN DO WHEN HE REALIZES YOU RAN AWAY WITH HIS DATABASE?
HE'LL DECLARE WAR.
THEN HE'LL KILL US ALL.

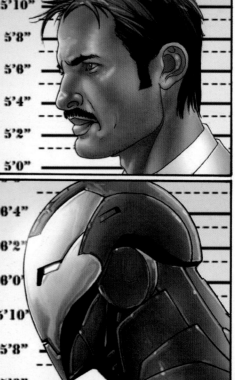

WORLD'S
MOST
WANTED

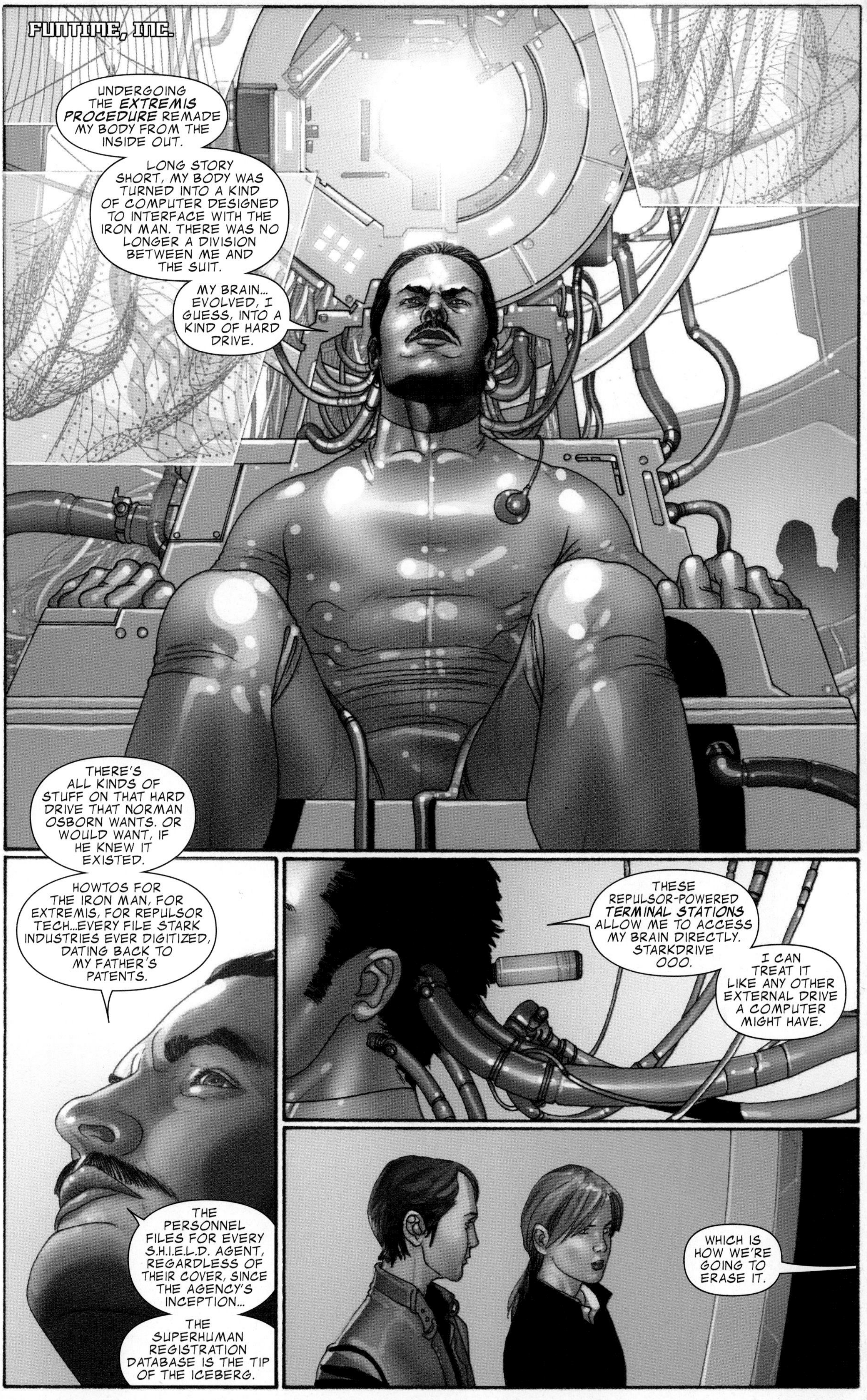
FUNTIME, INC.
UNDERGOING THE EXTREMIS PROCEDURE REMADE MY BODY FROM THE INSIDE OUT.
LONG STORY SHORT, MY BODY WAS TURNED INTO A KIND OF COMPUTER DESIGNED TO INTERFACE WITH THE IRON MAN. THERE WAS NO LONGER A DIVISION BETWEEN ME AND THE SUIT.
MY BRAIN... EVOLVED, I GUESS, INTO A KIND OF HARD DRIVE.
THERE'S ALL KINDS OF STUFF ON THAT HARD DRIVE THAT NORMAN OSBORN WANTS. OR WOULD WANT, IF HE KNEW IT EXISTED.
HOWTOS FOR THE IRON MAN, FOR EXTREMIS, FOR REPULSOR TECH...EVERY FILE STARK INDUSTRIES EVER DIGITIZED, DATING BACK TO MY FATHER'S PATENTS.
THE PERSONNEL FILES FOR EVERY S.H.I.E.L.D. AGENT, REGARDLESS OF THEIR COVER, SINCE THE AGENCY'S INCEPTION...
THE SUPERHUMAN REGISTRATION DATABASE IS THE TIP OF THE ICEBERG.
THESE REPULSOR-POWERED TERMINAL STATIONS ALLOW ME TO ACCESS MY BRAIN DIRECTLY. STARKDRIVE OOO.
I CAN TREAT IT LIKE ANY OTHER EXTERNAL DRIVE A COMPUTER MIGHT HAVE.
WHICH IS HOW WE'RE GOING TO ERASE IT.

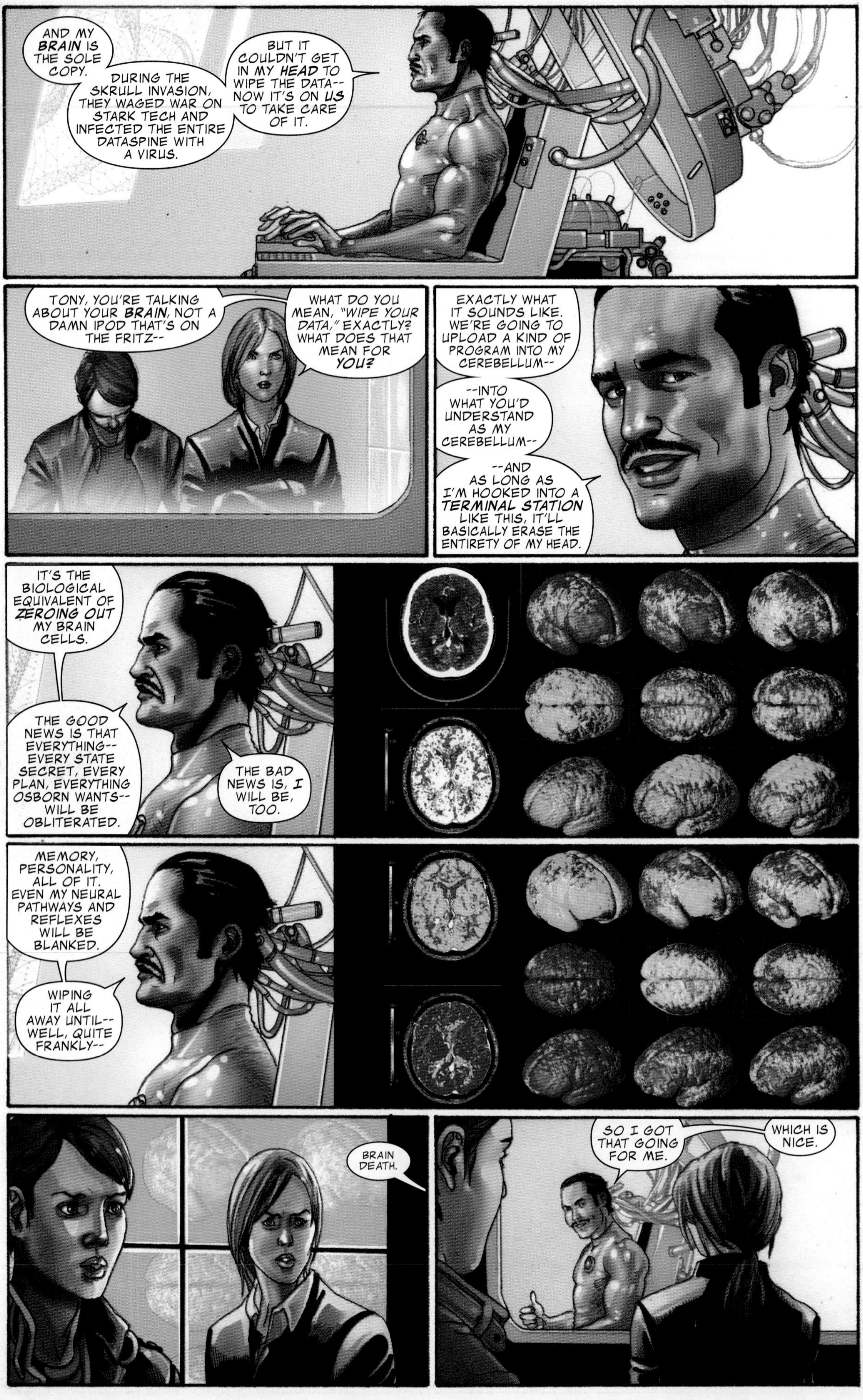
AND MY BRAIN IS THE SOLE COPY.
DURING THE SKRULL INVASION, THEY WAGED WAR ON STARK TECH AND INFECTED THE ENTIRE DATASPINE WITH A VIRUS.
BUT IT COULDN'T GET IN MY HEAD TO WIPE THE DATA-- NOW IT'S ON US TO TAKE CARE OF IT.
TONY, YOU'RE TALKING ABOUT YOUR BRAIN, NOT A DAMN IPOD THAT'S ON THE FRITZ--
WHAT DO YOU MEAN, "WIPE YOUR DATA," EXACTLY? WHAT DOES THAT MEAN FOR YOU?
EXACTLY WHAT IT SOUNDS LIKE. WE'RE GOING TO UPLOAD A KIND OF PROGRAM INTO MY CEREBELLUM--
--INTO WHAT YOU'D UNDERSTAND AS MY CEREBELLUM--
--AND AS LONG AS I'M HOOKED INTO A TERMINAL STATION LIKE THIS, IT'LL BASICALLY ERASE THE ENTIRETY OF MY HEAD.
IT'S THE BIOLOGICAL EQUIVALENT OF ZEROING OUT MY BRAIN CELLS.
THE GOOD NEWS IS THAT EVERYTHING-- EVERY STATE SECRET, EVERY PLAN, EVERYTHING OSBORN WANTS-- WILL BE OBLITERATED.
THE BAD NEWS IS, I WILL BE, TOO.
MEMORY, PERSONALITY, ALL OF IT. EVEN MY NEURAL PATHWAYS AND REFLEXES WILL BE BLANKED.
WIPING IT ALL AWAY UNTIL-- WELL, QUITE FRANKLY--
BRAIN DEATH.
SO I GOT THAT GOING FOR ME.
WHICH IS NICE.

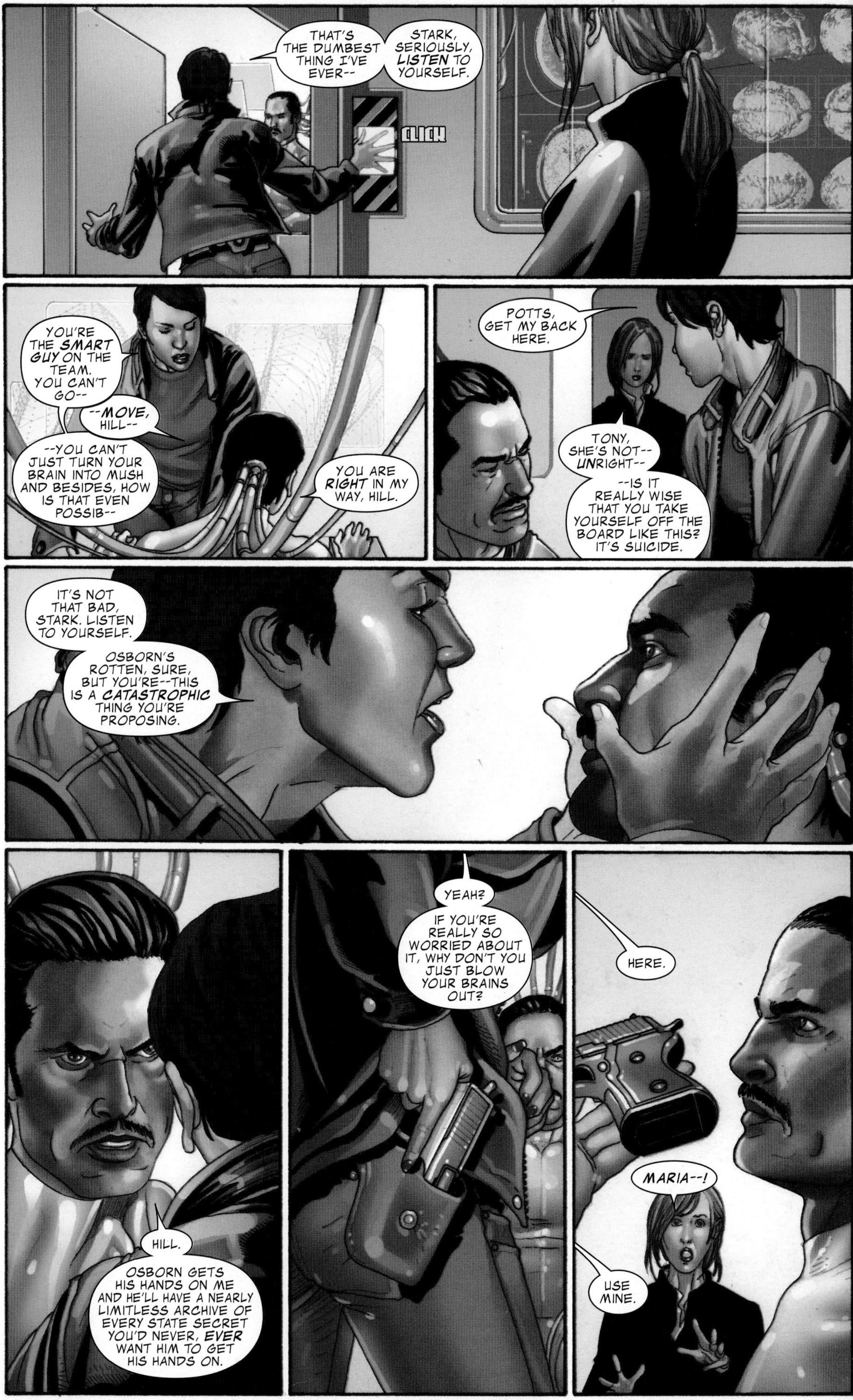
THAT'S THE DUMBEST THING I'VE EVER--
STARK, SERIOUSLY, LISTEN TO YOURSELF.
CLICK
YOU'RE THE SMART GUY ON THE TEAM. YOU CAN'T GO--
--MOVE, HILL--
--YOU CAN'T JUST TURN YOUR BRAIN INTO MUSH AND BESIDES, HOW IS THAT EVEN POSSIB--
YOU ARE RIGHT IN MY WAY, HILL.
POTTS, GET MY BACK HERE.
TONY, SHE'S NOT--UNRIGHT--
--IS IT REALLY WISE THAT YOU TAKE YOURSELF OFF THE BOARD LIKE THIS? IT'S SUICIDE.
IT'S NOT THAT BAD, STARK. LISTEN TO YOURSELF.
OSBORN'S ROTTEN, SURE, BUT YOU'RE--THIS IS A CATASTROPHIC THING YOU'RE PROPOSING.
HILL.
OSBORN GETS HIS HANDS ON ME AND HE'LL HAVE A NEARLY LIMITLESS ARCHIVE OF EVERY STATE SECRET YOU'D NEVER, EVER WANT HIM TO GET HIS HANDS ON.
YEAH?
IF YOU'RE REALLY SO WORRIED ABOUT IT, WHY DON'T YOU JUST BLOW YOUR BRAINS OUT?
HERE.
MARIA--!
USE MINE.

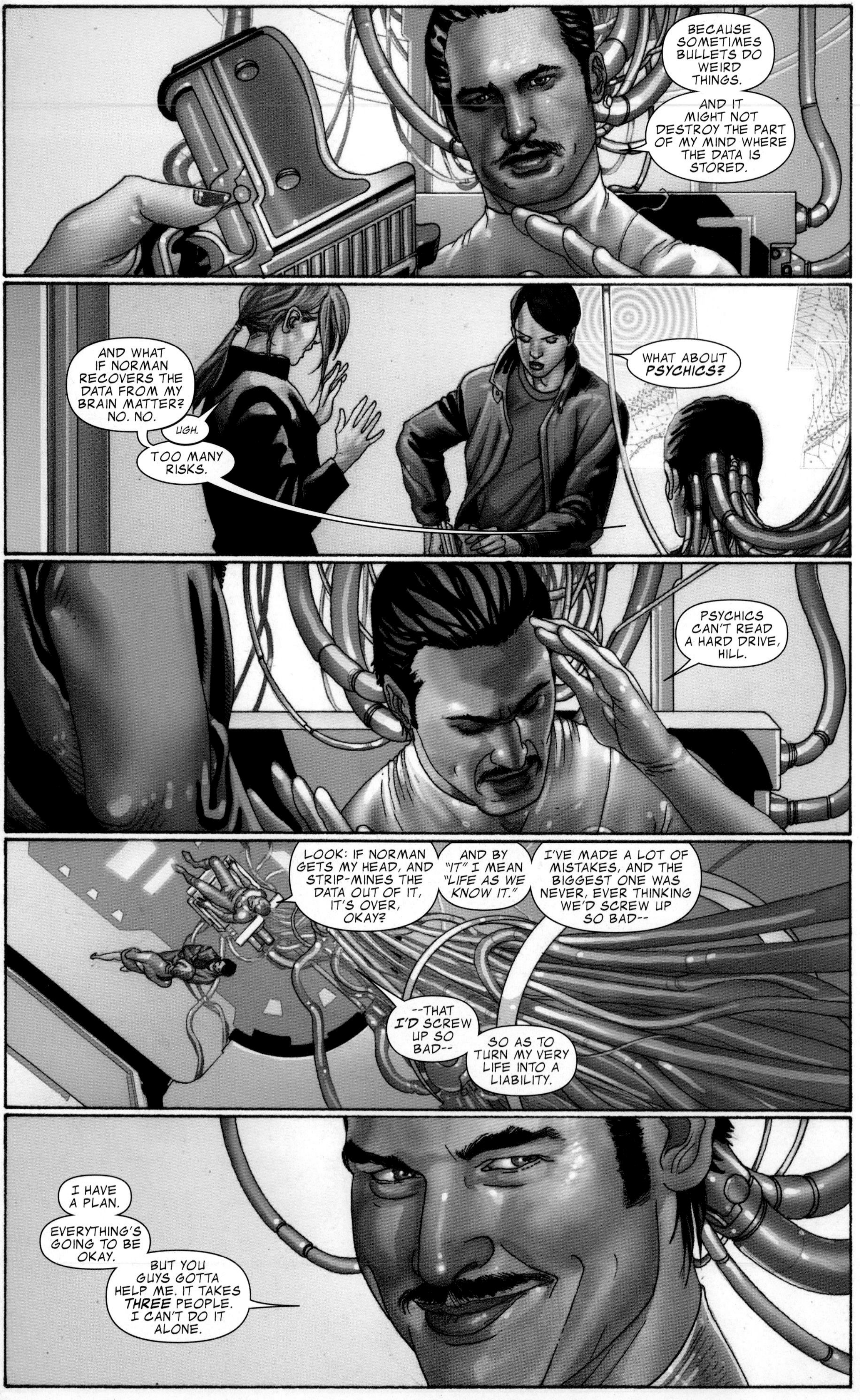
BECAUSE SOMETIMES BULLETS DO WEIRD THINGS.
AND IT MIGHT NOT DESTROY THE PART OF MY MIND WHERE THE DATA IS STORED.
AND WHAT IF NORMAN RECOVERS THE DATA FROM MY BRAIN MATTER? NO. NO.
UGH.
TOO MANY RISKS.
WHAT ABOUT PSYCHICS?
PSYCHICS CAN'T READ A HARD DRIVE, HILL.
LOOK: IF NORMAN GETS MY HEAD, AND STRIP-MINES THE DATA OUT OF IT, IT'S OVER, OKAY?
AND BY "IT" I MEAN "LIFE AS WE KNOW IT."
I'VE MADE A LOT OF MISTAKES, AND THE BIGGEST ONE WAS NEVER, EVER THINKING WE'D SCREW UP SO BAD--
--THAT I'D SCREW UP SO BAD--
SO AS TO TURN MY VERY LIFE INTO A LIABILITY.
I HAVE A PLAN.
EVERYTHING'S GOING TO BE OKAY.
BUT YOU GUYS GOTTA HELP ME. IT TAKES THREE PEOPLE. I CAN'T DO IT ALONE.

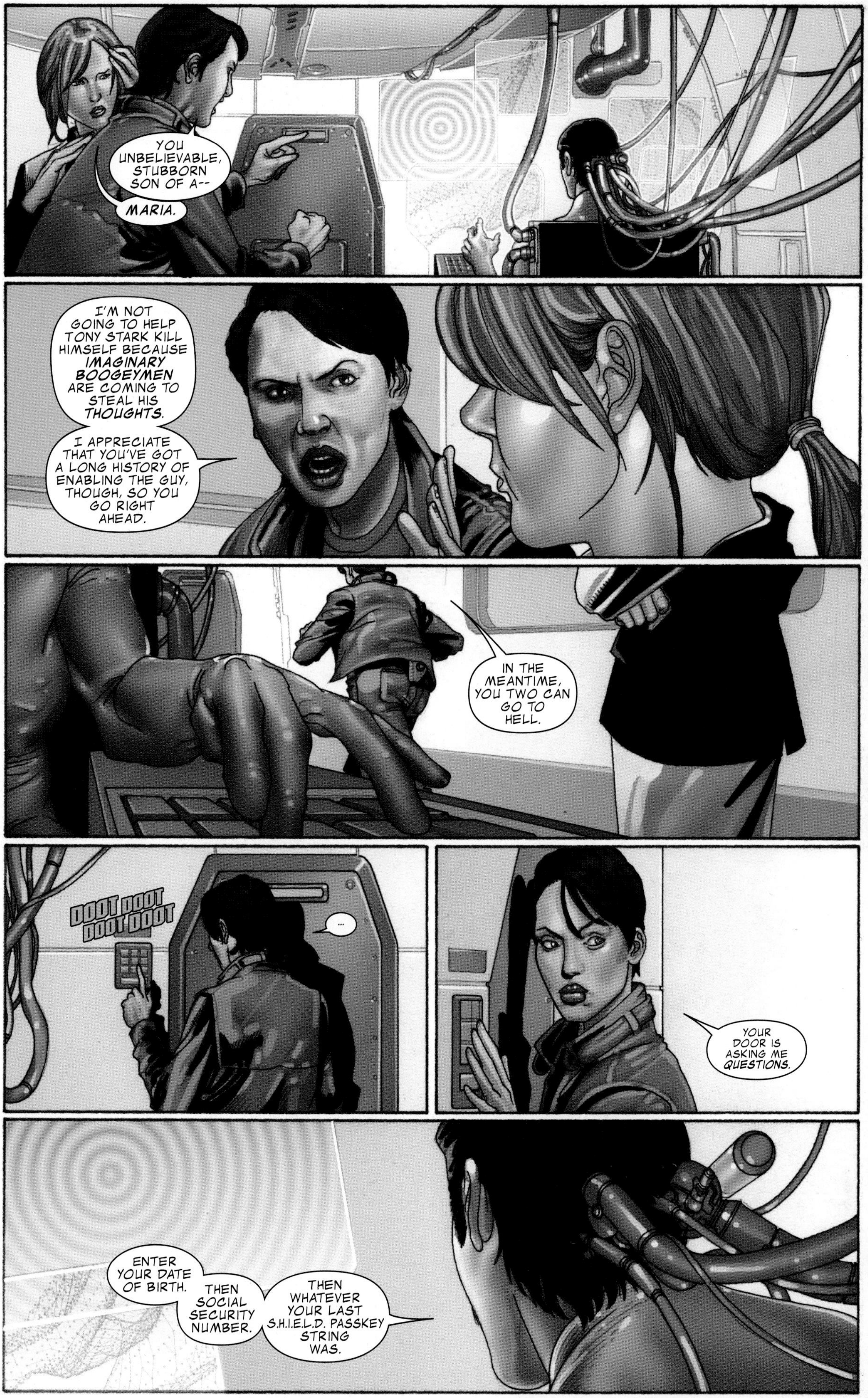
YOU UNBELIEVABLE, STUBBORN SON OF A--
MARIA.
I'M NOT GOING TO HELP TONY STARK KILL HIMSELF BECAUSE IMAGINARY BOOGEYMEN ARE COMING TO STEAL HIS THOUGHTS.
I APPRECIATE THAT YOU'VE GOT A LONG HISTORY OF ENABLING THE GUY, THOUGH, SO YOU GO RIGHT AHEAD.
IN THE MEANTIME, YOU TWO CAN GO TO HELL.
DOOT DOOT DOOT DOOT
...
YOUR DOOR IS ASKING ME QUESTIONS.
ENTER YOUR DATE OF BIRTH.
THEN SOCIAL SECURITY NUMBER.
THEN WHATEVER YOUR LAST S.H.I.E.L.D. PASSKEY STRING WAS.

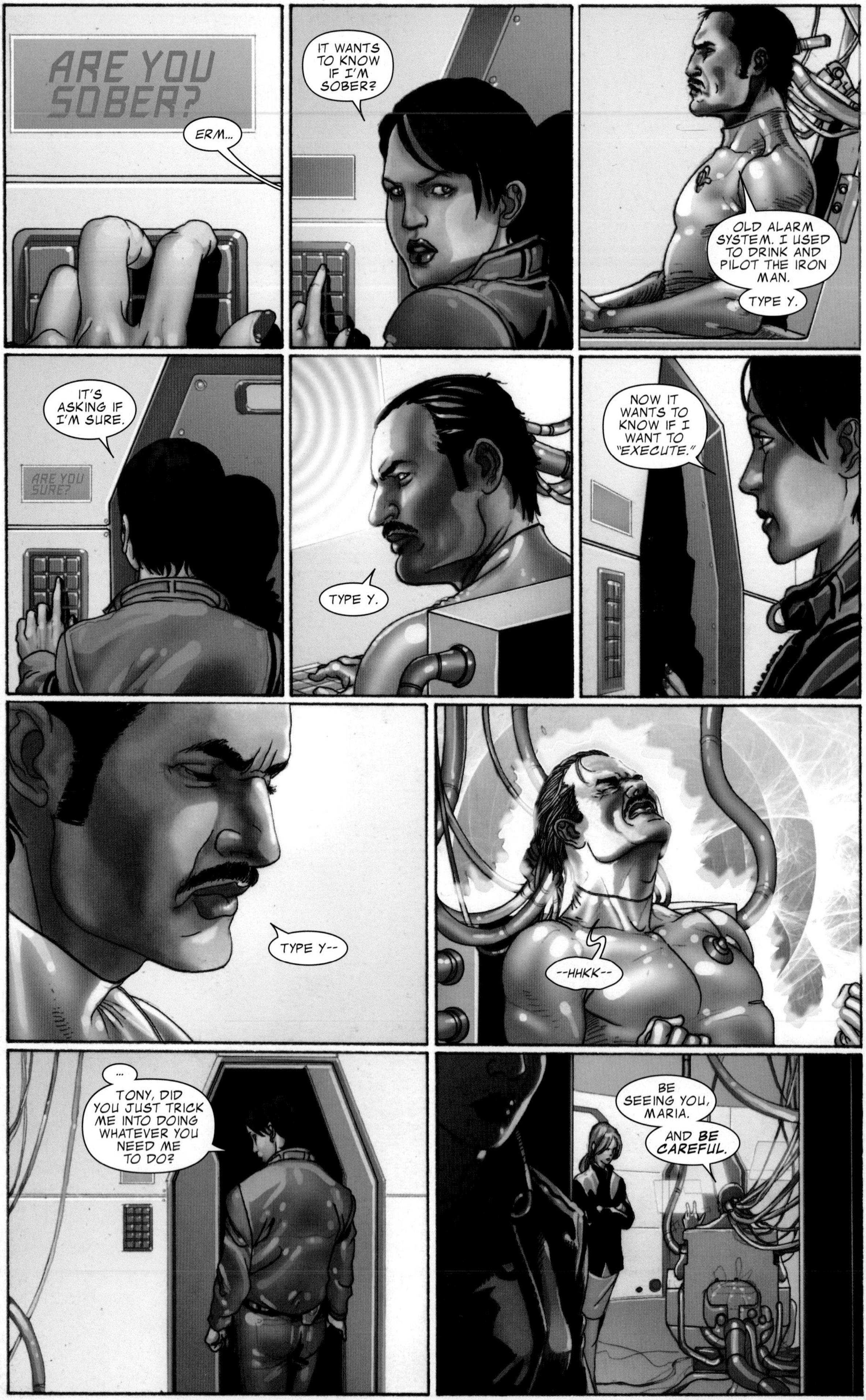
ARE YOU SOBER?
ERM...
IT WANTS TO KNOW IF I'M SOBER?
OLD ALARM SYSTEM. I USED TO DRINK AND PILOT THE IRON MAN.
TYPE Y.
IT'S ASKING IF I'M SURE.
ARE YOU SURE?
TYPE Y.
NOW IT WANTS TO KNOW IF I WANT TO "EXECUTE."
TYPE Y--
--HHKK--
... TONY, DID YOU JUST TRICK ME INTO DOING WHATEVER YOU NEED ME TO DO?
BE SEEING YOU, MARIA.
AND BE CAREFUL.

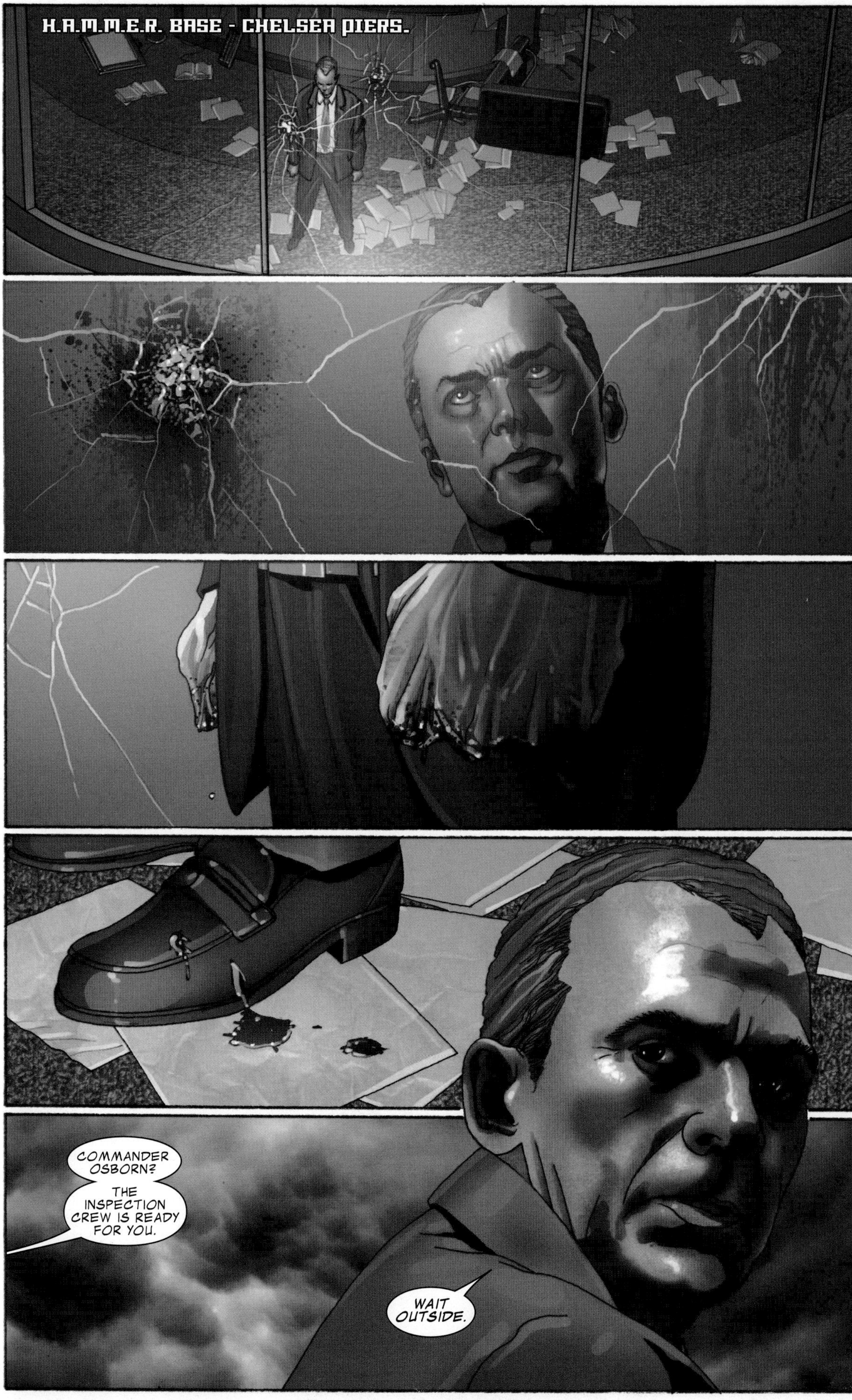

H.A.M.M.E.R. BASE - CHELSEA PIERS.
COMMANDER OSBORN?
THE INSPECTION CREW IS READY FOR YOU.
WAIT OUTSIDE.

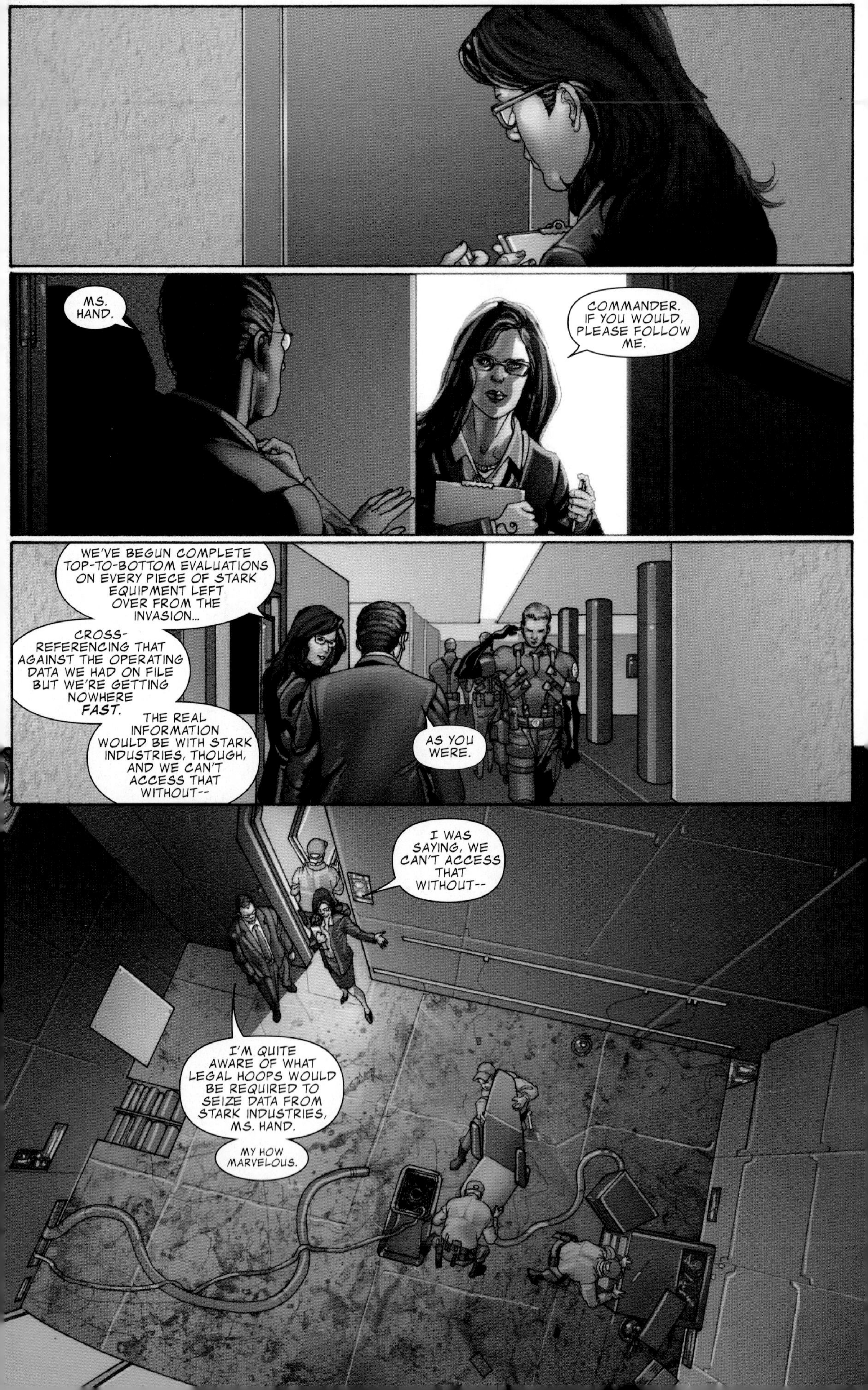
MS. HAND.
COMMANDER. IF YOU WOULD, PLEASE FOLLOW ME.
WE'VE BEGUN COMPLETE TOP-TO-BOTTOM EVALUATIONS ON EVERY PIECE OF STARK EQUIPMENT LEFT OVER FROM THE INVASION...
CROSS-REFERENCING THAT AGAINST THE OPERATING DATA WE HAD ON FILE BUT WE'RE GETTING NOWHERE FAST.
THE REAL INFORMATION WOULD BE WITH STARK INDUSTRIES, THOUGH, AND WE CAN'T ACCESS THAT WITHOUT--
AS YOU WERE.
I WAS SAYING, WE CAN'T ACCESS THAT WITHOUT--
I'M QUITE AWARE OF WHAT LEGAL HOOPS WOULD BE REQUIRED TO SEIZE DATA FROM STARK INDUSTRIES, MS. HAND.
MY HOW MARVELOUS.

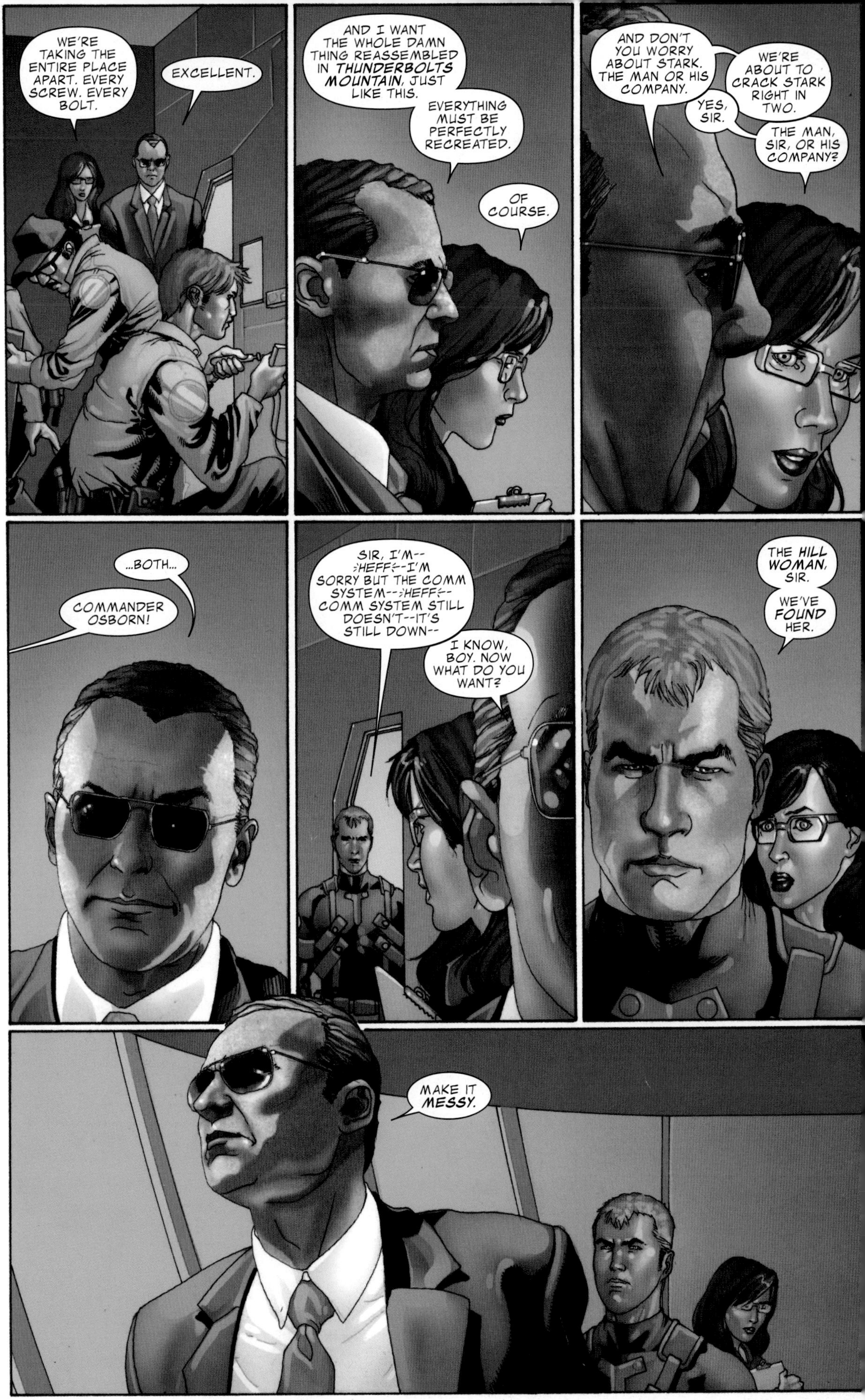
WE'RE TAKING THE ENTIRE PLACE APART. EVERY SCREW. EVERY BOLT.
EXCELLENT.
AND I WANT THE WHOLE DAMN THING REASSEMBLED IN THUNDERBOLTS MOUNTAIN, JUST LIKE THIS.
EVERYTHING MUST BE PERFECTLY RECREATED.
OF COURSE.
AND DON'T YOU WORRY ABOUT STARK. THE MAN OR HIS COMPANY.
YES, SIR.
WE'RE ABOUT TO CRACK STARK RIGHT IN TWO.
THE MAN, SIR, OR HIS COMPANY?
COMMANDER OSBORN!
...BOTH...
SIR, I'M-- HEFF --I'M SORRY BUT THE COMM SYSTEM-- HEFF -- COMM SYSTEM STILL DOESN'T--IT'S STILL DOWN--
I KNOW, BOY. NOW WHAT DO YOU WANT?
THE HILL WOMAN, SIR.
WE'VE FOUND HER.
MAKE IT MESSY.

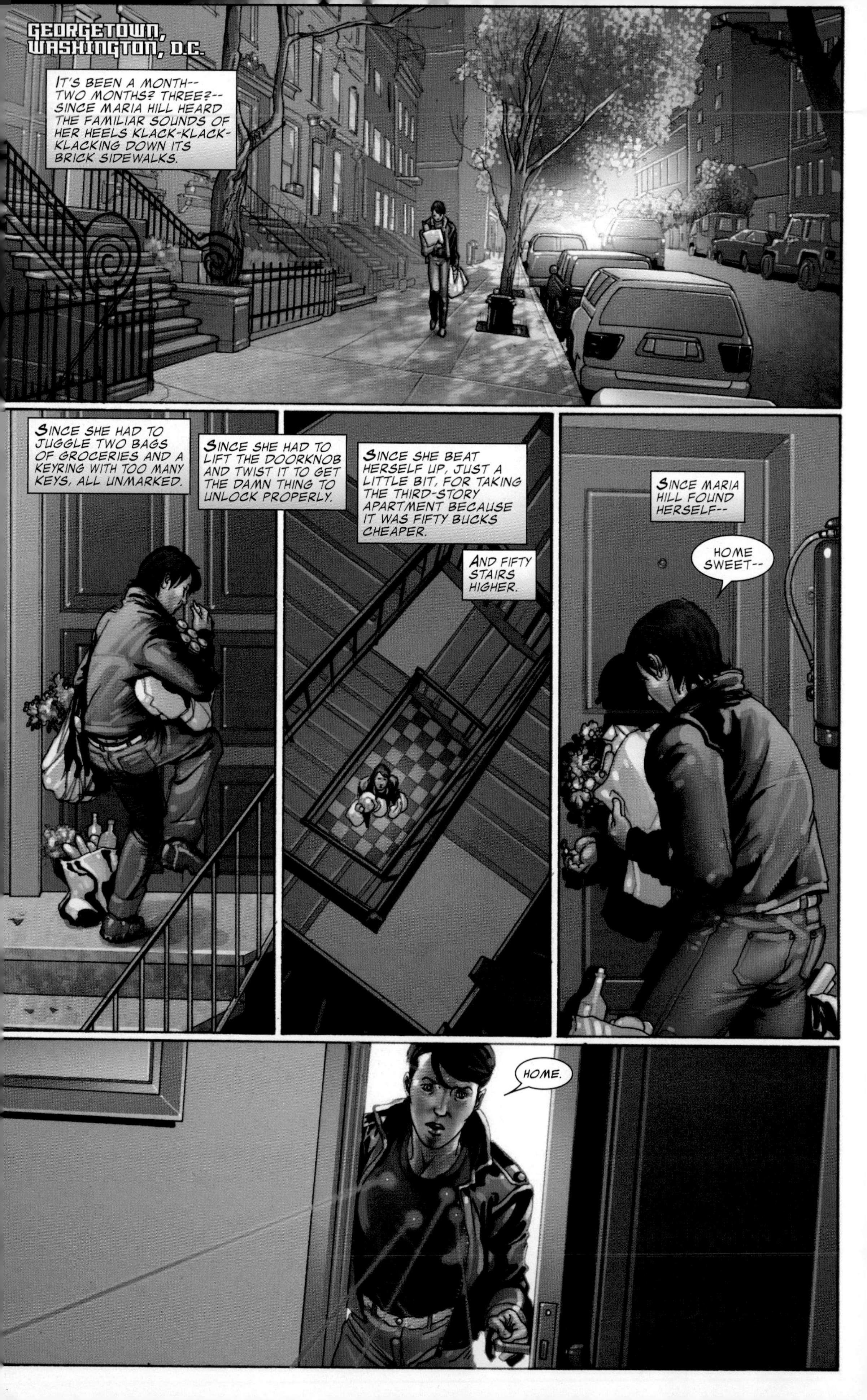
GEORGETOWN, WASHINGTON, D.C.
IT'S BEEN A MONTH-- TWO MONTHS? THREE?-- SINCE MARIA HILL HEARD THE FAMILIAR SOUNDS OF HER HEELS KLACK-KLACK-KLACKING DOWN ITS BRICK SIDEWALKS.
SINCE SHE HAD TO JUGGLE TWO BAGS OF GROCERIES AND A KEYRING WITH TOO MANY KEYS, ALL UNMARKED.
SINCE SHE HAD TO LIFT THE DOORKNOB AND TWIST IT TO GET THE DAMN THING TO UNLOCK PROPERLY.
SINCE SHE BEAT HERSELF UP, JUST A LITTLE BIT, FOR TAKING THE THIRD-STORY APARTMENT BECAUSE IT WAS FIFTY BUCKS CHEAPER.
AND FIFTY STAIRS HIGHER.
SINCE MARIA HILL FOUND HERSELF--
HOME SWEET--
HOME.

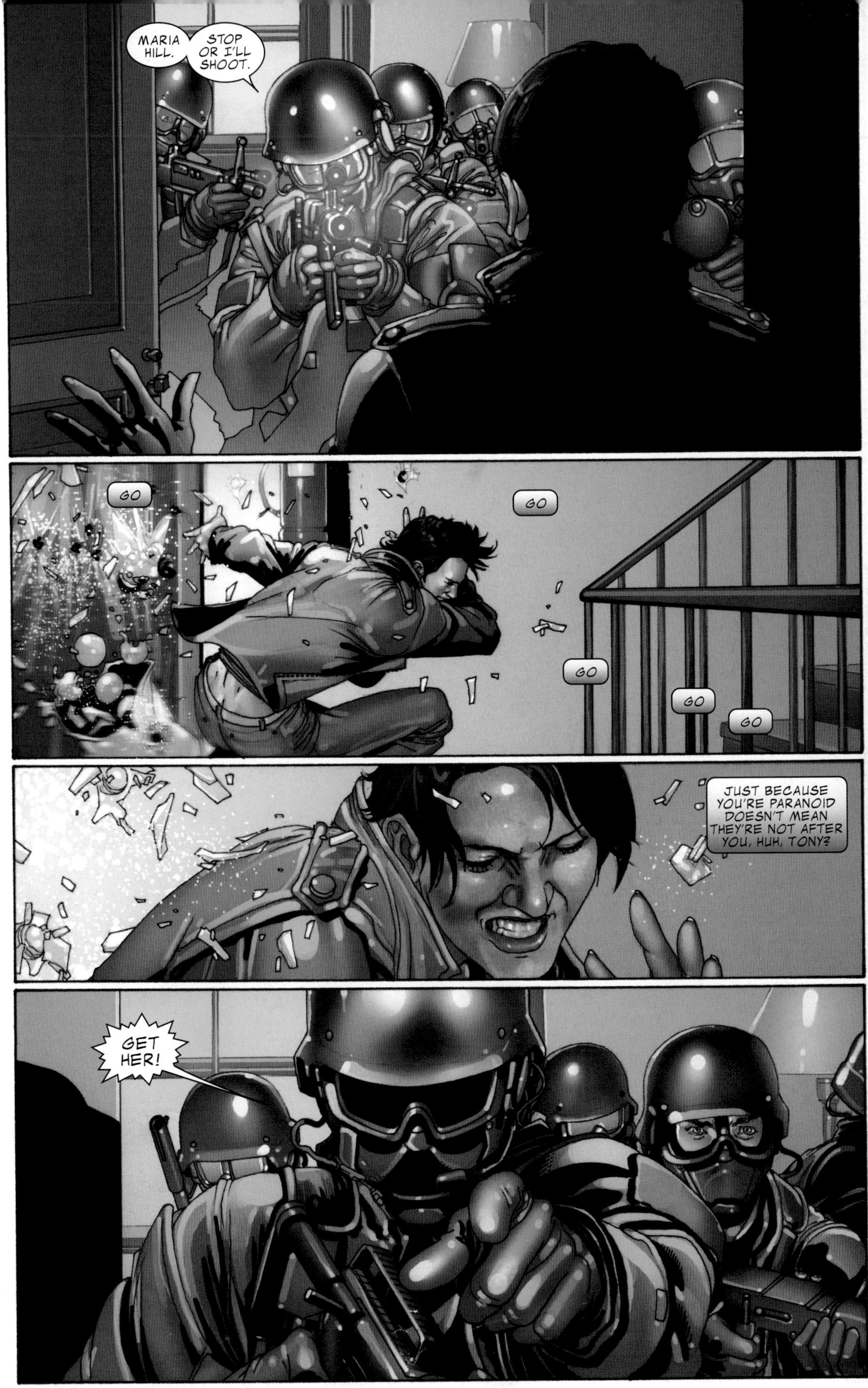
MARIA HILL.
STOP OR I'LL SHOOT.
GO
GO
GO
GO
GO
JUST BECAUSE YOU'RE PARANOID DOESN'T MEAN THEY'RE NOT AFTER YOU, HUH, TONY?
GET HER!

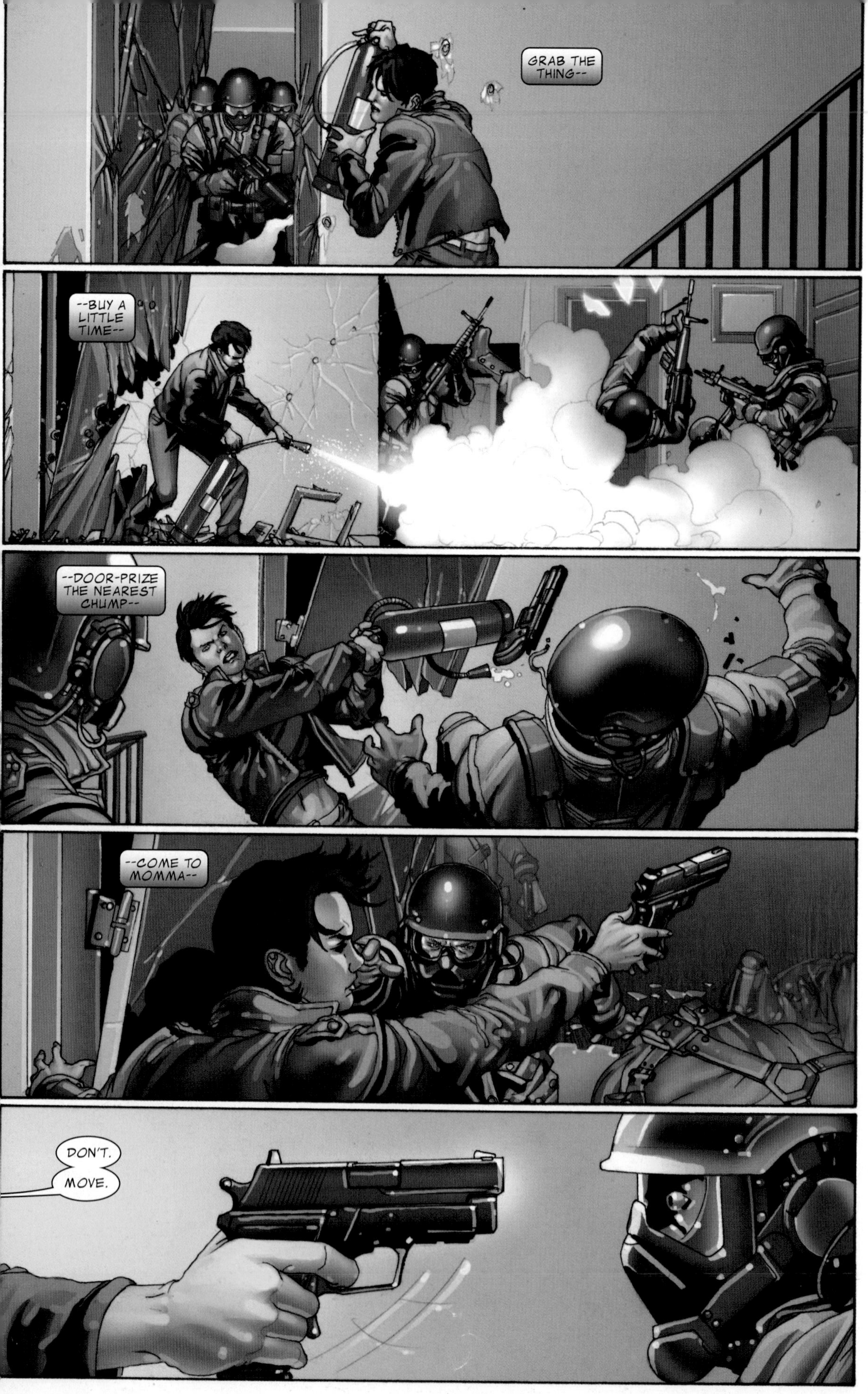
GRAB THE THING--
--BUY A LITTLE TIME--
--DOOR-PRIZE THE NEAREST CHUMP--
--COME TO MOMMA--
DON'T.
MOVE.

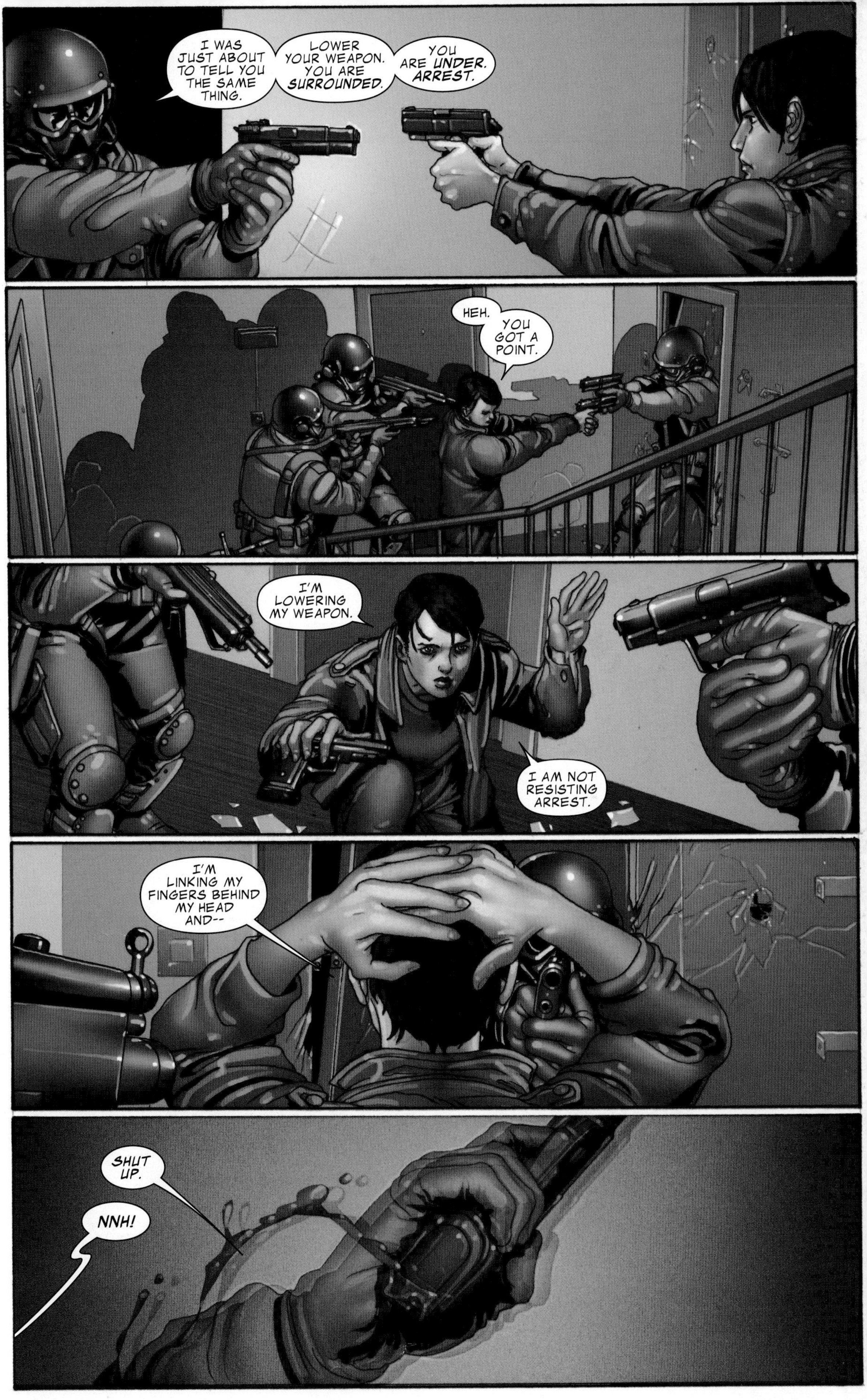

I WAS JUST ABOUT TO TELL YOU THE SAME THING.
LOWER YOUR WEAPON. YOU ARE SURROUNDED.
YOU ARE UNDER. ARREST.
HEH. YOU GOT A POINT.
I'M LOWERING MY WEAPON.
I AM NOT RESISTING ARREST.
I'M LINKING MY FINGERS BEHIND MY HEAD AND--
SHUT UP.
NNH!

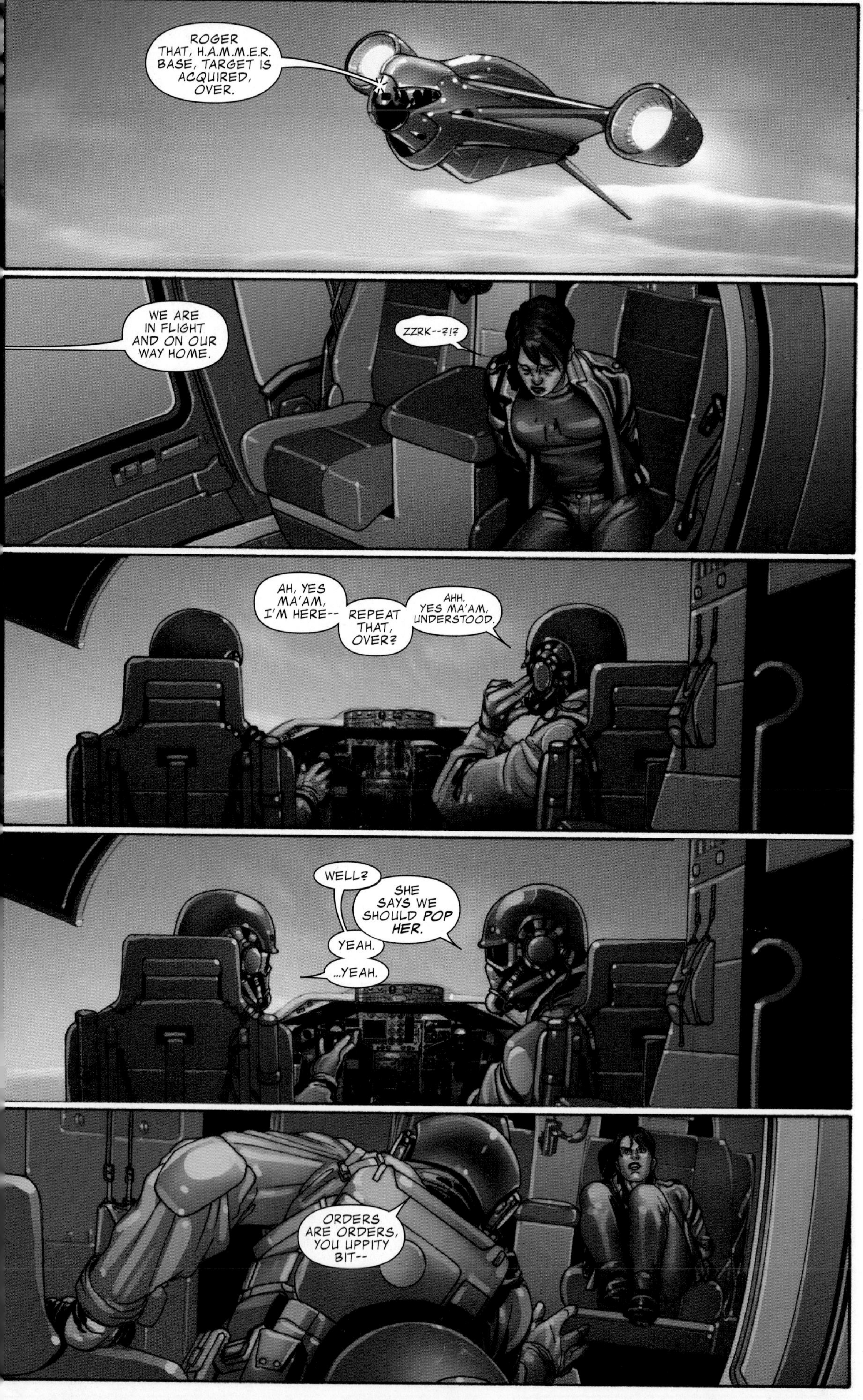
ROGER THAT, H.A.M.M.E.R. BASE, TARGET IS ACQUIRED, OVER.
WE ARE IN FLIGHT AND ON OUR WAY HOME.
ZZRK--?!?
AH, YES MA'AM, I'M HERE--
REPEAT THAT, OVER?
AHH. YES MA'AM, UNDERSTOOD.
WELL?
SHE SAYS WE SHOULD *POP HER*.
YEAH.
...YEAH.
ORDERS ARE ORDERS, YOU UPPITY BIT--

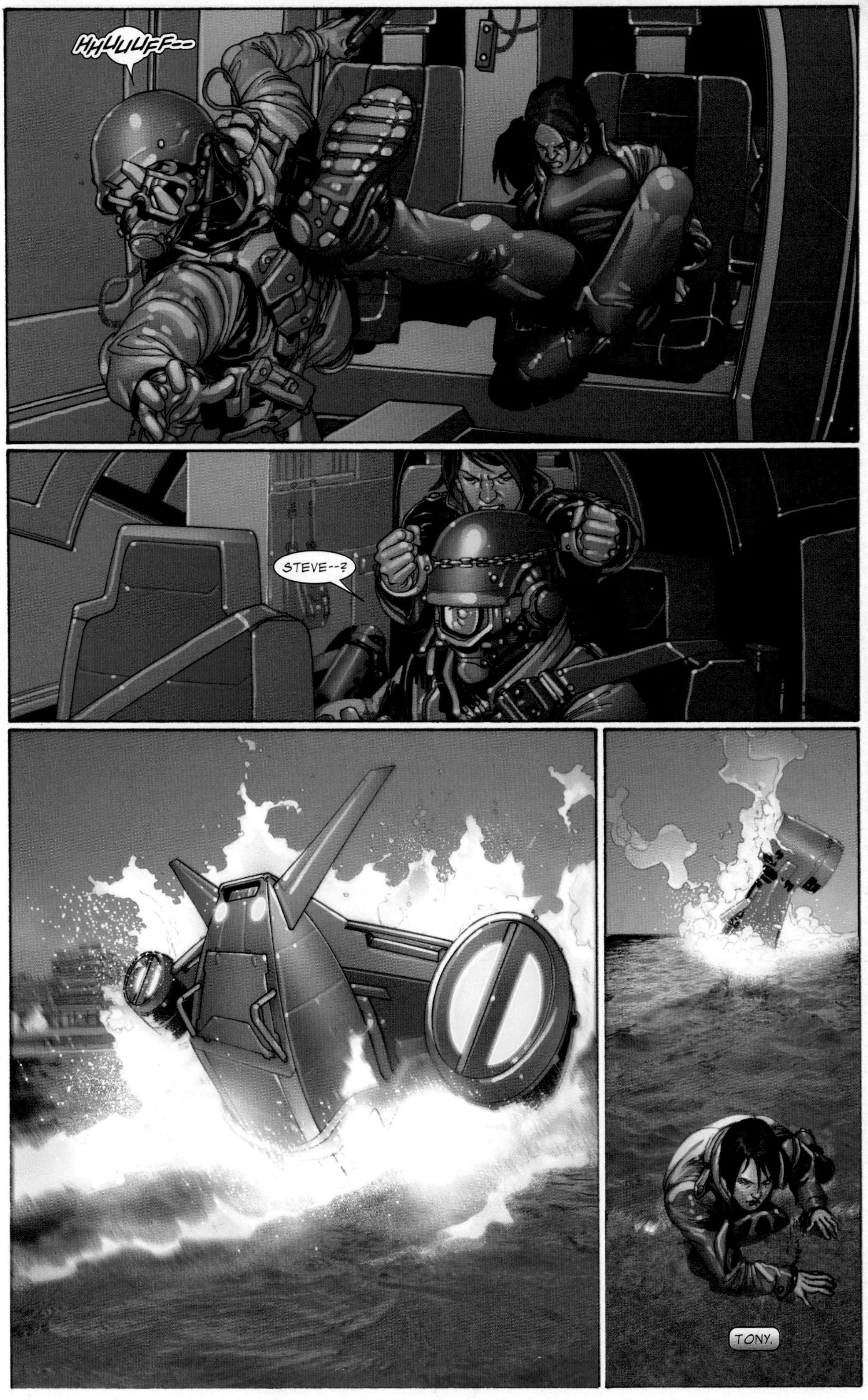
HHUUUFF--
STEVE--?
TONY.

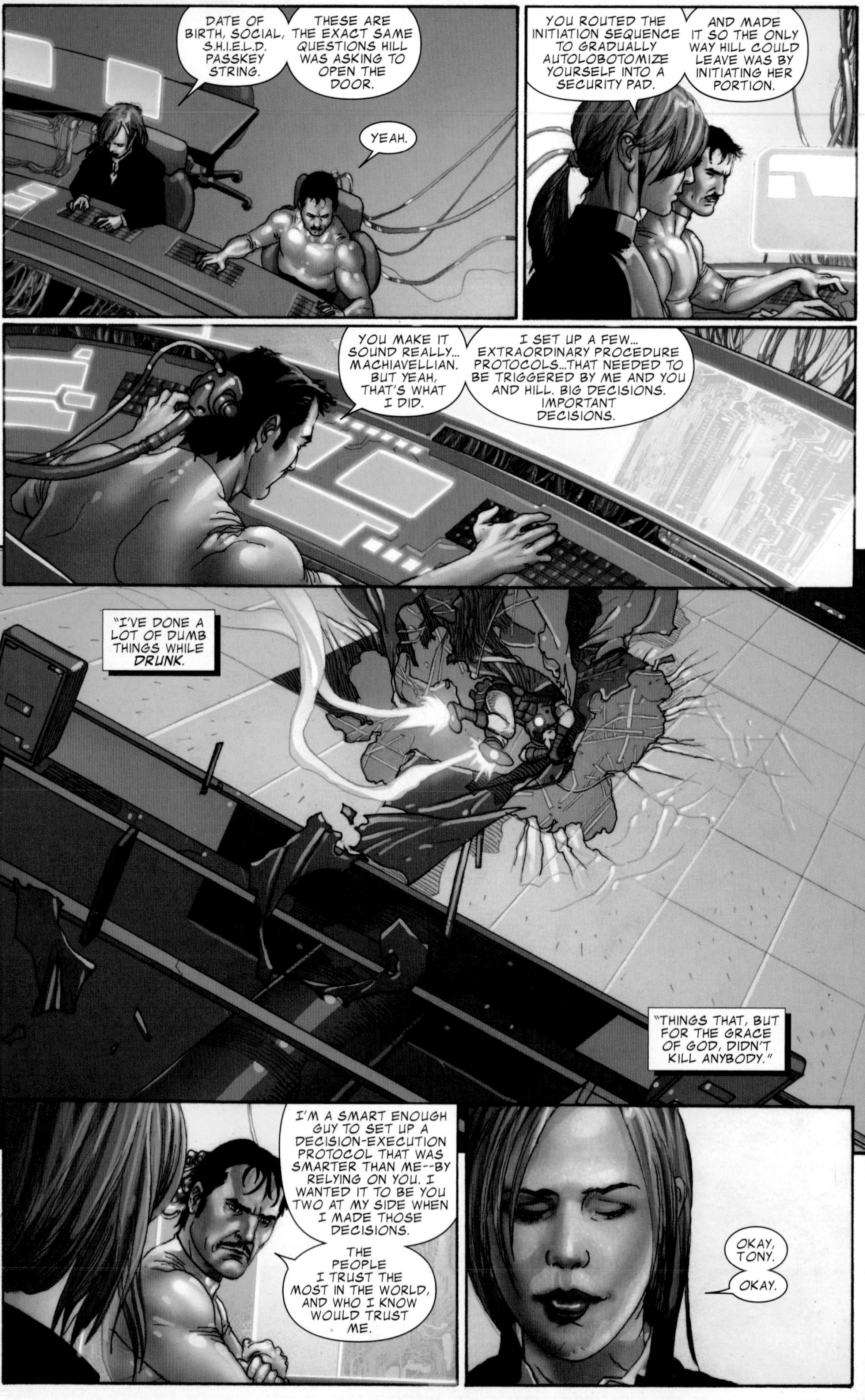
DATE OF BIRTH, SOCIAL, S.H.I.E.L.D. PASSKEY STRING.
THESE ARE THE EXACT SAME QUESTIONS HILL WAS ASKING TO OPEN THE DOOR.
YEAH.
YOU ROUTED THE INITIATION SEQUENCE TO GRADUALLY AUTOLOBOTOMIZE YOURSELF INTO A SECURITY PAD.
AND MADE IT SO THE ONLY WAY HILL COULD LEAVE WAS BY INITIATING HER PORTION.
YOU MAKE IT SOUND REALLY... MACHIAVELLIAN. BUT YEAH, THAT'S WHAT I DID.
I SET UP A FEW... EXTRAORDINARY PROCEDURE PROTOCOLS...THAT NEEDED TO BE TRIGGERED BY ME AND YOU AND HILL. BIG DECISIONS. IMPORTANT DECISIONS.
"I'VE DONE A LOT OF DUMB THINGS WHILE *DRUNK*.
"THINGS THAT, BUT FOR THE GRACE OF GOD, DIDN'T KILL ANYBODY."
I'M A SMART ENOUGH GUY TO SET UP A DECISION-EXECUTION PROTOCOL THAT WAS SMARTER THAN ME--BY RELYING ON YOU. I WANTED IT TO BE YOU TWO AT MY SIDE WHEN I MADE THOSE DECISIONS.
THE PEOPLE I TRUST THE MOST IN THE WORLD, AND WHO I KNOW WOULD TRUST ME.
OKAY, TONY.
OKAY.

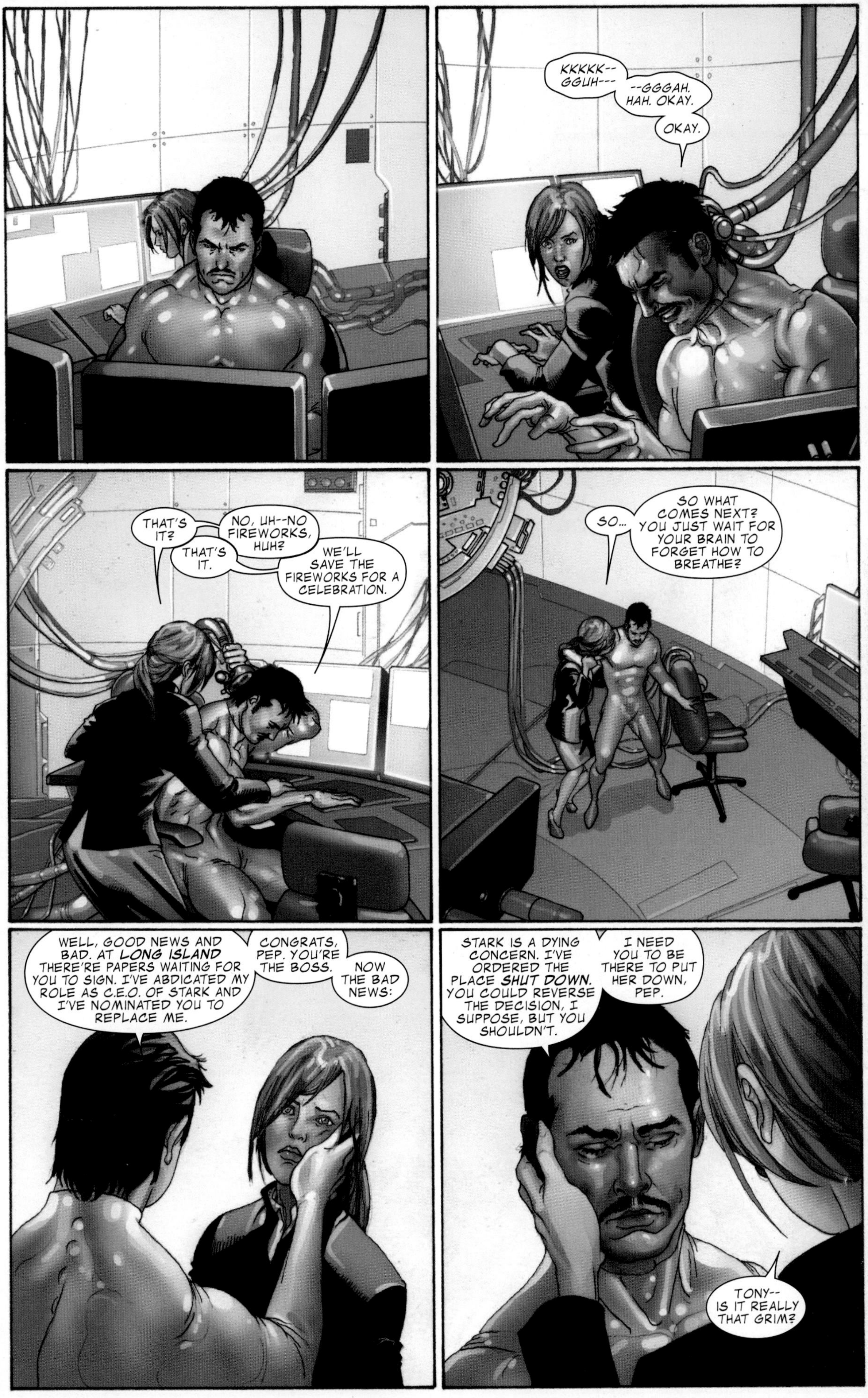
KKKKK--
GGUH---
--GGGAH. HAH. OKAY.
OKAY.
THAT'S IT?
NO, UH--NO FIREWORKS, HUH?
THAT'S IT.
WE'LL SAVE THE FIREWORKS FOR A CELEBRATION.
SO...
SO WHAT COMES NEXT? YOU JUST WAIT FOR YOUR BRAIN TO FORGET HOW TO BREATHE?
WELL, GOOD NEWS AND BAD. AT LONG ISLAND THERE'RE PAPERS WAITING FOR YOU TO SIGN. I'VE ABDICATED MY ROLE AS C.E.O. OF STARK AND I'VE NOMINATED YOU TO REPLACE ME.
CONGRATS, PEP. YOU'RE THE BOSS.
NOW THE BAD NEWS:
STARK IS A DYING CONCERN. I'VE ORDERED THE PLACE SHUT DOWN. YOU COULD REVERSE THE DECISION, I SUPPOSE, BUT YOU SHOULDN'T.
I NEED YOU TO BE THERE TO PUT HER DOWN, PEP.
TONY-- IS IT REALLY THAT GRIM?

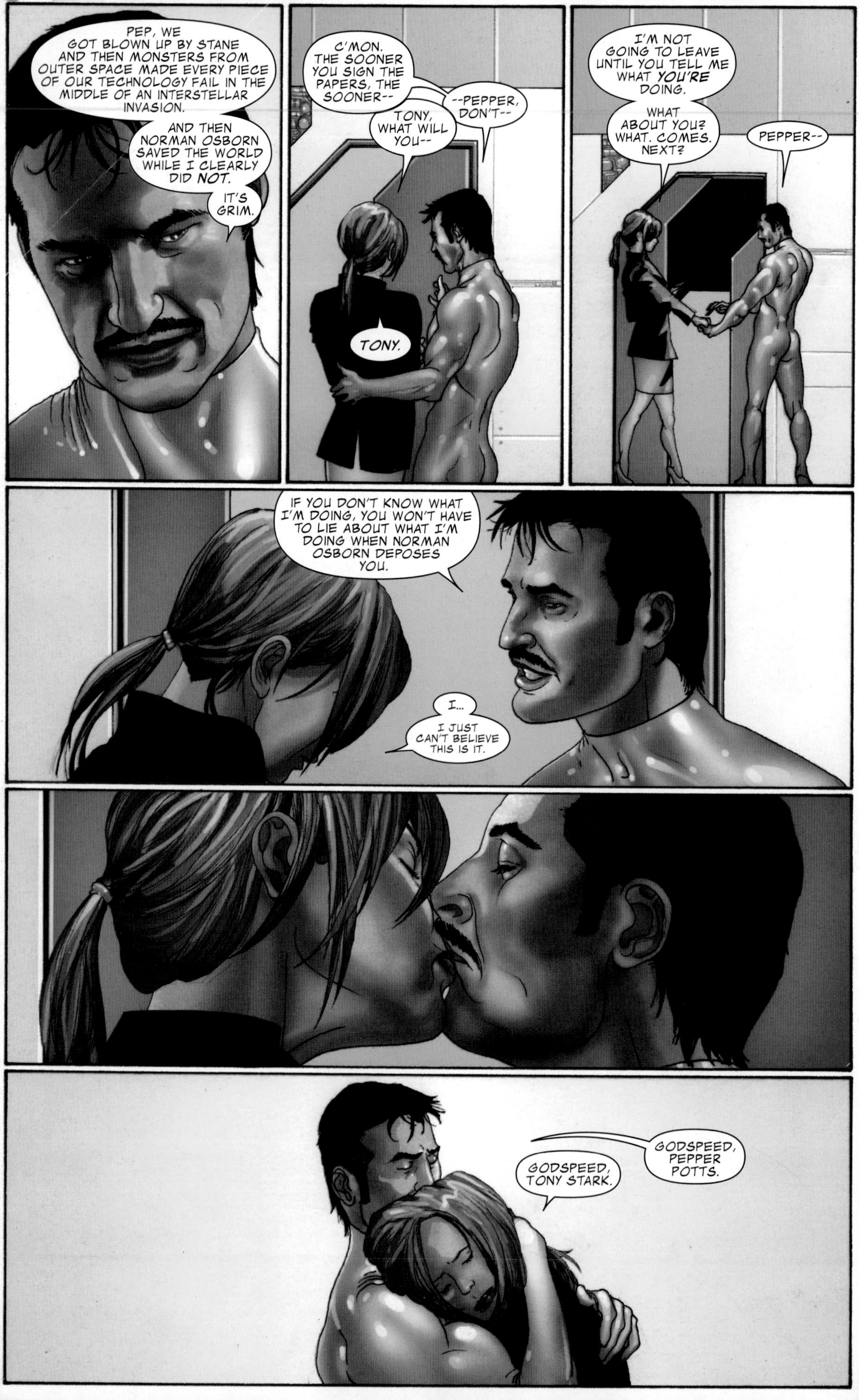
PEP, WE GOT BLOWN UP BY STANE AND THEN MONSTERS FROM OUTER SPACE MADE EVERY PIECE OF OUR TECHNOLOGY FAIL IN THE MIDDLE OF AN INTERSTELLAR INVASION.
AND THEN NORMAN OSBORN SAVED THE WORLD WHILE I CLEARLY DID NOT.
IT'S GRIM.
C'MON. THE SOONER YOU SIGN THE PAPERS, THE SOONER--
TONY, WHAT WILL YOU--
--PEPPER, DON'T--
TONY.
I'M NOT GOING TO LEAVE UNTIL YOU TELL ME WHAT YOU'RE DOING.
WHAT ABOUT YOU? WHAT. COMES. NEXT?
PEPPER--
IF YOU DON'T KNOW WHAT I'M DOING, YOU WON'T HAVE TO LIE ABOUT WHAT I'M DOING WHEN NORMAN OSBORN DEPOSES YOU.
I... I JUST CAN'T BELIEVE THIS IS IT.
GODSPEED, TONY STARK.
GODSPEED, PEPPER POTTS.

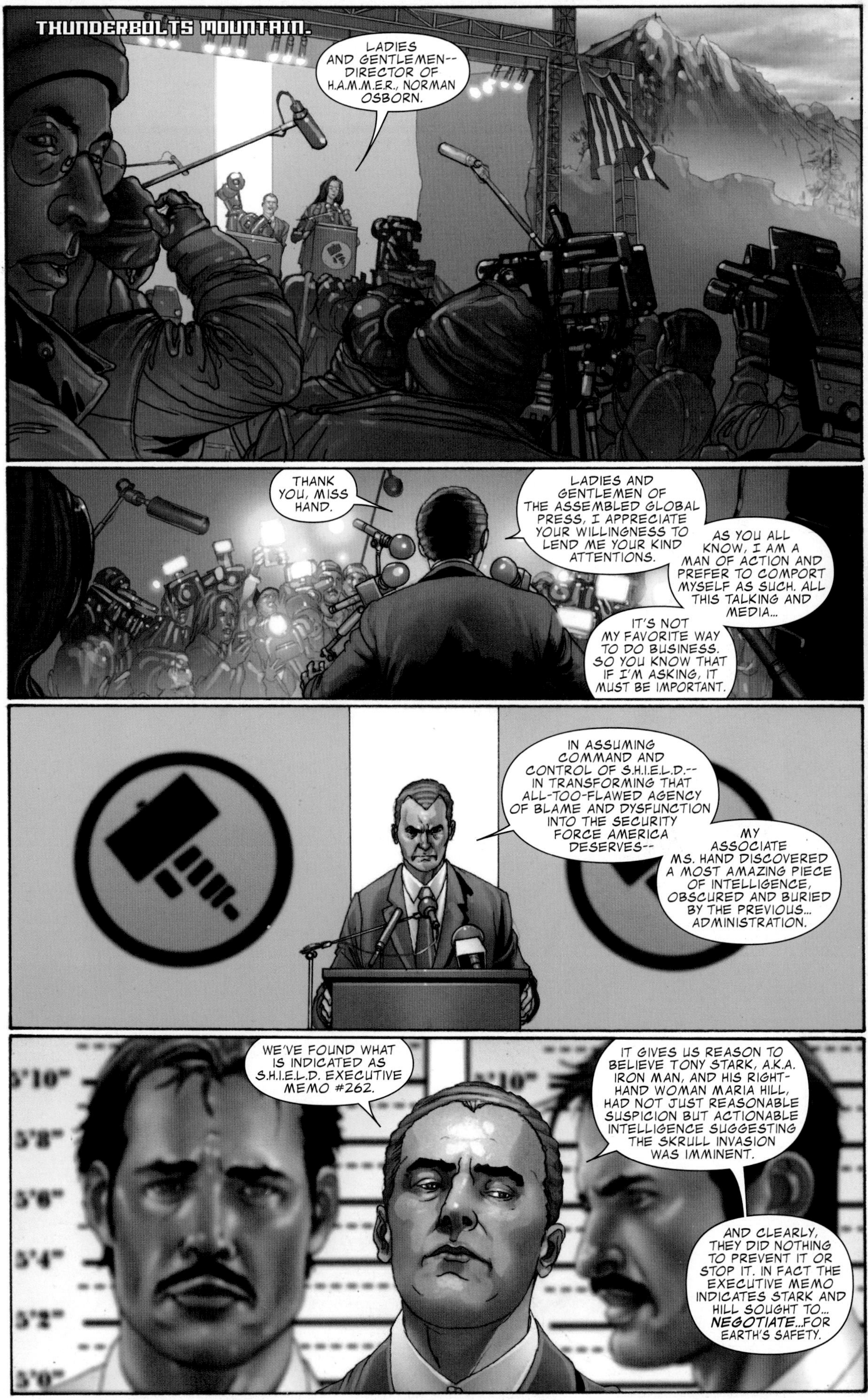
THUNDERBOLTS MOUNTAIN.
LADIES AND GENTLEMEN-- DIRECTOR OF H.A.M.M.E.R., NORMAN OSBORN.
THANK YOU, MISS HAND.
LADIES AND GENTLEMEN OF THE ASSEMBLED GLOBAL PRESS, I APPRECIATE YOUR WILLINGNESS TO LEND ME YOUR KIND ATTENTIONS.
AS YOU ALL KNOW, I AM A MAN OF ACTION AND PREFER TO COMPORT MYSELF AS SUCH. ALL THIS TALKING AND MEDIA...
IT'S NOT MY FAVORITE WAY TO DO BUSINESS. SO YOU KNOW THAT IF I'M ASKING, IT MUST BE IMPORTANT.
IN ASSUMING COMMAND AND CONTROL OF S.H.I.E.L.D.-- IN TRANSFORMING THAT ALL-TOO-FLAWED AGENCY OF BLAME AND DYSFUNCTION INTO THE SECURITY FORCE AMERICA DESERVES--
MY ASSOCIATE MS. HAND DISCOVERED A MOST AMAZING PIECE OF INTELLIGENCE, OBSCURED AND BURIED BY THE PREVIOUS... ADMINISTRATION.
WE'VE FOUND WHAT IS INDICATED AS S.H.I.E.L.D. EXECUTIVE MEMO #262.
IT GIVES US REASON TO BELIEVE TONY STARK, A.K.A. IRON MAN, AND HIS RIGHT-HAND WOMAN MARIA HILL, HAD NOT JUST REASONABLE SUSPICION BUT ACTIONABLE INTELLIGENCE SUGGESTING THE SKRULL INVASION WAS IMMINENT.
AND CLEARLY, THEY DID NOTHING TO PREVENT IT OR STOP IT. IN FACT THE EXECUTIVE MEMO INDICATES STARK AND HILL SOUGHT TO... NEGOTIATE...FOR EARTH'S SAFETY.

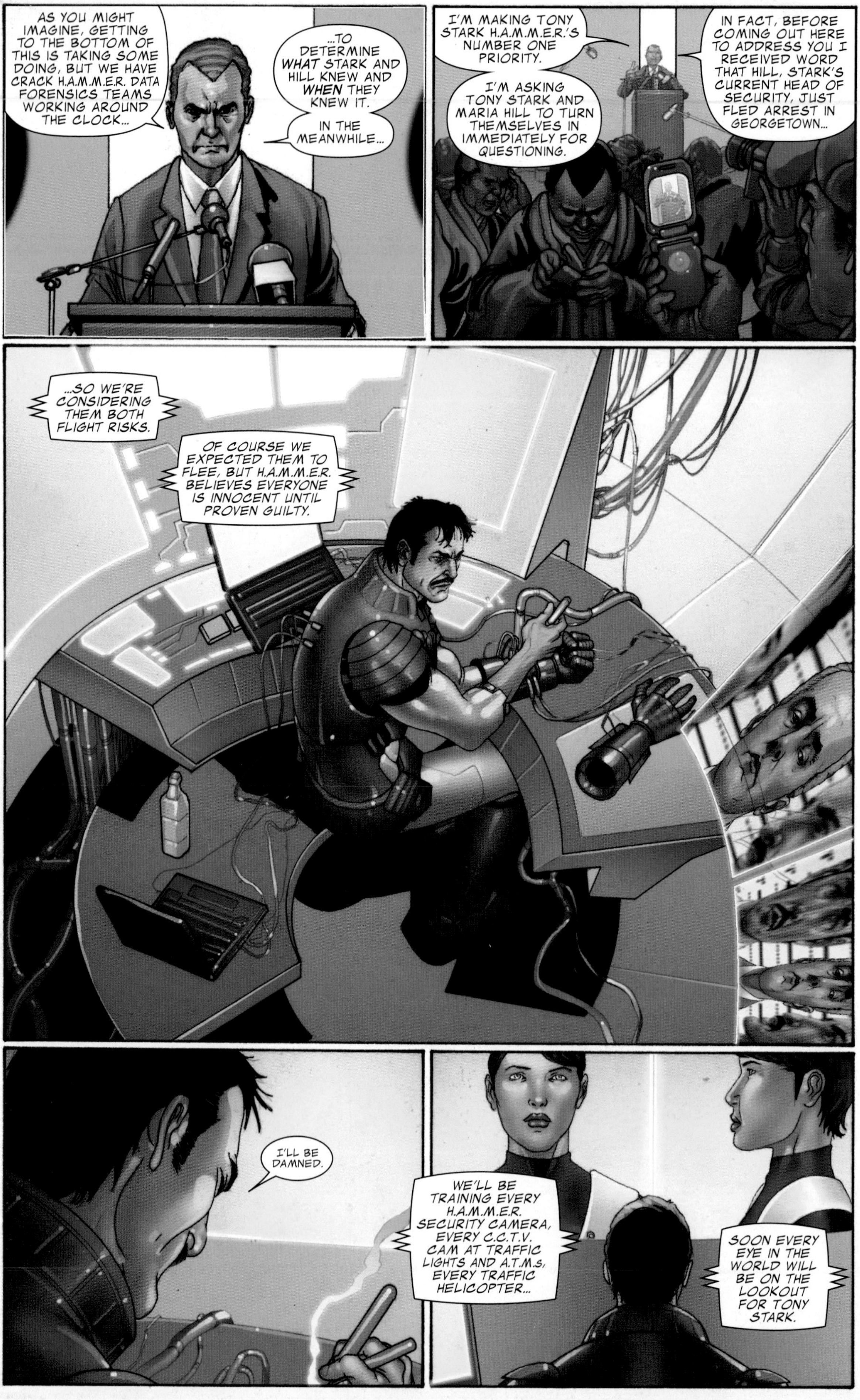

AS YOU MIGHT IMAGINE, GETTING TO THE BOTTOM OF THIS IS TAKING SOME DOING, BUT WE HAVE CRACK H.A.M.M.E.R. DATA FORENSICS TEAMS WORKING AROUND THE CLOCK...
...TO DETERMINE WHAT STARK AND HILL KNEW AND WHEN THEY KNEW IT.
IN THE MEANWHILE...
I'M MAKING TONY STARK H.A.M.M.E.R.'S NUMBER ONE PRIORITY.
I'M ASKING TONY STARK AND MARIA HILL TO TURN THEMSELVES IN IMMEDIATELY FOR QUESTIONING.
IN FACT, BEFORE COMING OUT HERE TO ADDRESS YOU I RECEIVED WORD THAT HILL, STARK'S CURRENT HEAD OF SECURITY, JUST FLED ARREST IN GEORGETOWN...
...SO WE'RE CONSIDERING THEM BOTH FLIGHT RISKS.
OF COURSE WE EXPECTED THEM TO FLEE, BUT H.A.M.M.E.R. BELIEVES EVERYONE IS INNOCENT UNTIL PROVEN GUILTY.
I'LL BE DAMNED.
WE'LL BE TRAINING EVERY H.A.M.M.E.R. SECURITY CAMERA, EVERY C.C.T.V. CAM AT TRAFFIC LIGHTS AND A.T.M.s, EVERY TRAFFIC HELICOPTER...
SOON EVERY EYE IN THE WORLD WILL BE ON THE LOOKOUT FOR TONY STARK.

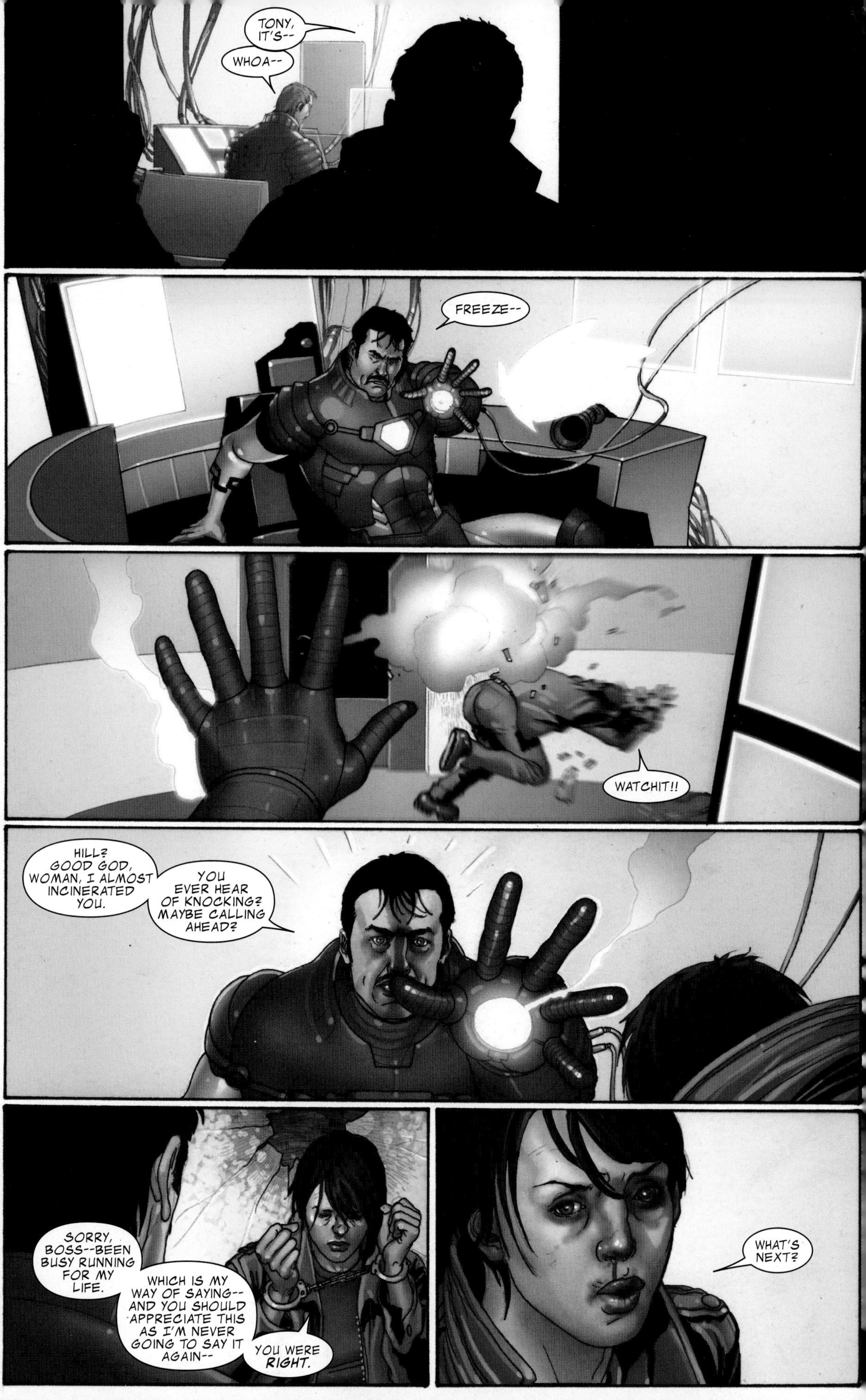
TONY, IT'S--
WHOA--
FREEZE--
WATCHIT!!
HILL? GOOD GOD, WOMAN, I ALMOST INCINERATED YOU.
YOU EVER HEAR OF KNOCKING? MAYBE CALLING AHEAD?
SORRY, BOSS--BEEN BUSY RUNNING FOR MY LIFE.
WHICH IS MY WAY OF SAYING-- AND YOU SHOULD APPRECIATE THIS AS I'M NEVER GOING TO SAY IT AGAIN--
YOU WERE RIGHT.
WHAT'S NEXT?

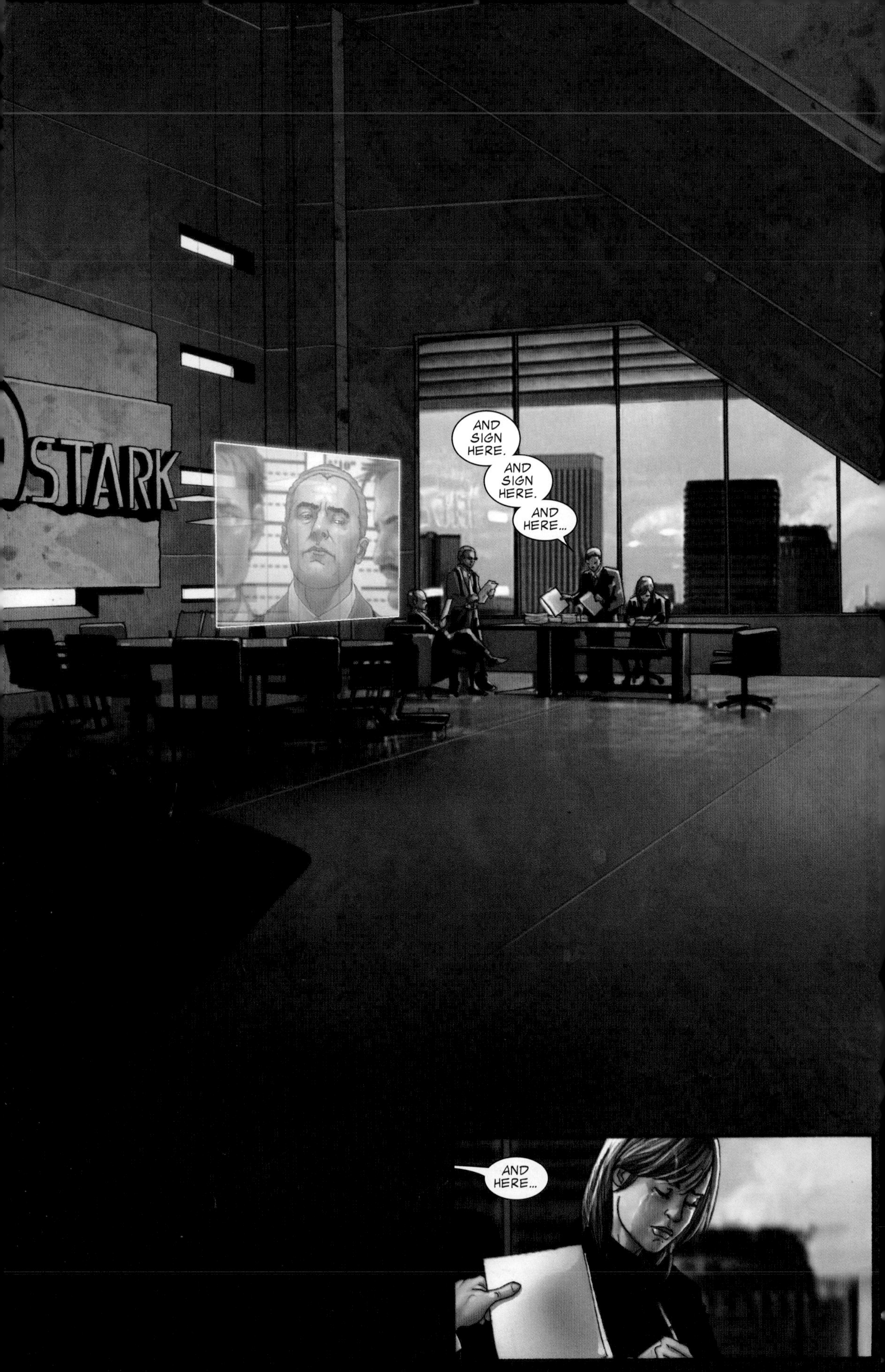
AND SIGN HERE.
AND SIGN HERE.
AND HERE...
STARK
AND HERE...

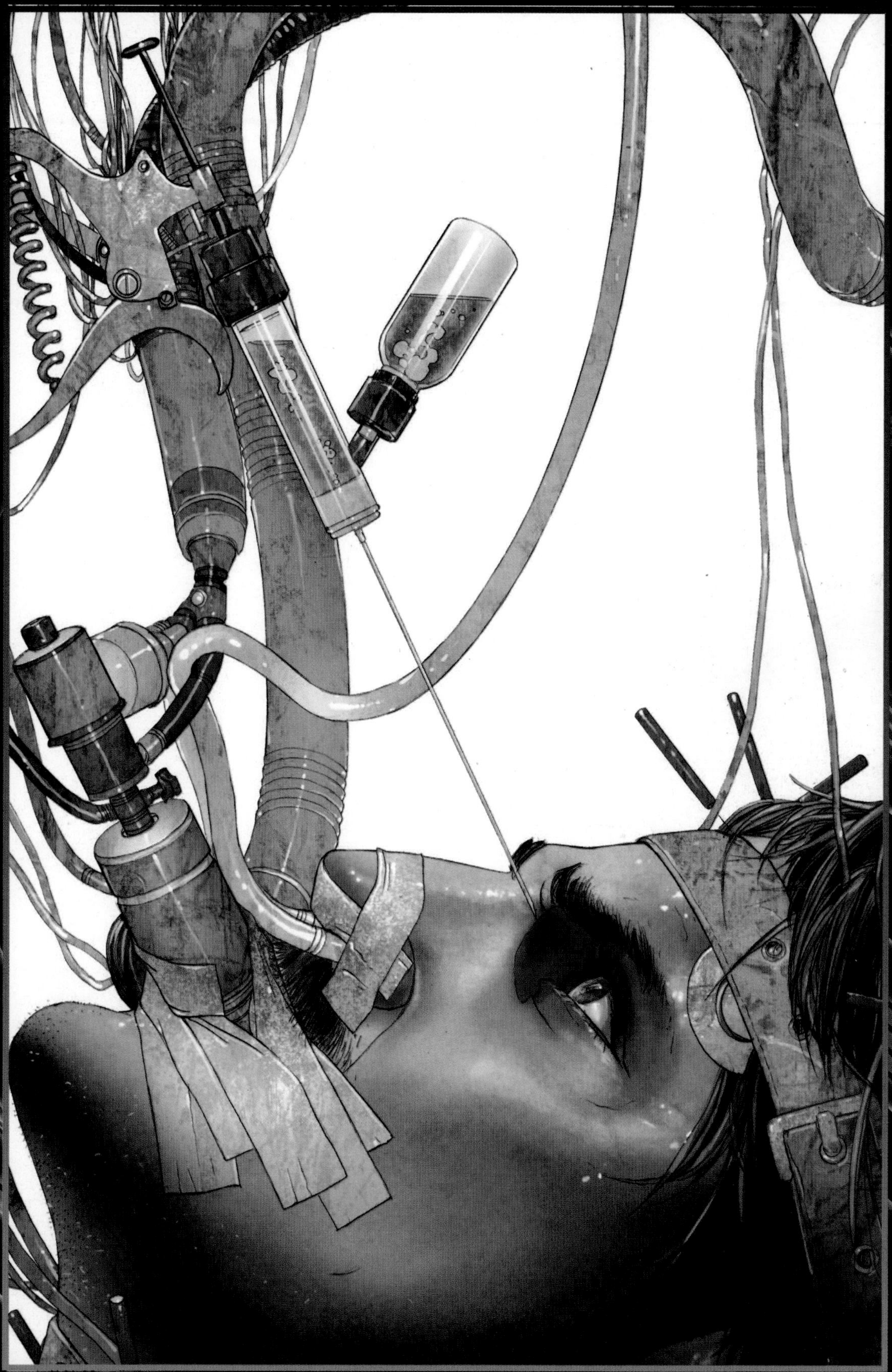

10

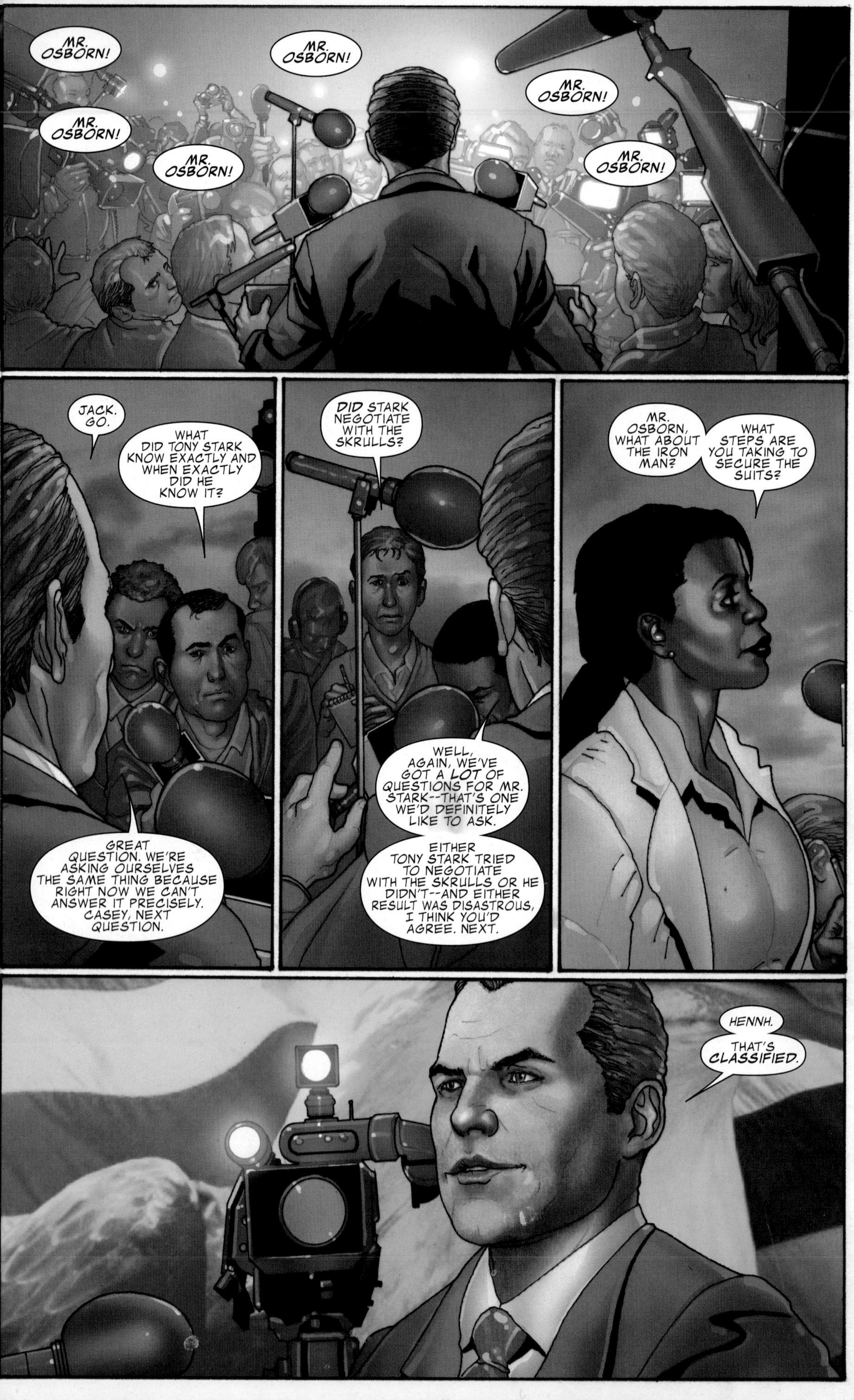
MR. OSBORN!
MR. OSBORN!
MR. OSBORN!
MR. OSBORN!
MR. OSBORN!
MR. OSBORN!
JACK. GO.
WHAT DID TONY STARK KNOW EXACTLY AND WHEN EXACTLY DID HE KNOW IT?
GREAT QUESTION. WE'RE ASKING OURSELVES THE SAME THING BECAUSE RIGHT NOW WE CAN'T ANSWER IT PRECISELY. CASEY, NEXT QUESTION.
DID STARK NEGOTIATE WITH THE SKRULLS?
WELL, AGAIN, WE'VE GOT A LOT OF QUESTIONS FOR MR. STARK--THAT'S ONE WE'D DEFINITELY LIKE TO ASK.
EITHER TONY STARK TRIED TO NEGOTIATE WITH THE SKRULLS OR HE DIDN'T--AND EITHER RESULT WAS DISASTROUS, I THINK YOU'D AGREE. NEXT.
MR. OSBORN, WHAT ABOUT THE IRON MAN?
WHAT STEPS ARE YOU TAKING TO SECURE THE SUITS?
HENNH.
THAT'S CLASSIFIED.

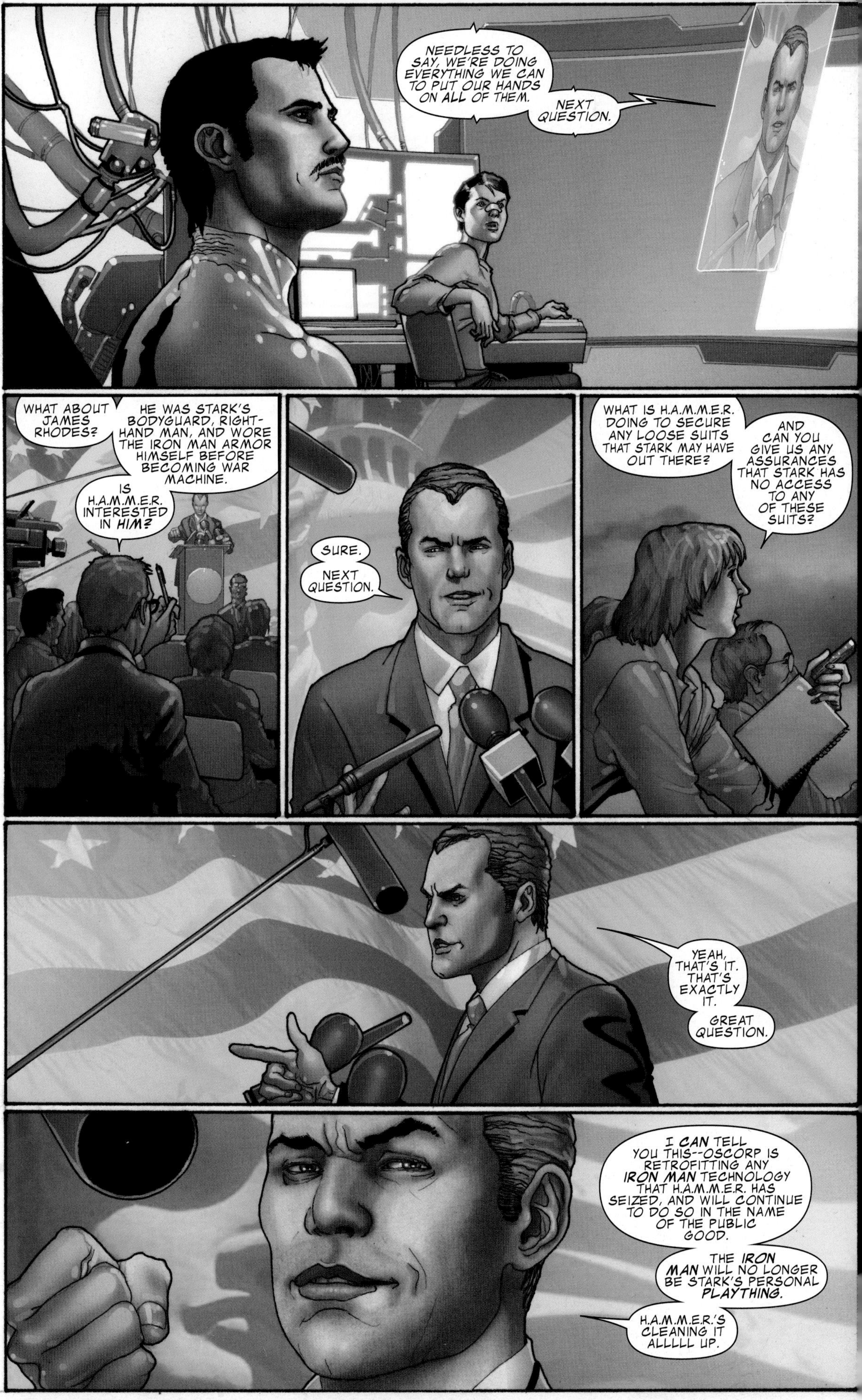
NEEDLESS TO SAY, WE'RE DOING EVERYTHING WE CAN TO PUT OUR HANDS ON ALL OF THEM.
NEXT QUESTION.
WHAT ABOUT JAMES RHODES?
HE WAS STARK'S BODYGUARD, RIGHT-HAND MAN, AND WORE THE IRON MAN ARMOR HIMSELF BEFORE BECOMING WAR MACHINE.
IS H.A.M.M.E.R. INTERESTED IN HIM?
SURE.
NEXT QUESTION.
WHAT IS H.A.M.M.E.R. DOING TO SECURE ANY LOOSE SUITS THAT STARK MAY HAVE OUT THERE?
AND CAN YOU GIVE US ANY ASSURANCES THAT STARK HAS NO ACCESS TO ANY OF THESE SUITS?
YEAH, THAT'S IT. THAT'S EXACTLY IT.
GREAT QUESTION.
I CAN TELL YOU THIS--OSCORP IS RETROFITTING ANY IRON MAN TECHNOLOGY THAT H.A.M.M.E.R. HAS SEIZED, AND WILL CONTINUE TO DO SO IN THE NAME OF THE PUBLIC GOOD.
THE IRON MAN WILL NO LONGER BE STARK'S PERSONAL PLAYTHING.
H.A.M.M.E.R.'S CLEANING IT ALLLLL UP.

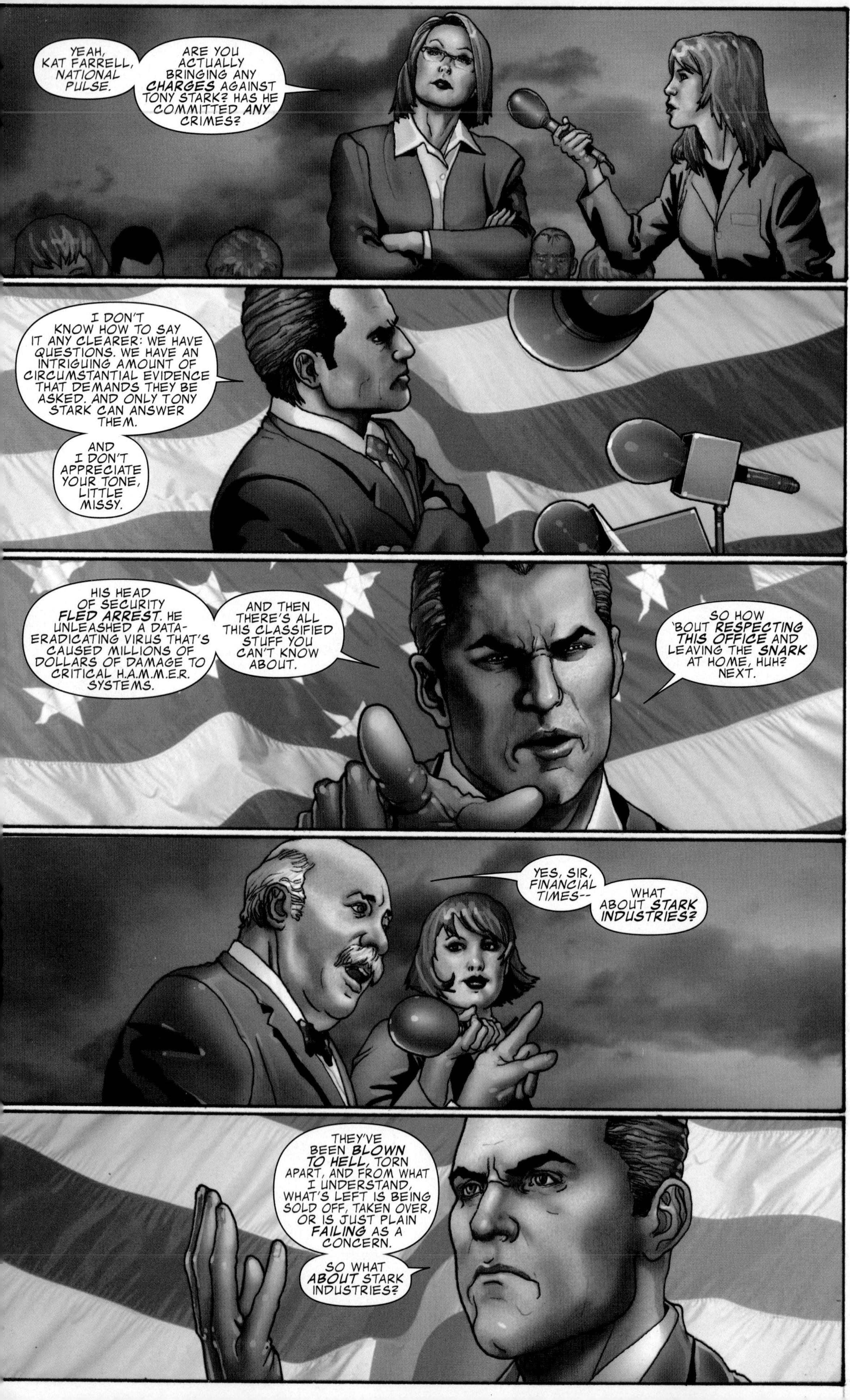

YEAH, KAT FARRELL, NATIONAL PULSE.
ARE YOU ACTUALLY BRINGING ANY CHARGES AGAINST TONY STARK? HAS HE COMMITTED ANY CRIMES?
I DON'T KNOW HOW TO SAY IT ANY CLEARER: WE HAVE QUESTIONS. WE HAVE AN INTRIGUING AMOUNT OF CIRCUMSTANTIAL EVIDENCE THAT DEMANDS THEY BE ASKED. AND ONLY TONY STARK CAN ANSWER THEM.
AND I DON'T APPRECIATE YOUR TONE, LITTLE MISSY.
HIS HEAD OF SECURITY FLED ARREST. HE UNLEASHED A DATA-ERADICATING VIRUS THAT'S CAUSED MILLIONS OF DOLLARS OF DAMAGE TO CRITICAL H.A.M.M.E.R. SYSTEMS.
AND THEN THERE'S ALL THIS CLASSIFIED STUFF YOU CAN'T KNOW ABOUT.
SO HOW 'BOUT RESPECTING THIS OFFICE AND LEAVING THE SNARK AT HOME, HUH? NEXT.
YES, SIR, FINANCIAL TIMES--
WHAT ABOUT STARK INDUSTRIES?
THEY'VE BEEN BLOWN TO HELL, TORN APART, AND FROM WHAT I UNDERSTAND, WHAT'S LEFT IS BEING SOLD OFF, TAKEN OVER, OR IS JUST PLAIN FAILING AS A CONCERN.
SO WHAT ABOUT STARK INDUSTRIES?

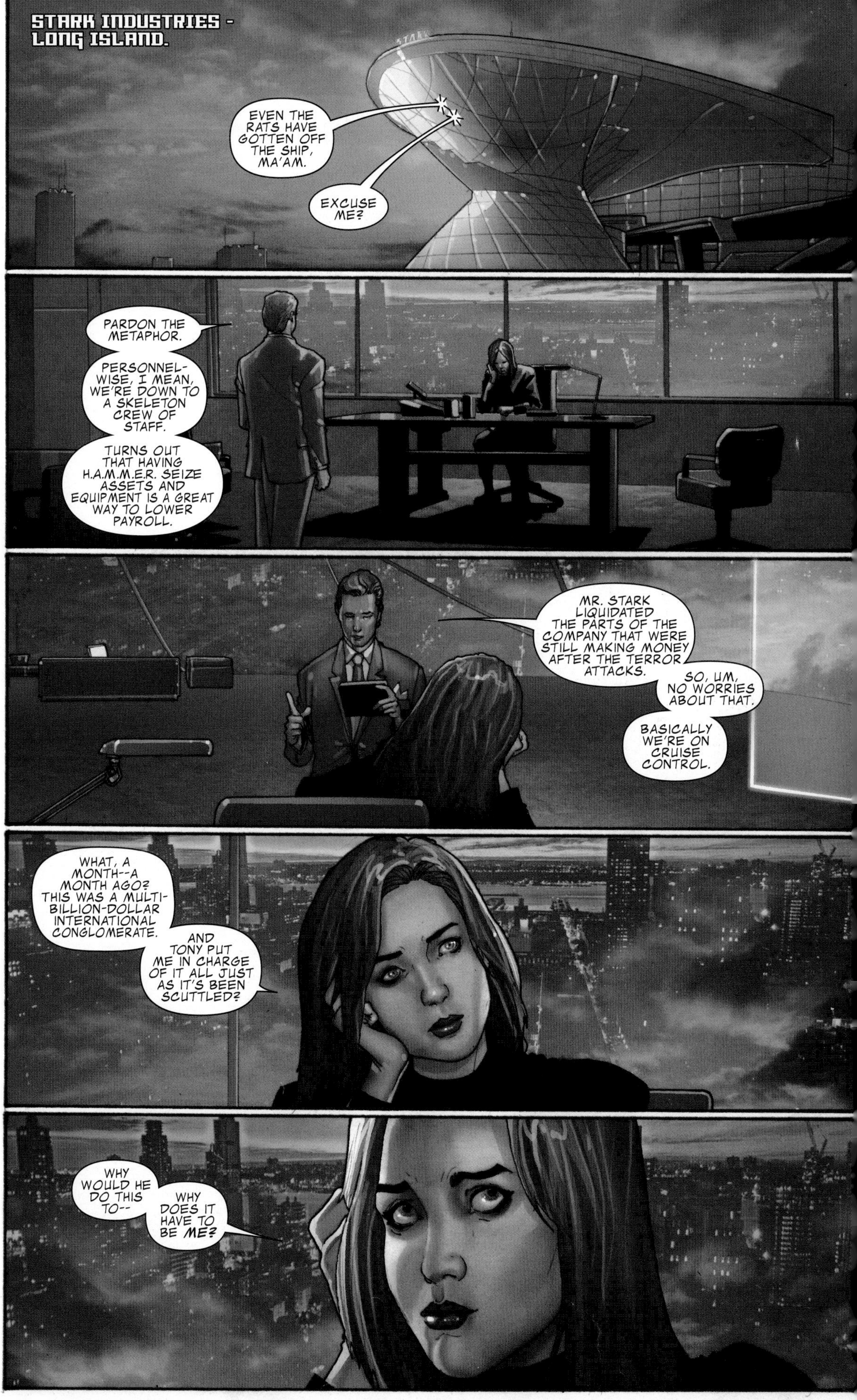
STARK INDUSTRIES - LONG ISLAND.
EVEN THE RATS HAVE GOTTEN OFF THE SHIP, MA'AM.
EXCUSE ME?
PARDON THE METAPHOR.
PERSONNEL-WISE, I MEAN, WE'RE DOWN TO A SKELETON CREW OF STAFF.
TURNS OUT THAT HAVING H.A.M.M.E.R. SEIZE ASSETS AND EQUIPMENT IS A GREAT WAY TO LOWER PAYROLL.
MR. STARK LIQUIDATED THE PARTS OF THE COMPANY THAT WERE STILL MAKING MONEY AFTER THE TERROR ATTACKS.
SO, UM, NO WORRIES ABOUT THAT.
BASICALLY WE'RE ON CRUISE CONTROL.
WHAT, A MONTH--A MONTH AGO? THIS WAS A MULTI-BILLION-DOLLAR INTERNATIONAL CONGLOMERATE.
AND TONY PUT ME IN CHARGE OF IT ALL JUST AS IT'S BEEN SCUTTLED?
WHY WOULD HE DO THIS TO--
WHY DOES IT HAVE TO BE *ME*?

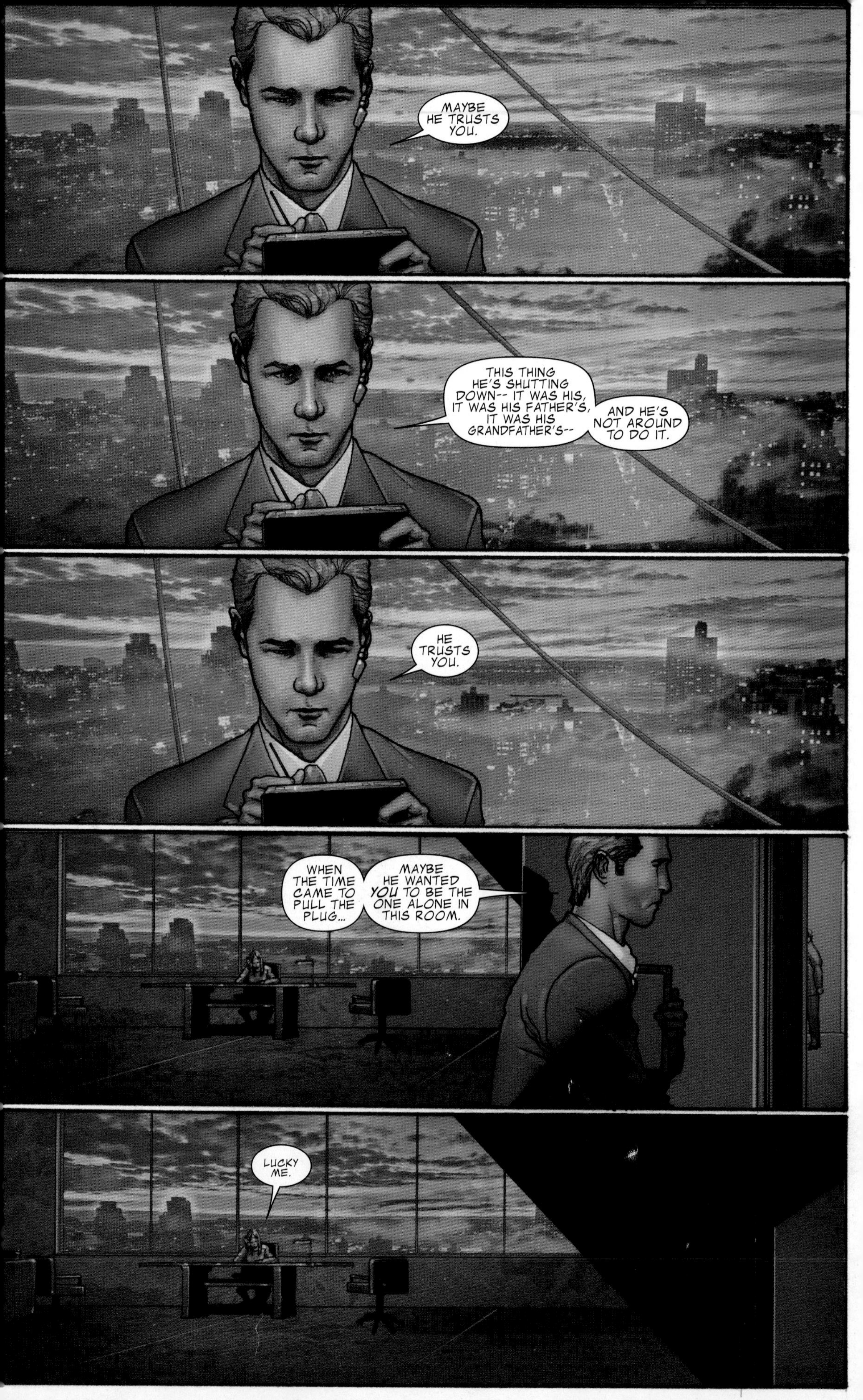
MAYBE HE TRUSTS YOU.
THIS THING HE'S SHUTTING DOWN-- IT WAS HIS, IT WAS HIS FATHER'S, IT WAS HIS GRANDFATHER'S--
AND HE'S NOT AROUND TO DO IT.
HE TRUSTS YOU.
WHEN THE TIME CAME TO PULL THE PLUG...
MAYBE HE WANTED *YOU* TO BE THE ONE ALONE IN THIS ROOM.
LUCKY ME.

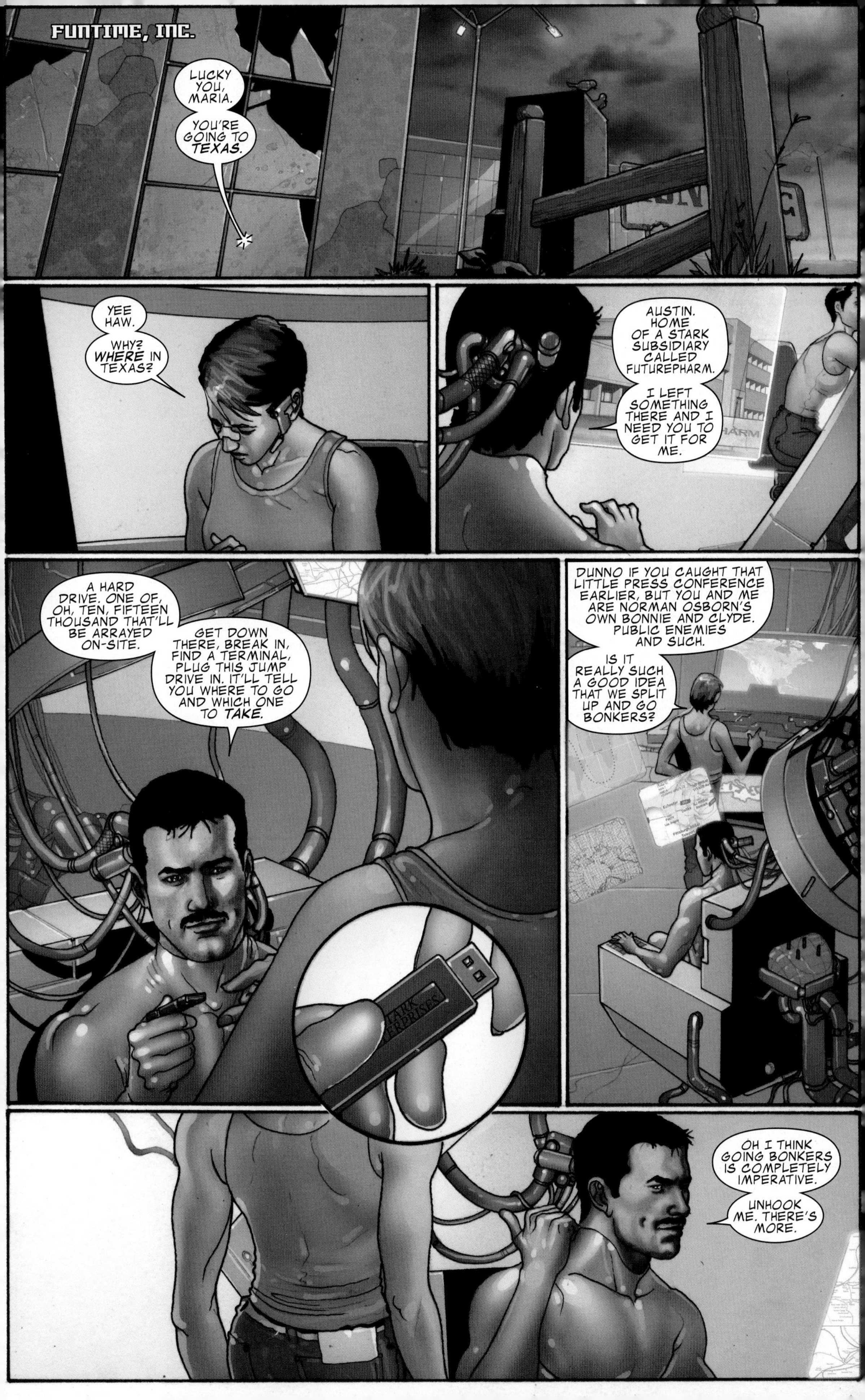
FUNTIME, INC.
LUCKY YOU, MARIA.
YOU'RE GOING TO TEXAS.
YEE HAW.
WHY? WHERE IN TEXAS?
AUSTIN. HOME OF A STARK SUBSIDIARY CALLED FUTUREPHARM.
I LEFT SOMETHING THERE AND I NEED YOU TO GET IT FOR ME.
A HARD DRIVE. ONE OF, OH, TEN, FIFTEEN THOUSAND THAT'LL BE ARRAYED ON-SITE.
GET DOWN THERE, BREAK IN, FIND A TERMINAL, PLUG THIS JUMP DRIVE IN. IT'LL TELL YOU WHERE TO GO AND WHICH ONE TO TAKE.
DUNNO IF YOU CAUGHT THAT LITTLE PRESS CONFERENCE EARLIER, BUT YOU AND ME ARE NORMAN OSBORN'S OWN BONNIE AND CLYDE. PUBLIC ENEMIES AND SUCH.
IS IT REALLY SUCH A GOOD IDEA THAT WE SPLIT UP AND GO BONKERS?
OH I THINK GOING BONKERS IS COMPLETELY IMPERATIVE.
UNHOOK ME. THERE'S MORE.

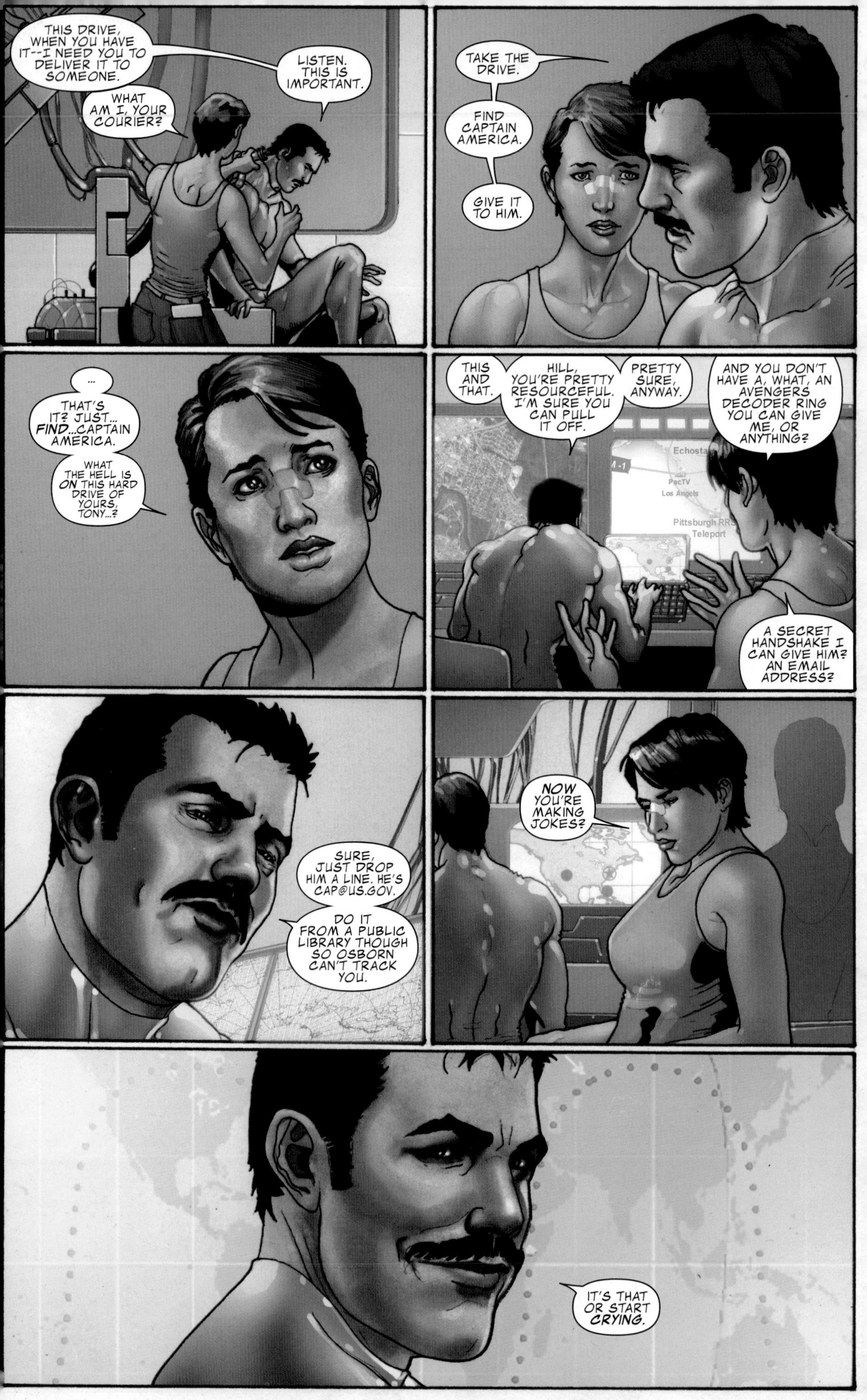
THIS DRIVE, WHEN YOU HAVE IT--I NEED YOU TO DELIVER IT TO SOMEONE.
LISTEN. THIS IS IMPORTANT.
WHAT AM I, YOUR COURIER?
TAKE THE DRIVE.
FIND CAPTAIN AMERICA.
GIVE IT TO HIM.
...
THAT'S IT? JUST... FIND...CAPTAIN AMERICA.
WHAT THE HELL IS ON THIS HARD DRIVE OF YOURS, TONY...?
THIS AND THAT.
HILL, YOU'RE PRETTY RESOURCEFUL. I'M SURE YOU CAN PULL IT OFF.
PRETTY SURE, ANYWAY.
AND YOU DON'T HAVE A, WHAT, AN AVENGERS DECODER RING YOU CAN GIVE ME, OR ANYTHING?
A SECRET HANDSHAKE I CAN GIVE HIM? AN EMAIL ADDRESS?
SURE, JUST DROP HIM A LINE. HE'S CAP@US.GOV.
DO IT FROM A PUBLIC LIBRARY THOUGH SO OSBORN CAN'T TRACK YOU.
NOW YOU'RE MAKING JOKES?
IT'S THAT OR START CRYING.

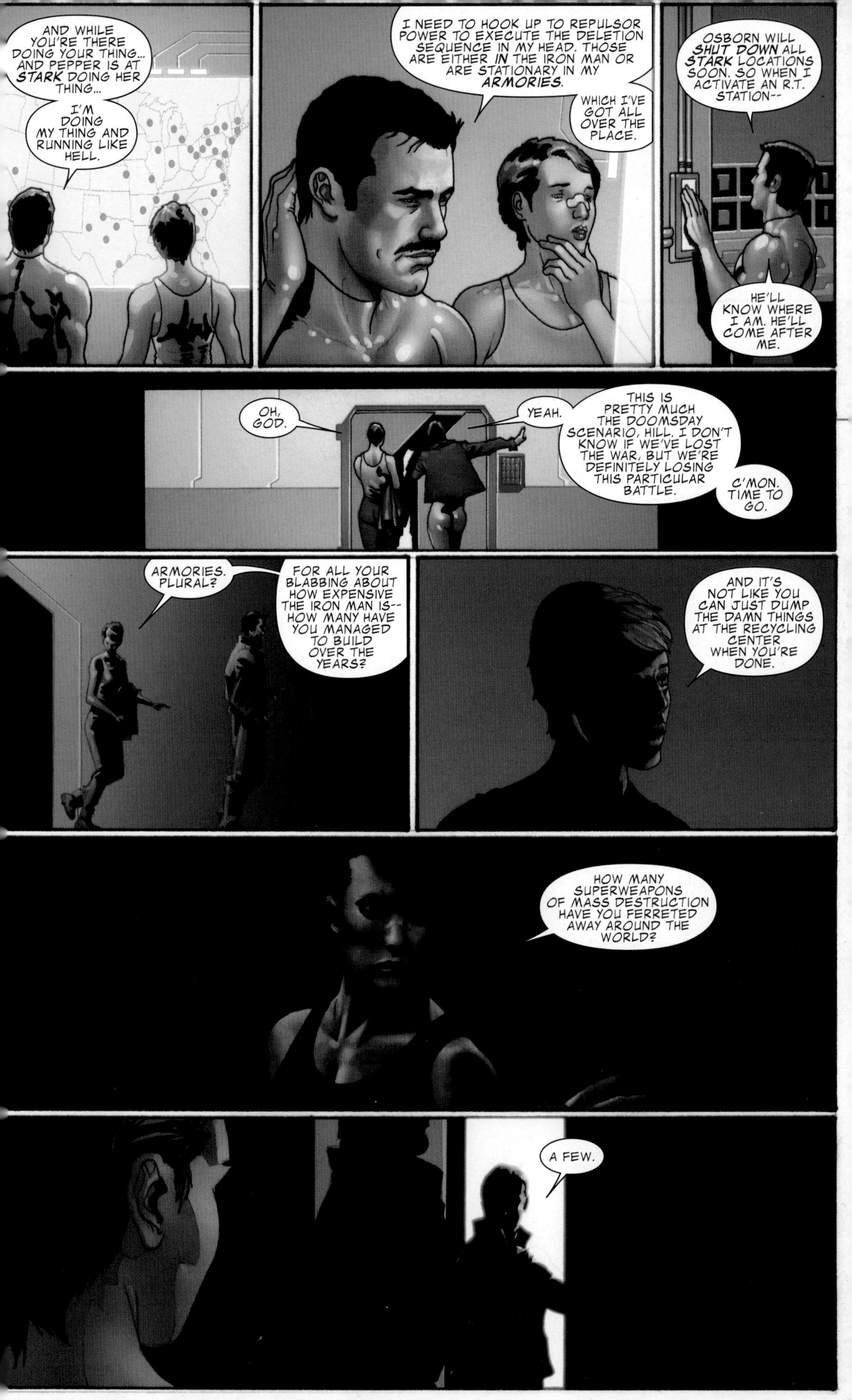
AND WHILE YOU'RE THERE DOING YOUR THING... AND PEPPER IS AT STARK DOING HER THING...
I'M DOING MY THING AND RUNNING LIKE HELL.
I NEED TO HOOK UP TO REPULSOR POWER TO EXECUTE THE DELETION SEQUENCE IN MY HEAD. THOSE ARE EITHER IN THE IRON MAN OR ARE STATIONARY IN MY ARMORIES.
WHICH I'VE GOT ALL OVER THE PLACE.
OSBORN WILL SHUT DOWN ALL STARK LOCATIONS SOON. SO WHEN I ACTIVATE AN R.T. STATION--
HE'LL KNOW WHERE I AM. HE'LL COME AFTER ME.
OH, GOD.
YEAH.
THIS IS PRETTY MUCH THE DOOMSDAY SCENARIO, HILL. I DON'T KNOW IF WE'VE LOST THE WAR, BUT WE'RE DEFINITELY LOSING THIS PARTICULAR BATTLE.
C'MON. TIME TO GO.
ARMORIES. PLURAL?
FOR ALL YOUR BLABBING ABOUT HOW EXPENSIVE THE IRON MAN IS-- HOW MANY HAVE YOU MANAGED TO BUILD OVER THE YEARS?
AND IT'S NOT LIKE YOU CAN JUST DUMP THE DAMN THINGS AT THE RECYCLING CENTER WHEN YOU'RE DONE.
HOW MANY SUPERWEAPONS OF MASS DESTRUCTION HAVE YOU FERRETED AWAY AROUND THE WORLD?
A FEW.

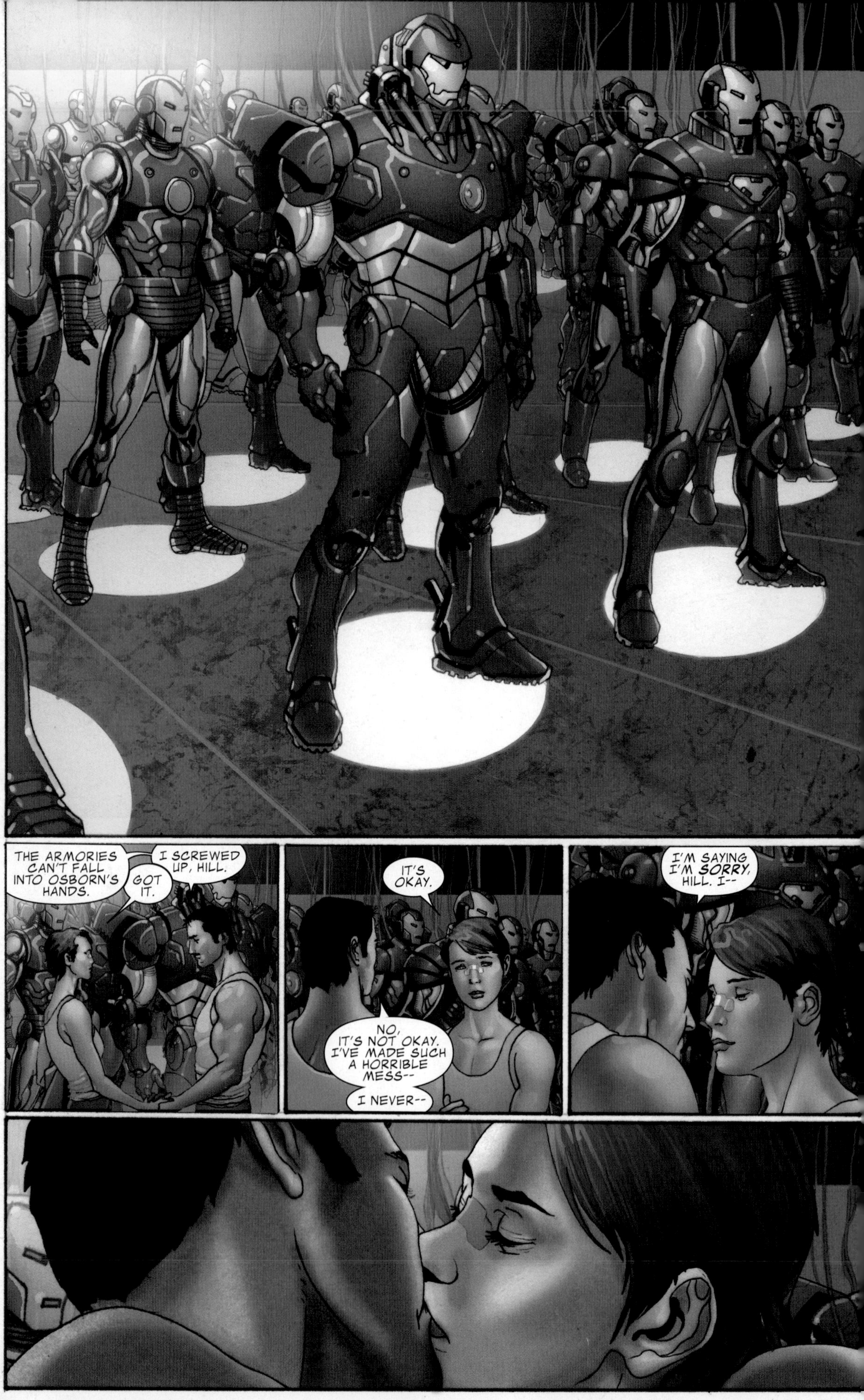
THE ARMORIES CAN'T FALL INTO OSBORN'S HANDS.
I SCREWED UP, HILL.
GOT IT.
IT'S OKAY.
NO, IT'S NOT OKAY. I'VE MADE SUCH A HORRIBLE MESS--
I NEVER--
I'M SAYING I'M SORRY, HILL. I--

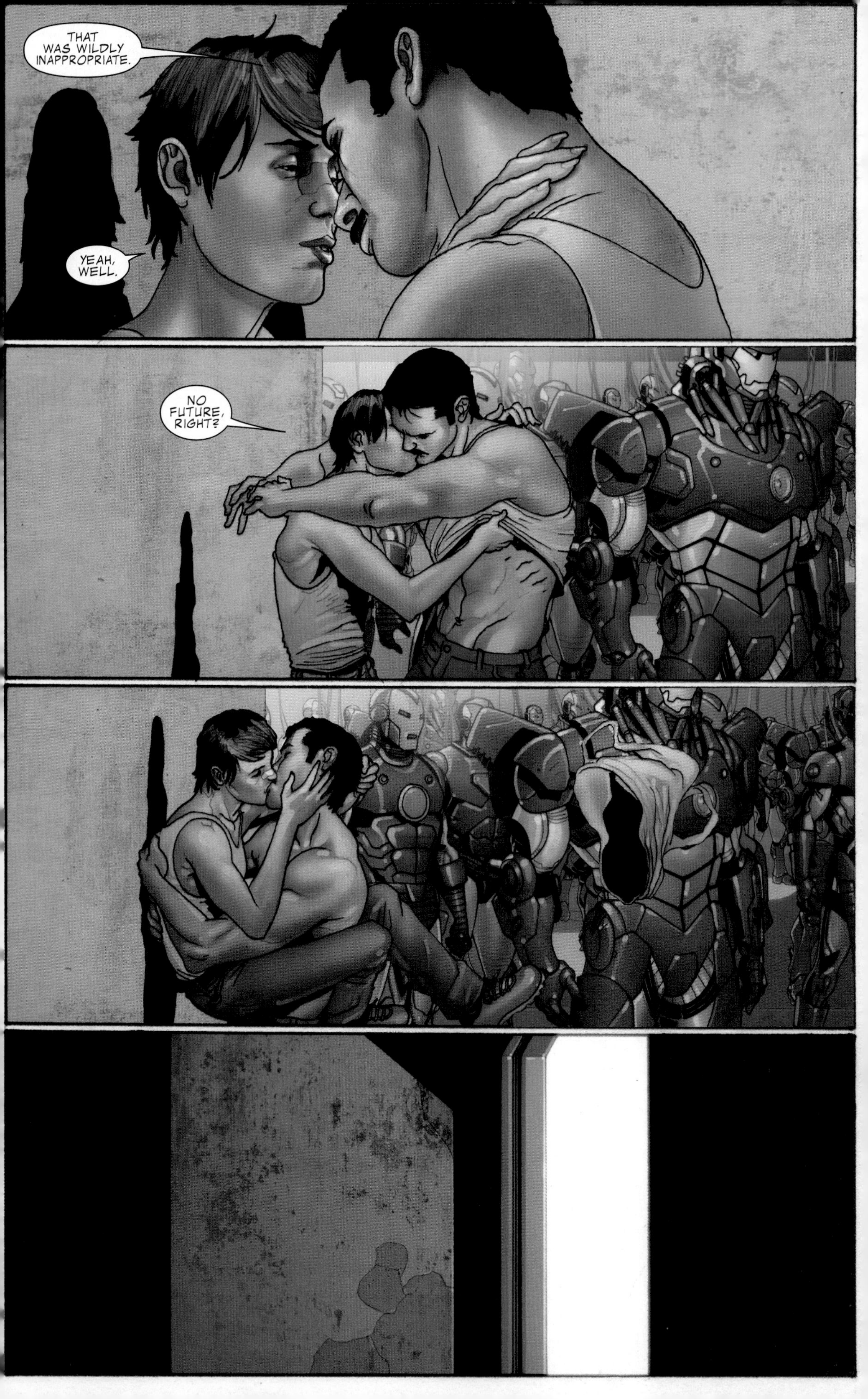
THAT WAS WILDLY INAPPROPRIATE.
YEAH, WELL.
NO FUTURE, RIGHT?

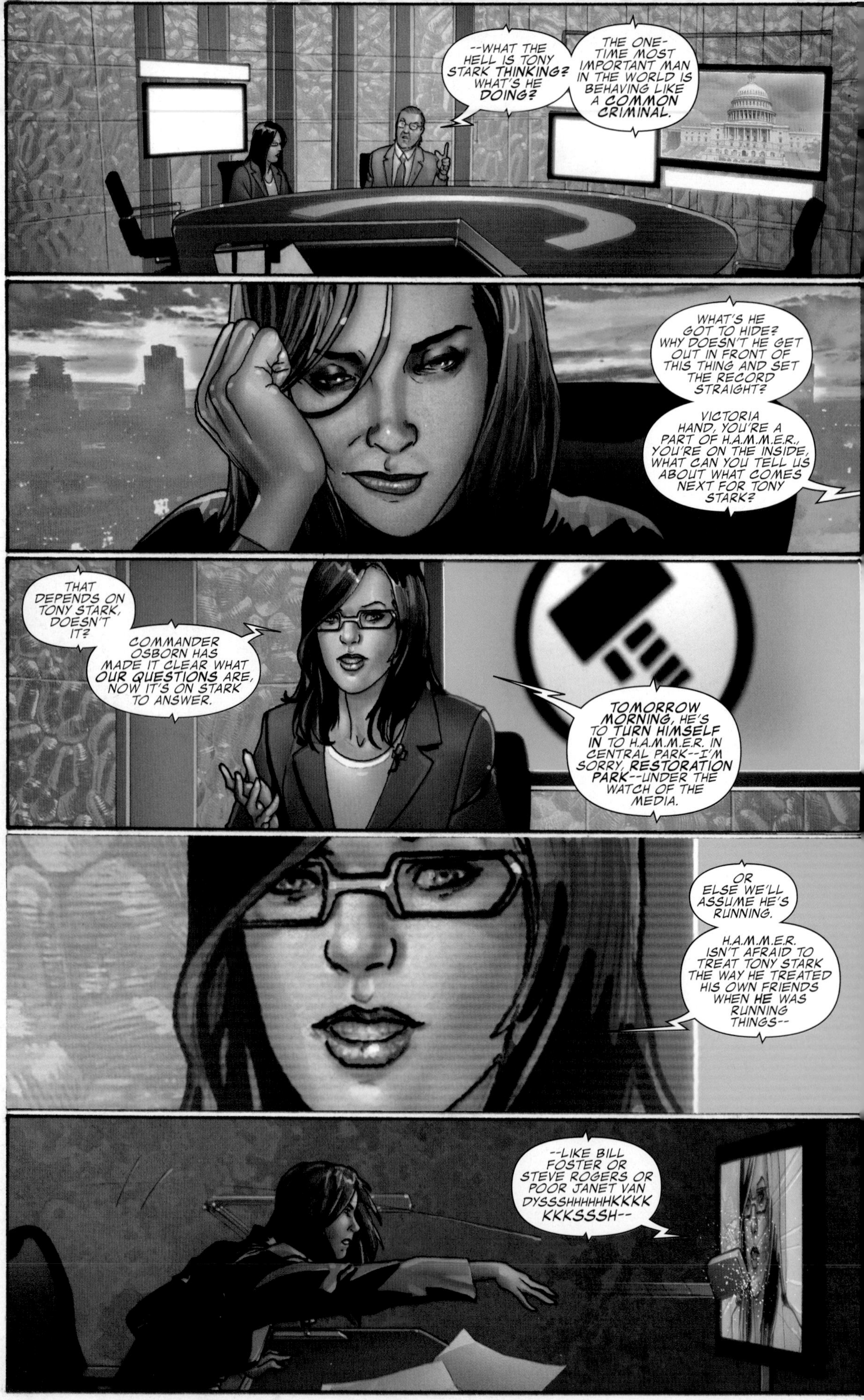
--WHAT THE HELL IS TONY STARK THINKING? WHAT'S HE DOING?
THE ONE-TIME MOST IMPORTANT MAN IN THE WORLD IS BEHAVING LIKE A COMMON CRIMINAL.
WHAT'S HE GOT TO HIDE? WHY DOESN'T HE GET OUT IN FRONT OF THIS THING AND SET THE RECORD STRAIGHT?
VICTORIA HAND, YOU'RE A PART OF H.A.M.M.E.R., YOU'RE ON THE INSIDE, WHAT CAN YOU TELL US ABOUT WHAT COMES NEXT FOR TONY STARK?
THAT DEPENDS ON TONY STARK, DOESN'T IT?
COMMANDER OSBORN HAS MADE IT CLEAR WHAT OUR QUESTIONS ARE, NOW IT'S ON STARK TO ANSWER.
TOMORROW MORNING, HE'S TO TURN HIMSELF IN TO H.A.M.M.E.R. IN CENTRAL PARK--I'M SORRY, RESTORATION PARK--UNDER THE WATCH OF THE MEDIA.
OR ELSE WE'LL ASSUME HE'S RUNNING.
H.A.M.M.E.R. ISN'T AFRAID TO TREAT TONY STARK THE WAY HE TREATED HIS OWN FRIENDS WHEN HE WAS RUNNING THINGS--
--LIKE BILL FOSTER OR STEVE ROGERS OR POOR JANET VAN DYSSSHHHHHHKKKK KKKSSSH--

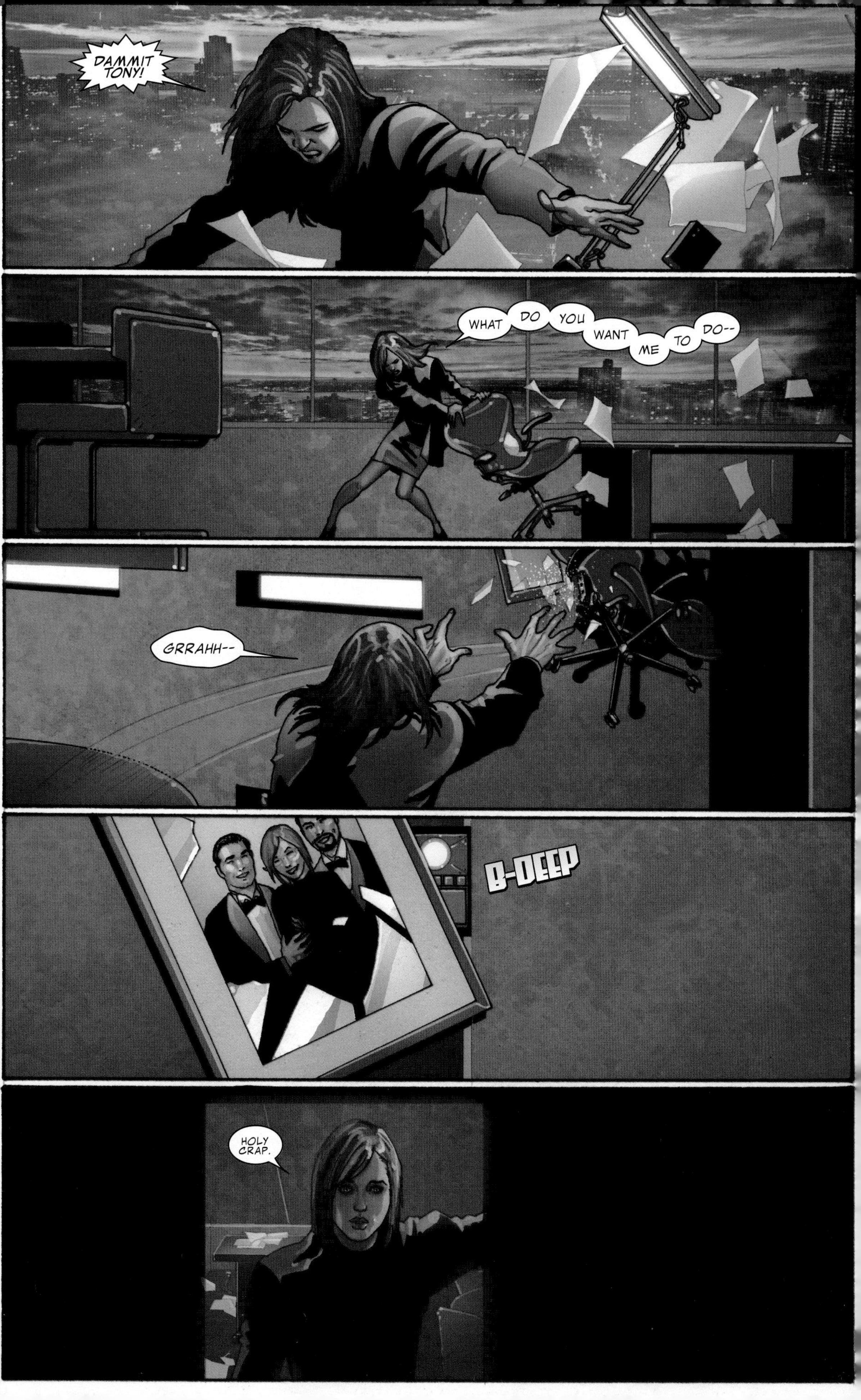
DAMMIT TONY!
WHAT DO YOU WANT ME TO DO--
GRRAHH--
B-DEEP
HOLY CRAP.

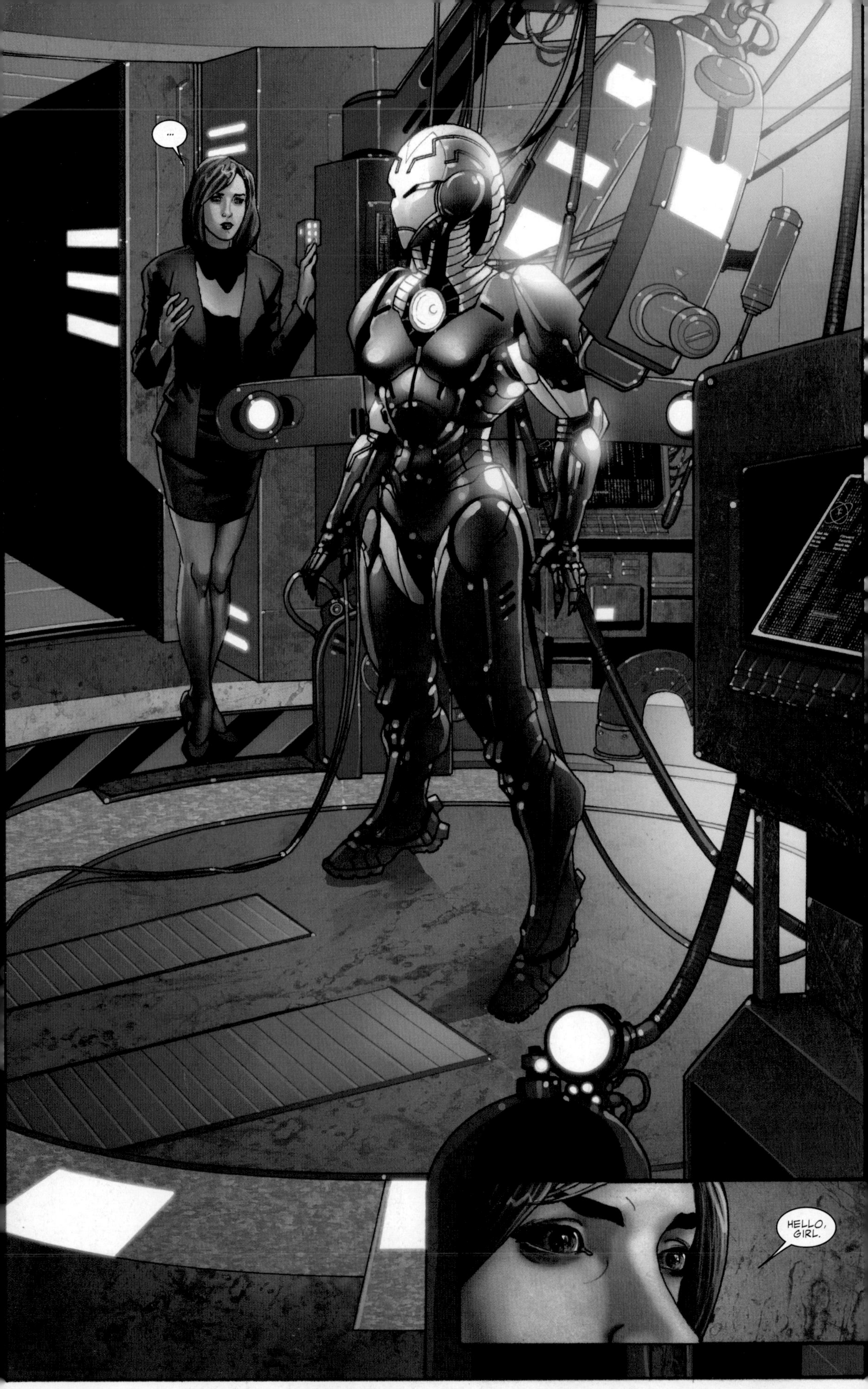
...
HELLO, GIRL.

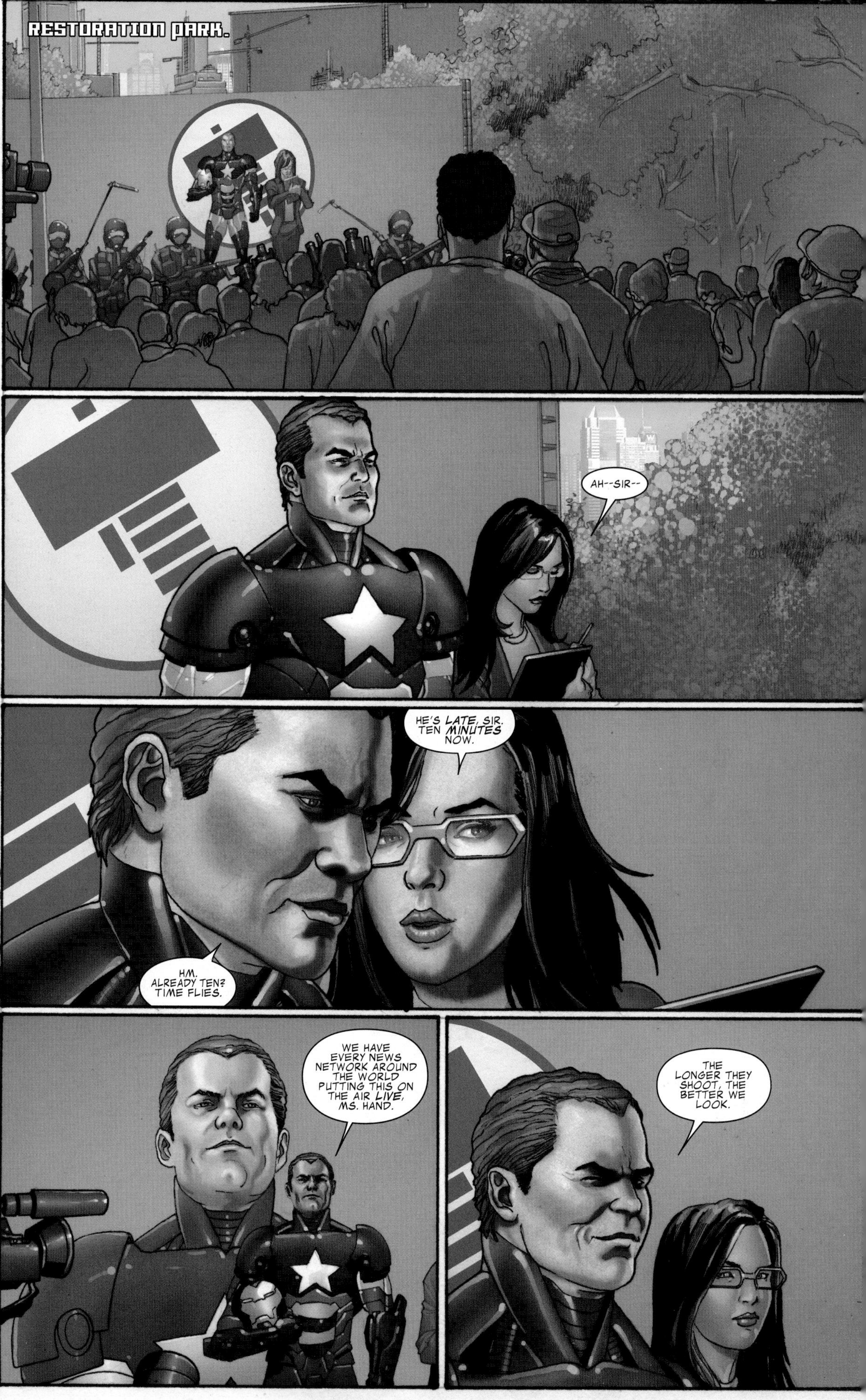
RESTORATION PARK.
AH--SIR--
HE'S LATE, SIR. TEN MINUTES NOW.
HM. ALREADY TEN? TIME FLIES.
WE HAVE EVERY NEWS NETWORK AROUND THE WORLD PUTTING THIS ON THE AIR LIVE, MS. HAND.
THE LONGER THEY SHOOT, THE BETTER WE LOOK.

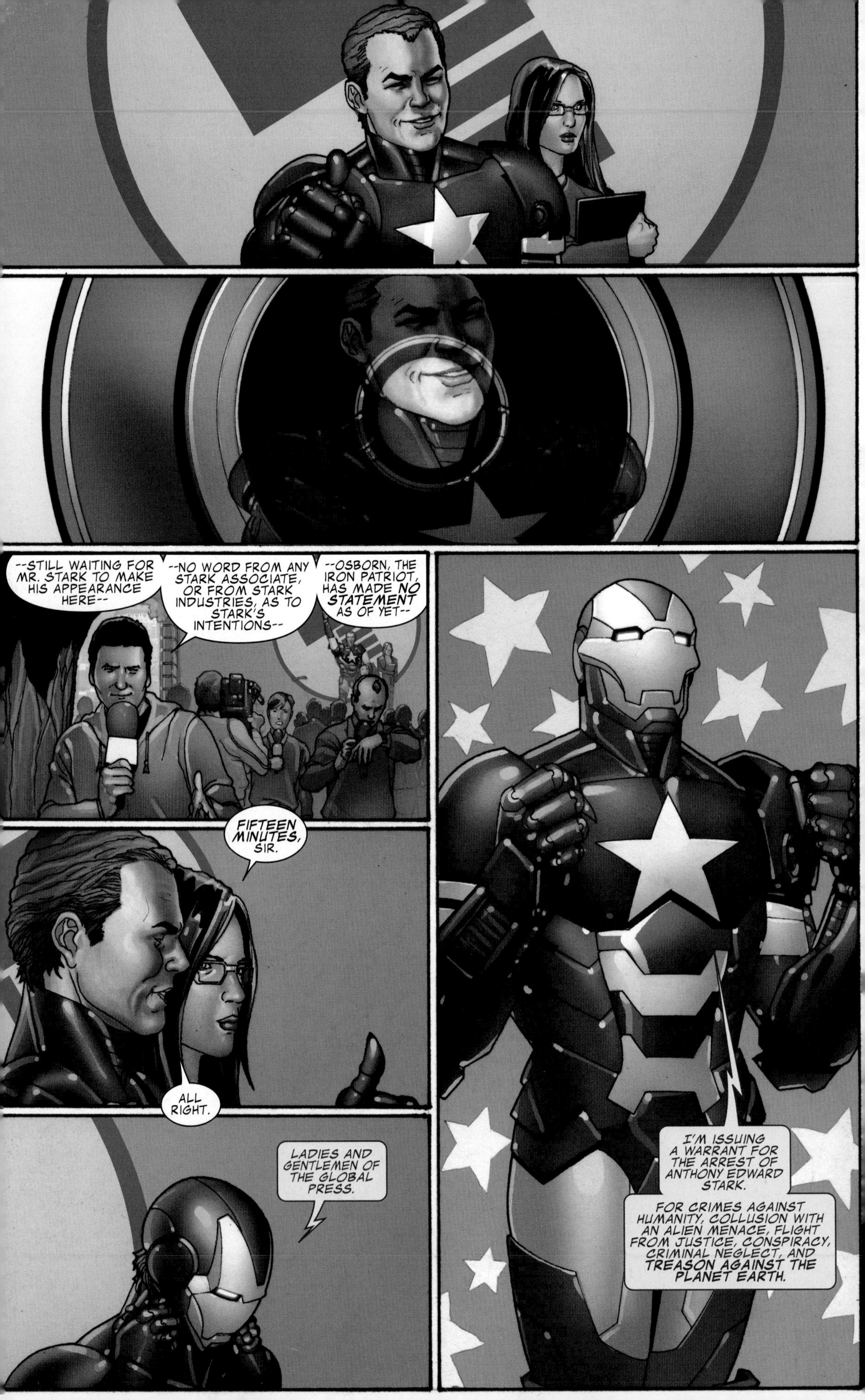
--STILL WAITING FOR MR. STARK TO MAKE HIS APPEARANCE HERE--
--NO WORD FROM ANY STARK ASSOCIATE, OR FROM STARK INDUSTRIES, AS TO STARK'S INTENTIONS--
--OSBORN, THE IRON PATRIOT, HAS MADE NO STATEMENT AS OF YET--
FIFTEEN MINUTES, SIR.
ALL RIGHT.
LADIES AND GENTLEMEN OF THE GLOBAL PRESS.
I'M ISSUING A WARRANT FOR THE ARREST OF ANTHONY EDWARD STARK.
FOR CRIMES AGAINST HUMANITY, COLLUSION WITH AN ALIEN MENACE, FLIGHT FROM JUSTICE, CONSPIRACY, CRIMINAL NEGLECT, AND TREASON AGAINST THE PLANET EARTH.

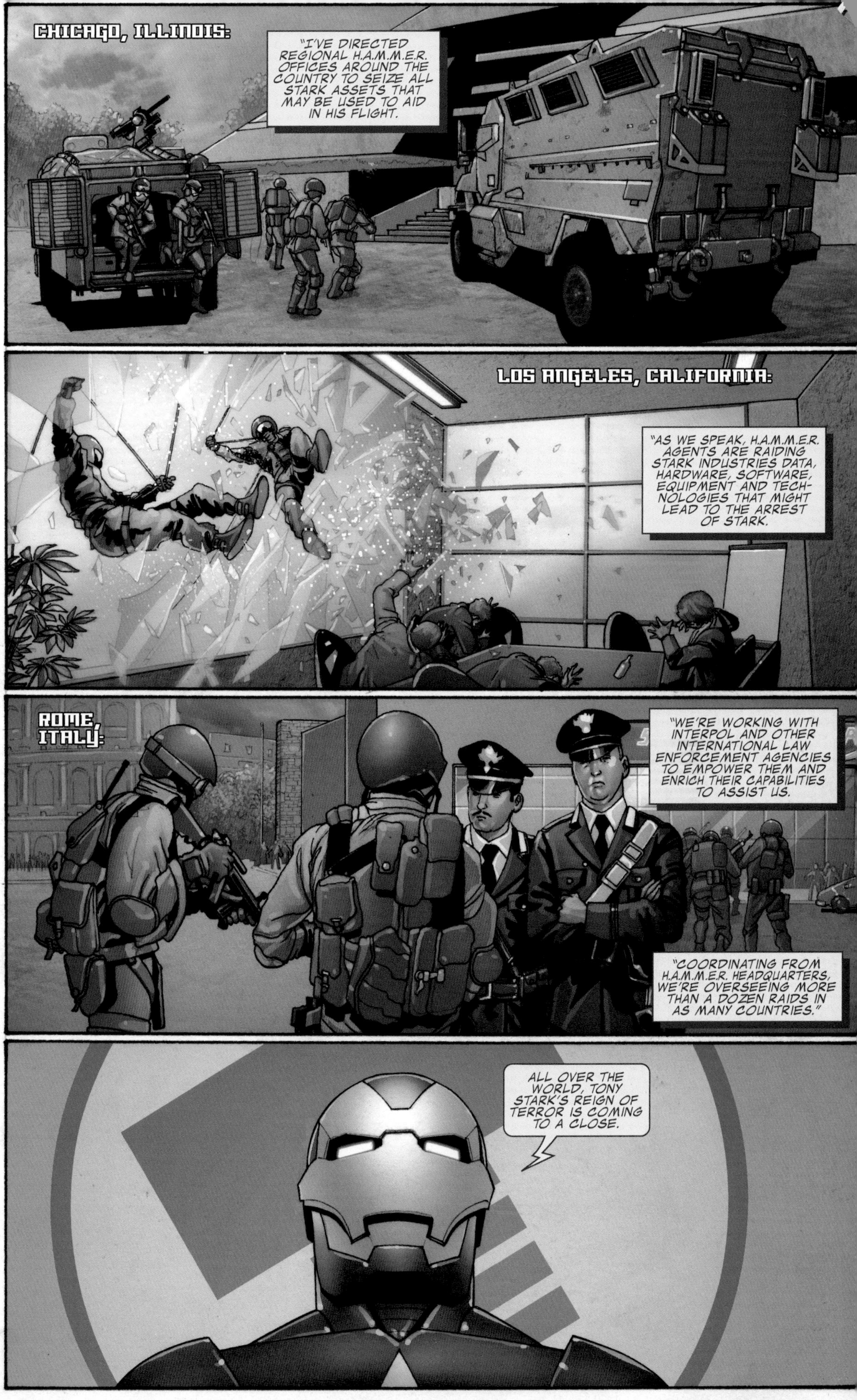

CHICAGO, ILLINOIS:
"I'VE DIRECTED REGIONAL H.A.M.M.E.R. OFFICES AROUND THE COUNTRY TO SEIZE ALL STARK ASSETS THAT MAY BE USED TO AID IN HIS FLIGHT.
LOS ANGELES, CALIFORNIA:
"AS WE SPEAK, H.A.M.M.E.R. AGENTS ARE RAIDING STARK INDUSTRIES DATA, HARDWARE, SOFTWARE, EQUIPMENT AND TECHNOLOGIES THAT MIGHT LEAD TO THE ARREST OF STARK.
ROME, ITALY:
"WE'RE WORKING WITH INTERPOL AND OTHER INTERNATIONAL LAW ENFORCEMENT AGENCIES TO EMPOWER THEM AND ENRICH THEIR CAPABILITIES TO ASSIST US.
"COORDINATING FROM H.A.M.M.E.R. HEADQUARTERS, WE'RE OVERSEEING MORE THAN A DOZEN RAIDS IN AS MANY COUNTRIES."
ALL OVER THE WORLD, TONY STARK'S REIGN OF TERROR IS COMING TO A CLOSE.

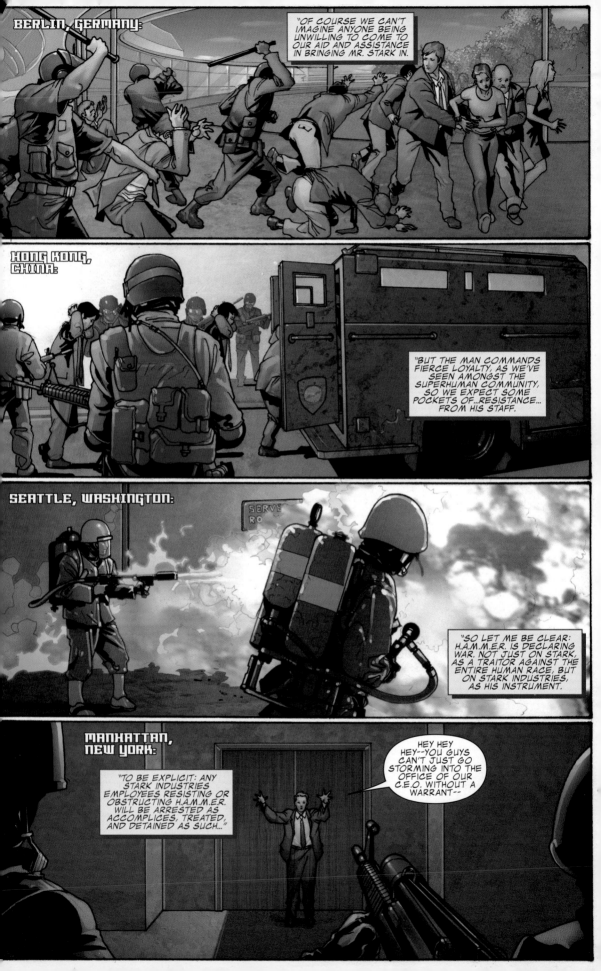

BERLIN, GERMANY:

"OF COURSE WE CAN'T IMAGINE ANYONE BEING UNWILLING TO COME TO OUR AID AND ASSISTANCE IN BRINGING MR. STARK IN."

HONG KONG, CHINA:

"BUT THE MAN COMMANDS FIERCE LOYALTY, AS WE'VE SEEN AMONGST THE SUPERHUMAN COMMUNITY, SO WE EXPECT SOME POCKETS OF...RESISTANCE... FROM HIS STAFF.

SEATTLE, WASHINGTON:

"SO LET ME BE CLEAR: H.A.M.M.E.R. IS DECLARING WAR. NOT JUST ON STARK, AS A TRAITOR AGAINST THE ENTIRE HUMAN RACE, BUT ON STARK INDUSTRIES, AS HIS INSTRUMENT.

MANHATTAN, NEW YORK:

"TO BE EXPLICIT: ANY STARK INDUSTRIES EMPLOYEES RESISTING OR OBSTRUCTING H.A.M.M.E.R. WILL BE ARRESTED AS ACCOMPLICES, TREATED, AND DETAINED AS SUCH..."

HEY HEY HEY--YOU GUYS CAN'T JUST GO STORMING INTO THE OFFICE OF OUR C.E.O. WITHOUT A WARRANT--

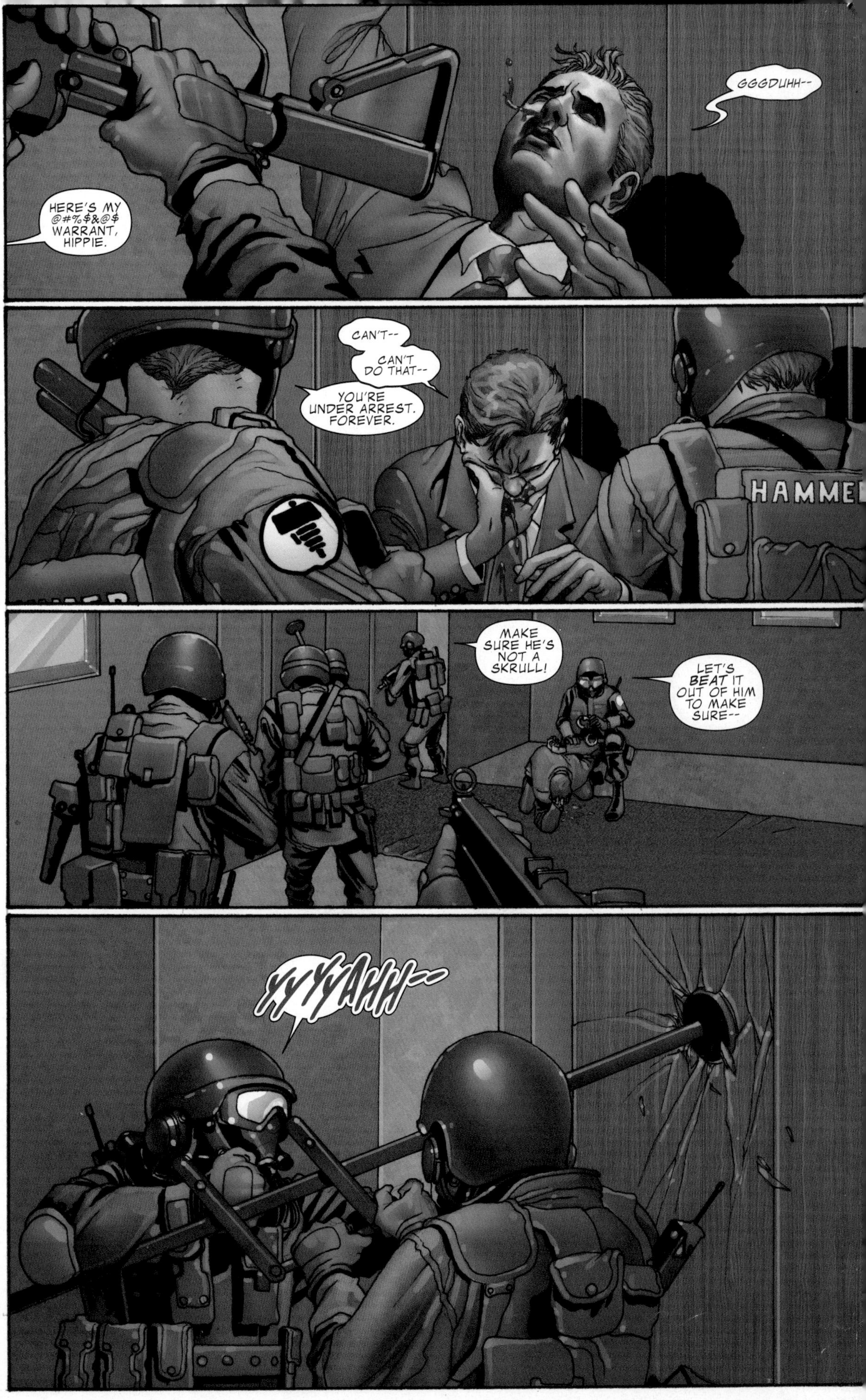
GGGDUHH--
HERE'S MY @#%$&@$ WARRANT, HIPPIE.
CAN'T--
CAN'T DO THAT--
YOU'RE UNDER ARREST. FOREVER.
HAMME
MAKE SURE HE'S NOT A SKRULL!
LET'S BEAT IT OUT OF HIM TO MAKE SURE--
YYYYAHH--

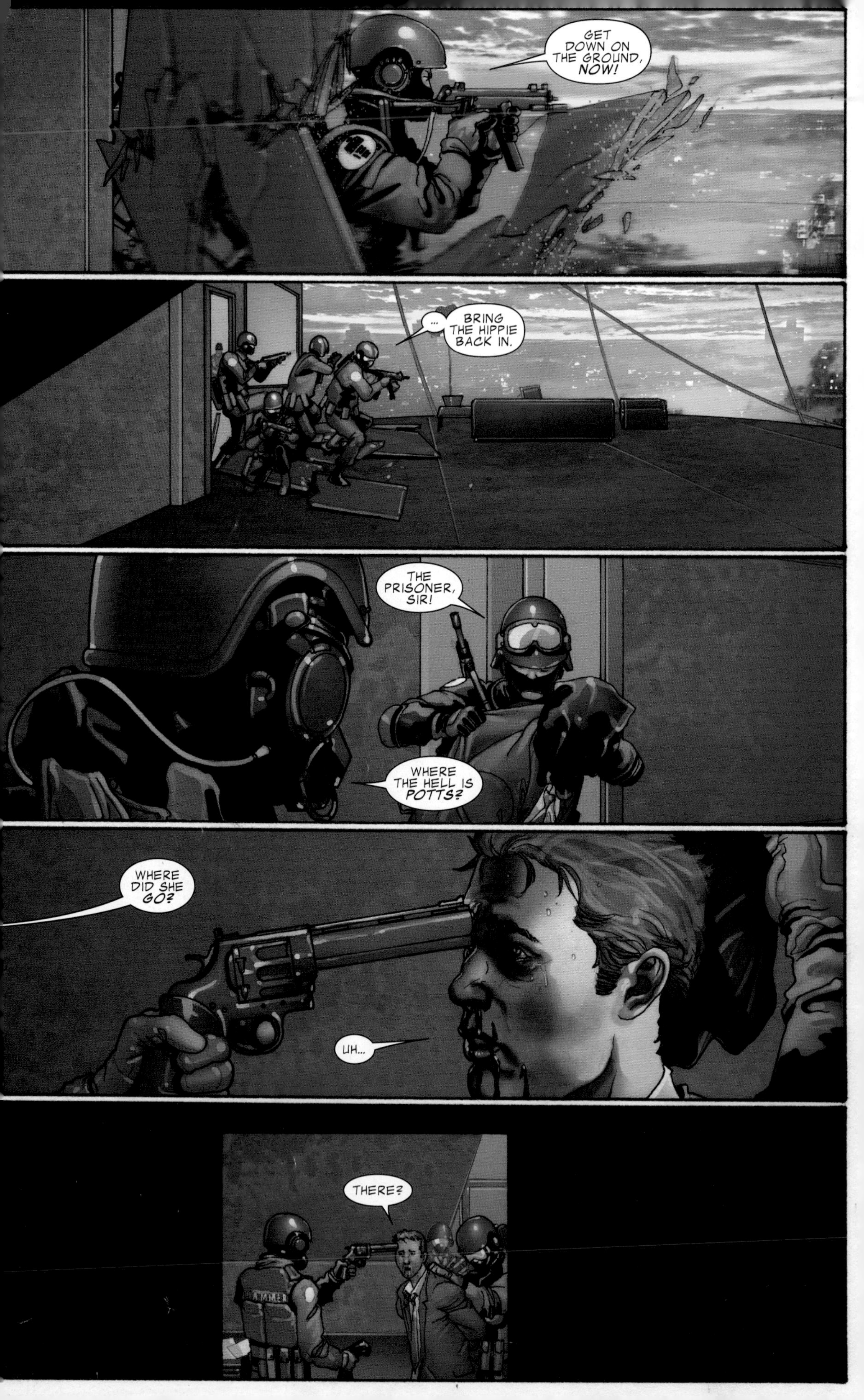
GET DOWN ON THE GROUND, NOW!
... BRING THE HIPPIE BACK IN.
THE PRISONER, SIR!
WHERE THE HELL IS POTTS?
WHERE DID SHE GO?
UH...
THERE?

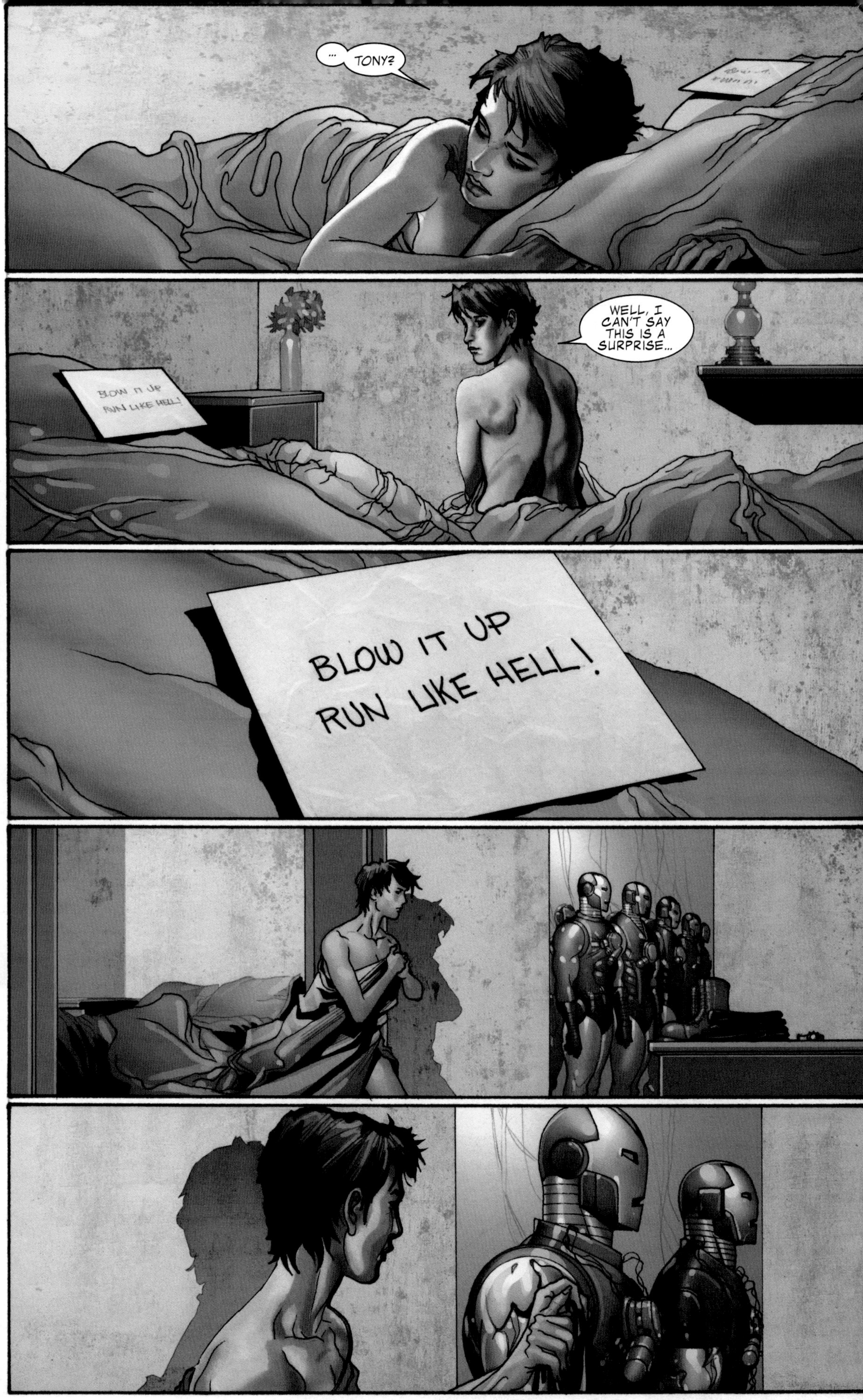
... TONY?
WELL, I CAN'T SAY THIS IS A SURPRISE...
BLOW IT UP
RUN LIKE HELL!
BLOW IT UP
RUN LIKE HELL!

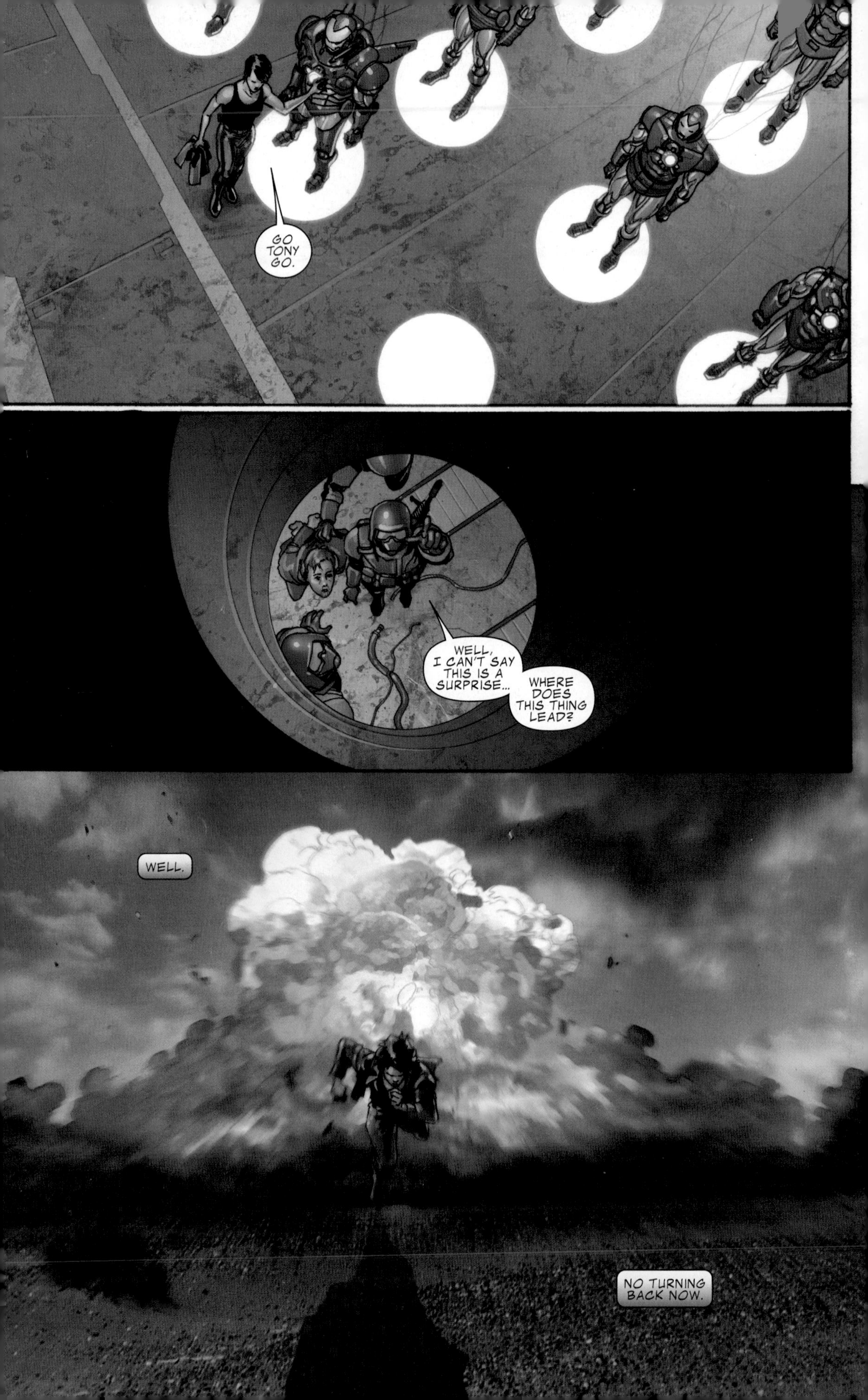
GO TONY GO.
WELL, I CAN'T SAY THIS IS A SURPRISE...
WHERE DOES THIS THING LEAD?
WELL.
NO TURNING BACK NOW.

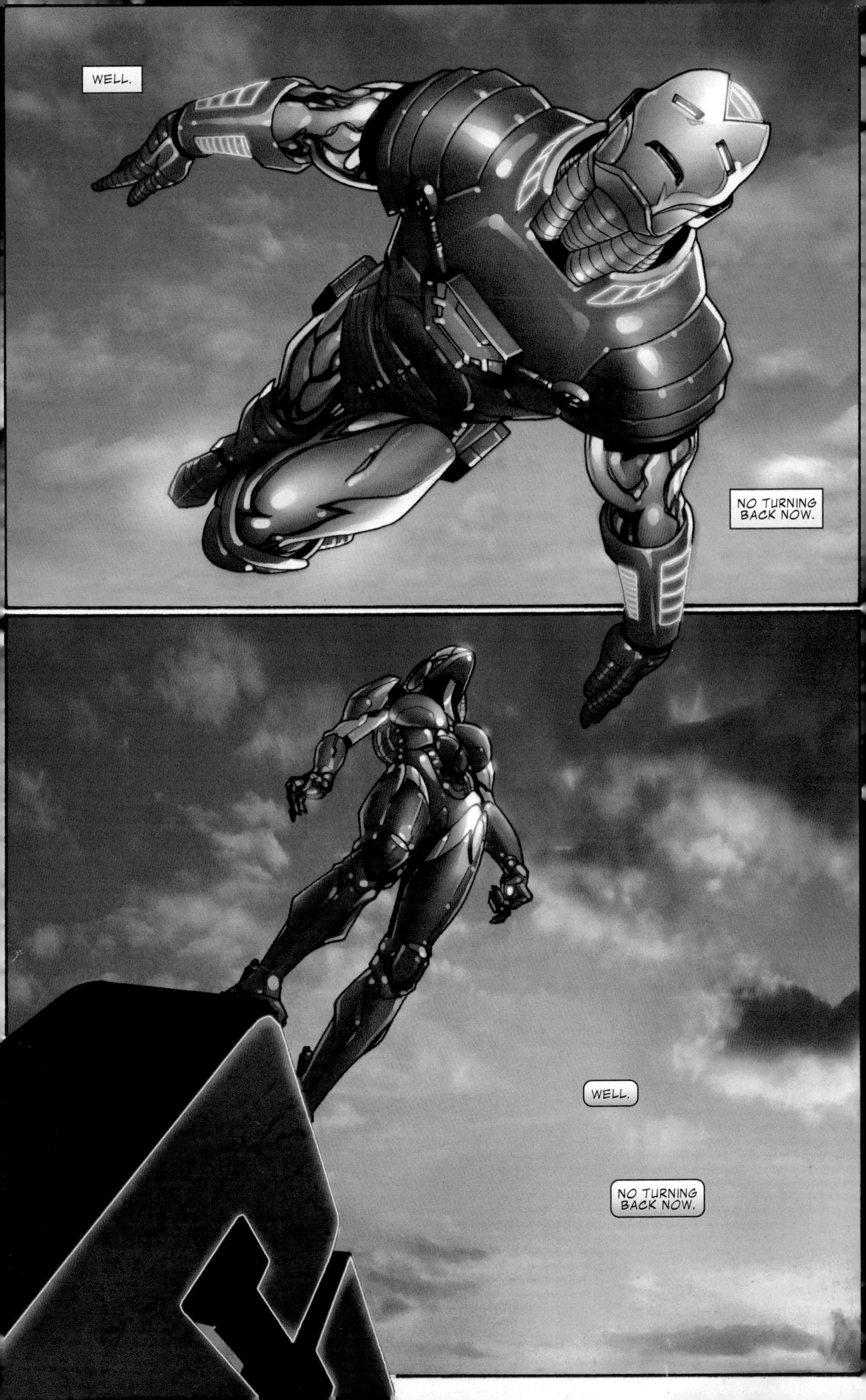
WELL.
NO TURNING BACK NOW.
WELL.
NO TURNING BACK NOW.

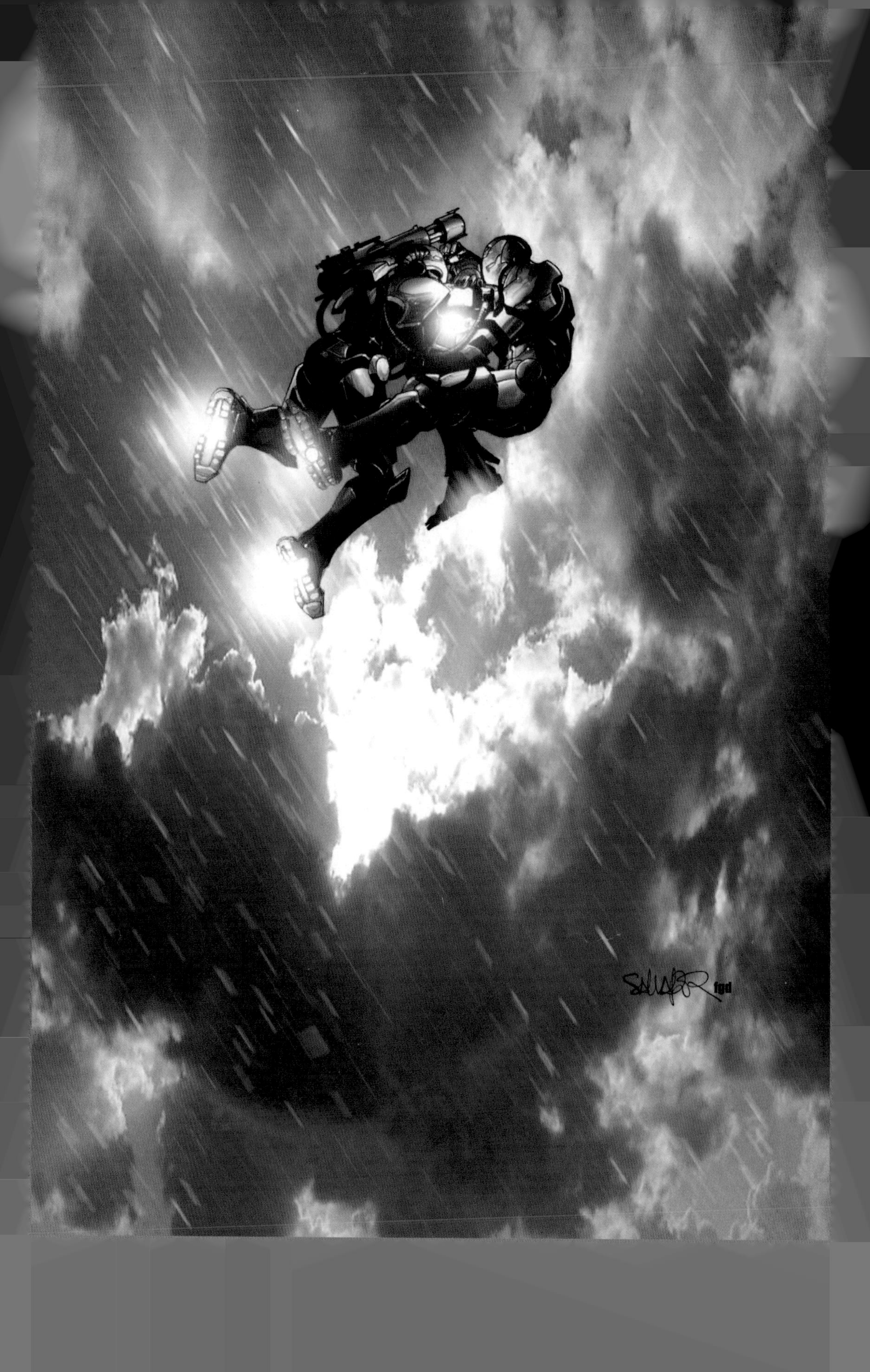

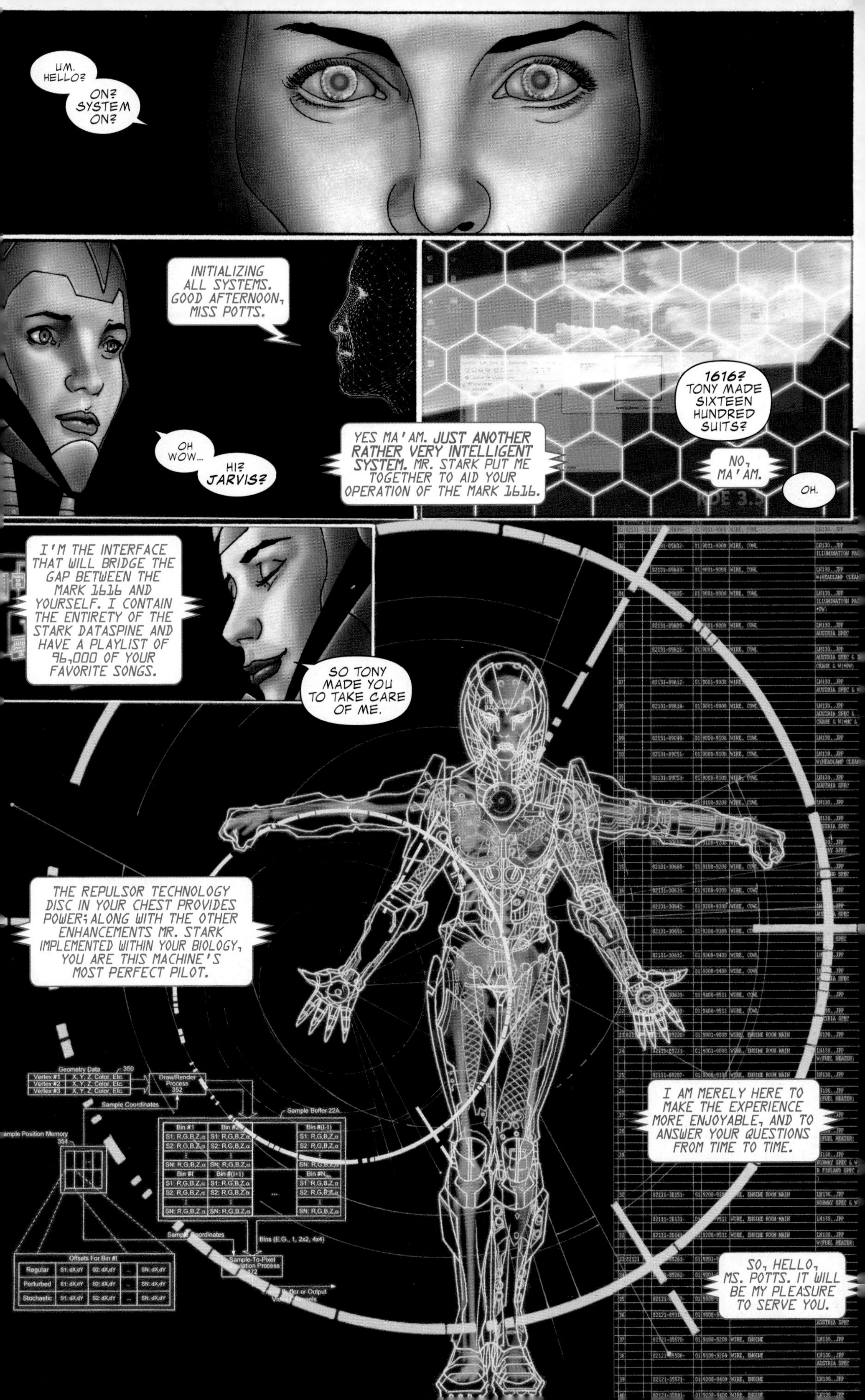
UM. HELLO?
ON? SYSTEM ON?
INITIALIZING ALL SYSTEMS. GOOD AFTERNOON, MISS POTTS.
OH WOW...
HI? JARVIS?
YES MA'AM. JUST ANOTHER RATHER VERY INTELLIGENT SYSTEM. MR. STARK PUT ME TOGETHER TO AID YOUR OPERATION OF THE MARK 1616.
1616? TONY MADE SIXTEEN HUNDRED SUITS?
NO, MA'AM.
OH.
I'M THE INTERFACE THAT WILL BRIDGE THE GAP BETWEEN THE MARK 1616 AND YOURSELF. I CONTAIN THE ENTIRETY OF THE STARK DATASPINE AND HAVE A PLAYLIST OF 96,000 OF YOUR FAVORITE SONGS.
SO TONY MADE YOU TO TAKE CARE OF ME.
THE REPULSOR TECHNOLOGY DISC IN YOUR CHEST PROVIDES POWER; ALONG WITH THE OTHER ENHANCEMENTS MR. STARK IMPLEMENTED WITHIN YOUR BIOLOGY, YOU ARE THIS MACHINE'S MOST PERFECT PILOT.
I AM MERELY HERE TO MAKE THE EXPERIENCE MORE ENJOYABLE, AND TO ANSWER YOUR QUESTIONS FROM TIME TO TIME.
SO, HELLO, MS. POTTS. IT WILL BE MY PLEASURE TO SERVE YOU.

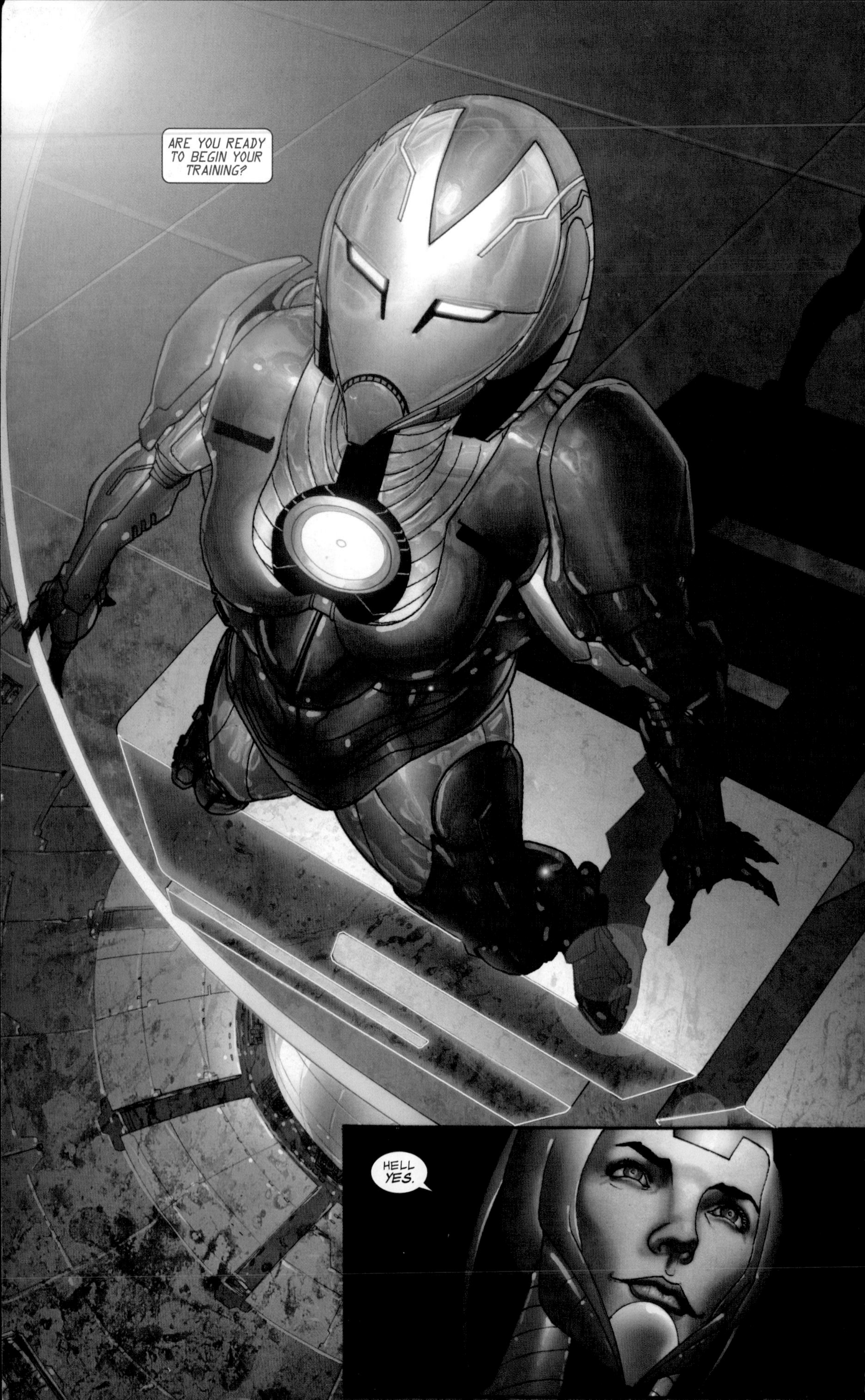
ARE YOU READY TO BEGIN YOUR TRAINING?
HELL YES.

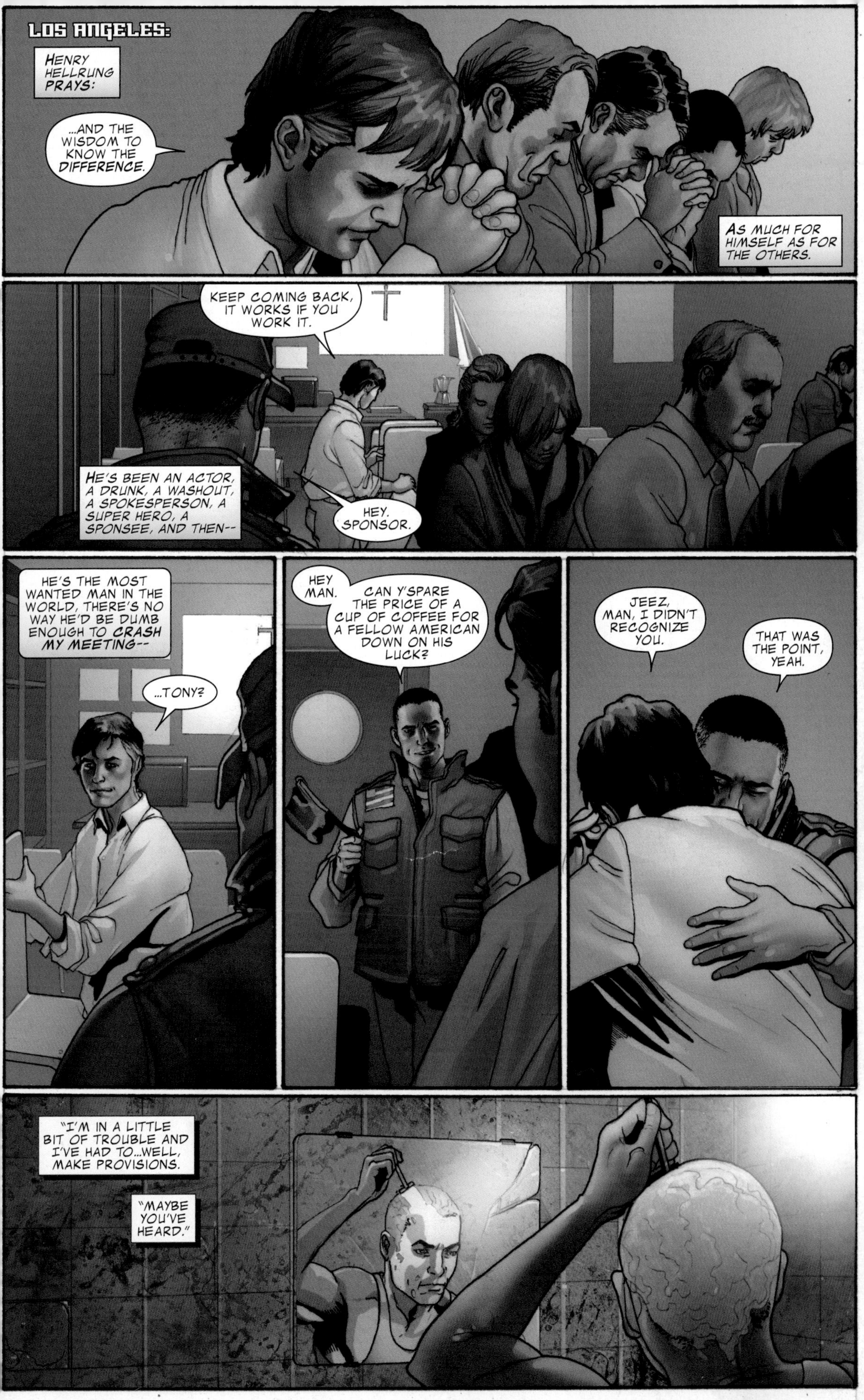
LOS ANGELES:
HENRY HELLRUNG PRAYS:
...AND THE WISDOM TO KNOW THE DIFFERENCE.
AS MUCH FOR HIMSELF AS FOR THE OTHERS.
KEEP COMING BACK, IT WORKS IF YOU WORK IT.
HE'S BEEN AN ACTOR, A DRUNK, A WASHOUT, A SPOKESPERSON, A SUPER HERO, A SPONSEE, AND THEN--
HEY. SPONSOR.
HE'S THE MOST WANTED MAN IN THE WORLD, THERE'S NO WAY HE'D BE DUMB ENOUGH TO CRASH MY MEETING--
...TONY?
HEY MAN.
CAN Y'SPARE THE PRICE OF A CUP OF COFFEE FOR A FELLOW AMERICAN DOWN ON HIS LUCK?
JEEZ, MAN, I DIDN'T RECOGNIZE YOU.
THAT WAS THE POINT, YEAH.
"I'M IN A LITTLE BIT OF TROUBLE AND I'VE HAD TO...WELL, MAKE PROVISIONS.
"MAYBE YOU'VE HEARD."

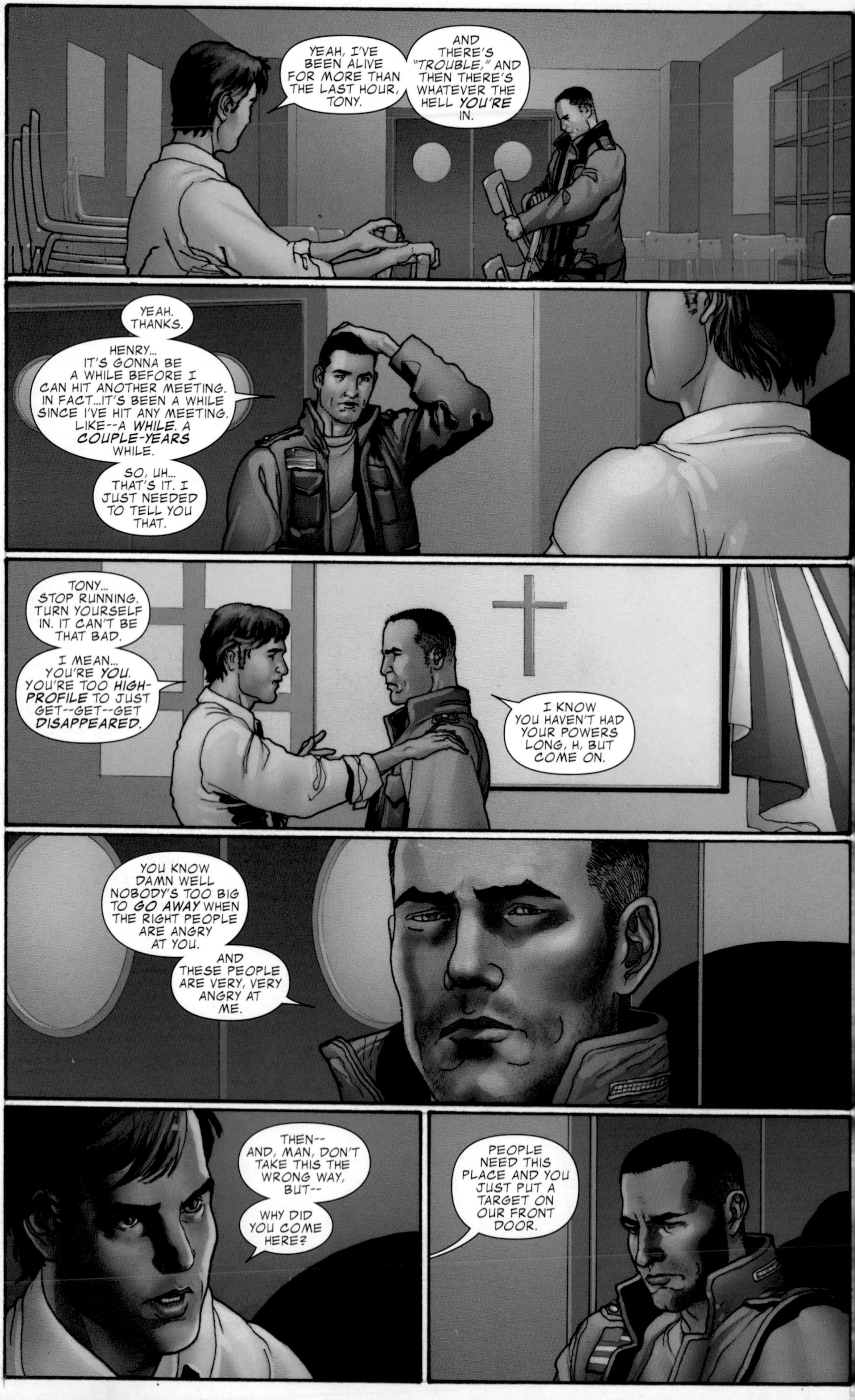

YEAH, I'VE BEEN ALIVE FOR MORE THAN THE LAST HOUR, TONY.
AND THERE'S "TROUBLE," AND THEN THERE'S WHATEVER THE HELL YOU'RE IN.
YEAH. THANKS.
HENRY... IT'S GONNA BE A WHILE BEFORE I CAN HIT ANOTHER MEETING. IN FACT...IT'S BEEN A WHILE SINCE I'VE HIT ANY MEETING. LIKE--A WHILE. A COUPLE-YEARS WHILE.
SO, UH... THAT'S IT. I JUST NEEDED TO TELL YOU THAT.
TONY... STOP RUNNING. TURN YOURSELF IN. IT CAN'T BE THAT BAD.
I MEAN... YOU'RE YOU. YOU'RE TOO HIGH-PROFILE TO JUST GET--GET--GET DISAPPEARED.
I KNOW YOU HAVEN'T HAD YOUR POWERS LONG, H, BUT COME ON.
YOU KNOW DAMN WELL NOBODY'S TOO BIG TO GO AWAY WHEN THE RIGHT PEOPLE ARE ANGRY AT YOU.
AND THESE PEOPLE ARE VERY, VERY ANGRY AT ME.
THEN-- AND, MAN, DON'T TAKE THIS THE WRONG WAY, BUT--
WHY DID YOU COME HERE?
PEOPLE NEED THIS PLACE AND YOU JUST PUT A TARGET ON OUR FRONT DOOR.

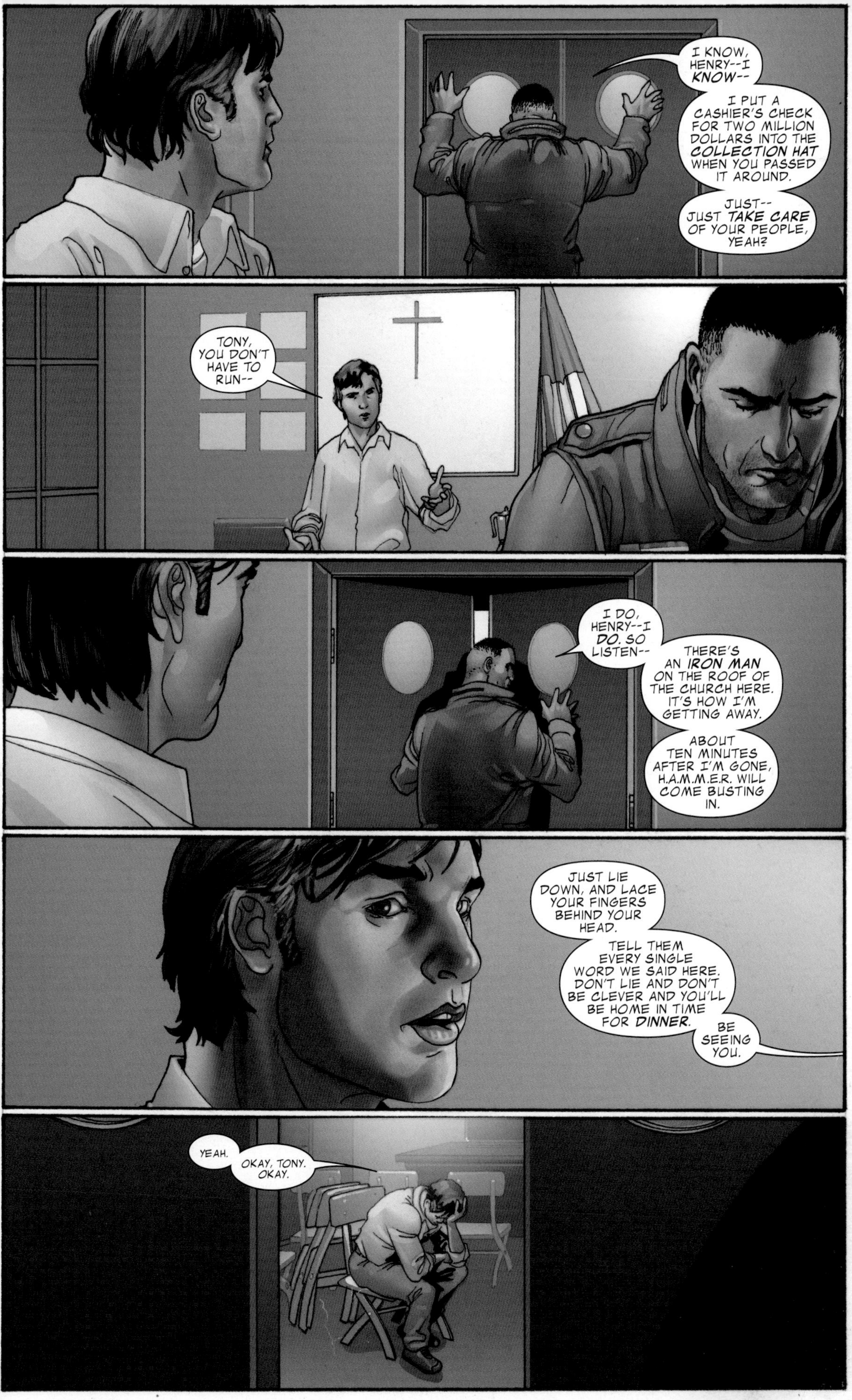

I KNOW, HENRY--I KNOW--
I PUT A CASHIER'S CHECK FOR TWO MILLION DOLLARS INTO THE COLLECTION HAT WHEN YOU PASSED IT AROUND.
JUST-- JUST TAKE CARE OF YOUR PEOPLE, YEAH?
TONY, YOU DON'T HAVE TO RUN--
I DO, HENRY--I DO. SO LISTEN--
THERE'S AN IRON MAN ON THE ROOF OF THE CHURCH HERE. IT'S HOW I'M GETTING AWAY.
ABOUT TEN MINUTES AFTER I'M GONE, H.A.M.M.E.R. WILL COME BUSTING IN.
JUST LIE DOWN, AND LACE YOUR FINGERS BEHIND YOUR HEAD.
TELL THEM EVERY SINGLE WORD WE SAID HERE. DON'T LIE AND DON'T BE CLEVER AND YOU'LL BE HOME IN TIME FOR DINNER.
BE SEEING YOU.
YEAH.
OKAY, TONY. OKAY.

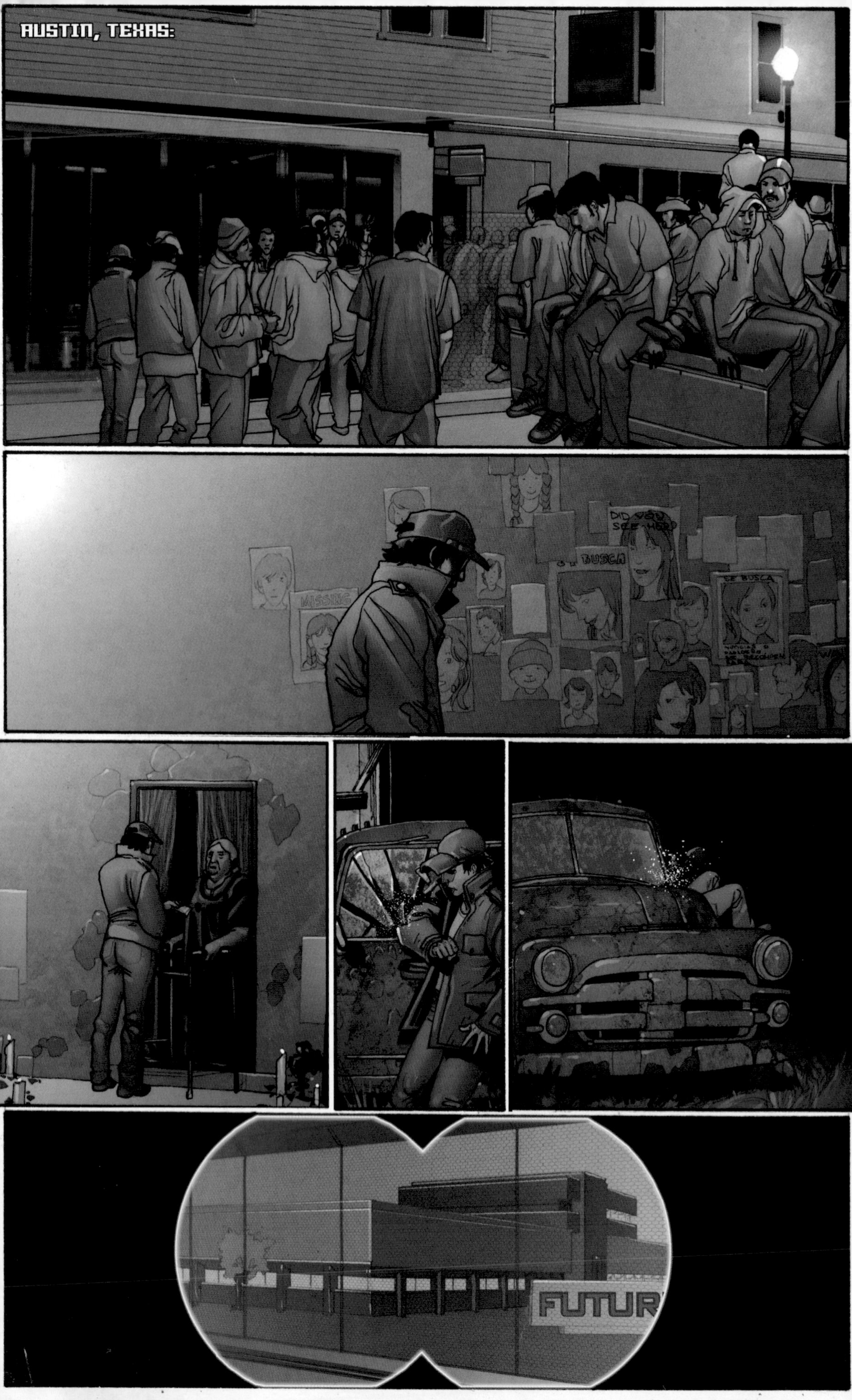
AUSTIN, TEXAS:
SE BUSCA
FUTUR

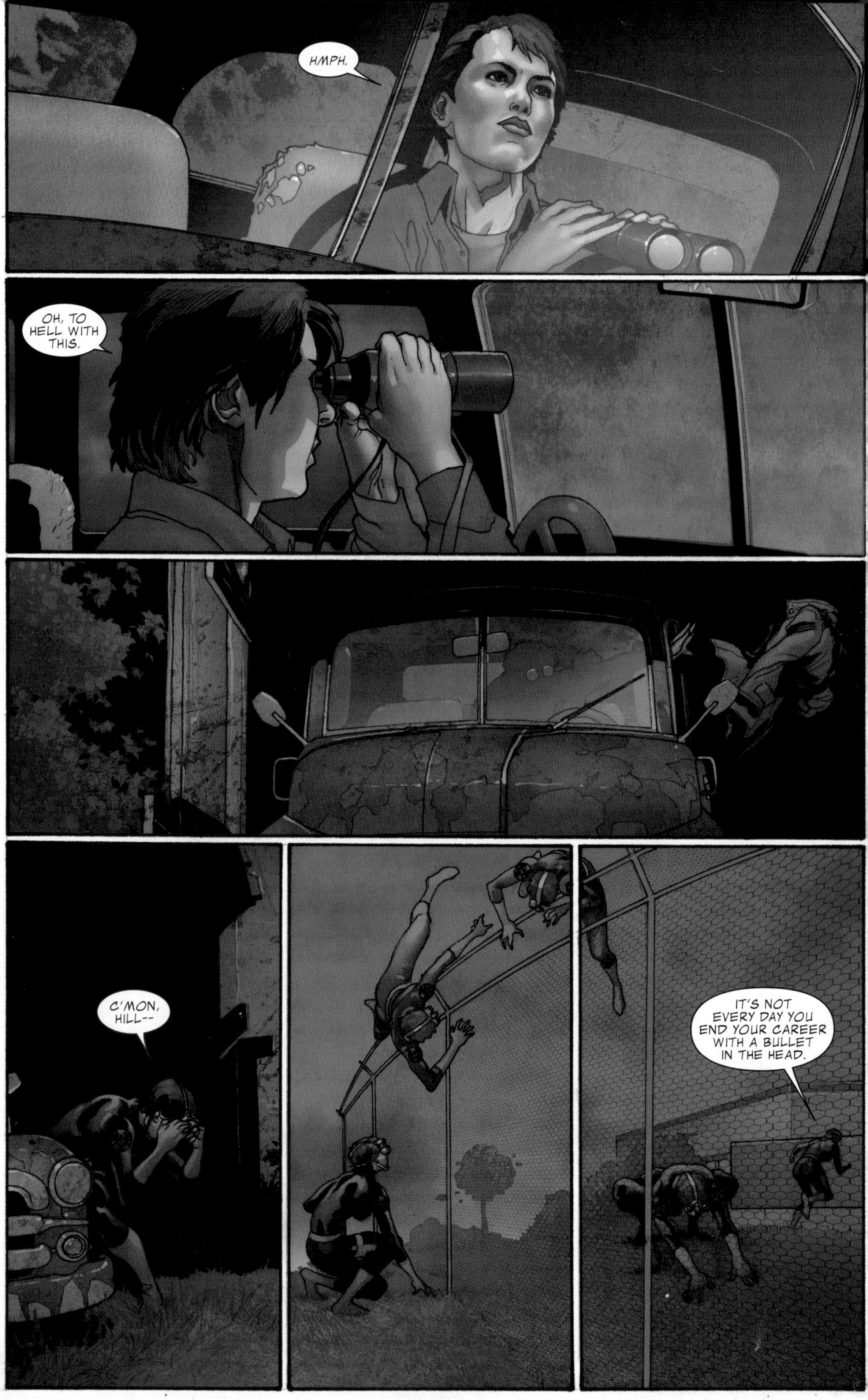
HMPH.
OH, TO HELL WITH THIS.
C'MON, HILL--
IT'S NOT EVERY DAY YOU END YOUR CAREER WITH A BULLET IN THE HEAD.

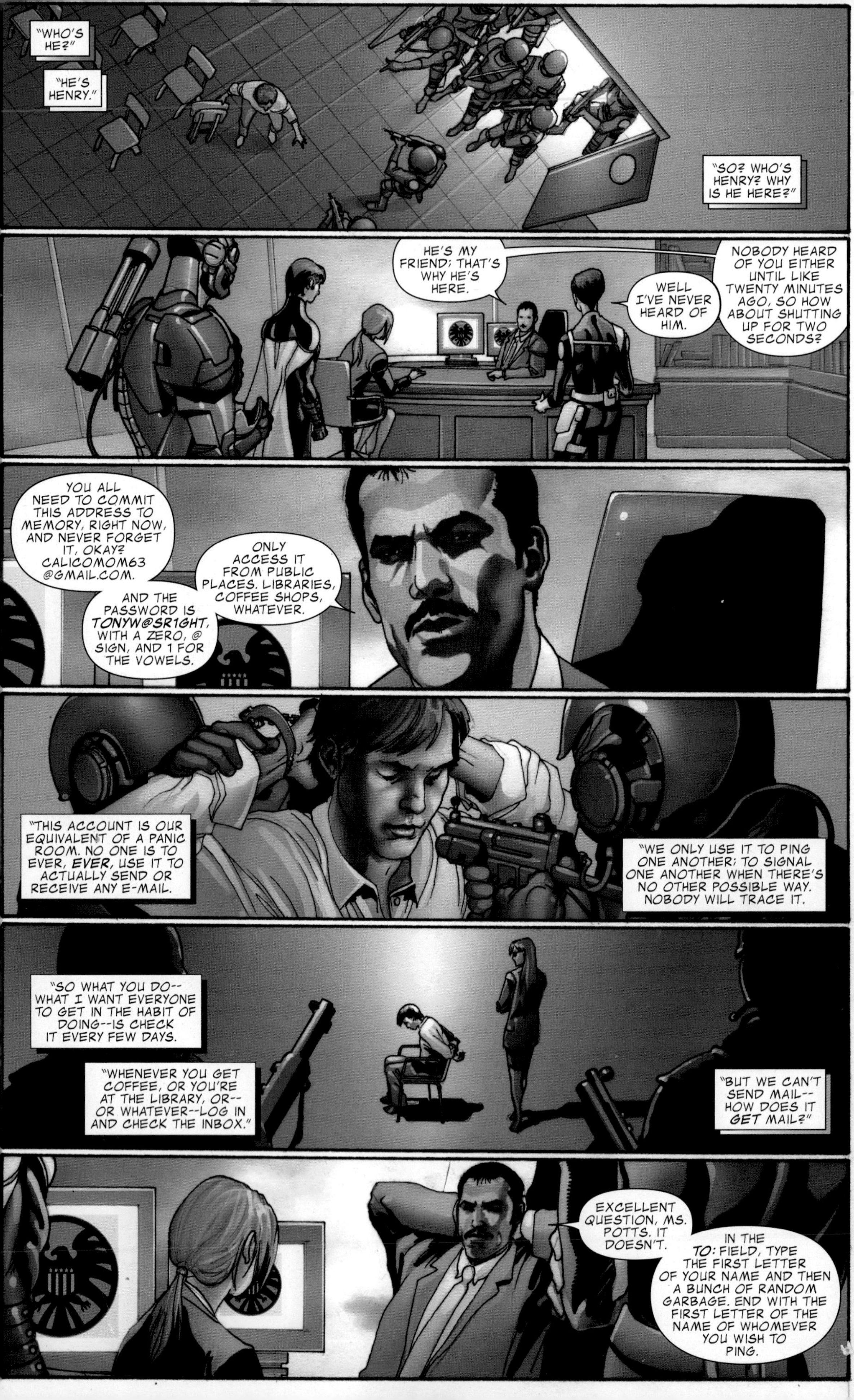
"WHO'S HE?"
"HE'S HENRY."
"SO? WHO'S HENRY? WHY IS HE HERE?"
HE'S MY FRIEND; THAT'S WHY HE'S HERE.
WELL I'VE NEVER HEARD OF HIM.
NOBODY HEARD OF YOU EITHER UNTIL LIKE TWENTY MINUTES AGO, SO HOW ABOUT SHUTTING UP FOR TWO SECONDS?
YOU ALL NEED TO COMMIT THIS ADDRESS TO MEMORY, RIGHT NOW, AND NEVER FORGET IT, OKAY? CALICOMOM63 @GMAIL.COM.
AND THE PASSWORD IS *TONYW@SR1GHT*, WITH A ZERO, @ SIGN, AND 1 FOR THE VOWELS.
ONLY ACCESS IT FROM PUBLIC PLACES. LIBRARIES, COFFEE SHOPS, WHATEVER.
"THIS ACCOUNT IS OUR EQUIVALENT OF A PANIC ROOM. NO ONE IS TO EVER, ***EVER***, USE IT TO ACTUALLY SEND OR RECEIVE ANY E-MAIL.
"WE ONLY USE IT TO PING ONE ANOTHER; TO SIGNAL ONE ANOTHER WHEN THERE'S NO OTHER POSSIBLE WAY. NOBODY WILL TRACE IT.
"SO WHAT YOU DO--WHAT I WANT EVERYONE TO GET IN THE HABIT OF DOING--IS CHECK IT EVERY FEW DAYS.
"WHENEVER YOU GET COFFEE, OR YOU'RE AT THE LIBRARY, OR--OR WHATEVER--LOG IN AND CHECK THE INBOX."
"BUT WE CAN'T SEND MAIL--HOW DOES IT *GET* MAIL?"
EXCELLENT QUESTION, MS. POTTS. IT DOESN'T.
IN THE *TO:* FIELD, TYPE THE FIRST LETTER OF YOUR NAME AND THEN A BUNCH OF RANDOM GARBAGE. END WITH THE FIRST LETTER OF THE NAME OF WHOMEVER YOU WISH TO PING.

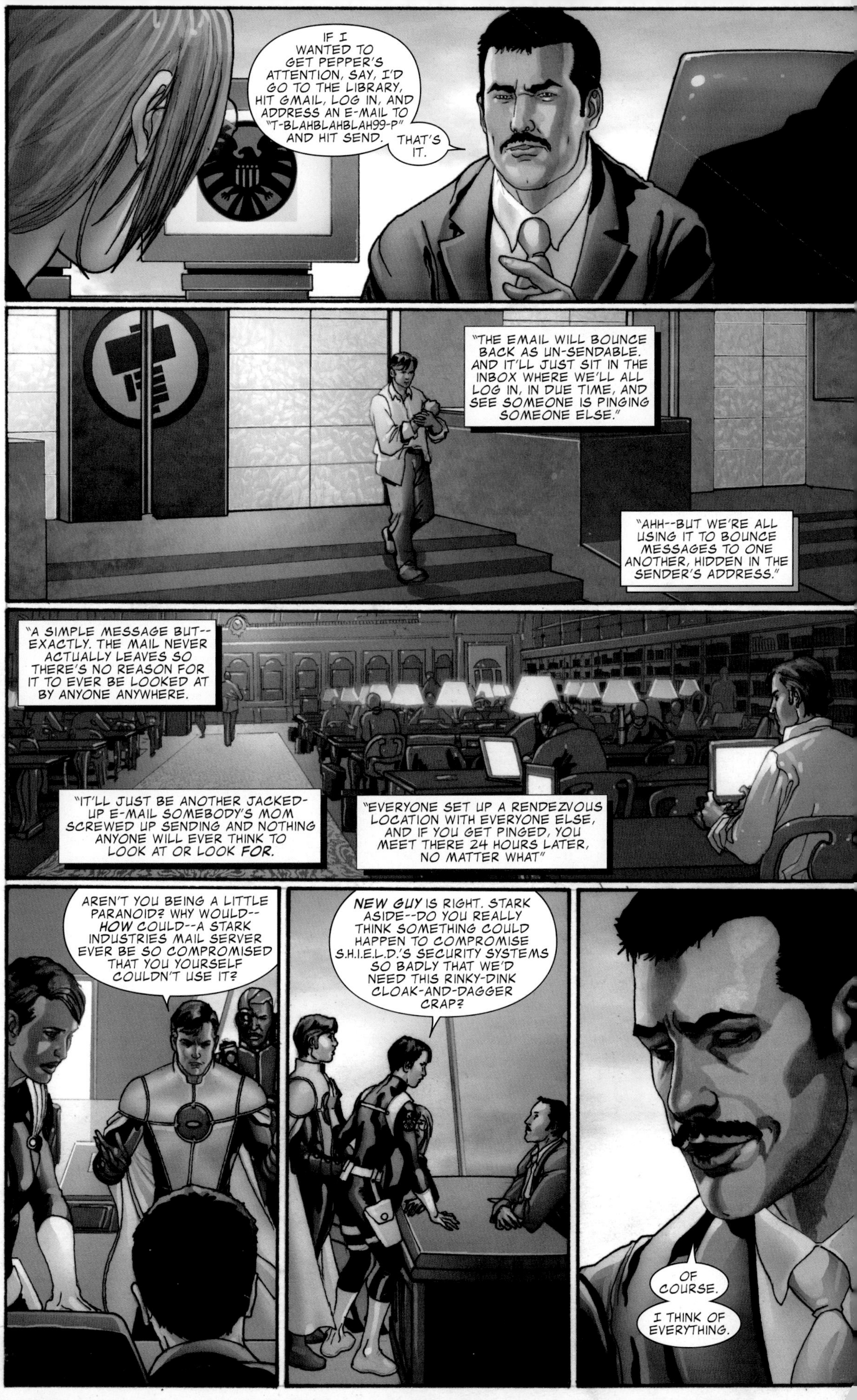
IF I WANTED TO GET PEPPER'S ATTENTION, SAY, I'D GO TO THE LIBRARY, HIT GMAIL, LOG IN, AND ADDRESS AN E-MAIL TO "T-BLAHBLAHBLAH99-P" AND HIT SEND.
THAT'S IT.
"THE EMAIL WILL BOUNCE BACK AS UN-SENDABLE. AND IT'LL JUST SIT IN THE INBOX WHERE WE'LL ALL LOG IN, IN DUE TIME, AND SEE SOMEONE IS PINGING SOMEONE ELSE."
"AHH--BUT WE'RE ALL USING IT TO BOUNCE MESSAGES TO ONE ANOTHER, HIDDEN IN THE SENDER'S ADDRESS."
"A SIMPLE MESSAGE BUT--EXACTLY. THE MAIL NEVER ACTUALLY LEAVES SO THERE'S NO REASON FOR IT TO EVER BE LOOKED AT BY ANYONE ANYWHERE.
"IT'LL JUST BE ANOTHER JACKED-UP E-MAIL SOMEBODY'S MOM SCREWED UP SENDING AND NOTHING ANYONE WILL EVER THINK TO LOOK AT OR LOOK FOR.
"EVERYONE SET UP A RENDEZVOUS LOCATION WITH EVERYONE ELSE, AND IF YOU GET PINGED, YOU MEET THERE 24 HOURS LATER, NO MATTER WHAT"
AREN'T YOU BEING A LITTLE PARANOID? WHY WOULD--HOW COULD--A STARK INDUSTRIES MAIL SERVER EVER BE SO COMPROMISED THAT YOU YOURSELF COULDN'T USE IT?
NEW GUY IS RIGHT. STARK ASIDE--DO YOU REALLY THINK SOMETHING COULD HAPPEN TO COMPROMISE S.H.I.E.L.D.'S SECURITY SYSTEMS SO BADLY THAT WE'D NEED THIS RINKY-DINK CLOAK-AND-DAGGER CRAP?
OF COURSE.
I THINK OF EVERYTHING.

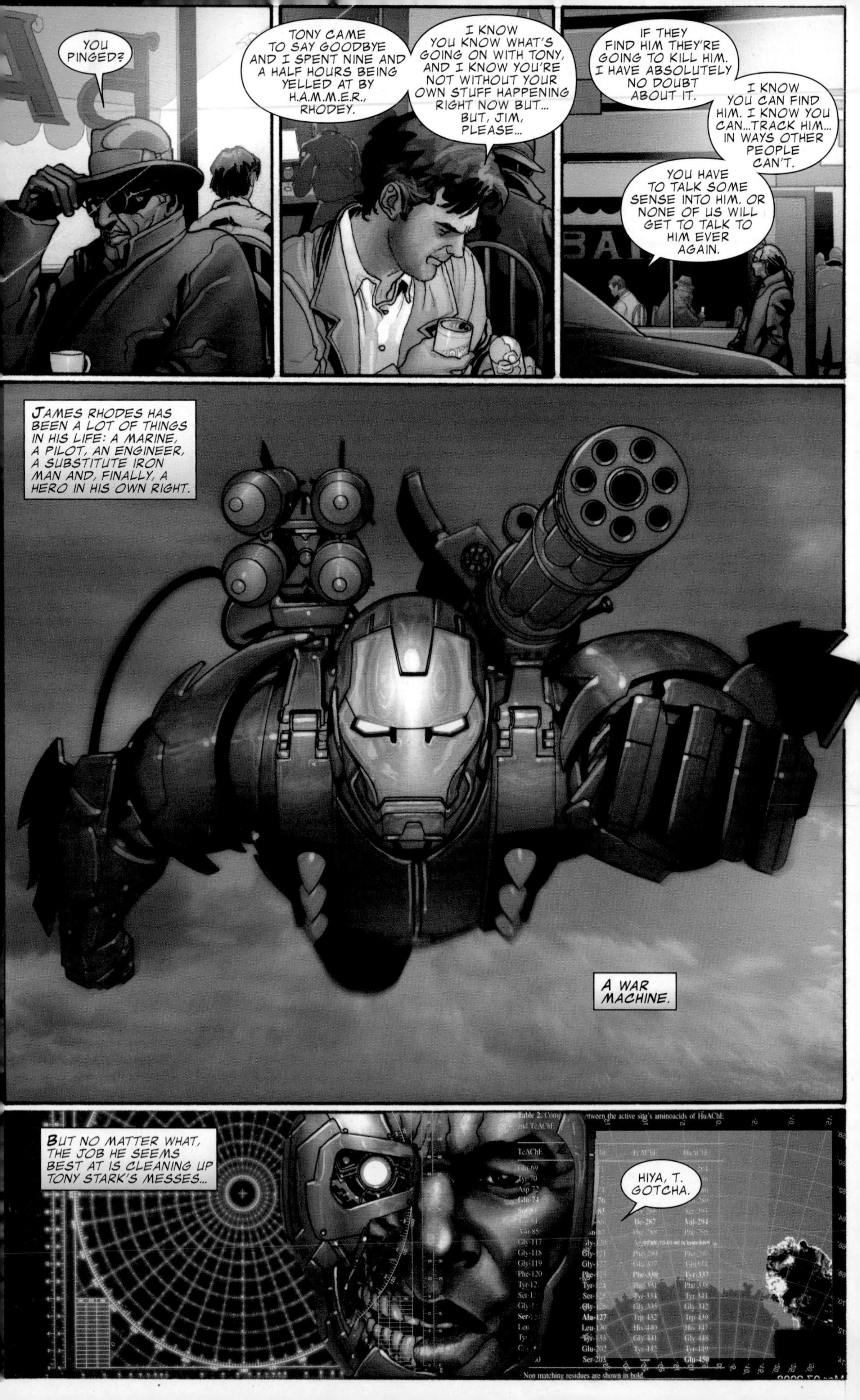
YOU PINGED?
TONY CAME TO SAY GOODBYE AND I SPENT NINE AND A HALF HOURS BEING YELLED AT BY H.A.M.M.E.R., RHODEY.
I KNOW YOU KNOW WHAT'S GOING ON WITH TONY, AND I KNOW YOU'RE NOT WITHOUT YOUR OWN STUFF HAPPENING RIGHT NOW BUT... BUT, JIM, PLEASE...
IF THEY FIND HIM THEY'RE GOING TO KILL HIM. I HAVE ABSOLUTELY NO DOUBT ABOUT IT.
I KNOW YOU CAN FIND HIM. I KNOW YOU CAN...TRACK HIM... IN WAYS OTHER PEOPLE CAN'T.
YOU HAVE TO TALK SOME SENSE INTO HIM. OR NONE OF US WILL GET TO TALK TO HIM EVER AGAIN.
JAMES RHODES HAS BEEN A LOT OF THINGS IN HIS LIFE: A MARINE, A PILOT, AN ENGINEER, A SUBSTITUTE IRON MAN AND, FINALLY, A HERO IN HIS OWN RIGHT.
A WAR MACHINE.
BUT NO MATTER WHAT, THE JOB HE SEEMS BEST AT IS CLEANING UP TONY STARK'S MESSES...
HIYA, T. GOTCHA.

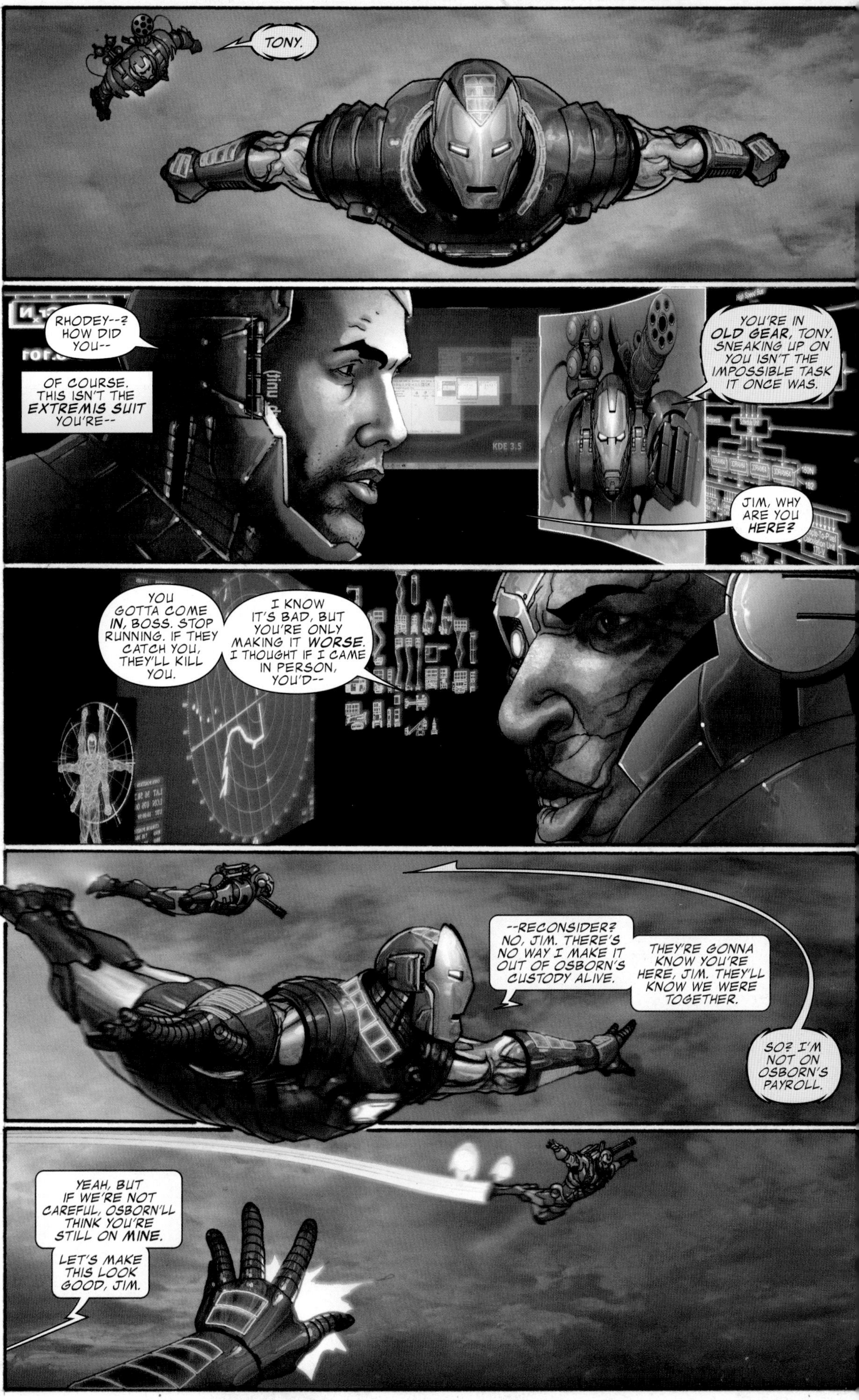
TONY.
RHODEY--? HOW DID YOU--
OF COURSE. THIS ISN'T THE EXTREMIS SUIT YOU'RE--
YOU'RE IN OLD GEAR, TONY. SNEAKING UP ON YOU ISN'T THE IMPOSSIBLE TASK IT ONCE WAS.
JIM, WHY ARE YOU HERE?
YOU GOTTA COME IN, BOSS. STOP RUNNING. IF THEY CATCH YOU, THEY'LL KILL YOU.
I KNOW IT'S BAD, BUT YOU'RE ONLY MAKING IT WORSE. I THOUGHT IF I CAME IN PERSON, YOU'D--
--RECONSIDER? NO, JIM. THERE'S NO WAY I MAKE IT OUT OF OSBORN'S CUSTODY ALIVE.
THEY'RE GONNA KNOW YOU'RE HERE, JIM. THEY'LL KNOW WE WERE TOGETHER.
SO? I'M NOT ON OSBORN'S PAYROLL.
YEAH, BUT IF WE'RE NOT CAREFUL, OSBORN'LL THINK YOU'RE STILL ON MINE.
LET'S MAKE THIS LOOK GOOD, JIM.

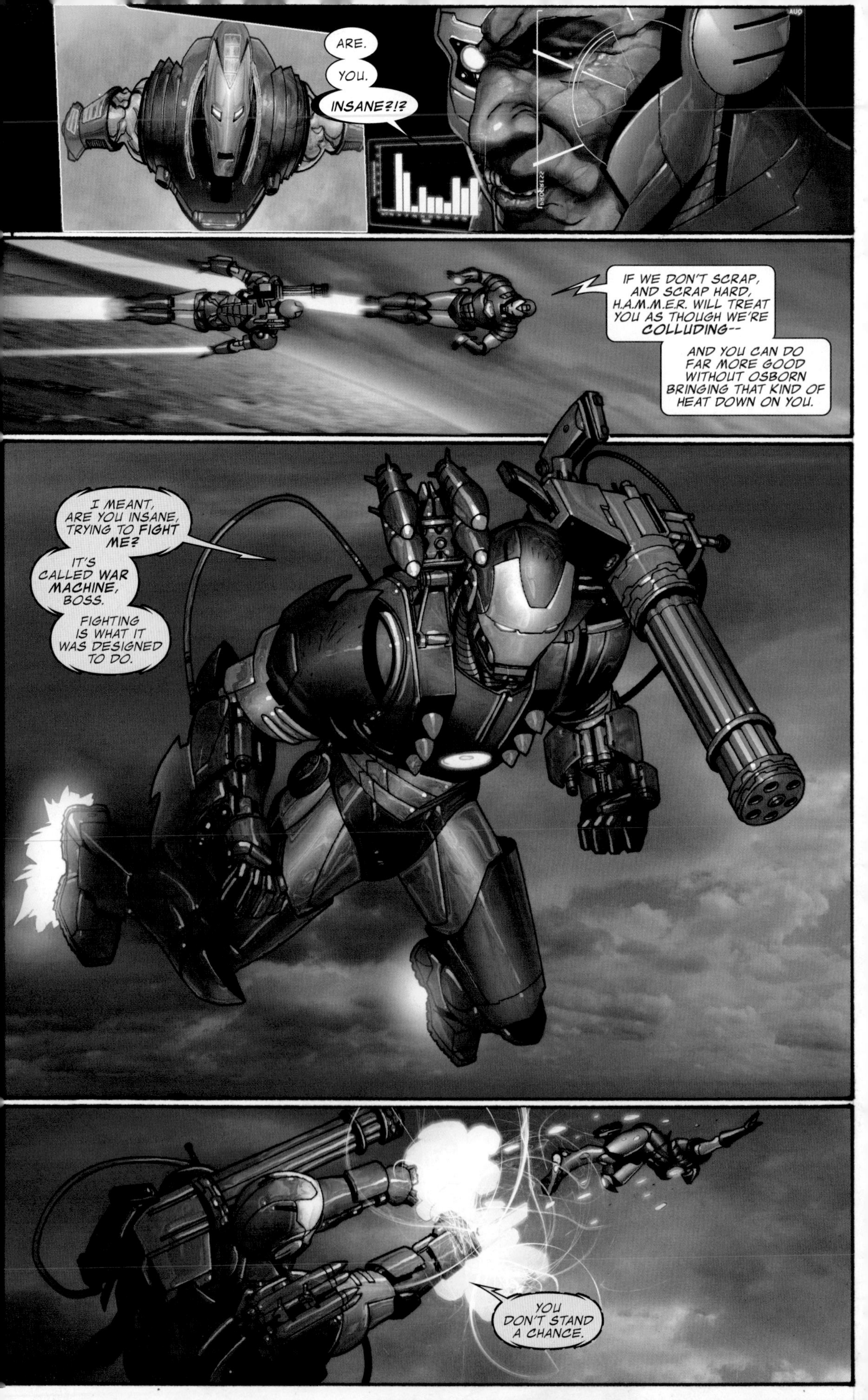
ARE.
YOU.
INSANE?!?
IF WE DON'T SCRAP, AND SCRAP HARD, H.A.M.M.E.R. WILL TREAT YOU AS THOUGH WE'RE COLLUDING--
AND YOU CAN DO FAR MORE GOOD WITHOUT OSBORN BRINGING THAT KIND OF HEAT DOWN ON YOU.
I MEANT, ARE YOU INSANE, TRYING TO FIGHT ME?
IT'S CALLED WAR MACHINE, BOSS.
FIGHTING IS WHAT IT WAS DESIGNED TO DO.
YOU DON'T STAND A CHANCE.

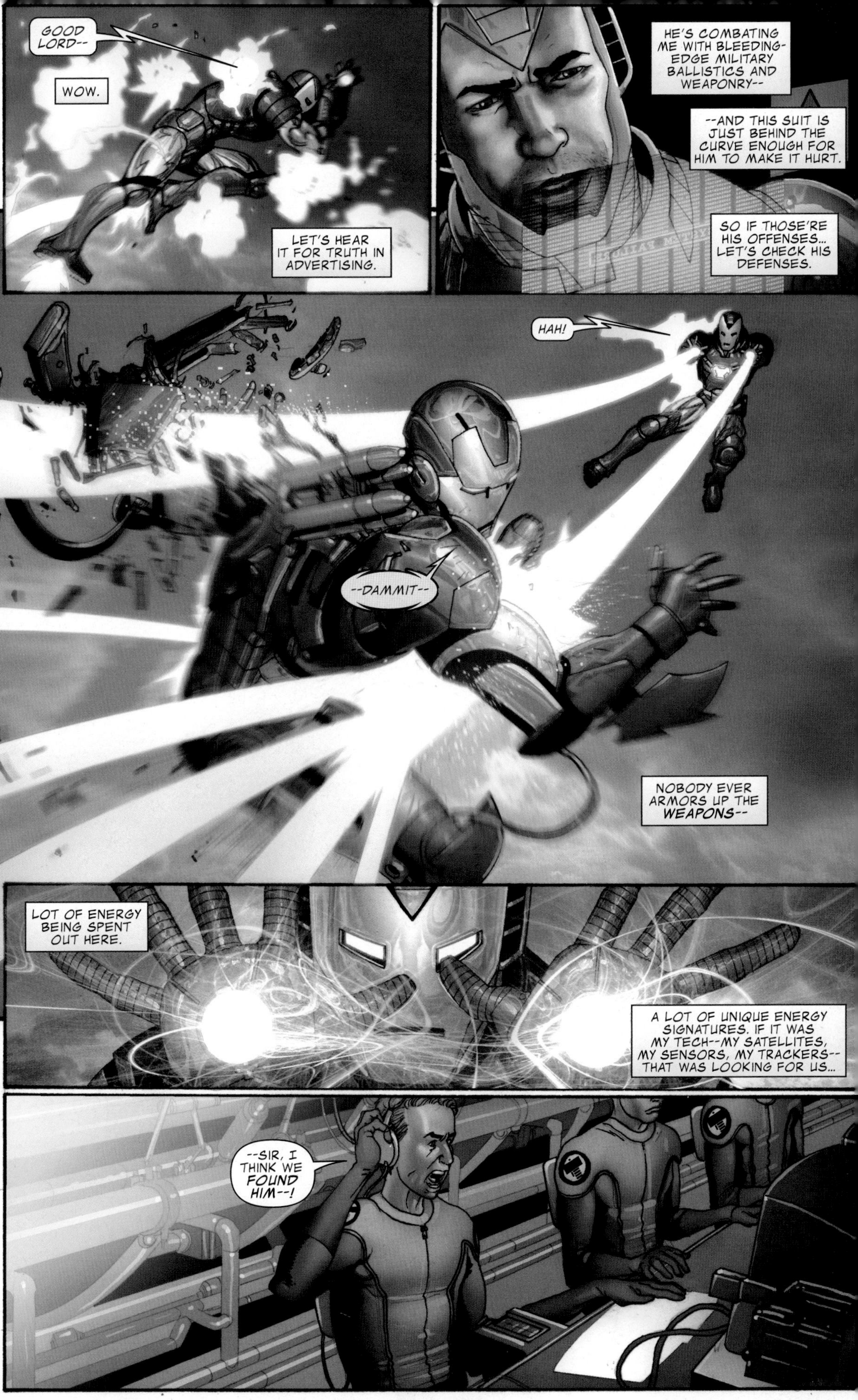
GOOD LORD--
WOW.
LET'S HEAR IT FOR TRUTH IN ADVERTISING.
HE'S COMBATING ME WITH BLEEDING-EDGE MILITARY BALLISTICS AND WEAPONRY--
--AND THIS SUIT IS JUST BEHIND THE CURVE ENOUGH FOR HIM TO MAKE IT HURT.
SO IF THOSE'RE HIS OFFENSES... LET'S CHECK HIS DEFENSES.
HAH!
--DAMMIT--
NOBODY EVER ARMORS UP THE WEAPONS--
LOT OF ENERGY BEING SPENT OUT HERE.
A LOT OF UNIQUE ENERGY SIGNATURES. IF IT WAS MY TECH--MY SATELLITES, MY SENSORS, MY TRACKERS--THAT WAS LOOKING FOR US...
--SIR, I THINK WE FOUND HIM--!

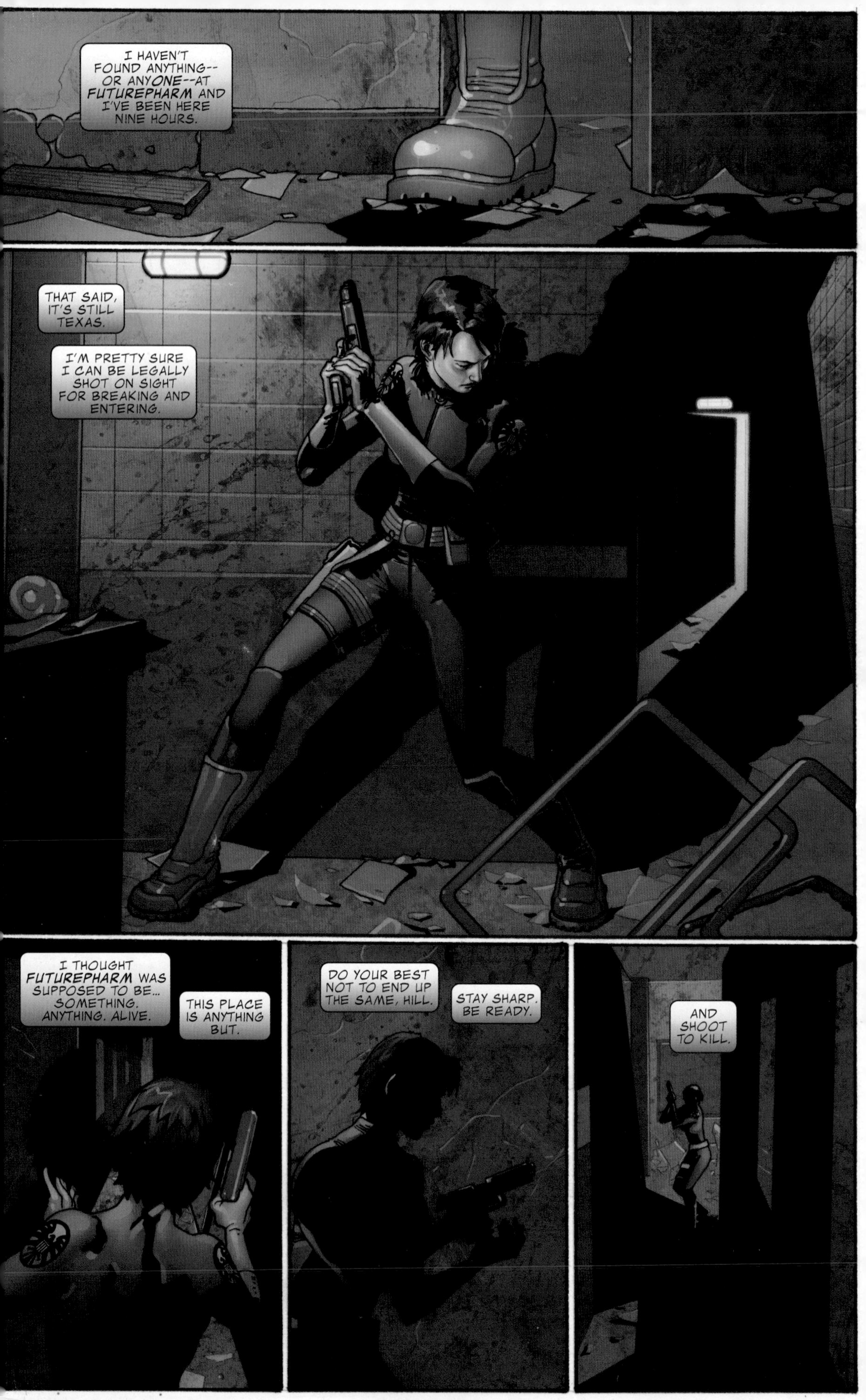
I HAVEN'T FOUND ANYTHING-- OR ANYONE--AT FUTUREPHARM AND I'VE BEEN HERE NINE HOURS.
THAT SAID, IT'S STILL TEXAS.
I'M PRETTY SURE I CAN BE LEGALLY SHOT ON SIGHT FOR BREAKING AND ENTERING.
I THOUGHT FUTUREPHARM WAS SUPPOSED TO BE... SOMETHING. ANYTHING. ALIVE.
THIS PLACE IS ANYTHING BUT.
DO YOUR BEST NOT TO END UP THE SAME, HILL.
STAY SHARP. BE READY.
AND SHOOT TO KILL.

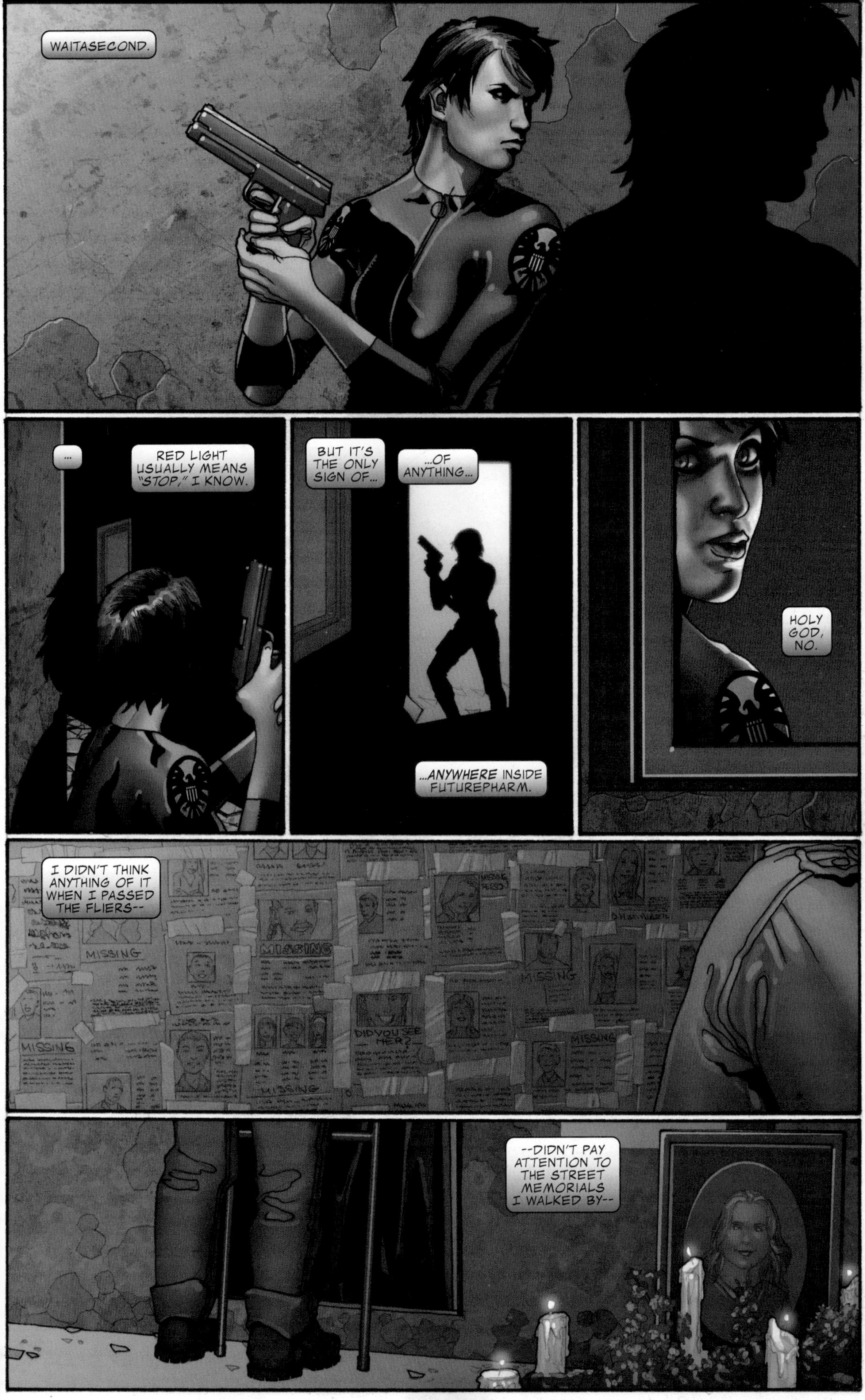

WAITASECOND.
...
RED LIGHT USUALLY MEANS "STOP," I KNOW.
BUT IT'S THE ONLY SIGN OF...
...OF ANYTHING...
...ANYWHERE INSIDE FUTUREPHARM.
HOLY GOD, NO.
I DIDN'T THINK ANYTHING OF IT WHEN I PASSED THE FLIERS--
MISSING
MISSING
DID YOU SEE HER?
MISSING
MISSING
MISSING
--DIDN'T PAY ATTENTION TO THE STREET MEMORIALS I WALKED BY--

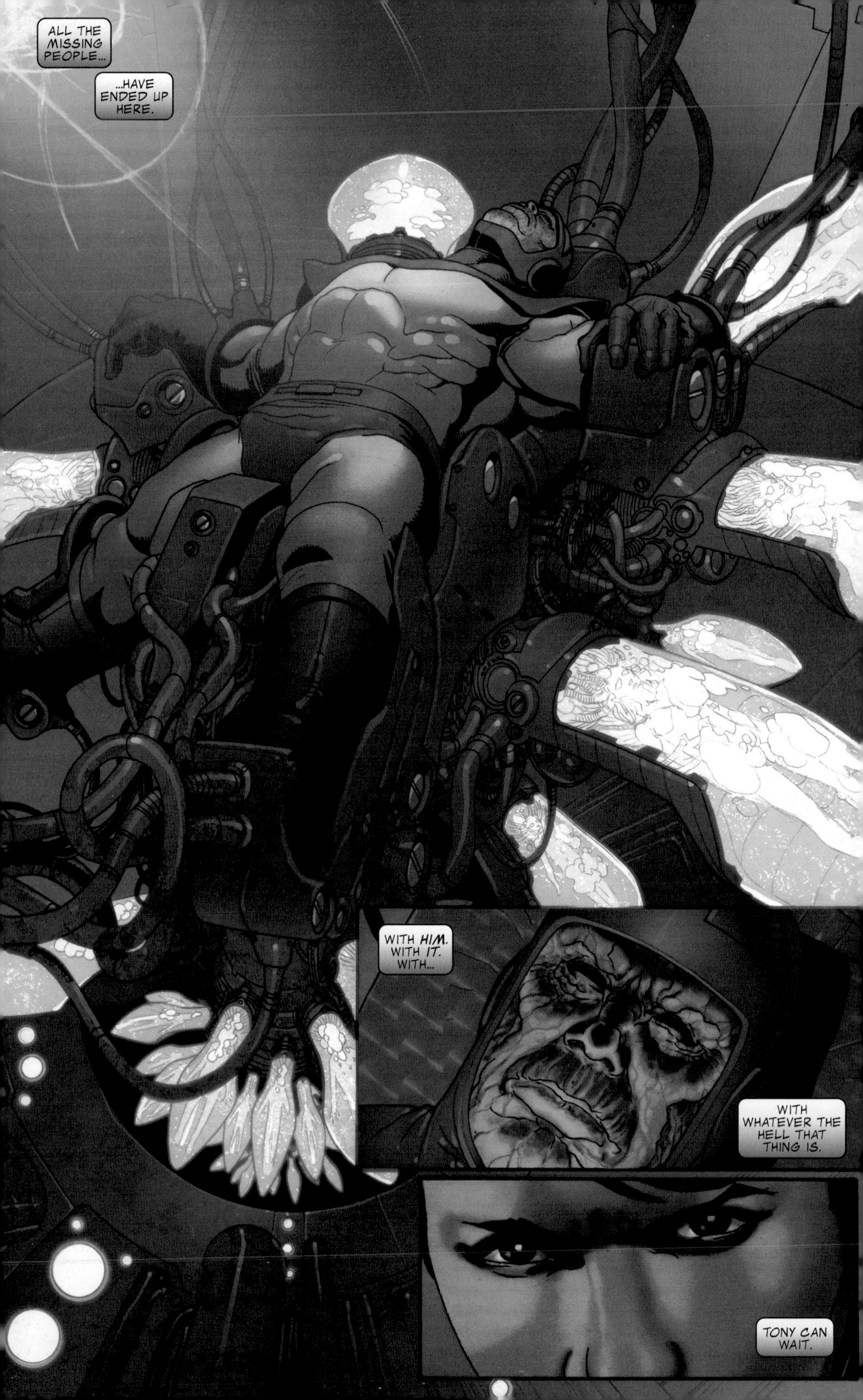
ALL THE MISSING PEOPLE...
...HAVE ENDED UP HERE.
WITH *HIM*. WITH *IT*. WITH...
WITH WHATEVER THE HELL THAT THING IS.
TONY CAN WAIT.

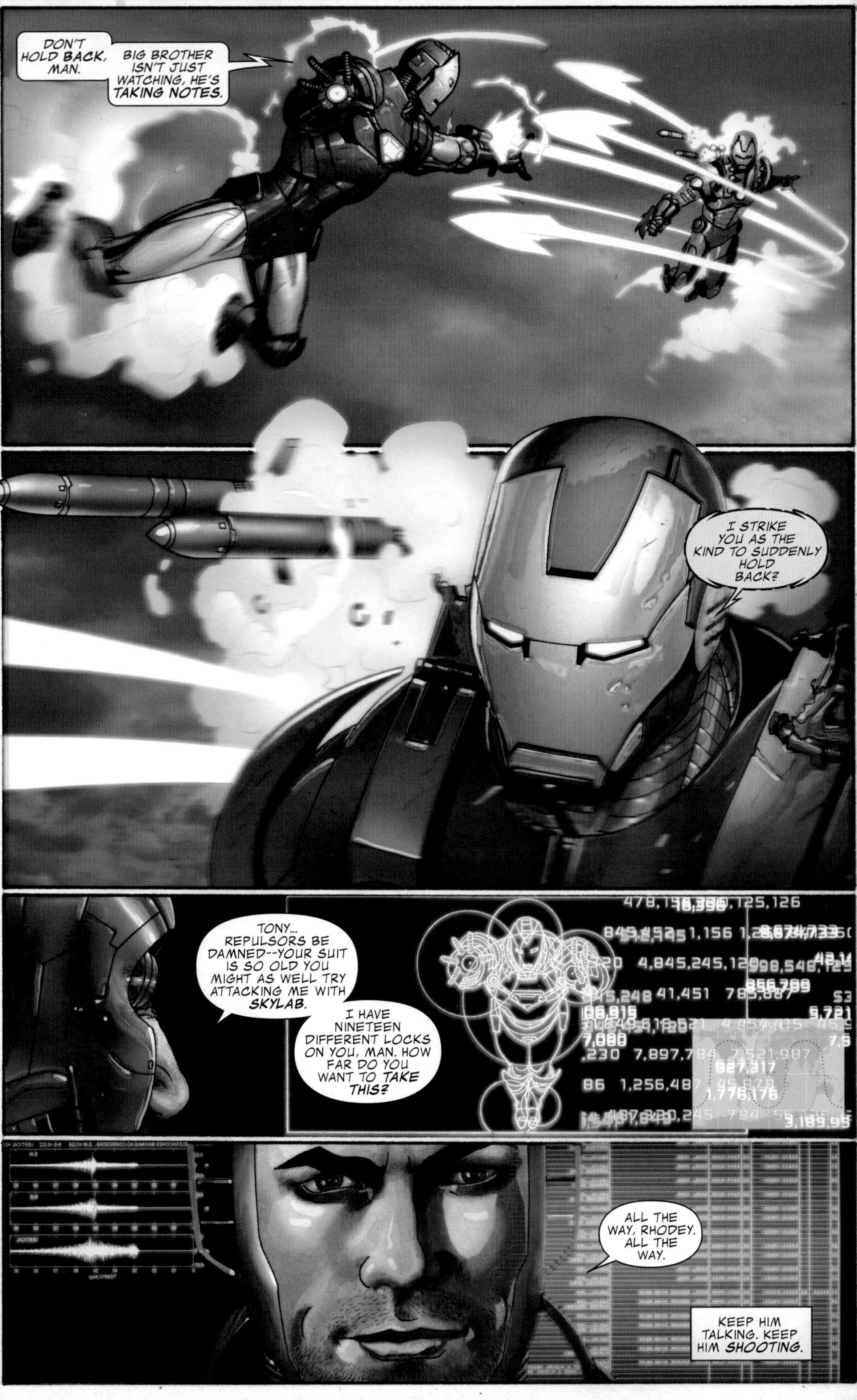
DON'T HOLD BACK, MAN.
BIG BROTHER ISN'T JUST WATCHING, HE'S TAKING NOTES.
I STRIKE YOU AS THE KIND TO SUDDENLY HOLD BACK?
TONY... REPULSORS BE DAMNED--YOUR SUIT IS SO OLD YOU MIGHT AS WELL TRY ATTACKING ME WITH SKYLAB.
I HAVE NINETEEN DIFFERENT LOCKS ON YOU, MAN. HOW FAR DO YOU WANT TO TAKE THIS?
ALL THE WAY, RHODEY. ALL THE WAY.
KEEP HIM TALKING. KEEP HIM SHOOTING.

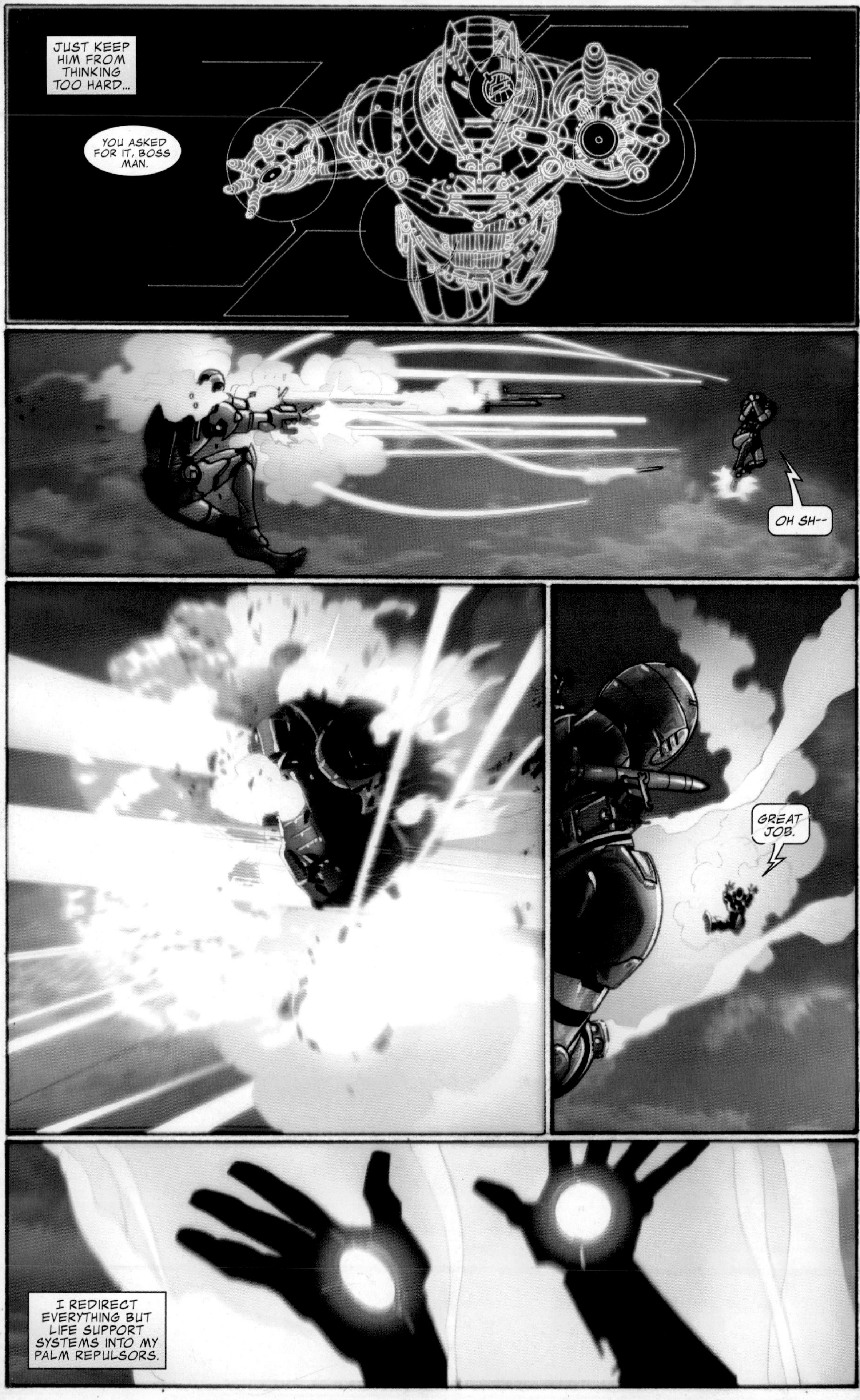
JUST KEEP HIM FROM THINKING TOO HARD...
YOU ASKED FOR IT, BOSS MAN.
OH SH--
GREAT JOB.
I REDIRECT EVERYTHING BUT LIFE SUPPORT SYSTEMS INTO MY PALM REPULSORS.

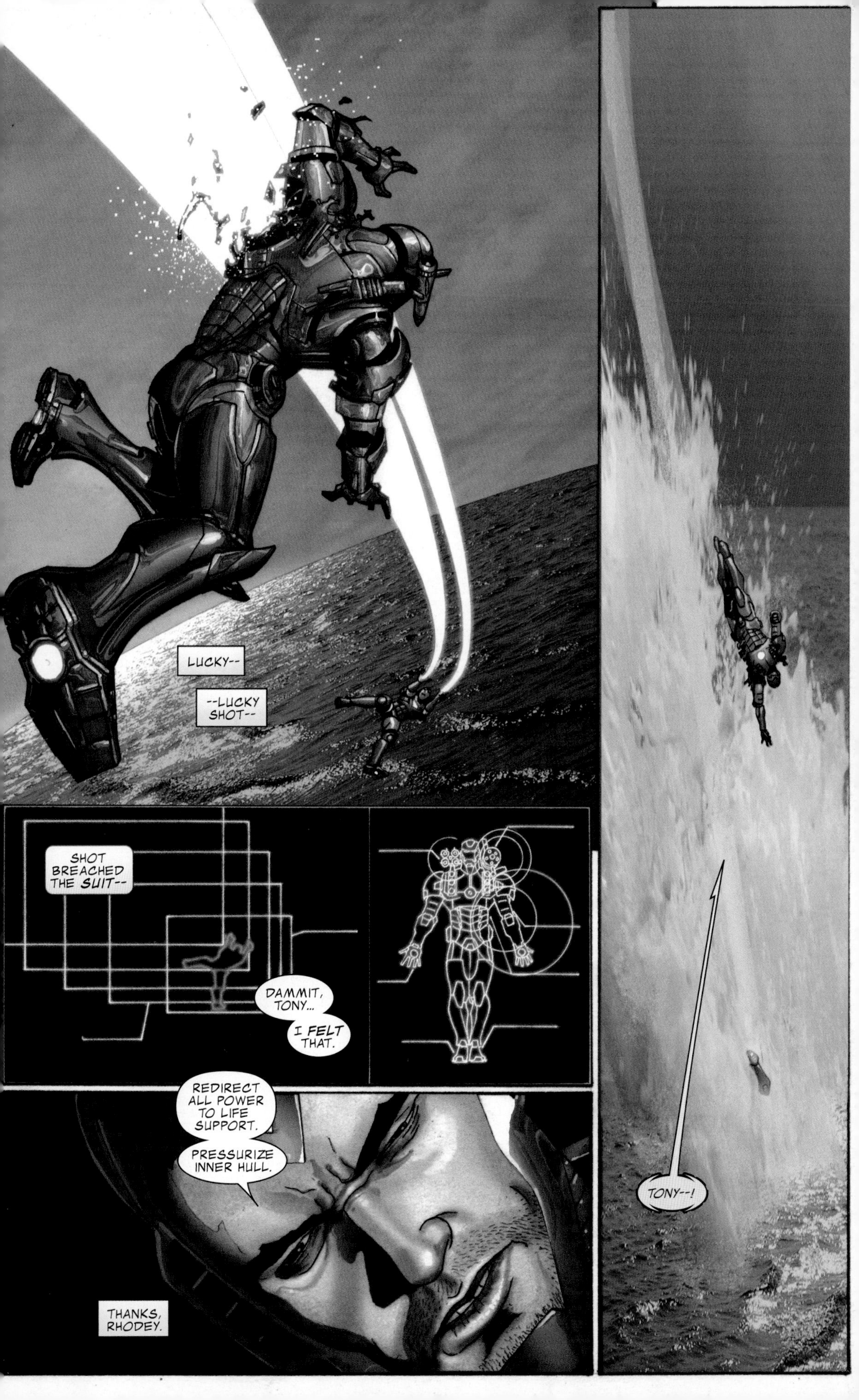

LUCKY--
--LUCKY SHOT--
SHOT BREACHED THE SUIT--
DAMMIT, TONY...
I FELT THAT.
REDIRECT ALL POWER TO LIFE SUPPORT.
PRESSURIZE INNER HULL.
THANKS, RHODEY.
TONY--!

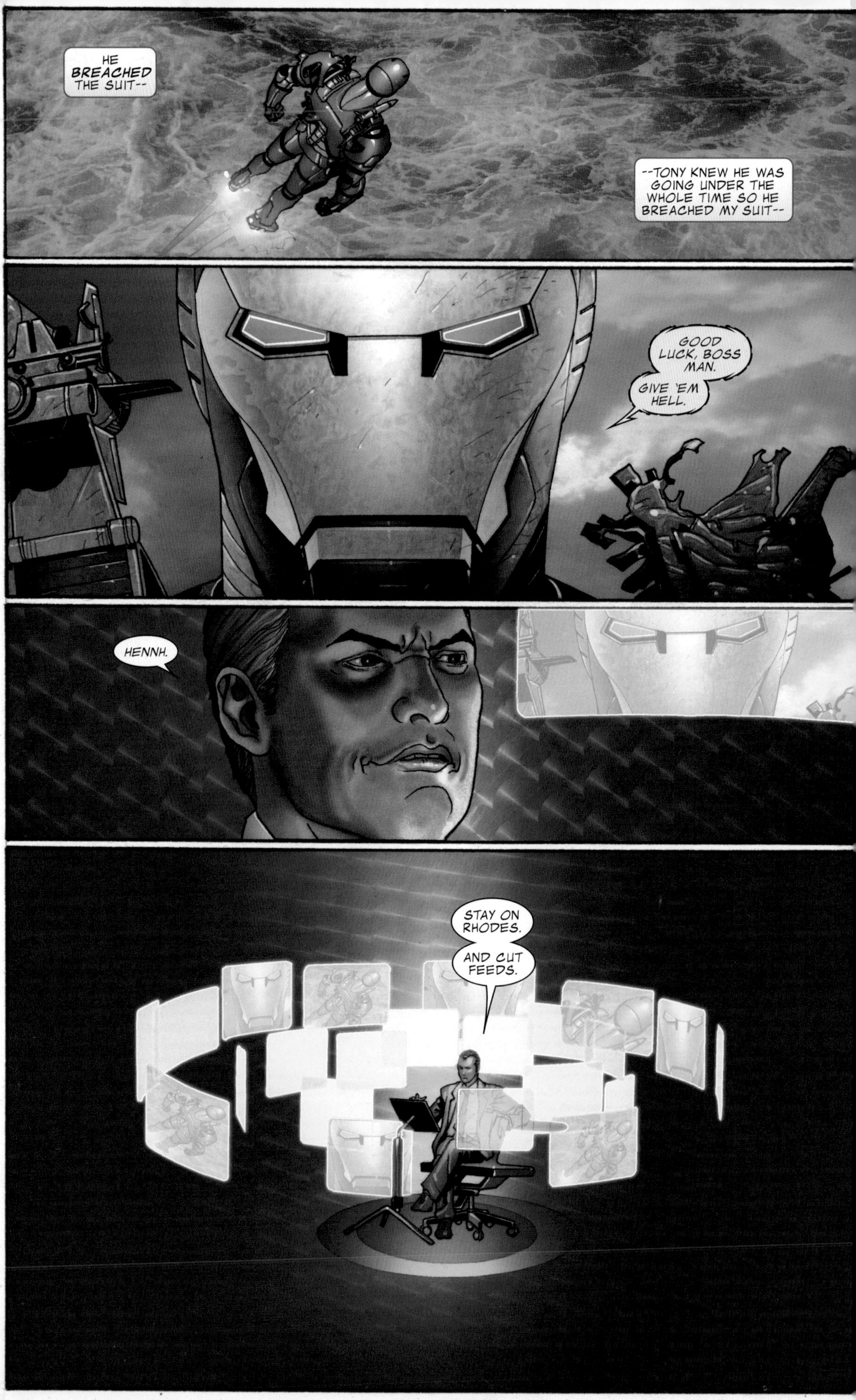
HE BREACHED THE SUIT--
--TONY KNEW HE WAS GOING UNDER THE WHOLE TIME SO HE BREACHED MY SUIT--
GOOD LUCK, BOSS MAN.
GIVE 'EM HELL.
HENNH.
STAY ON RHODES.
AND CUT FEEDS.

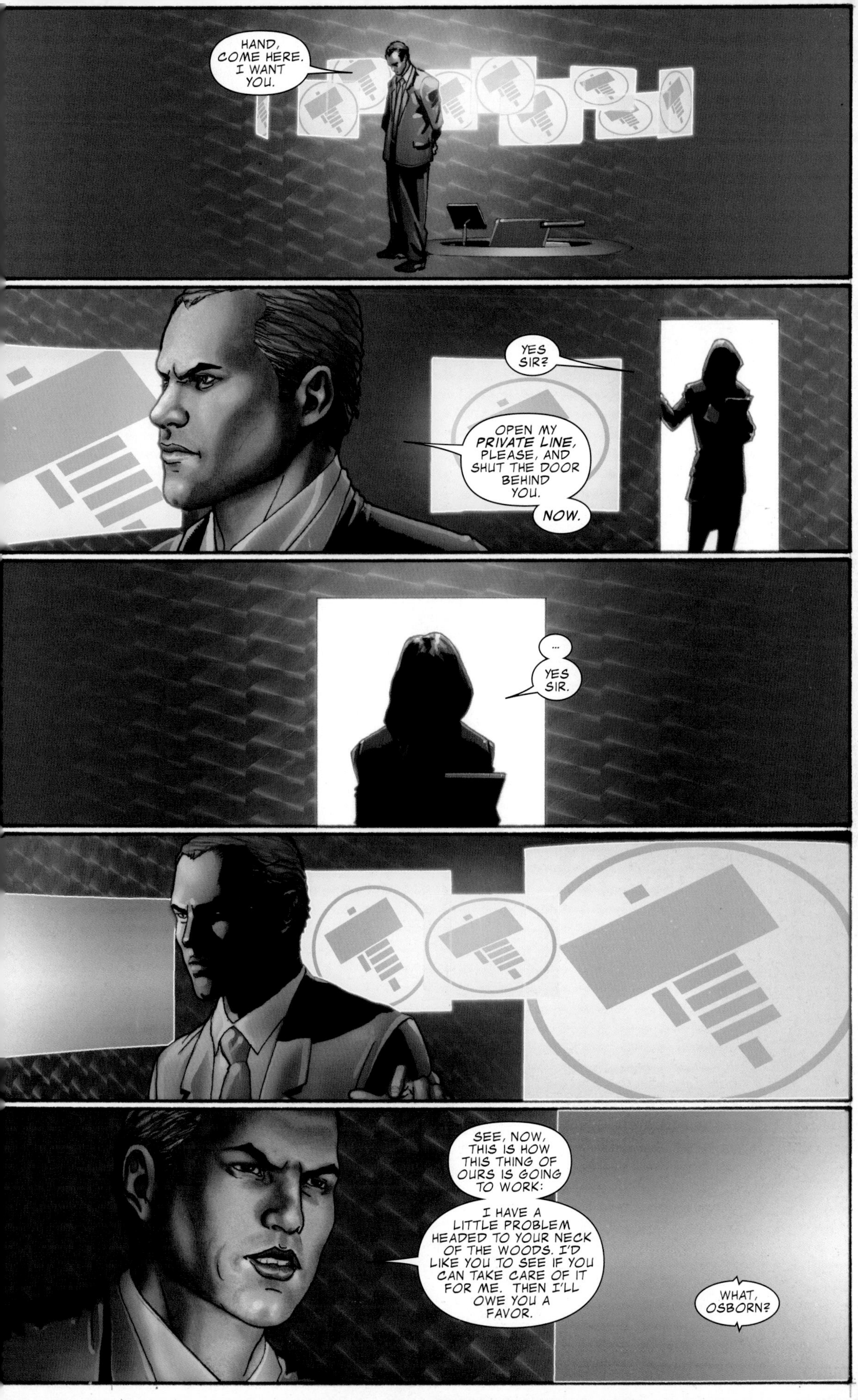
HAND, COME HERE. I WANT YOU.
YES SIR?
OPEN MY PRIVATE LINE, PLEASE, AND SHUT THE DOOR BEHIND YOU.
NOW.
...
YES SIR.
SEE, NOW, THIS IS HOW THIS THING OF OURS IS GOING TO WORK:
I HAVE A LITTLE PROBLEM HEADED TO YOUR NECK OF THE WOODS. I'D LIKE YOU TO SEE IF YOU CAN TAKE CARE OF IT FOR ME. THEN I'LL OWE YOU A FAVOR.
WHAT, OSBORN?

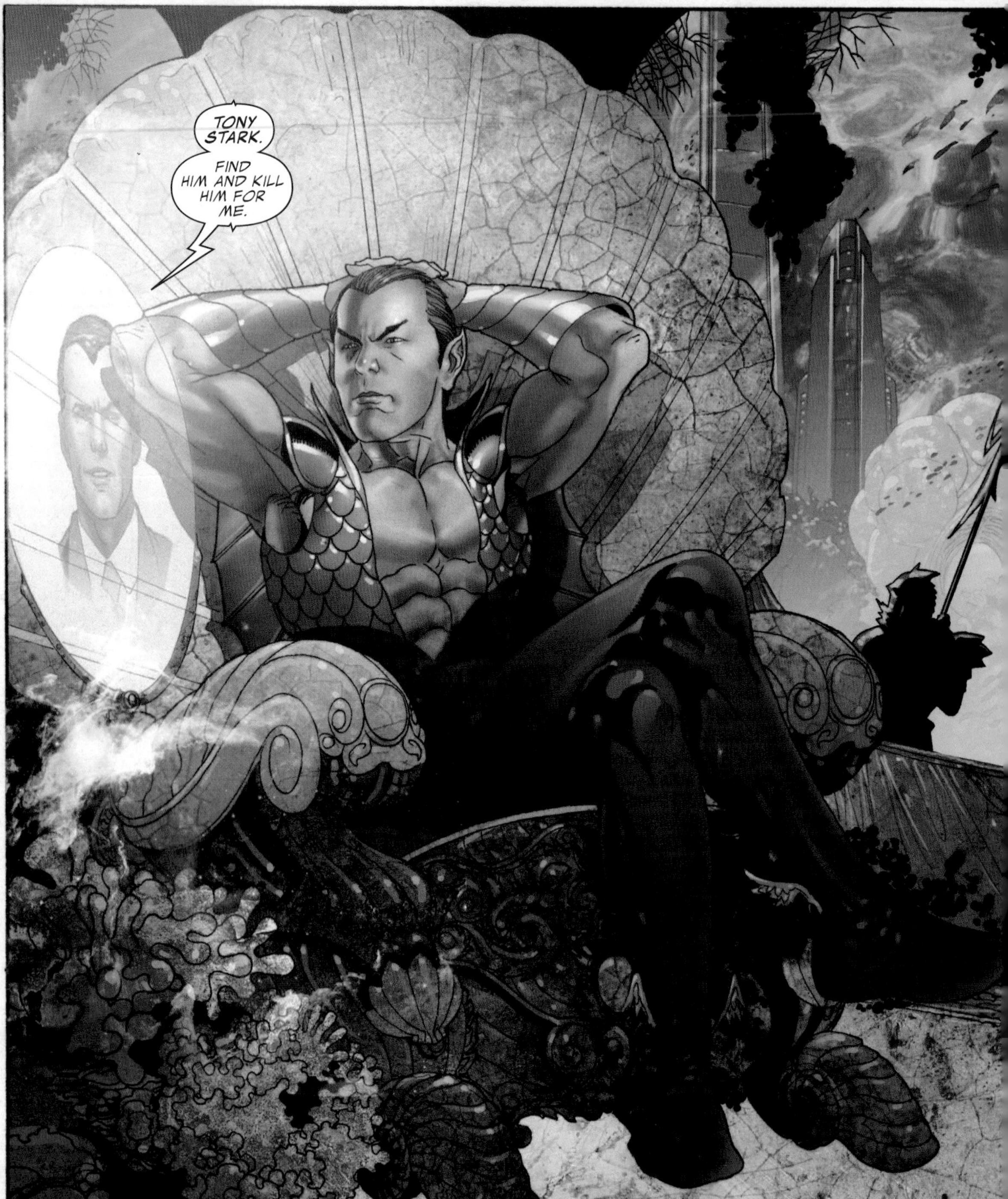
TONY STARK.
FIND HIM AND KILL HIM FOR ME.

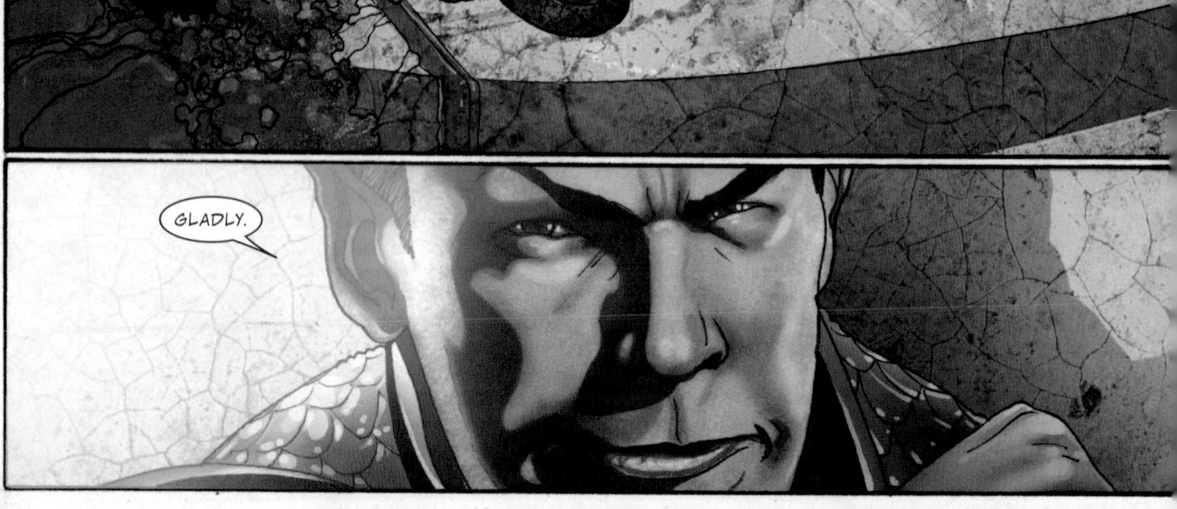
GLADLY.

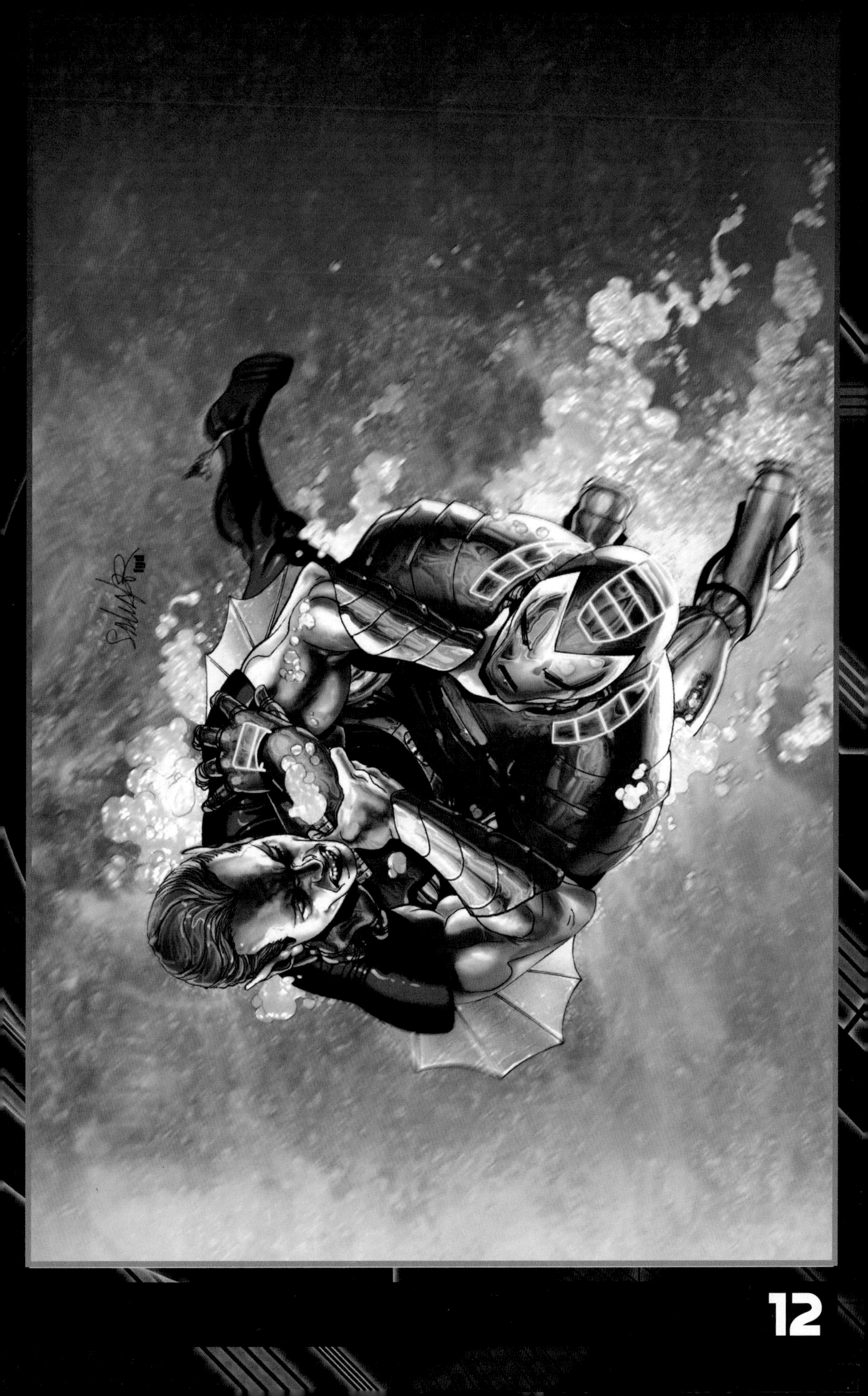

12

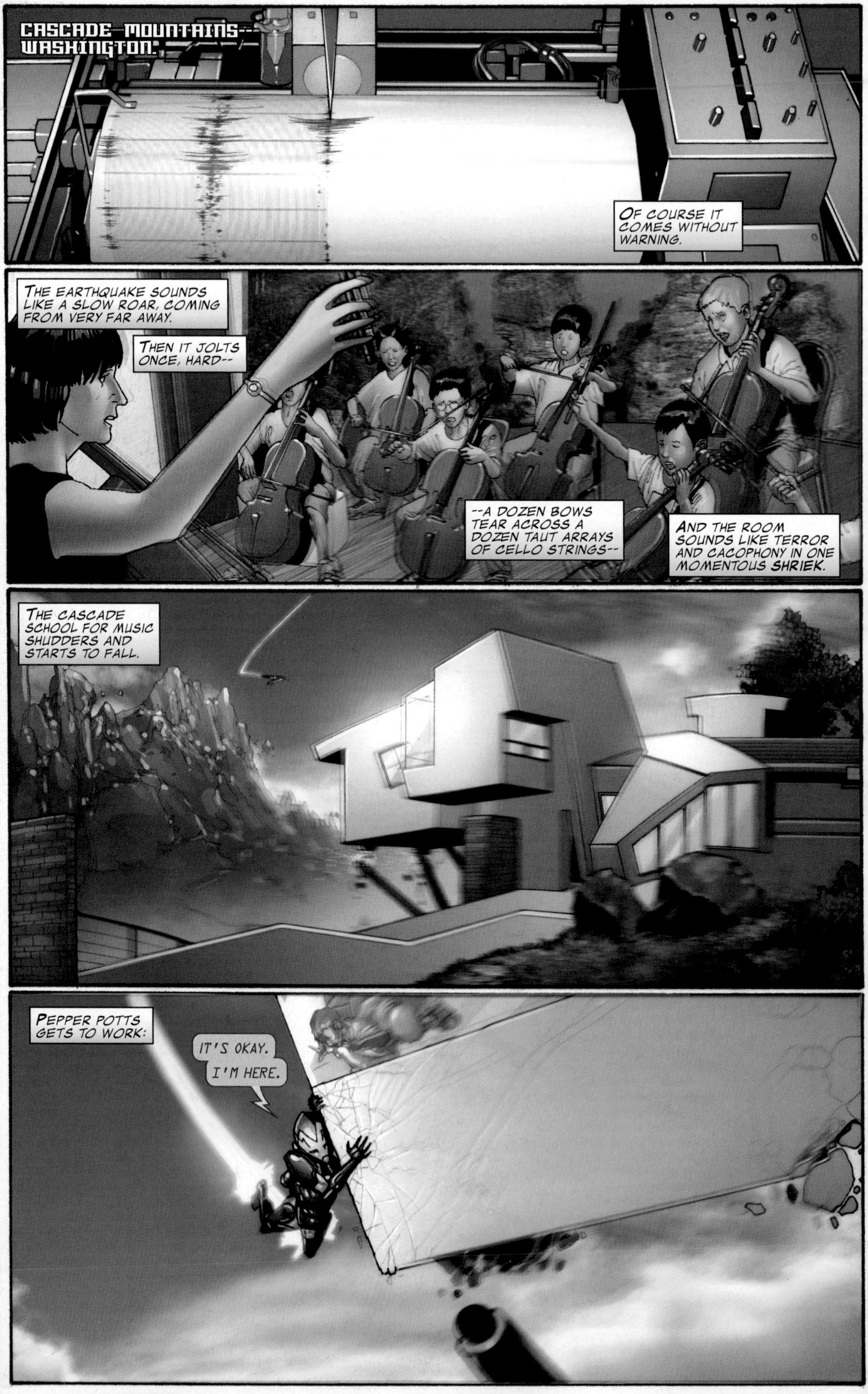

CASCADE MOUNTAINS--
WASHINGTON.
OF COURSE IT COMES WITHOUT WARNING.
THE EARTHQUAKE SOUNDS LIKE A SLOW ROAR, COMING FROM VERY FAR AWAY.
THEN IT JOLTS ONCE, HARD--
--A DOZEN BOWS TEAR ACROSS A DOZEN TAUT ARRAYS OF CELLO STRINGS--
AND THE ROOM SOUNDS LIKE TERROR AND CACOPHONY IN ONE MOMENTOUS SHRIEK.
THE CASCADE SCHOOL FOR MUSIC SHUDDERS AND STARTS TO FALL.
PEPPER POTTS GETS TO WORK:
IT'S OKAY. I'M HERE.

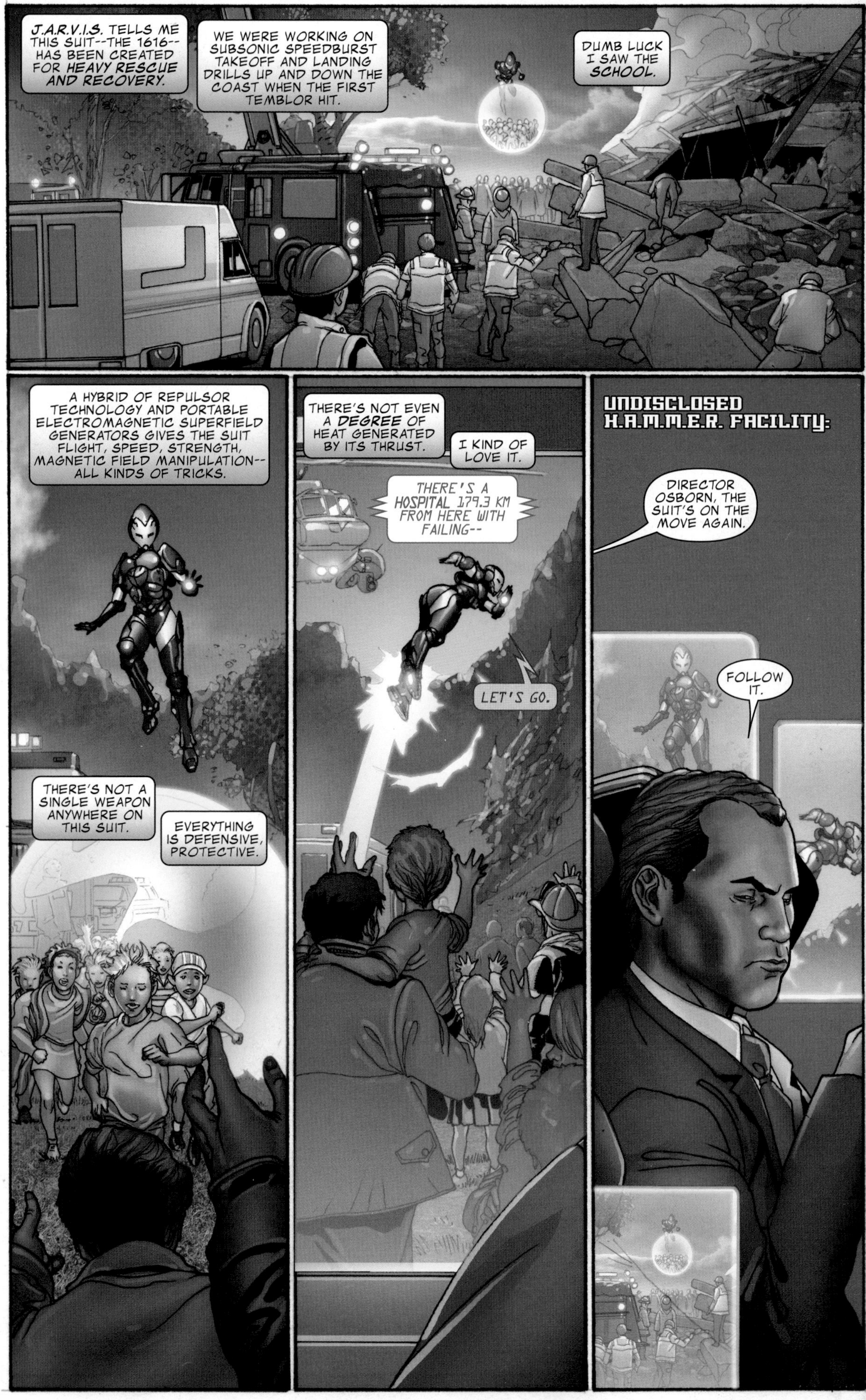
J.A.R.V.I.S. TELLS ME THIS SUIT--THE 1616--HAS BEEN CREATED FOR HEAVY RESCUE AND RECOVERY.
WE WERE WORKING ON SUBSONIC SPEEDBURST TAKEOFF AND LANDING DRILLS UP AND DOWN THE COAST WHEN THE FIRST TEMBLOR HIT.
DUMB LUCK I SAW THE SCHOOL.
A HYBRID OF REPULSOR TECHNOLOGY AND PORTABLE ELECTROMAGNETIC SUPERFIELD GENERATORS GIVES THE SUIT FLIGHT, SPEED, STRENGTH, MAGNETIC FIELD MANIPULATION--ALL KINDS OF TRICKS.
THERE'S NOT A SINGLE WEAPON ANYWHERE ON THIS SUIT.
EVERYTHING IS DEFENSIVE, PROTECTIVE.
THERE'S NOT EVEN A DEGREE OF HEAT GENERATED BY ITS THRUST.
I KIND OF LOVE IT.
THERE'S A HOSPITAL 179.3 KM FROM HERE WITH FAILING--
LET'S GO.
UNDISCLOSED H.A.M.M.E.R. FACILITY:
DIRECTOR OSBORN, THE SUIT'S ON THE MOVE AGAIN.
FOLLOW IT.

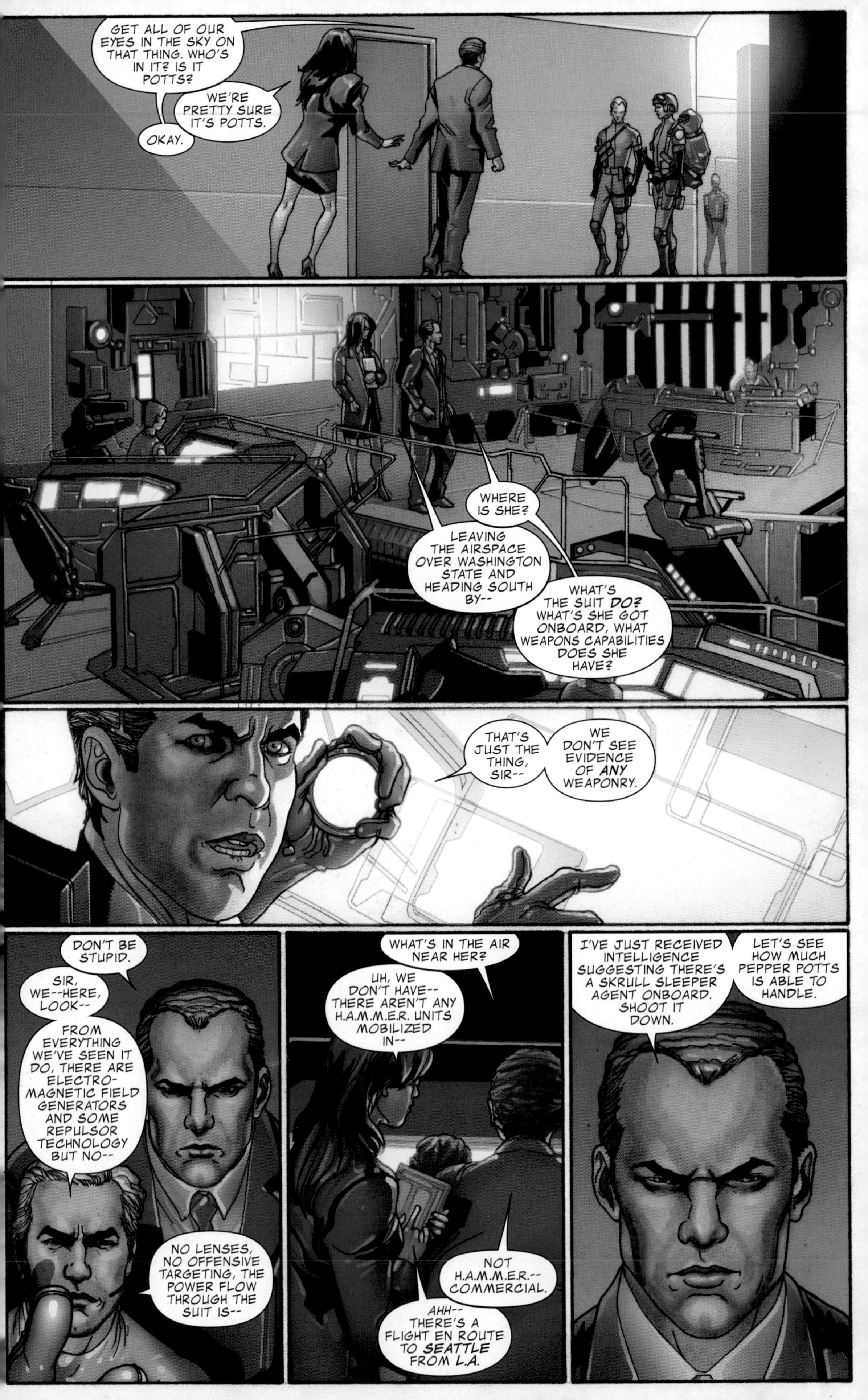
GET ALL OF OUR EYES IN THE SKY ON THAT THING. WHO'S IN IT? IS IT POTTS?
WE'RE PRETTY SURE IT'S POTTS.
OKAY.
WHERE IS SHE?
LEAVING THE AIRSPACE OVER WASHINGTON STATE AND HEADING SOUTH BY--
WHAT'S THE SUIT *DO?* WHAT'S SHE GOT ONBOARD, WHAT WEAPONS CAPABILITIES DOES SHE HAVE?
THAT'S JUST THE THING, SIR--
WE DON'T SEE EVIDENCE OF *ANY* WEAPONRY.
DON'T BE STUPID.
SIR, WE--HERE, LOOK--
FROM EVERYTHING WE'VE SEEN IT DO, THERE ARE ELECTRO-MAGNETIC FIELD GENERATORS AND SOME REPULSOR TECHNOLOGY BUT NO--
NO LENSES, NO OFFENSIVE TARGETING, THE POWER FLOW THROUGH THE SUIT IS--
WHAT'S IN THE AIR NEAR HER?
UH, WE DON'T HAVE-- THERE AREN'T ANY H.A.M.M.E.R. UNITS MOBILIZED IN--
NOT H.A.M.M.E.R.-- COMMERCIAL.
AHH-- THERE'S A FLIGHT EN ROUTE TO *SEATTLE* FROM *L.A.*
I'VE JUST RECEIVED INTELLIGENCE SUGGESTING THERE'S A SKRULL SLEEPER AGENT ONBOARD. SHOOT IT DOWN.
LET'S SEE HOW MUCH PEPPER POTTS IS ABLE TO HANDLE.

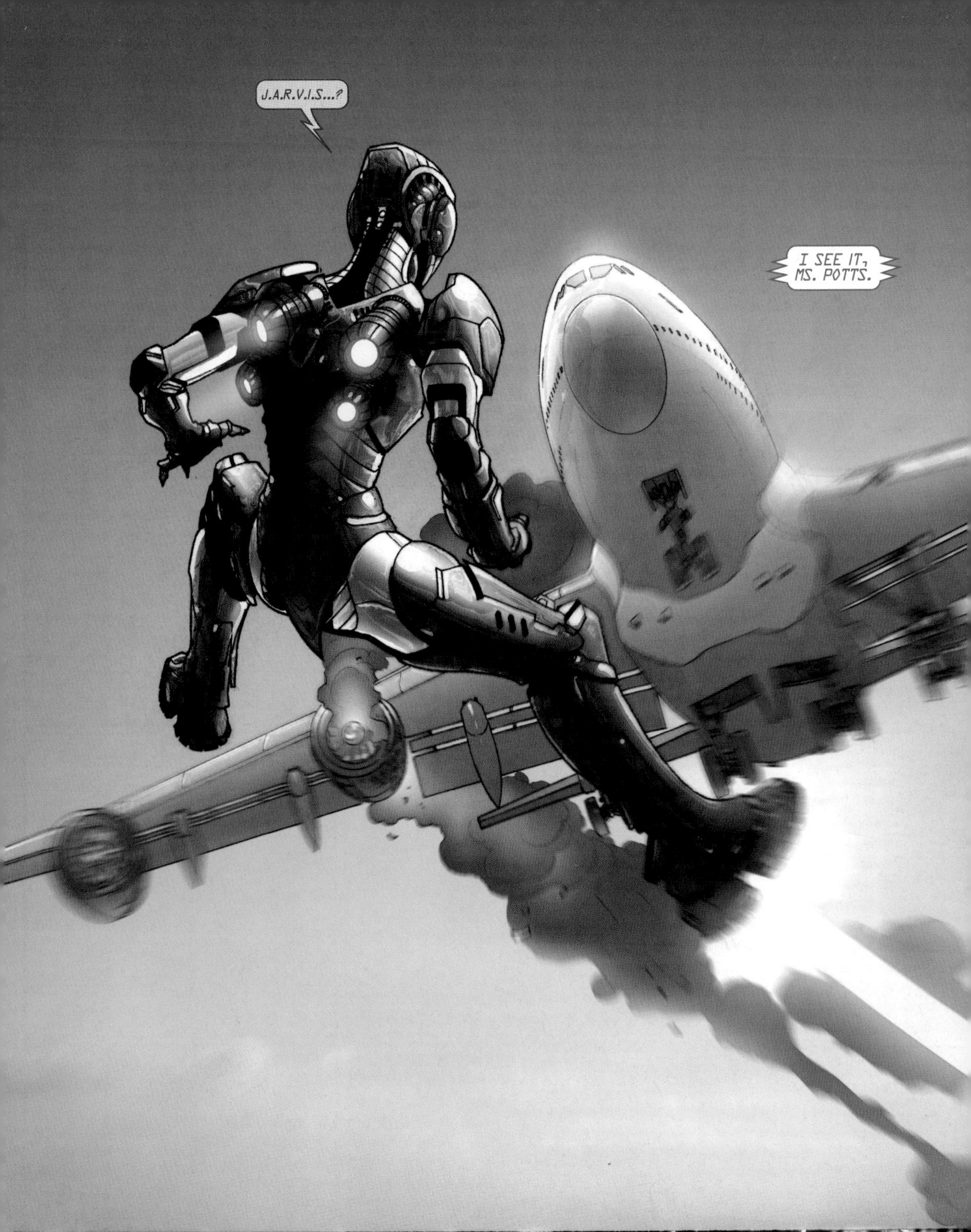
J.A.R.V.I.S...?
I SEE IT, MS. POTTS.

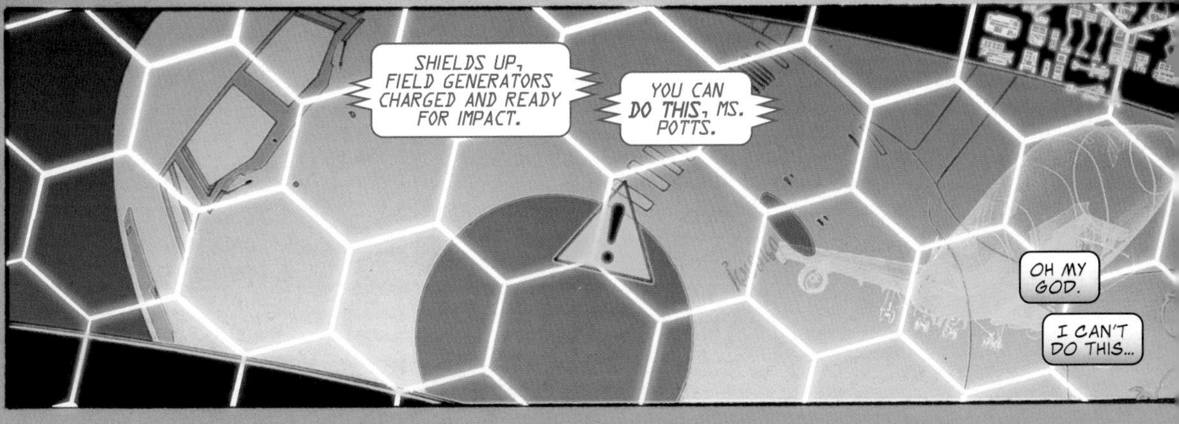
SHIELDS UP, FIELD GENERATORS CHARGED AND READY FOR IMPACT.
YOU CAN DO THIS, MS. POTTS.
OH MY GOD.
I CAN'T DO THIS...

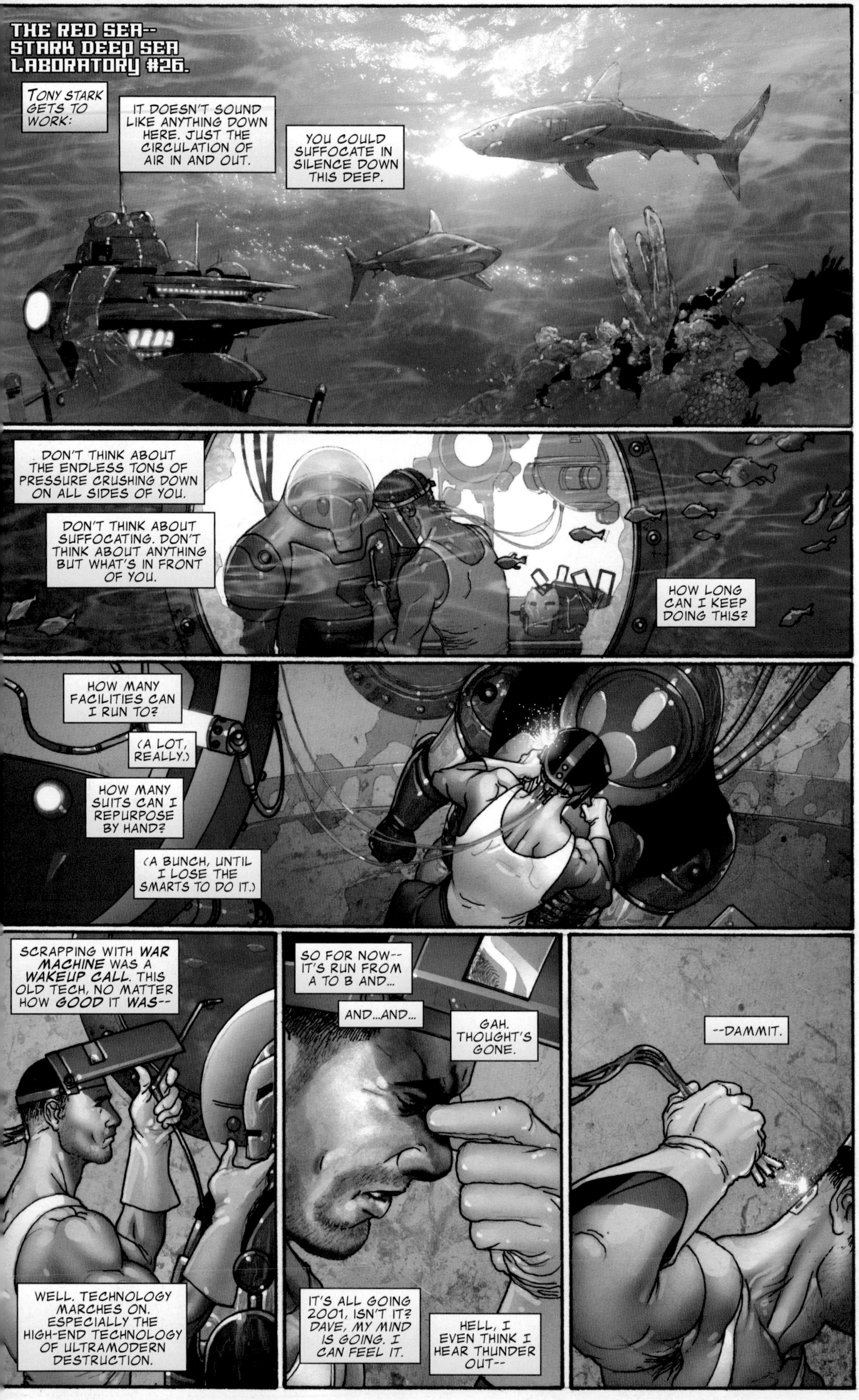
THE RED SEA-- STARK DEEP SEA LABORATORY #26.
TONY STARK GETS TO WORK:
IT DOESN'T SOUND LIKE ANYTHING DOWN HERE. JUST THE CIRCULATION OF AIR IN AND OUT.
YOU COULD SUFFOCATE IN SILENCE DOWN THIS DEEP.
DON'T THINK ABOUT THE ENDLESS TONS OF PRESSURE CRUSHING DOWN ON ALL SIDES OF YOU.
DON'T THINK ABOUT SUFFOCATING. DON'T THINK ABOUT ANYTHING BUT WHAT'S IN FRONT OF YOU.
HOW LONG CAN I KEEP DOING THIS?
HOW MANY FACILITIES CAN I RUN TO?
(A LOT, REALLY.)
HOW MANY SUITS CAN I REPURPOSE BY HAND?
(A BUNCH, UNTIL I LOSE THE SMARTS TO DO IT.)
SCRAPPING WITH WAR MACHINE WAS A WAKEUP CALL. THIS OLD TECH, NO MATTER HOW GOOD IT WAS--
WELL. TECHNOLOGY MARCHES ON. ESPECIALLY THE HIGH-END TECHNOLOGY OF ULTRAMODERN DESTRUCTION.
SO FOR NOW-- IT'S RUN FROM A TO B AND...
AND...AND...
GAH. THOUGHT'S GONE.
IT'S ALL GOING 2001, ISN'T IT? DAVE, MY MIND IS GOING. I CAN FEEL IT.
HELL, I EVEN THINK I HEAR THUNDER OUT--
--DAMMIT.

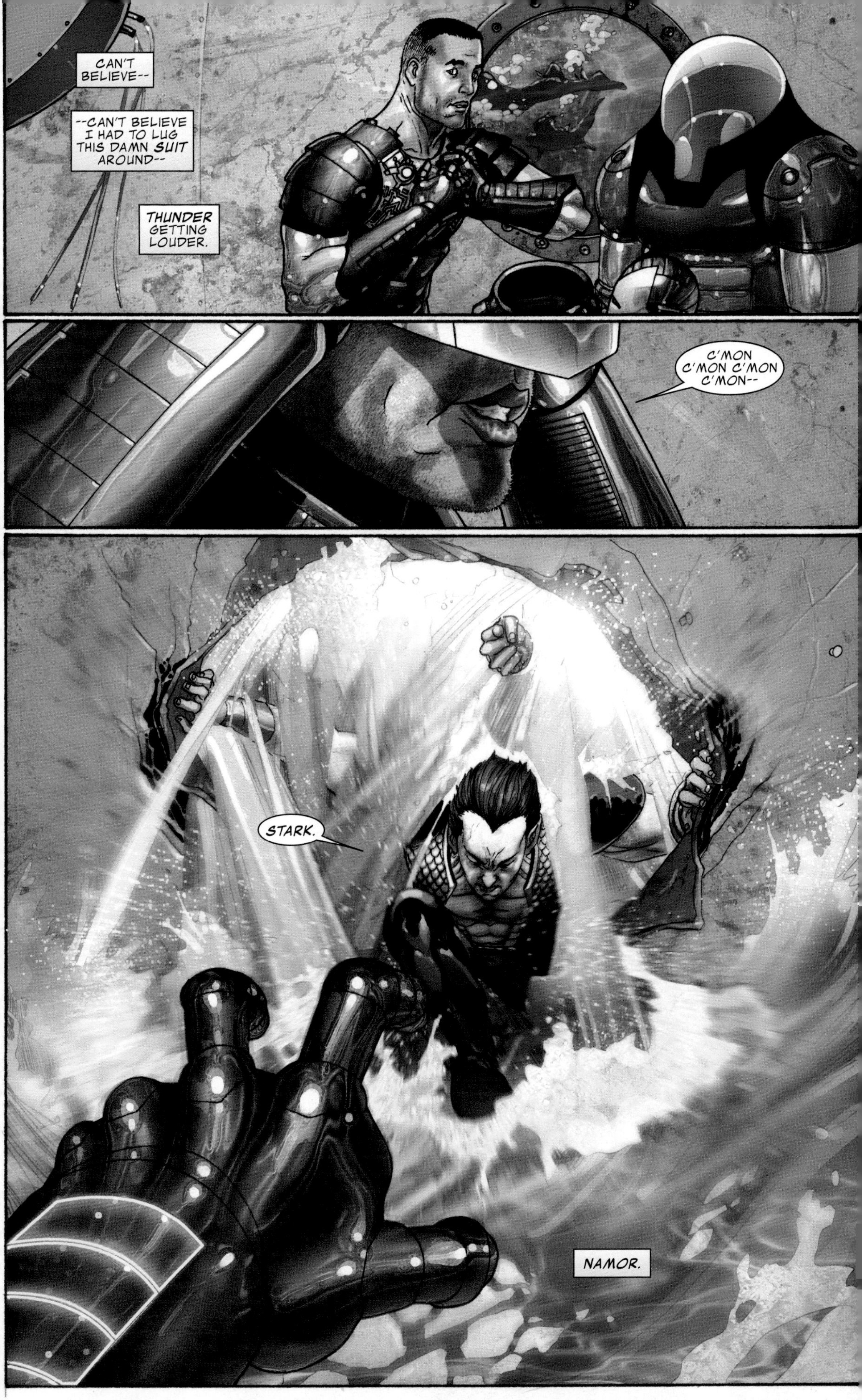
CAN'T BELIEVE--
--CAN'T BELIEVE I HAD TO LUG THIS DAMN SUIT AROUND--
THUNDER GETTING LOUDER.
C'MON C'MON C'MON C'MON--
STARK.
NAMOR.

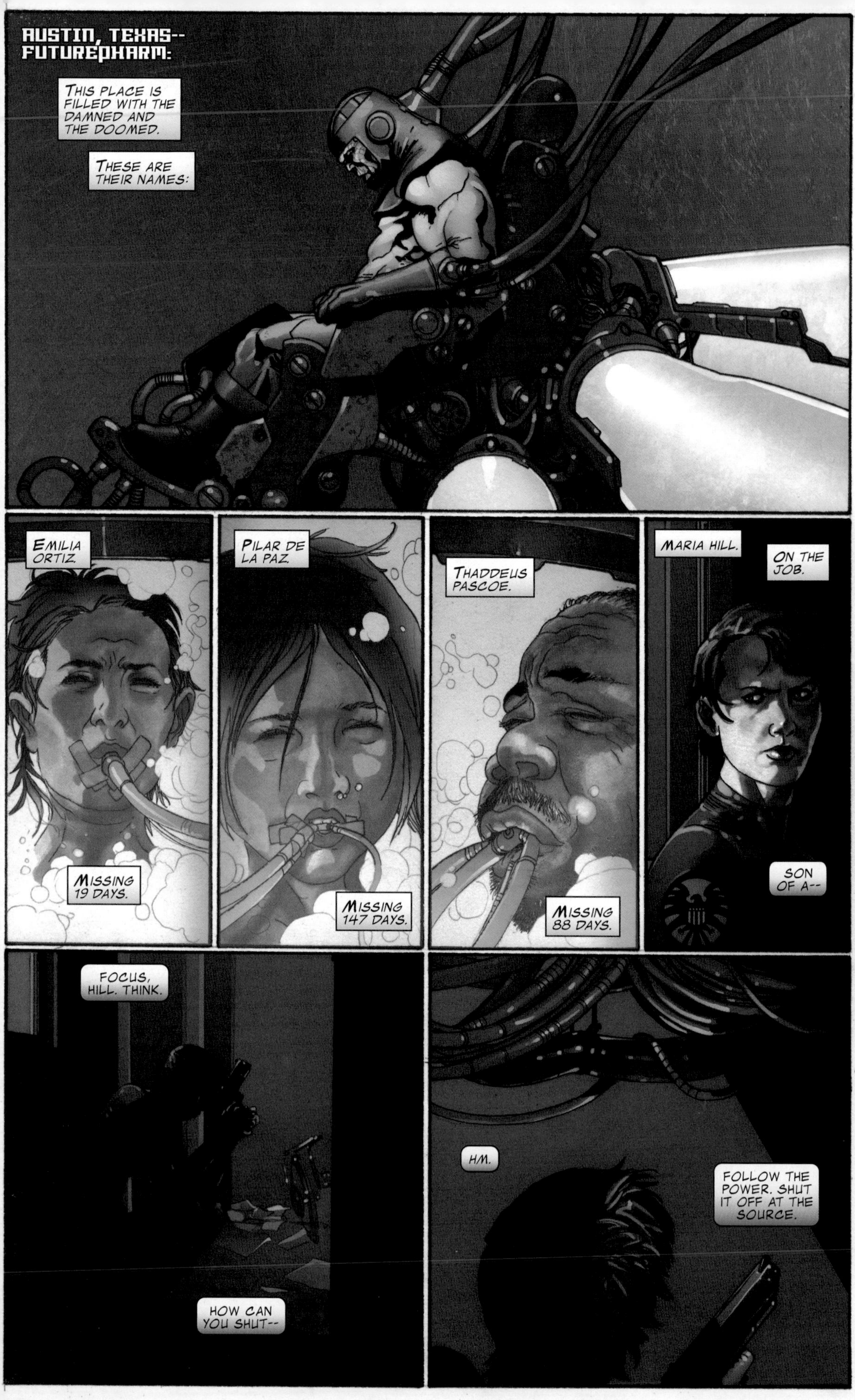
AUSTIN, TEXAS--
FUTUREPHARM:
THIS PLACE IS FILLED WITH THE DAMNED AND THE DOOMED.
THESE ARE THEIR NAMES:
EMILIA ORTIZ.
MISSING 19 DAYS.
PILAR DE LA PAZ.
MISSING 147 DAYS.
THADDEUS PASCOE.
MISSING 88 DAYS.
MARIA HILL.
ON THE JOB.
SON OF A--
FOCUS, HILL. THINK.
HOW CAN YOU SHUT--
HM.
FOLLOW THE POWER. SHUT IT OFF AT THE SOURCE.

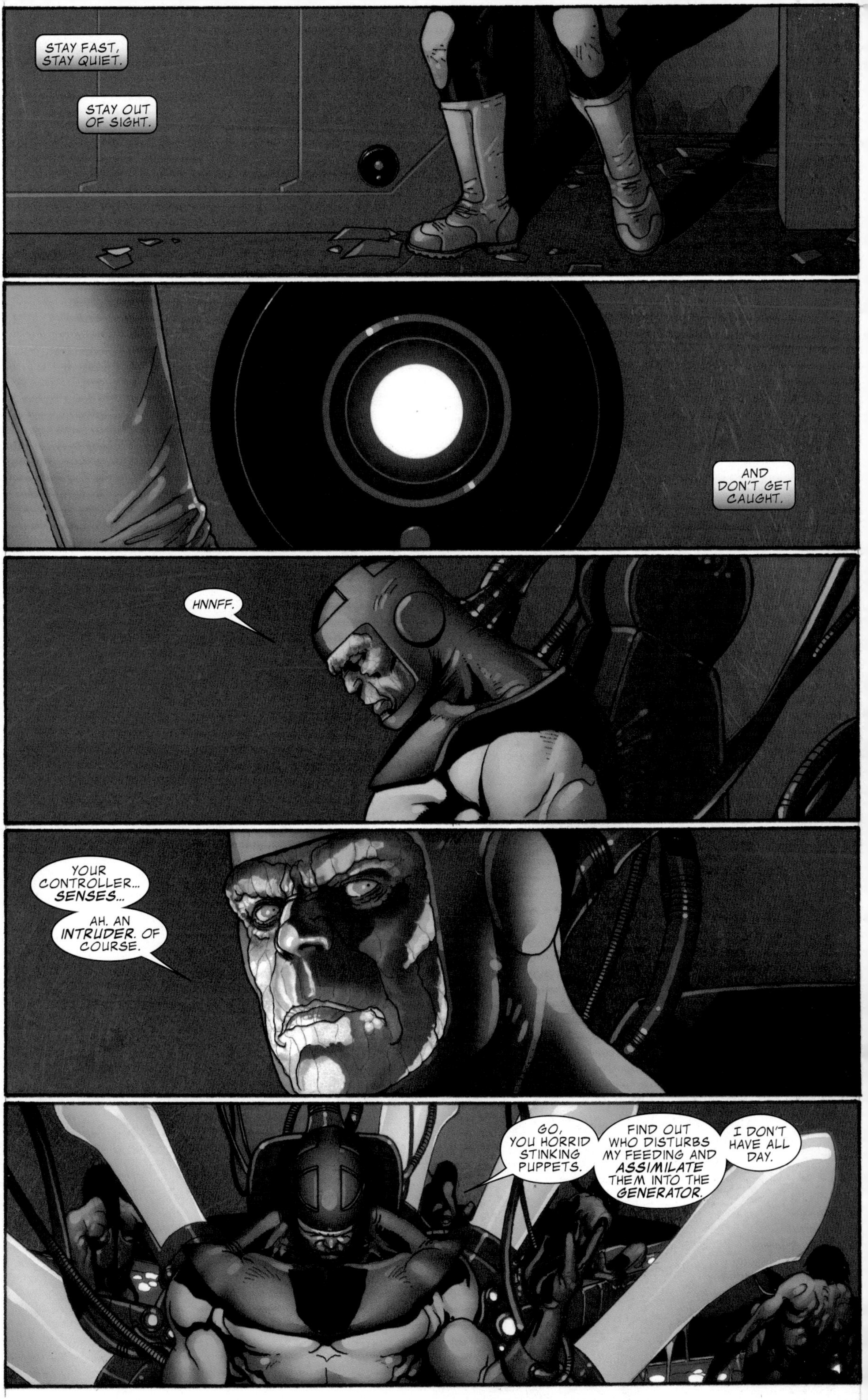
STAY FAST, STAY QUIET.
STAY OUT OF SIGHT.
AND DON'T GET CAUGHT.
HNNFF.
YOUR CONTROLLER... SENSES...
AH. AN INTRUDER. OF COURSE.
GO, YOU HORRID STINKING PUPPETS.
FIND OUT WHO DISTURBS MY FEEDING AND ASSIMILATE THEM INTO THE GENERATOR.
I DON'T HAVE ALL DAY.

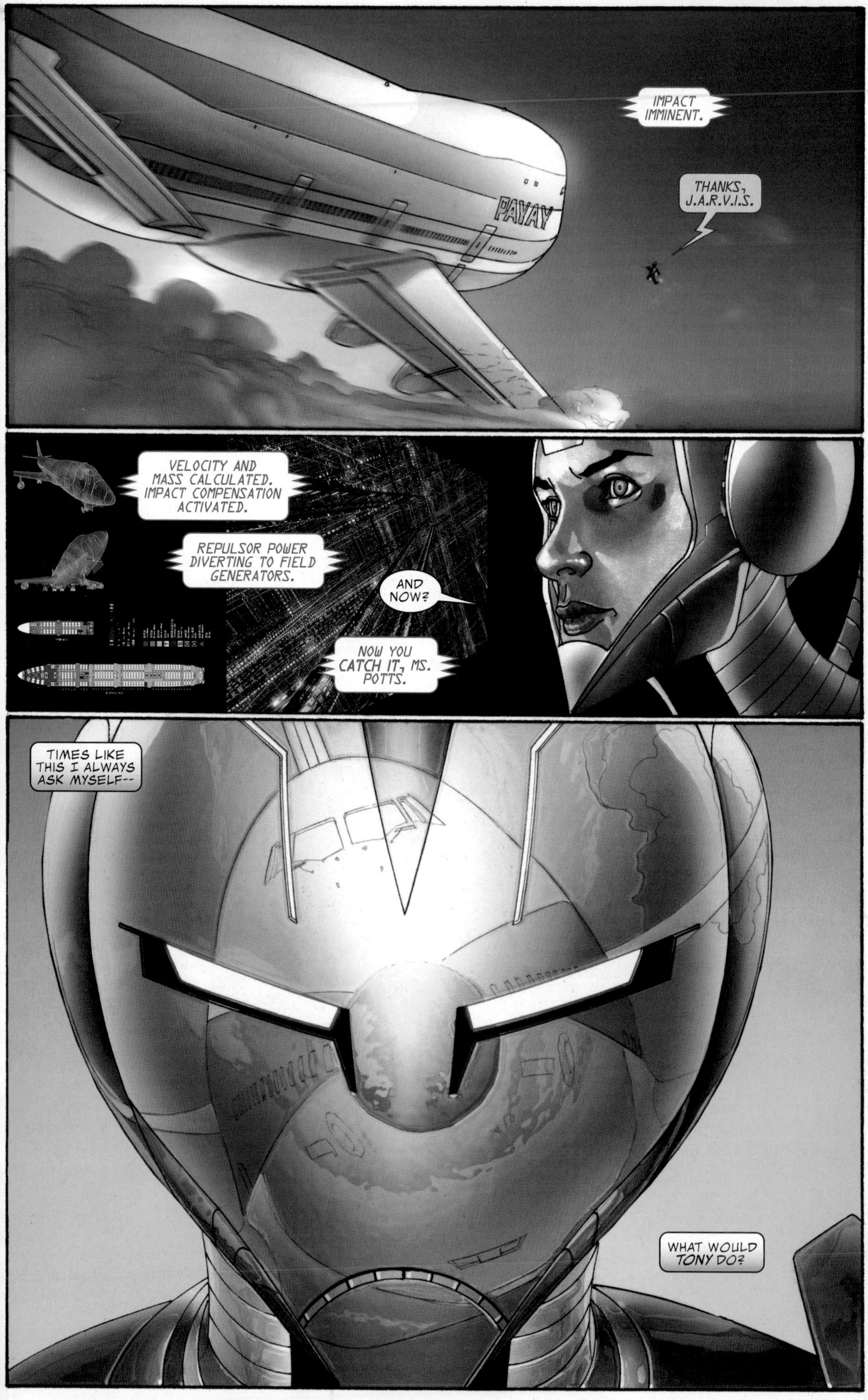
IMPACT IMMINENT.
THANKS, J.A.R.V.I.S.
PAYAY
VELOCITY AND MASS CALCULATED. IMPACT COMPENSATION ACTIVATED.
REPULSOR POWER DIVERTING TO FIELD GENERATORS.
AND NOW?
NOW YOU CATCH IT, MS. POTTS.
TIMES LIKE THIS I ALWAYS ASK MYSELF--
WHAT WOULD TONY DO?

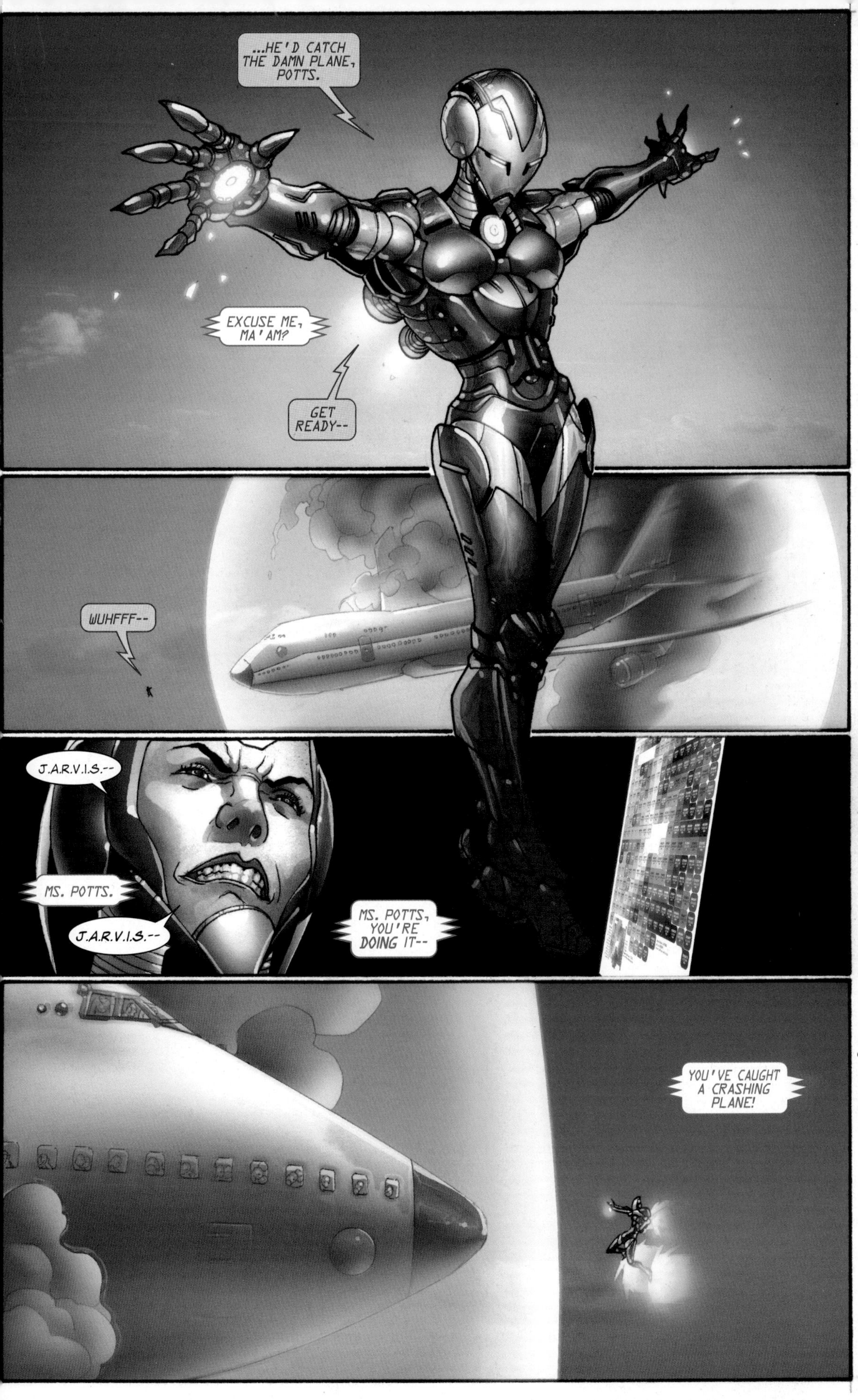
...HE'D CATCH THE DAMN PLANE, POTTS.
EXCUSE ME, MA'AM?
GET READY--
WUHFFF--
J.A.R.V.I.S.--
MS. POTTS.
J.A.R.V.I.S.--
MS. POTTS, YOU'RE DOING IT--
YOU'VE CAUGHT A CRASHING PLANE!

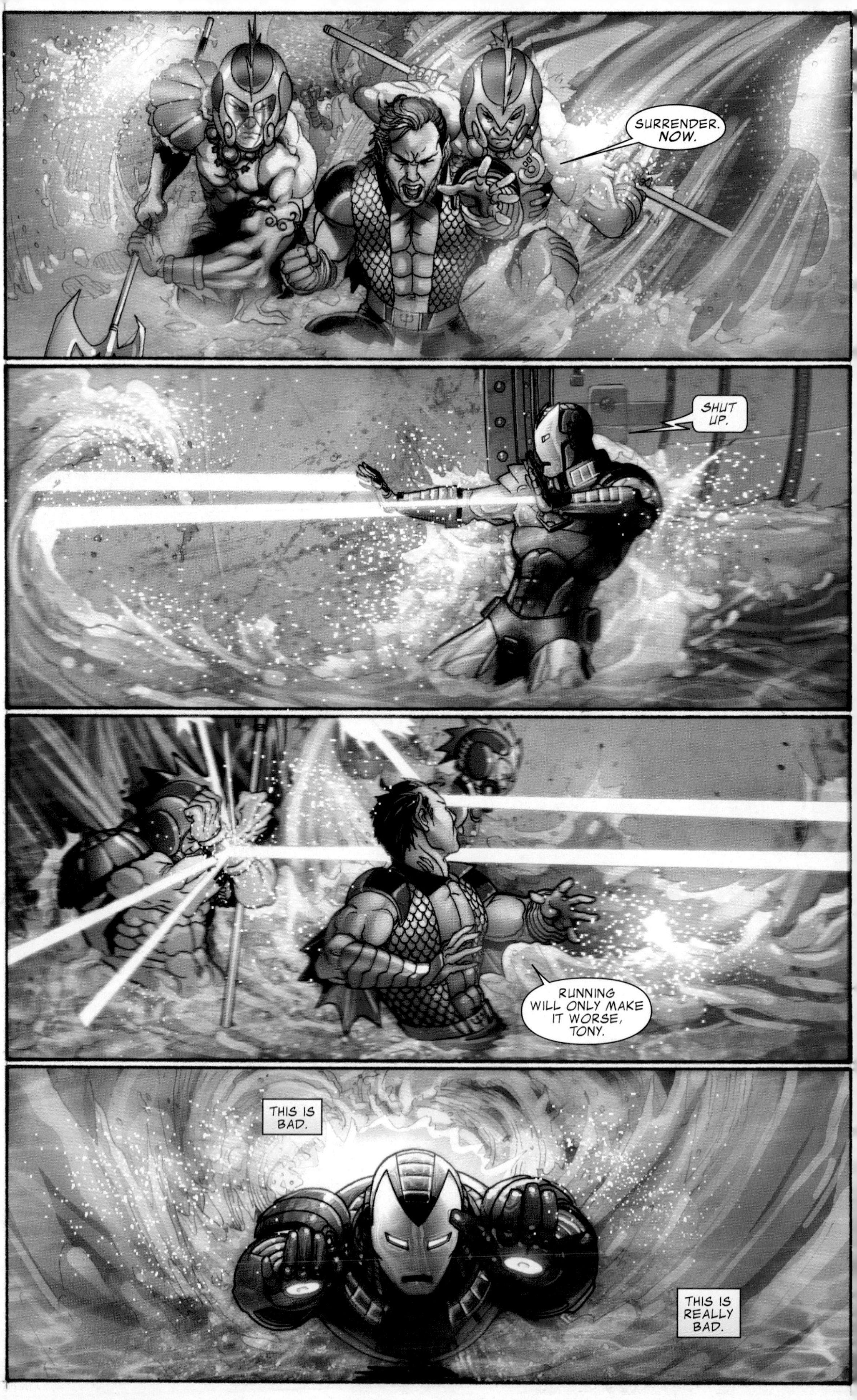
SURRENDER. NOW.
SHUT UP.
RUNNING WILL ONLY MAKE IT WORSE, TONY.
THIS IS BAD.
THIS IS REALLY BAD.

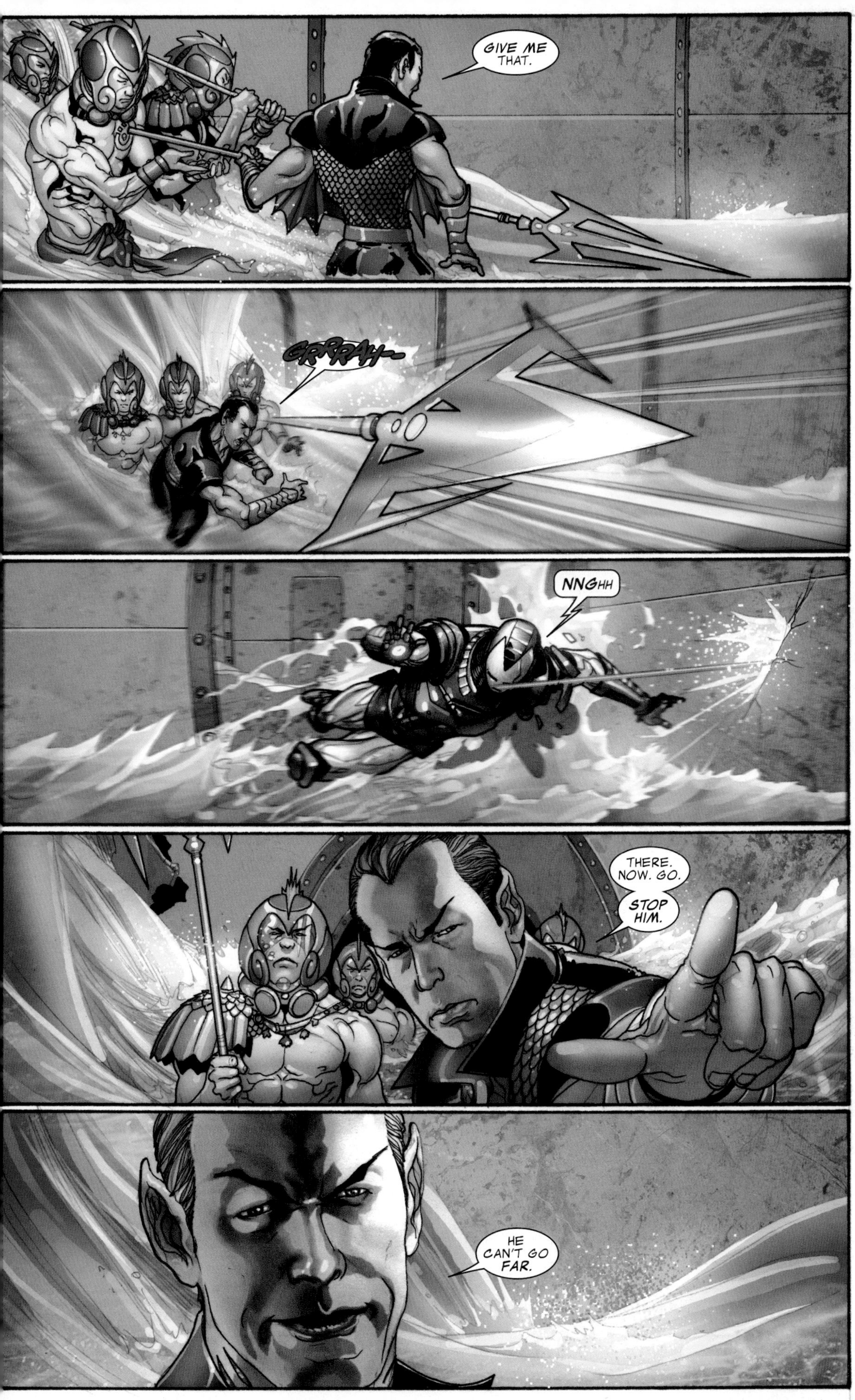
GIVE ME THAT.
GRRRAH--
NNGHH
THERE. NOW. GO.
STOP HIM.
HE CAN'T GO FAR.

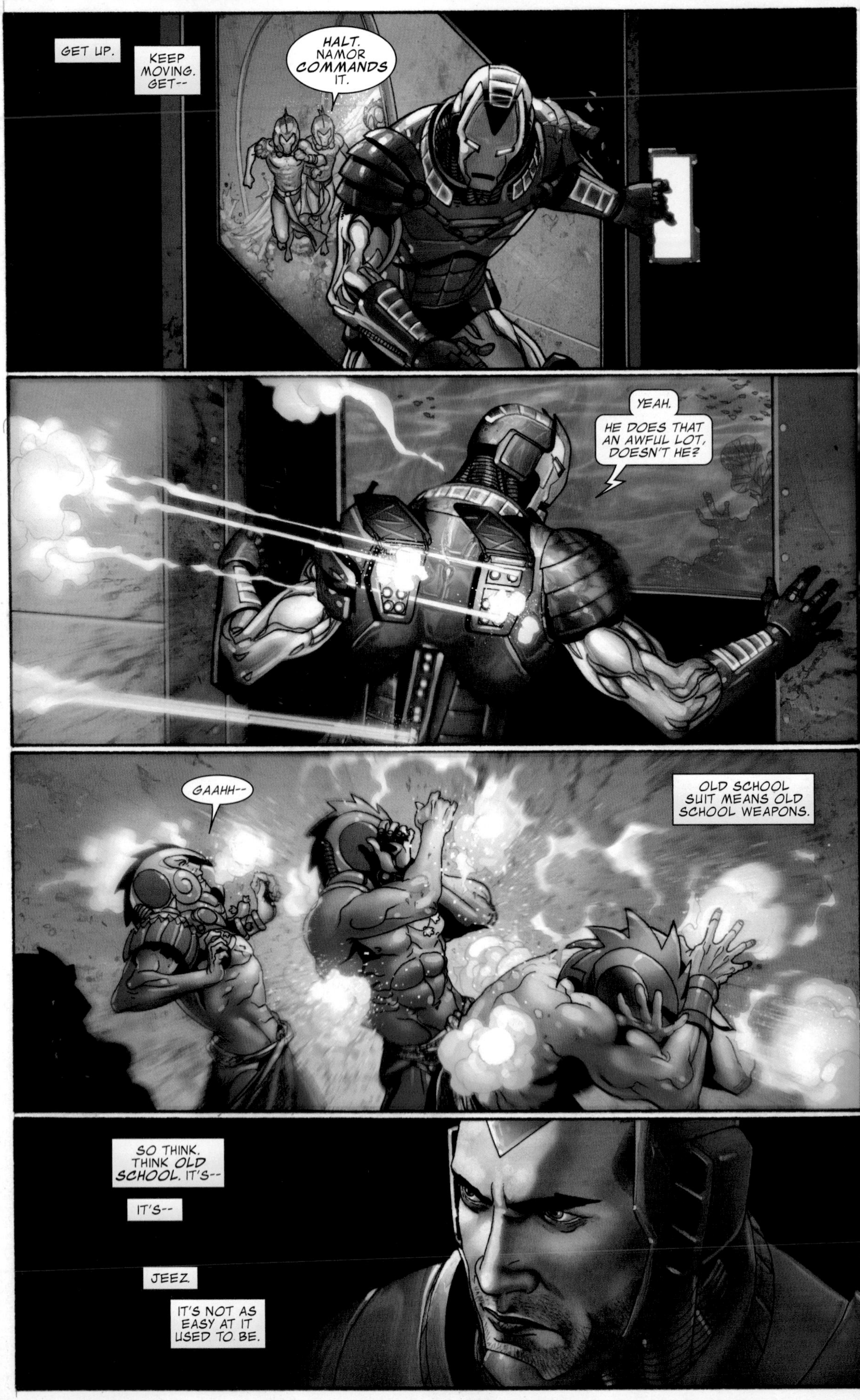
GET UP.
KEEP MOVING. GET--
HALT. NAMOR COMMANDS IT.
YEAH.
HE DOES THAT AN AWFUL LOT, DOESN'T HE?
GAAHH--
OLD SCHOOL SUIT MEANS OLD SCHOOL WEAPONS.
SO THINK. THINK OLD SCHOOL. IT'S--
IT'S--
JEEZ.
IT'S NOT AS EASY AT IT USED TO BE.

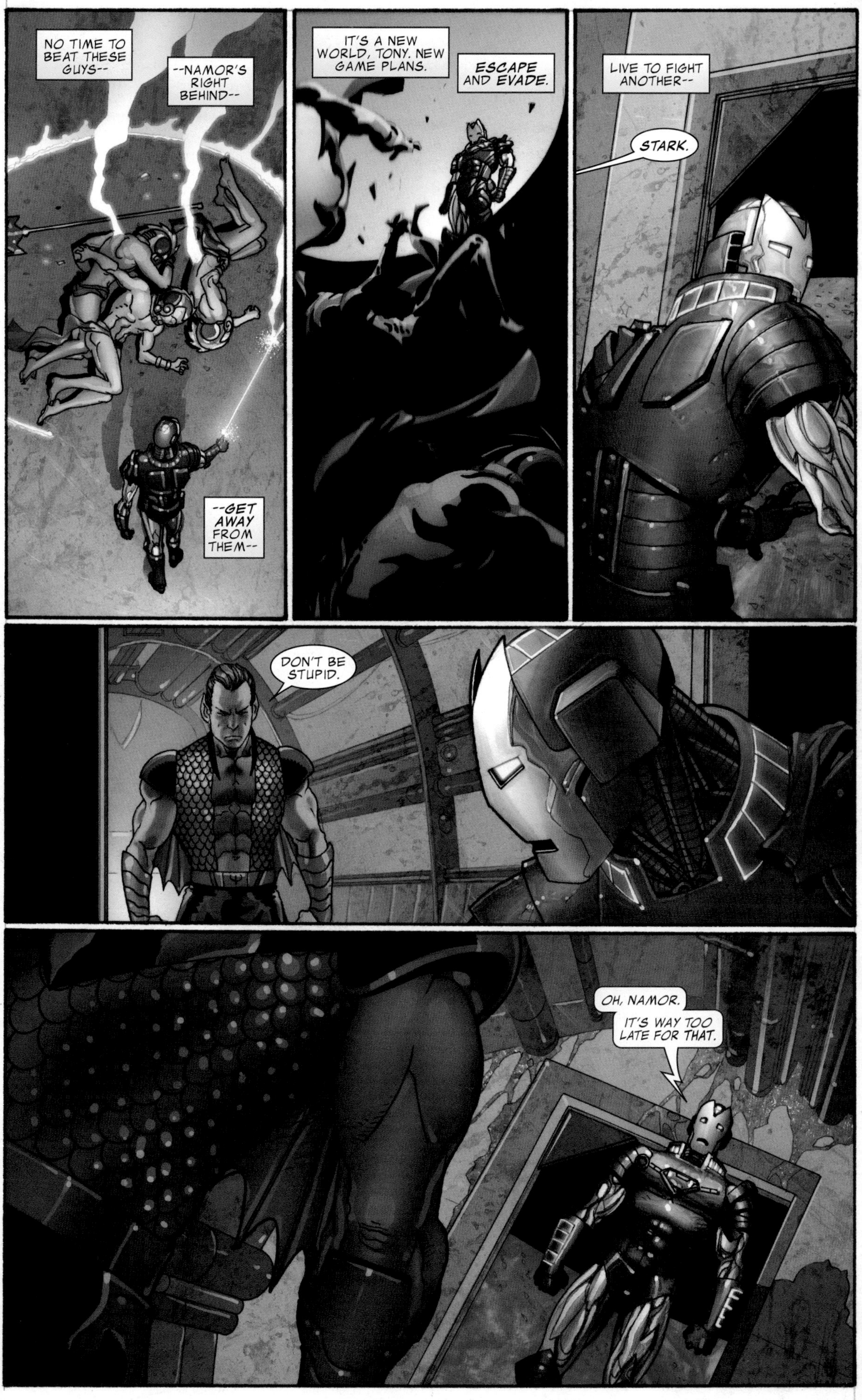
NO TIME TO BEAT THESE GUYS--
--NAMOR'S RIGHT BEHIND--
--GET AWAY FROM THEM--
IT'S A NEW WORLD, TONY. NEW GAME PLANS.
ESCAPE AND EVADE.
LIVE TO FIGHT ANOTHER--
STARK.
DON'T BE STUPID.
OH, NAMOR.
IT'S WAY TOO LATE FOR THAT.

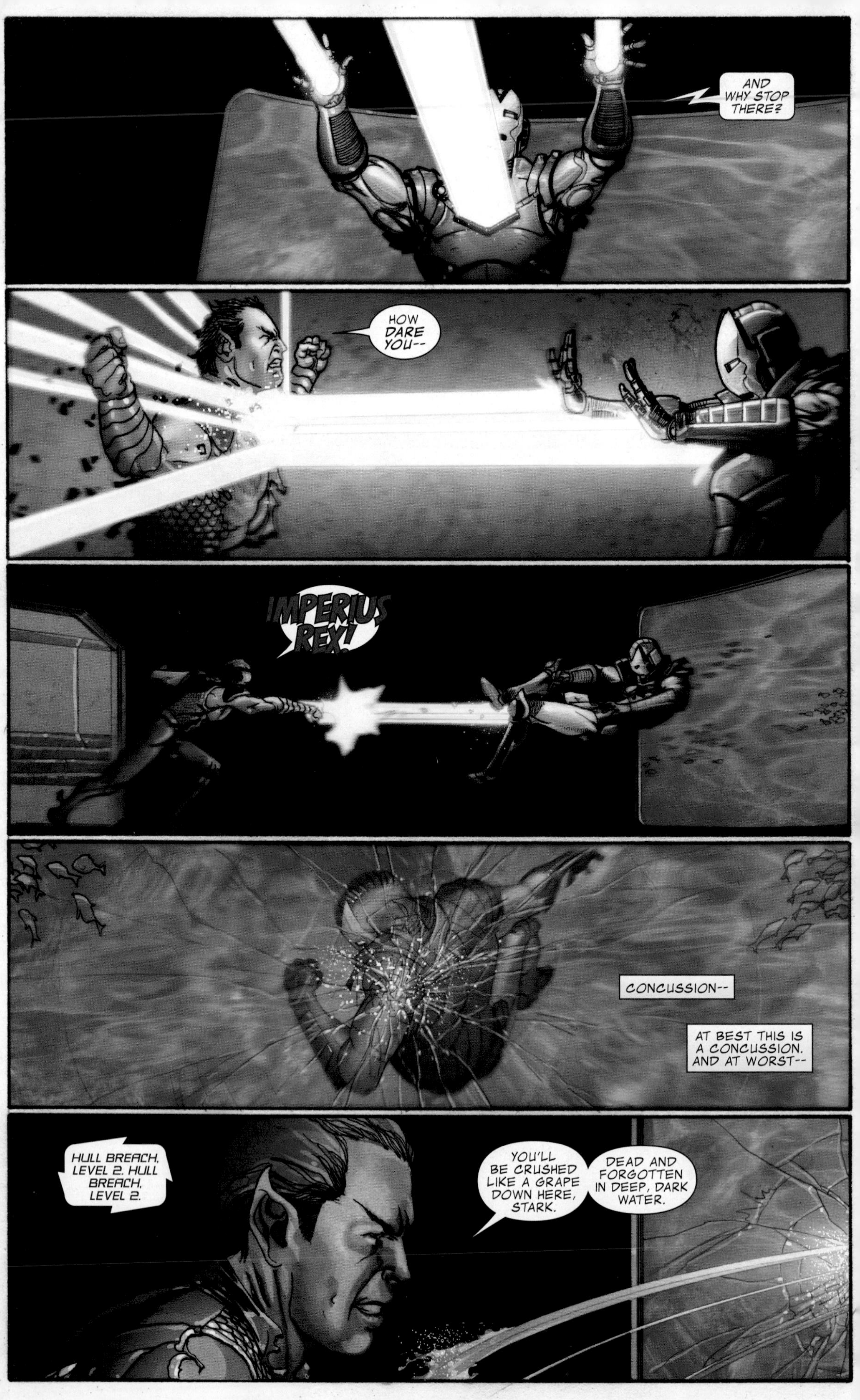
AND WHY STOP THERE?
HOW DARE YOU--
IMPERIUS REX!
CONCUSSION--
AT BEST THIS IS A CONCUSSION. AND AT WORST--
HULL BREACH, LEVEL 2. HULL BREACH, LEVEL 2.
YOU'LL BE CRUSHED LIKE A GRAPE DOWN HERE, STARK.
DEAD AND FORGOTTEN IN DEEP, DARK WATER.

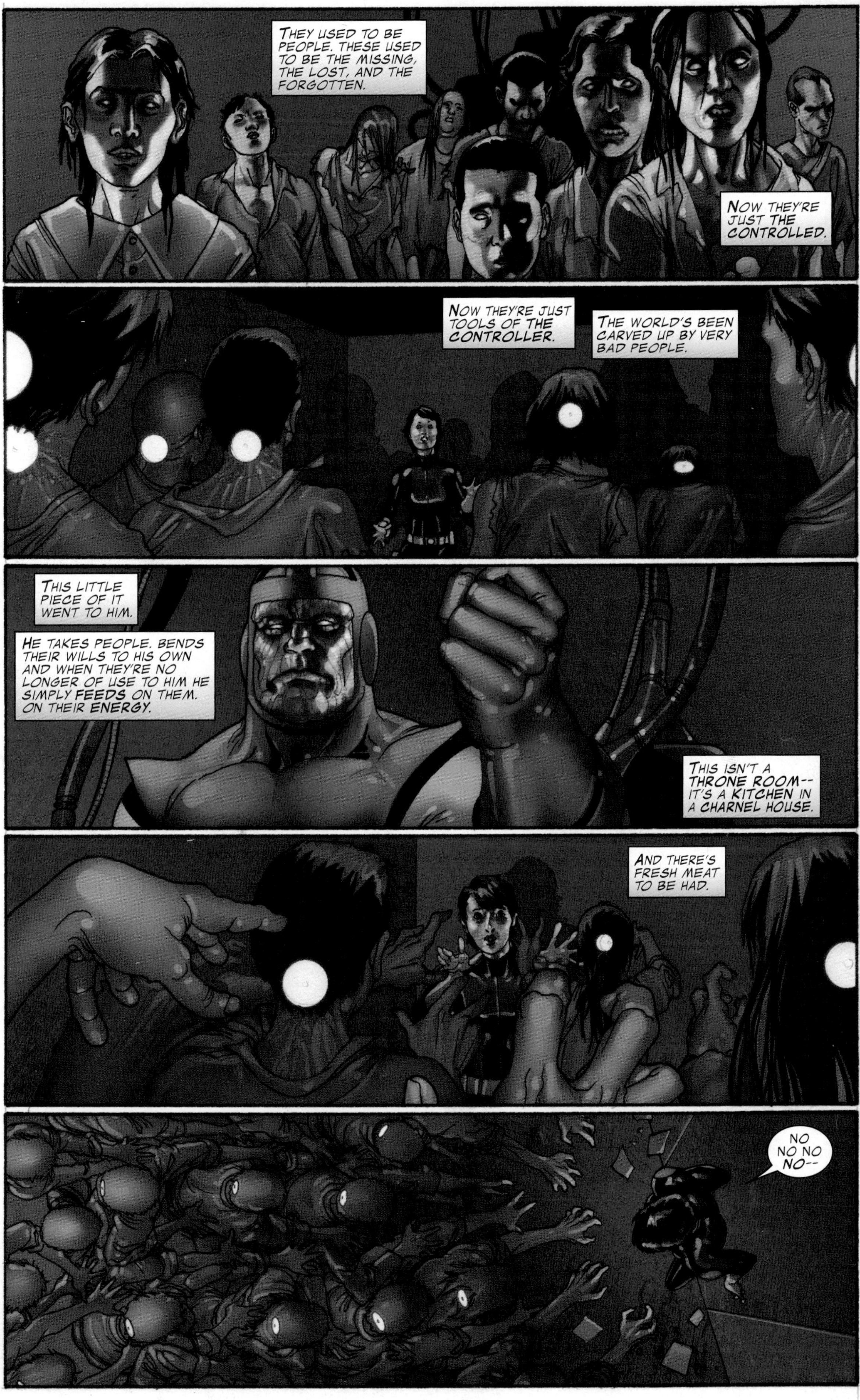
THEY USED TO BE PEOPLE. THESE USED TO BE THE MISSING, THE LOST, AND THE FORGOTTEN.
NOW THEY'RE JUST THE CONTROLLED.
NOW THEY'RE JUST TOOLS OF THE CONTROLLER.
THE WORLD'S BEEN CARVED UP BY VERY BAD PEOPLE.
THIS LITTLE PIECE OF IT WENT TO HIM.
HE TAKES PEOPLE. BENDS THEIR WILLS TO HIS OWN AND WHEN THEY'RE NO LONGER OF USE TO HIM HE SIMPLY FEEDS ON THEM. ON THEIR ENERGY.
THIS ISN'T A THRONE ROOM-- IT'S A KITCHEN IN A CHARNEL HOUSE.
AND THERE'S FRESH MEAT TO BE HAD.
NO NO NO NO--

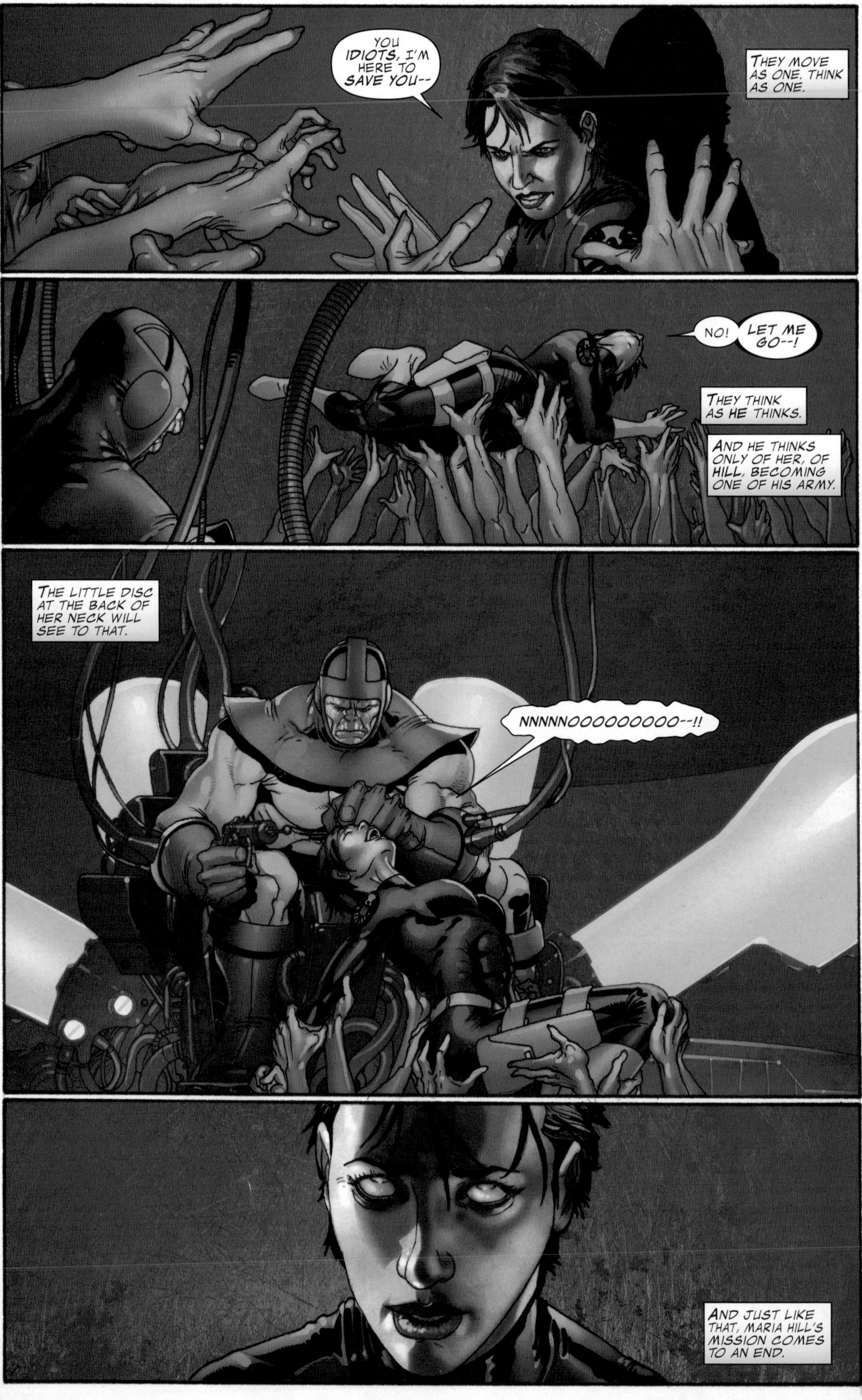
YOU IDIOTS, I'M HERE TO SAVE YOU--
THEY MOVE AS ONE. THINK AS ONE.
NO!
LET ME GO--!
THEY THINK AS HE THINKS.
AND HE THINKS ONLY OF HER, OF HILL, BECOMING ONE OF HIS ARMY.
THE LITTLE DISC AT THE BACK OF HER NECK WILL SEE TO THAT.
NNNNNOOOOOOOOOO--!!
AND JUST LIKE THAT, MARIA HILL'S MISSION COMES TO AN END.

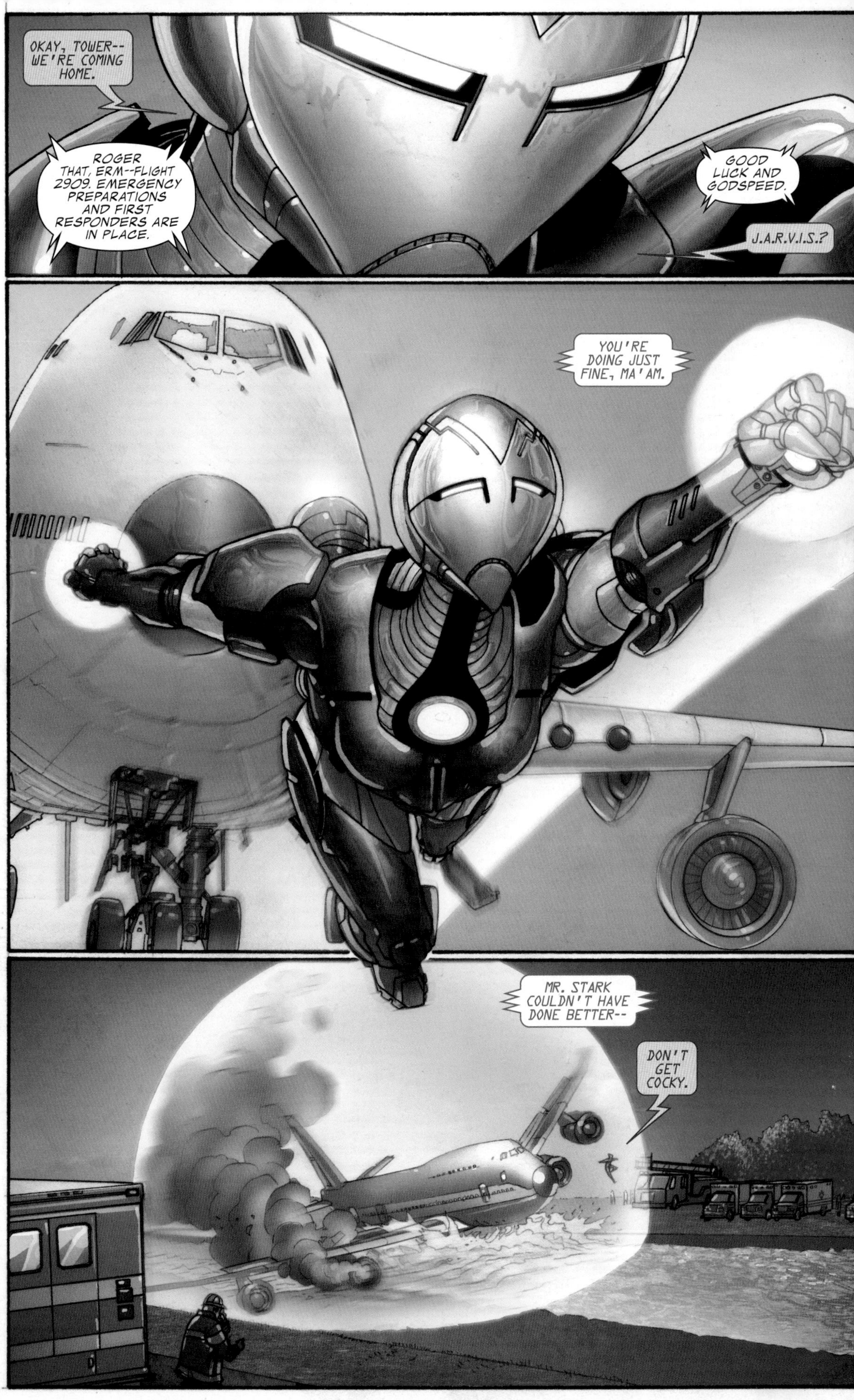
OKAY, TOWER--WE'RE COMING HOME.
ROGER THAT, ERM--FLIGHT 2909. EMERGENCY PREPARATIONS AND FIRST RESPONDERS ARE IN PLACE.
GOOD LUCK AND GODSPEED.
J.A.R.V.I.S.?
YOU'RE DOING JUST FINE, MA'AM.
MR. STARK COULDN'T HAVE DONE BETTER--
DON'T GET COCKY.

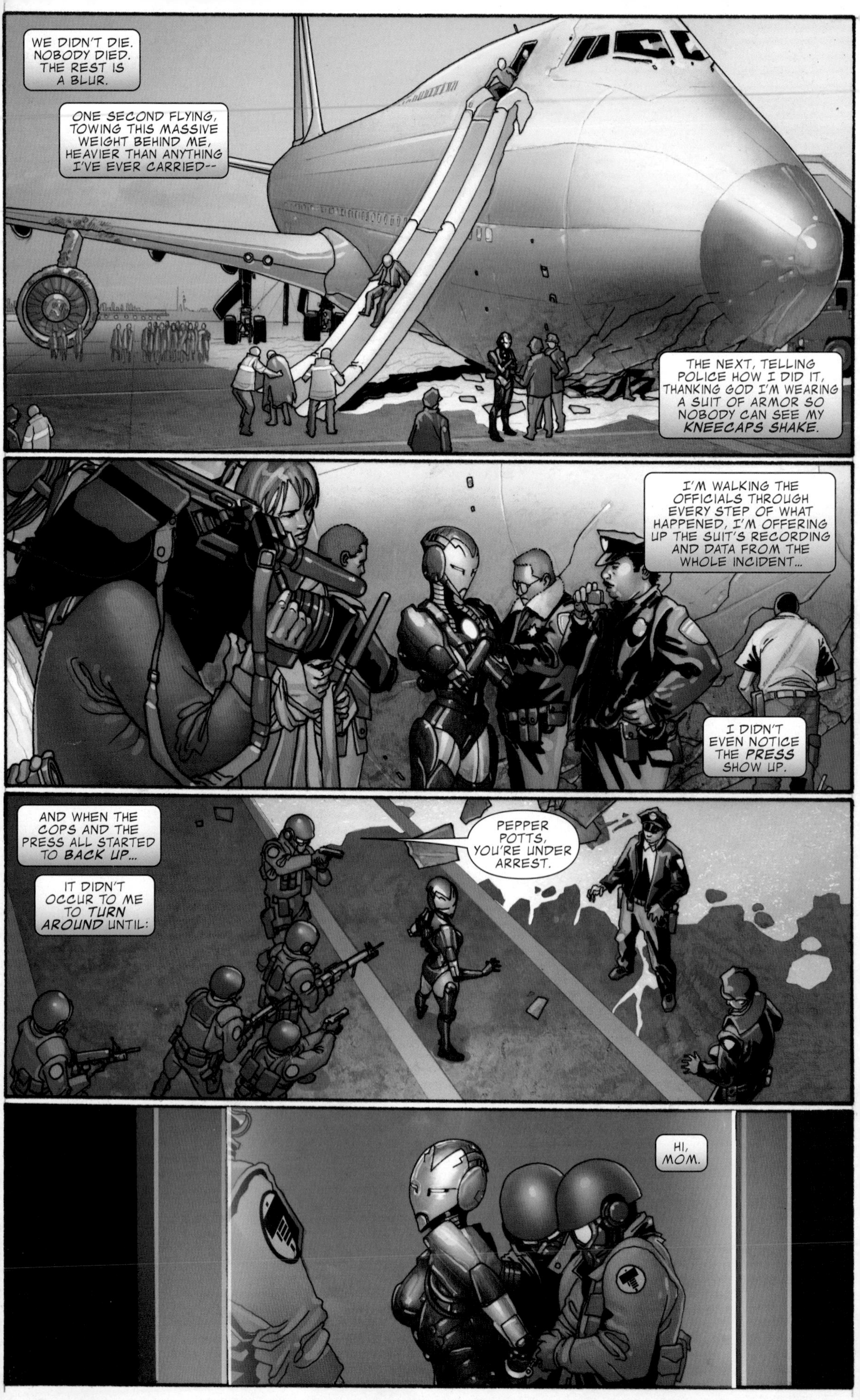
WE DIDN'T DIE. NOBODY DIED. THE REST IS A BLUR.
ONE SECOND FLYING, TOWING THIS MASSIVE WEIGHT BEHIND ME, HEAVIER THAN ANYTHING I'VE EVER CARRIED--
THE NEXT, TELLING POLICE HOW I DID IT, THANKING GOD I'M WEARING A SUIT OF ARMOR SO NOBODY CAN SEE MY KNEECAPS SHAKE.
I'M WALKING THE OFFICIALS THROUGH EVERY STEP OF WHAT HAPPENED, I'M OFFERING UP THE SUIT'S RECORDING AND DATA FROM THE WHOLE INCIDENT...
I DIDN'T EVEN NOTICE THE PRESS SHOW UP.
AND WHEN THE COPS AND THE PRESS ALL STARTED TO BACK UP...
IT DIDN'T OCCUR TO ME TO TURN AROUND UNTIL:
PEPPER POTTS, YOU'RE UNDER ARREST.
HI, MOM.

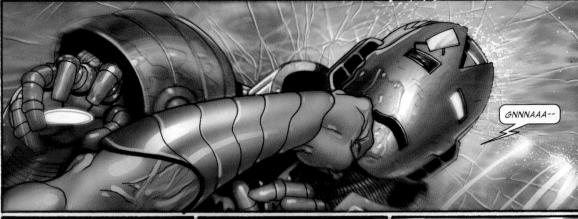

GNNNAAA--

HE'S BEATING THE SUIT OPEN--

--BEATING THE HULL OPEN--

--ONE PUNCH AT A TIME--

--EVEN UNLOADING WHAT REPULSOR POWER I HAVE LEFT INTO HIM--

--START *RUNNING* FROM HIM--

--LIVE TO FIGHT ANOTHER DAY--

--HE'S RELENTLESS--

--STOP FIGHTING HIM, TONY--

WASTE PIPE RELAY 53

HYDRAULICS CHANNEL

LIQUID HYDROGEN CHANNEL

SEWAGE RELAY 11

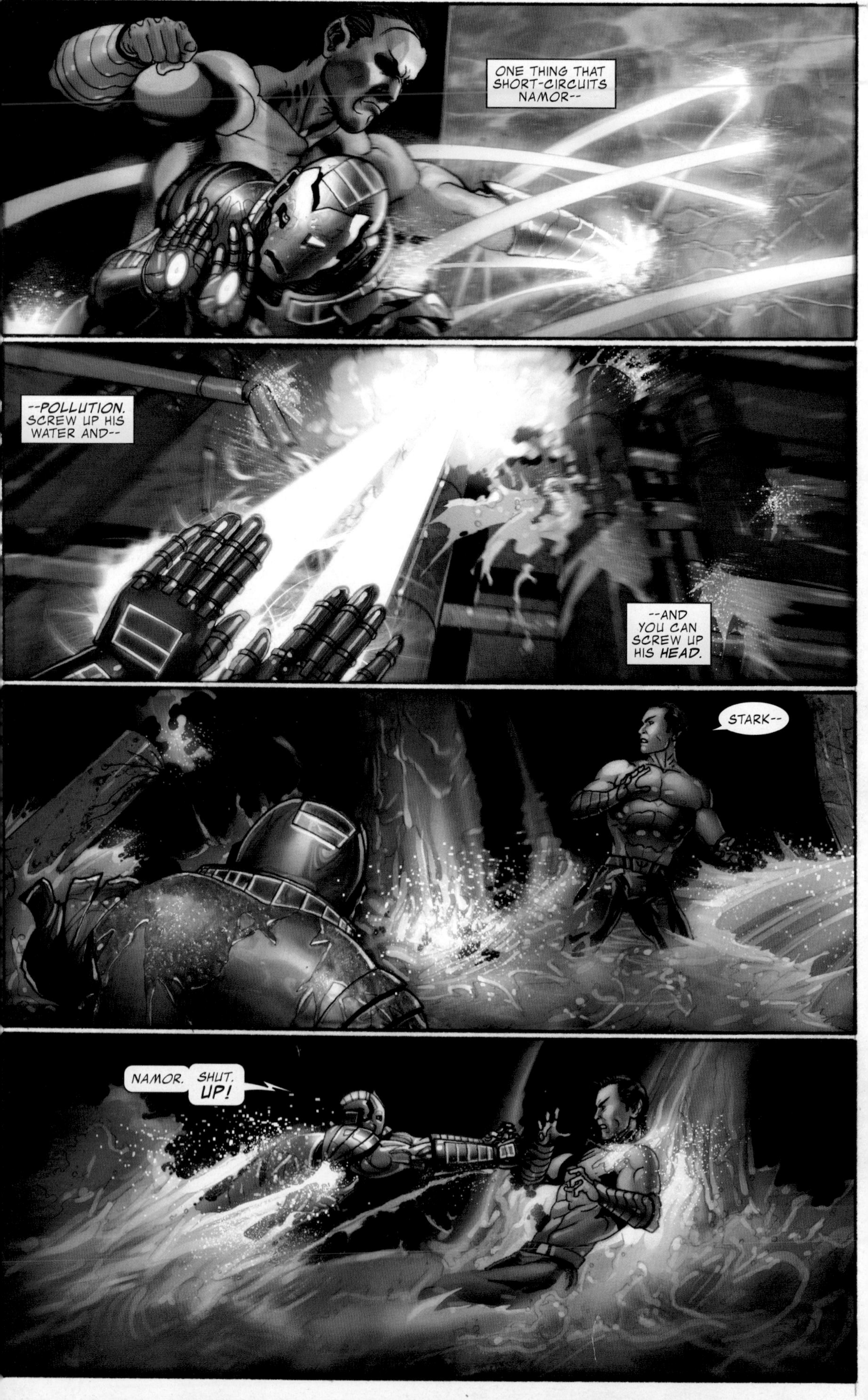
ONE THING THAT SHORT-CIRCUITS NAMOR--
--POLLUTION. SCREW UP HIS WATER AND--
--AND YOU CAN SCREW UP HIS HEAD.
STARK--
NAMOR.
SHUT. UP!

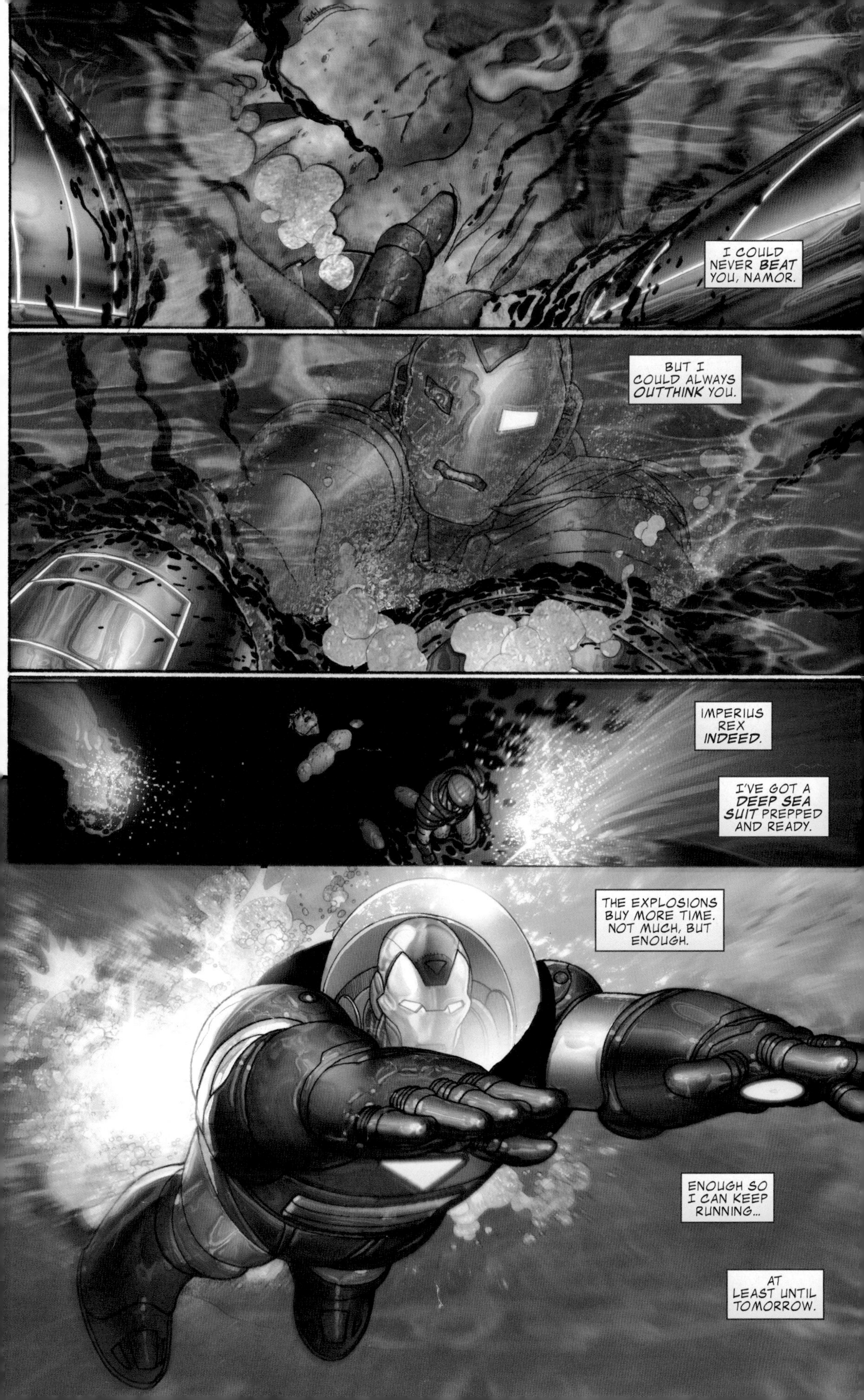
I COULD NEVER BEAT YOU, NAMOR.
BUT I COULD ALWAYS OUTTHINK YOU.
IMPERIUS REX INDEED.
I'VE GOT A DEEP SEA SUIT PREPPED AND READY.
THE EXPLOSIONS BUY MORE TIME. NOT MUCH, BUT ENOUGH.
ENOUGH SO I CAN KEEP RUNNING...
AT LEAST UNTIL TOMORROW.

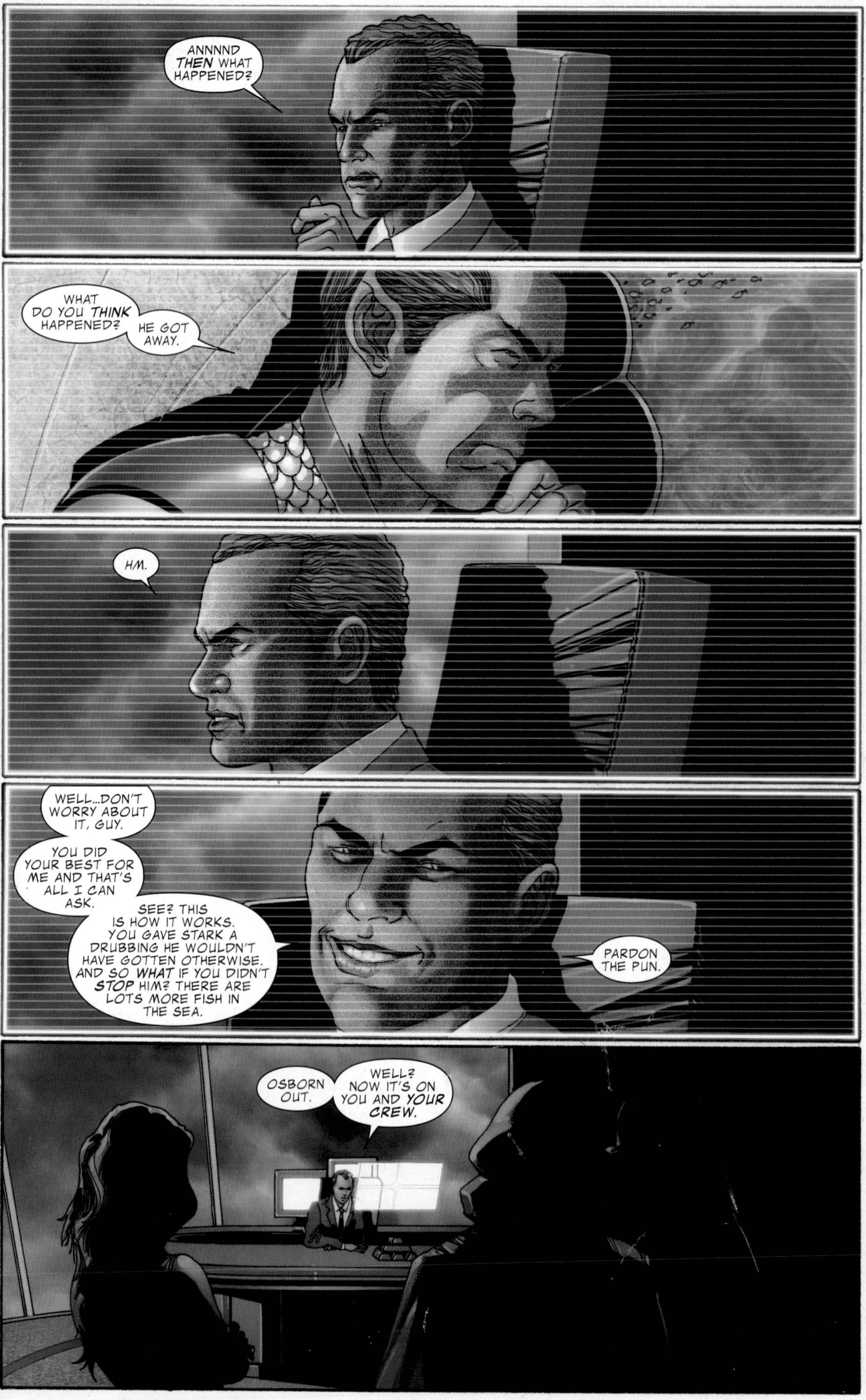
ANNNND *THEN* WHAT HAPPENED?
WHAT DO YOU *THINK* HAPPENED?
HE GOT AWAY.
HM.
WELL...DON'T WORRY ABOUT IT, GUY.
YOU DID YOUR BEST FOR ME AND THAT'S ALL I CAN ASK.
SEE? THIS IS HOW IT WORKS. YOU GAVE STARK A DRUBBING HE WOULDN'T HAVE GOTTEN OTHERWISE. AND SO *WHAT* IF YOU DIDN'T *STOP* HIM? THERE ARE LOTS MORE FISH IN THE SEA.
PARDON THE PUN.
OSBORN OUT.
WELL? NOW IT'S ON YOU AND *YOUR CREW.*

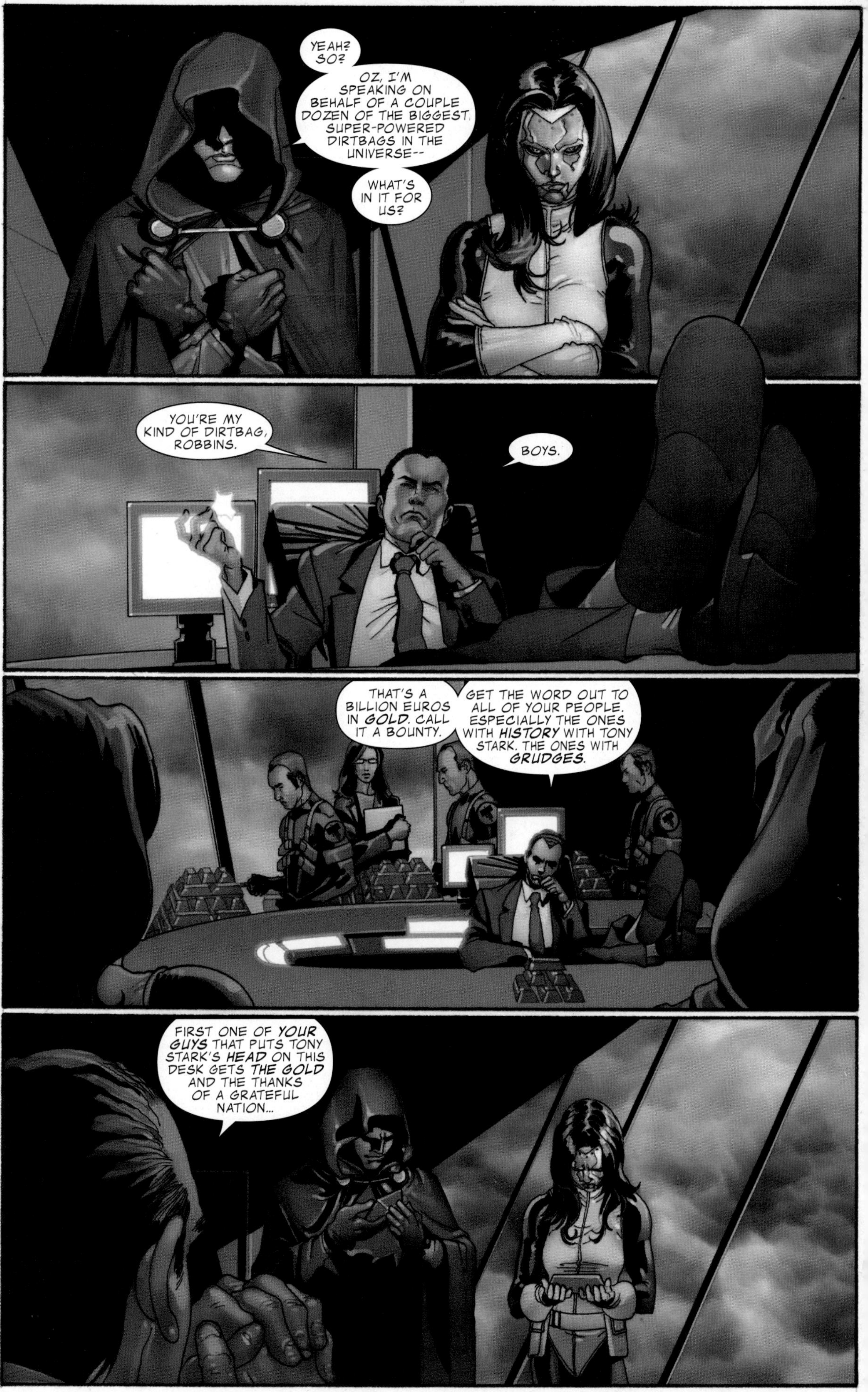
YEAH? SO?
OZ, I'M SPEAKING ON BEHALF OF A COUPLE DOZEN OF THE BIGGEST, SUPER-POWERED DIRTBAGS IN THE UNIVERSE--
WHAT'S IN IT FOR US?
YOU'RE MY KIND OF DIRTBAG, ROBBINS.
BOYS.
THAT'S A BILLION EUROS IN GOLD. CALL IT A BOUNTY.
GET THE WORD OUT TO ALL OF YOUR PEOPLE. ESPECIALLY THE ONES WITH HISTORY WITH TONY STARK. THE ONES WITH GRUDGES.
FIRST ONE OF YOUR GUYS THAT PUTS TONY STARK'S HEAD ON THIS DESK GETS THE GOLD AND THE THANKS OF A GRATEFUL NATION...

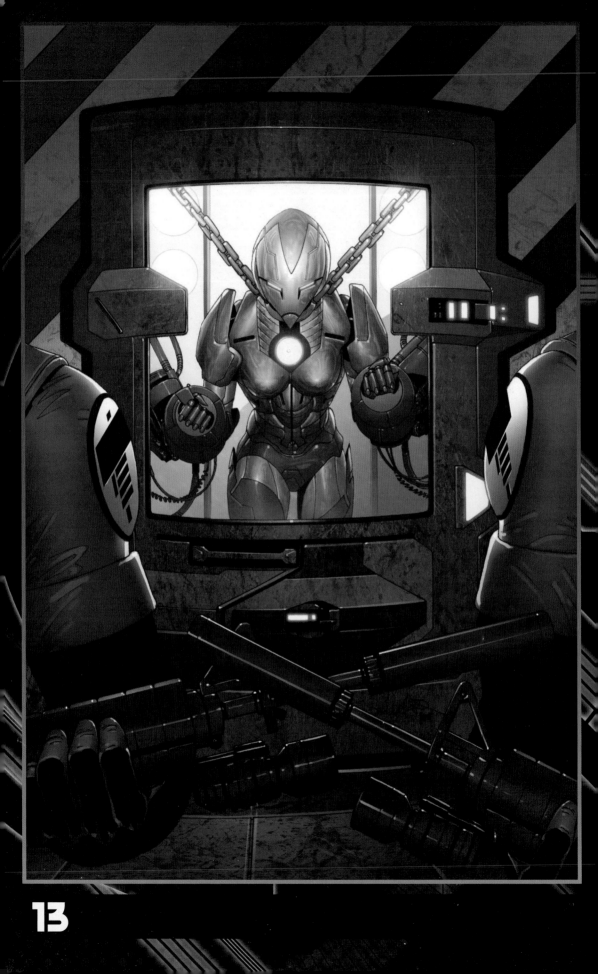

13

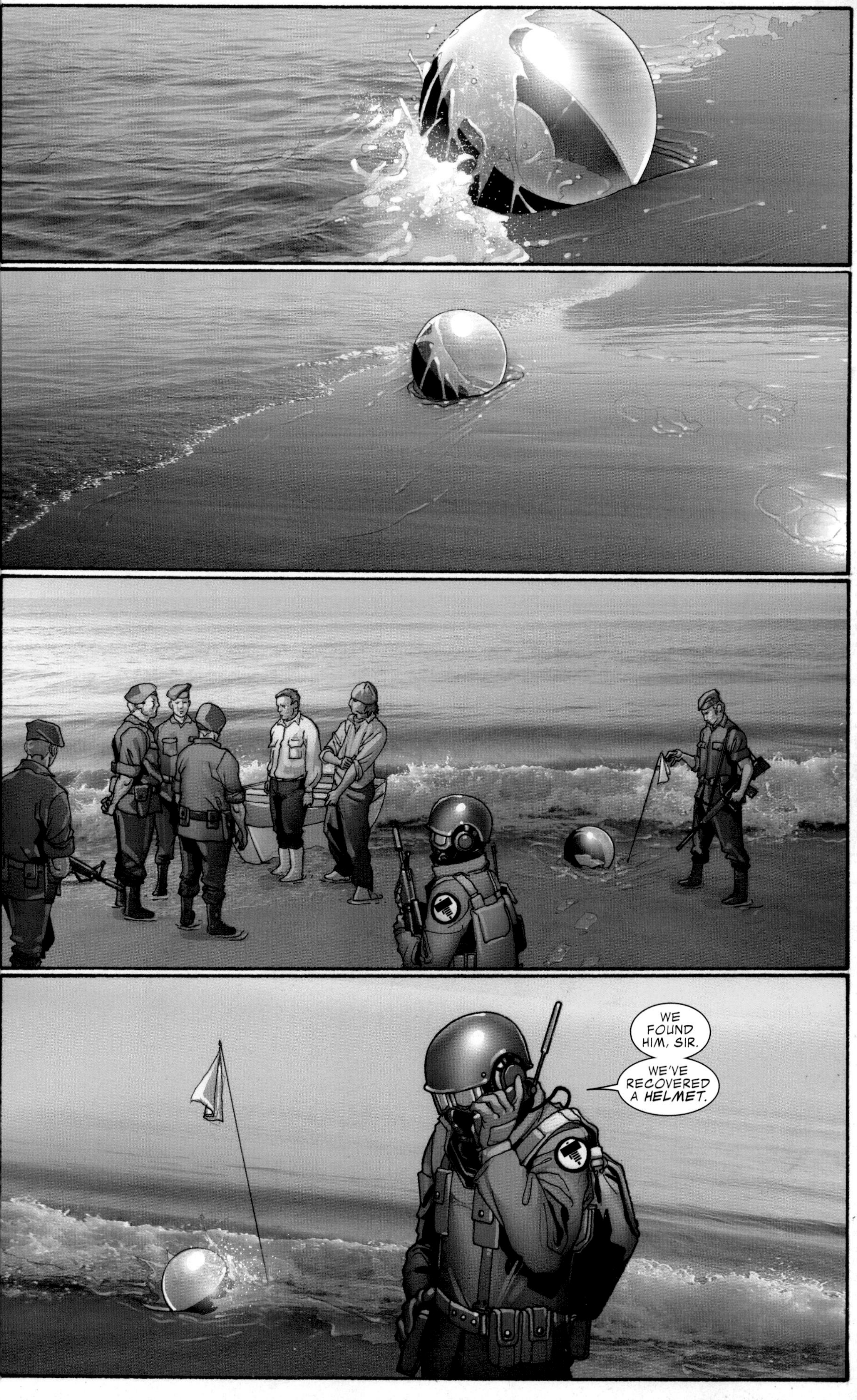
WE FOUND HIM, SIR.
WE'VE RECOVERED A HELMET.

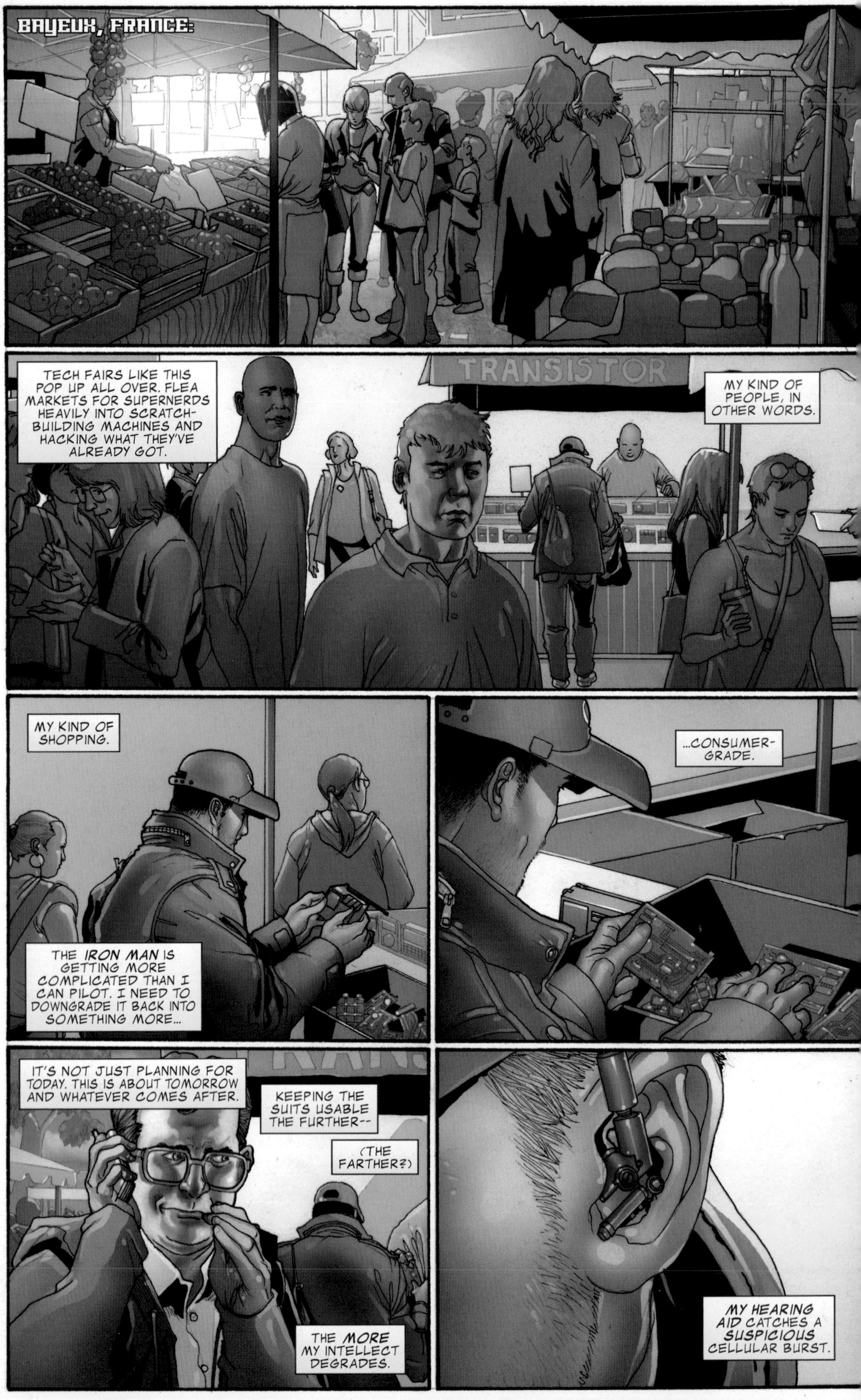
BAYEUX, FRANCE:
TECH FAIRS LIKE THIS POP UP ALL OVER. FLEA MARKETS FOR SUPERNERDS HEAVILY INTO SCRATCH-BUILDING MACHINES AND HACKING WHAT THEY'VE ALREADY GOT.
TRANSISTOR
MY KIND OF PEOPLE, IN OTHER WORDS.
MY KIND OF SHOPPING.
THE IRON MAN IS GETTING MORE COMPLICATED THAN I CAN PILOT. I NEED TO DOWNGRADE IT BACK INTO SOMETHING MORE...
...CONSUMER-GRADE.
IT'S NOT JUST PLANNING FOR TODAY. THIS IS ABOUT TOMORROW AND WHATEVER COMES AFTER.
KEEPING THE SUITS USABLE THE FURTHER--
(THE FARTHER?)
THE MORE MY INTELLECT DEGRADES.
MY HEARING AID CATCHES A SUSPICIOUS CELLULAR BURST.

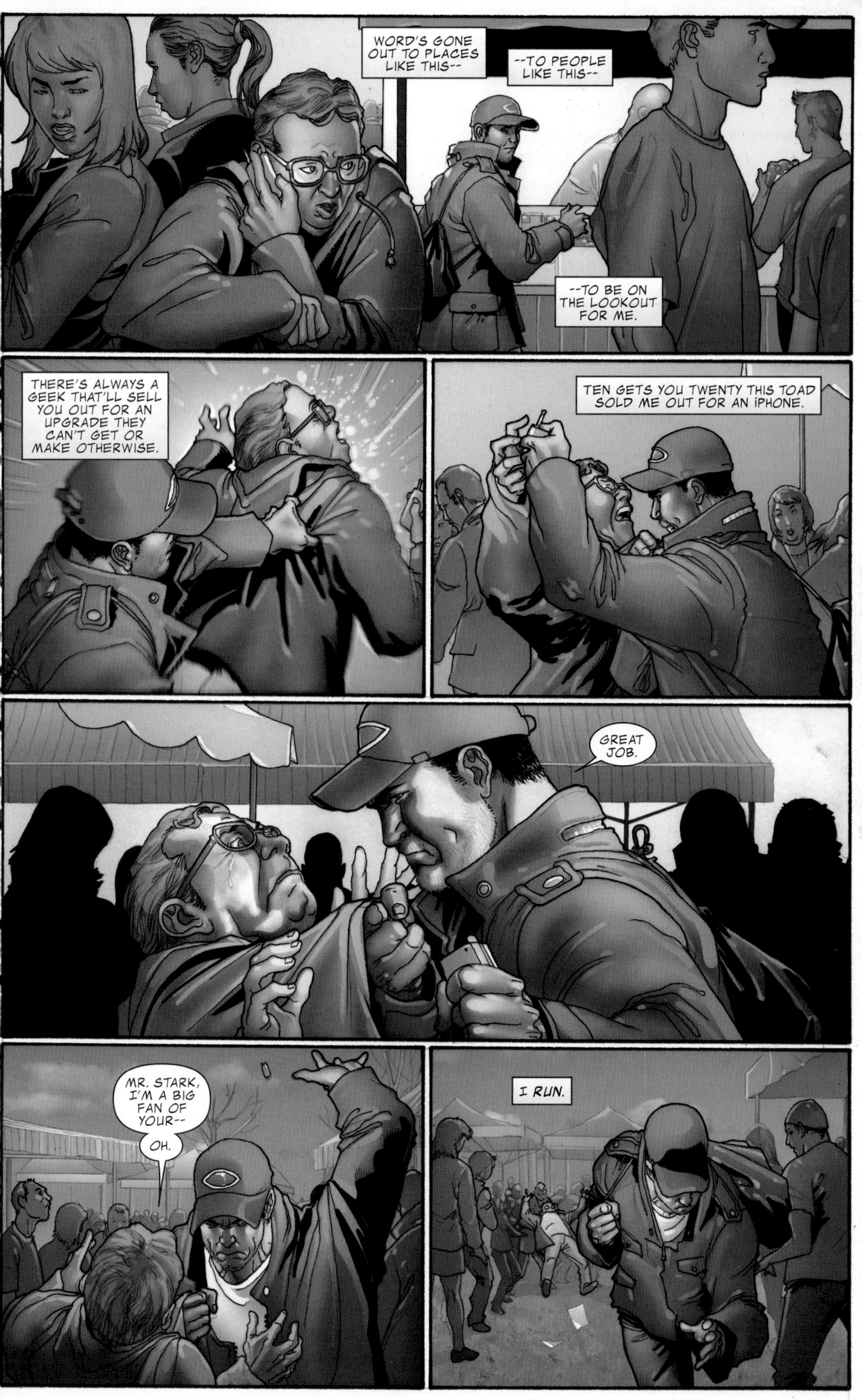
WORD'S GONE OUT TO PLACES LIKE THIS--
--TO PEOPLE LIKE THIS--
--TO BE ON THE LOOKOUT FOR ME.
THERE'S ALWAYS A GEEK THAT'LL SELL YOU OUT FOR AN UPGRADE THEY CAN'T GET OR MAKE OTHERWISE.
TEN GETS YOU TWENTY THIS TOAD SOLD ME OUT FOR AN iPHONE.
GREAT JOB.
MR. STARK, I'M A BIG FAN OF YOUR--
OH.
I RUN.

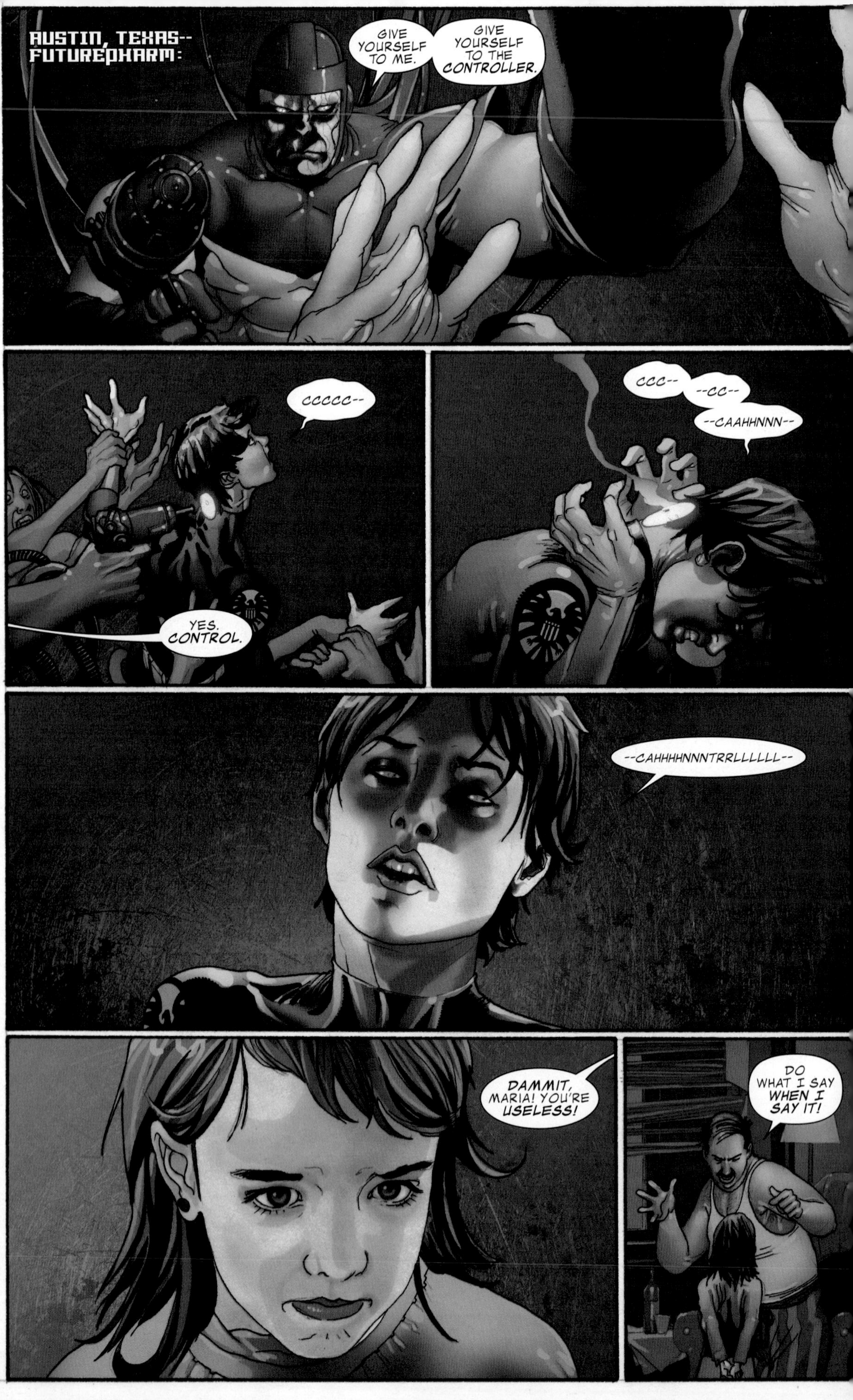
AUSTIN, TEXAS--
FUTUREPHARM:
GIVE YOURSELF TO ME.
GIVE YOURSELF TO THE CONTROLLER.
CCCCC--
YES. CONTROL.
CCC--
--CC--
--CAAHHNNN--
--CAHHHHNNNTRRLLLLLL--
DAMMIT, MARIA! YOU'RE USELESS!
DO WHAT I SAY WHEN I SAY IT!

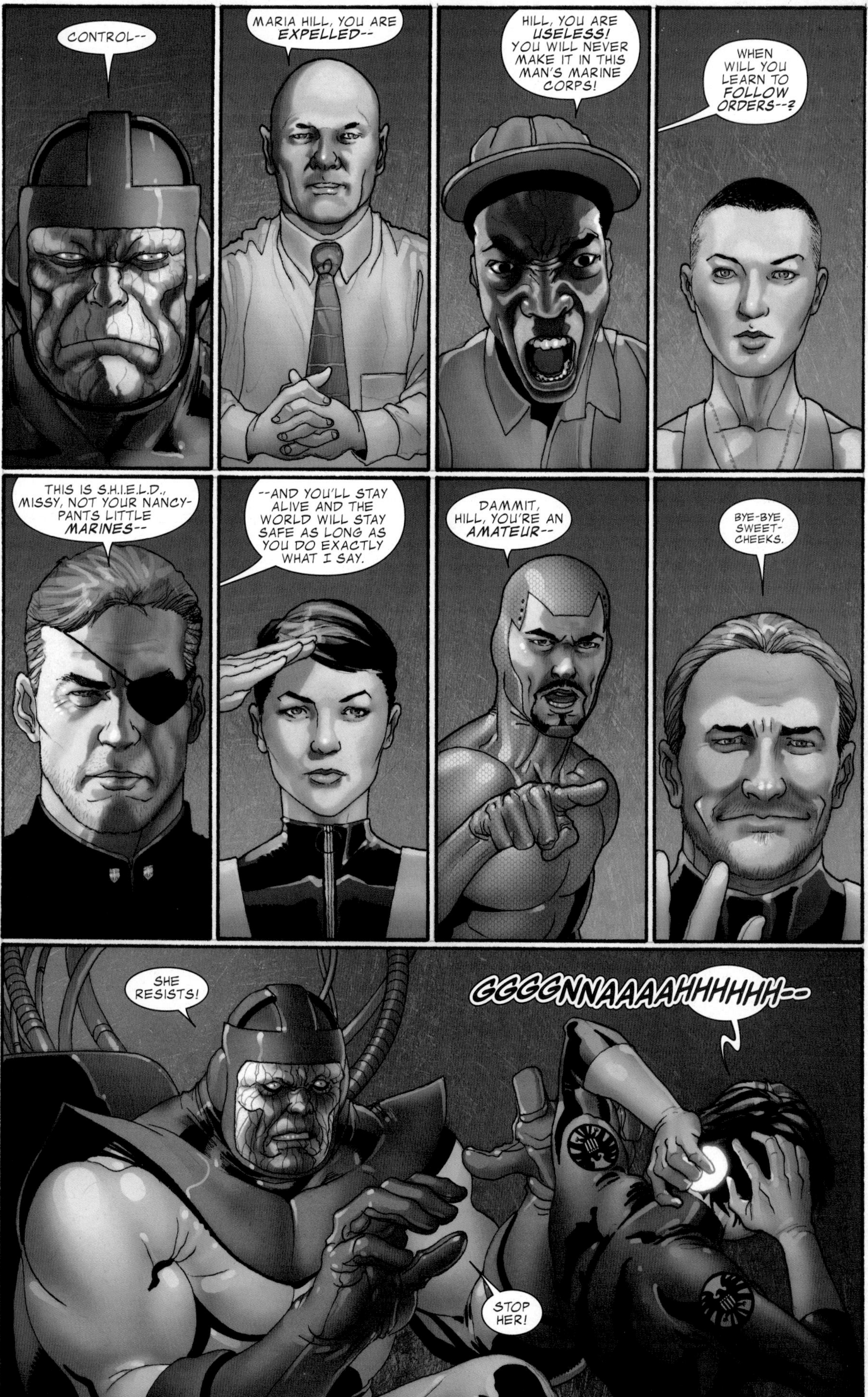
CONTROL--
MARIA HILL, YOU ARE EXPELLED--
HILL, YOU ARE USELESS! YOU WILL NEVER MAKE IT IN THIS MAN'S MARINE CORPS!
WHEN WILL YOU LEARN TO FOLLOW ORDERS--?
THIS IS S.H.I.E.L.D., MISSY, NOT YOUR NANCY-PANTS LITTLE MARINES--
--AND YOU'LL STAY ALIVE AND THE WORLD WILL STAY SAFE AS LONG AS YOU DO EXACTLY WHAT I SAY.
DAMMIT, HILL, YOU'RE AN AMATEUR--
BYE-BYE, SWEET-CHEEKS.
SHE RESISTS!
GGGGNNAAAAHHHHHH--
STOP HER!

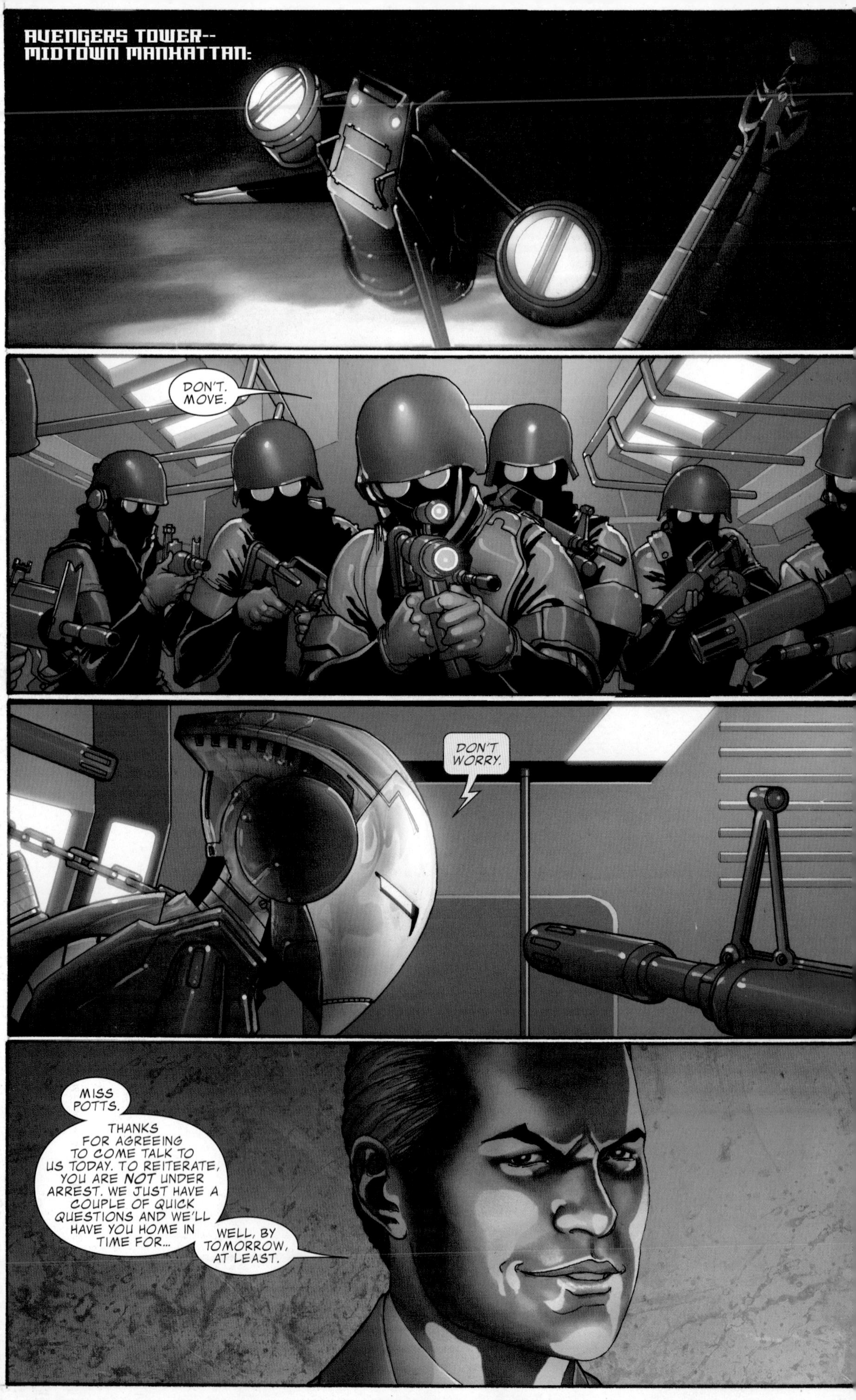
AVENGERS TOWER--
MIDTOWN MANHATTAN:
DON'T. MOVE.
DON'T WORRY.
MISS POTTS.
THANKS FOR AGREEING TO COME TALK TO US TODAY. TO REITERATE, YOU ARE NOT UNDER ARREST. WE JUST HAVE A COUPLE OF QUICK QUESTIONS AND WE'LL HAVE YOU HOME IN TIME FOR...
WELL, BY TOMORROW, AT LEAST.

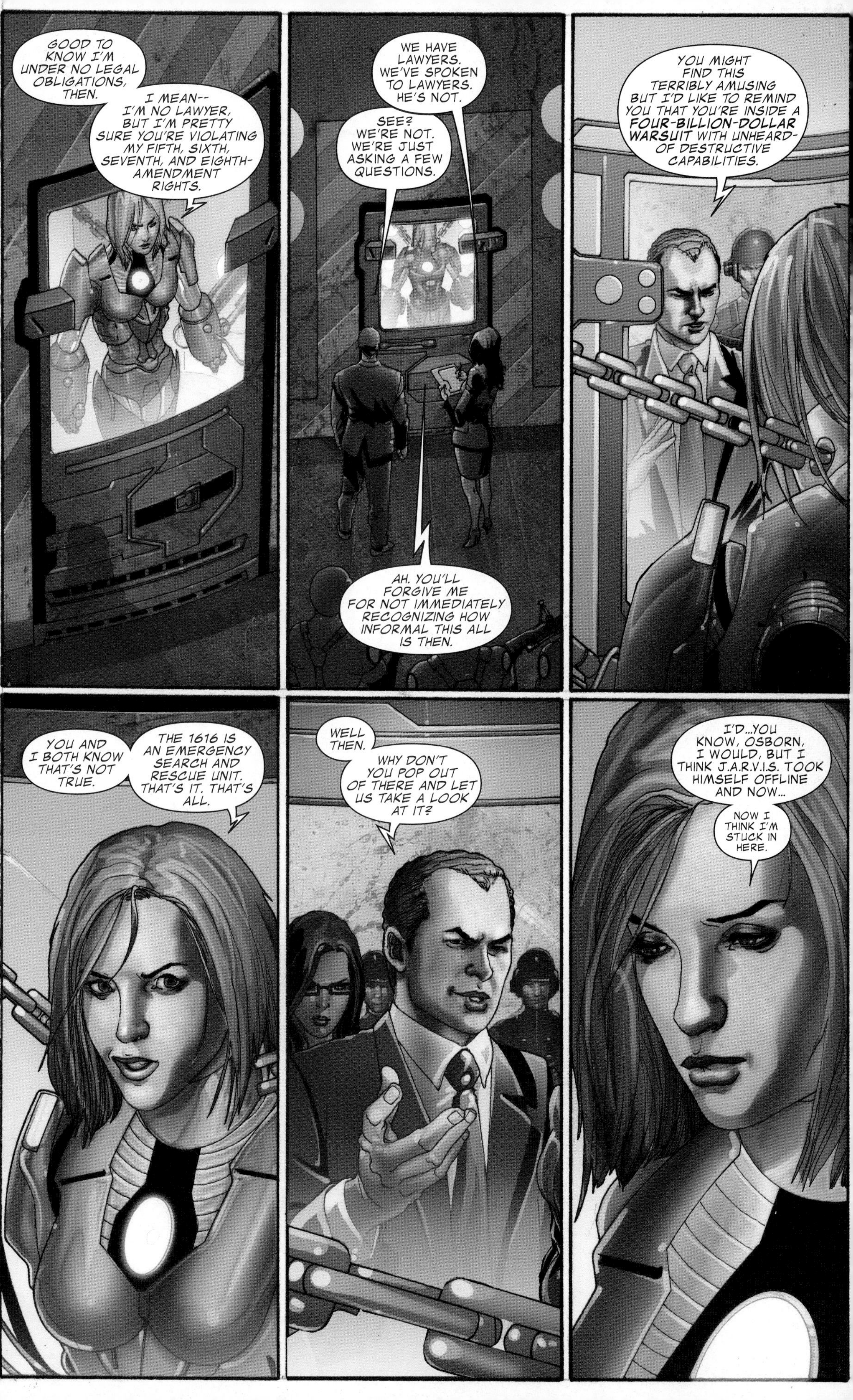
GOOD TO KNOW I'M UNDER NO LEGAL OBLIGATIONS, THEN.
I MEAN-- I'M NO LAWYER, BUT I'M PRETTY SURE YOU'RE VIOLATING MY FIFTH, SIXTH, SEVENTH, AND EIGHTH-AMENDMENT RIGHTS.
WE HAVE LAWYERS. WE'VE SPOKEN TO LAWYERS. HE'S NOT.
SEE? WE'RE NOT. WE'RE JUST ASKING A FEW QUESTIONS.
AH. YOU'LL FORGIVE ME FOR NOT IMMEDIATELY RECOGNIZING HOW INFORMAL THIS ALL IS THEN.
YOU MIGHT FIND THIS TERRIBLY AMUSING BUT I'D LIKE TO REMIND YOU THAT YOU'RE INSIDE A **FOUR-BILLION-DOLLAR WARSUIT** WITH UNHEARD-OF DESTRUCTIVE CAPABILITIES.
YOU AND I BOTH KNOW THAT'S NOT TRUE.
THE 1616 IS AN EMERGENCY SEARCH AND RESCUE UNIT. THAT'S IT. THAT'S ALL.
WELL THEN.
WHY DON'T YOU POP OUT OF THERE AND LET US TAKE A LOOK AT IT?
I'D...YOU KNOW, OSBORN, I WOULD, BUT I THINK J.A.R.V.I.S. TOOK HIMSELF OFFLINE AND NOW...
NOW I THINK I'M STUCK IN HERE.

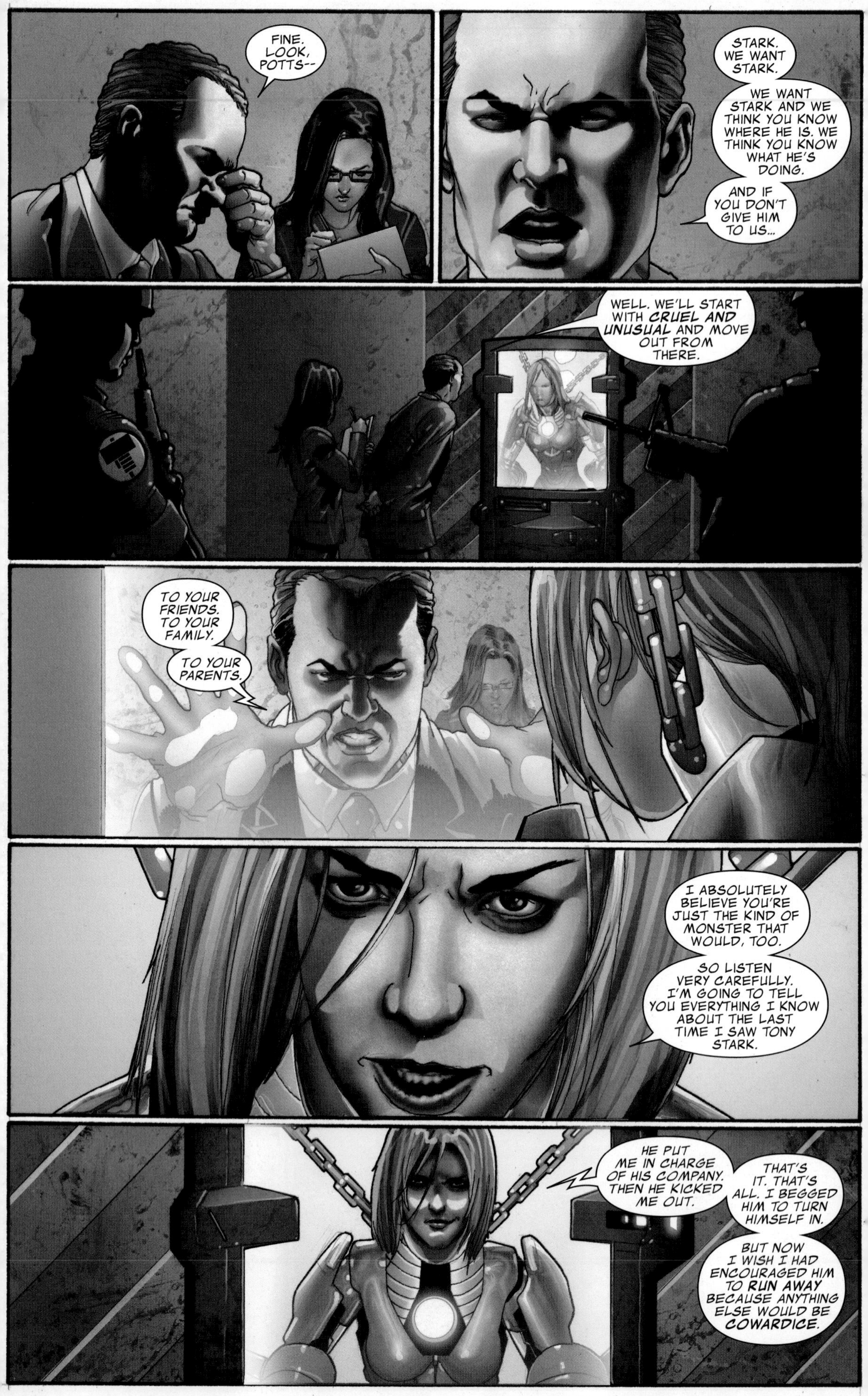

FINE. LOOK, POTTS--
STARK. WE WANT STARK.
WE WANT STARK AND WE THINK YOU KNOW WHERE HE IS. WE THINK YOU KNOW WHAT HE'S DOING.
AND IF YOU DON'T GIVE HIM TO US...
WELL. WE'LL START WITH **CRUEL AND UNUSUAL** AND MOVE OUT FROM THERE.
TO YOUR FRIENDS. TO YOUR FAMILY.
TO YOUR PARENTS.
I ABSOLUTELY BELIEVE YOU'RE JUST THE KIND OF MONSTER THAT WOULD, TOO.
SO LISTEN VERY CAREFULLY. I'M GOING TO TELL YOU EVERYTHING I KNOW ABOUT THE LAST TIME I SAW TONY STARK.
HE PUT ME IN CHARGE OF HIS COMPANY. THEN HE KICKED ME OUT.
THAT'S IT. THAT'S ALL. I BEGGED HIM TO TURN HIMSELF IN.
BUT NOW I WISH I HAD ENCOURAGED HIM TO **RUN AWAY** BECAUSE ANYTHING ELSE WOULD BE **COWARDICE**.

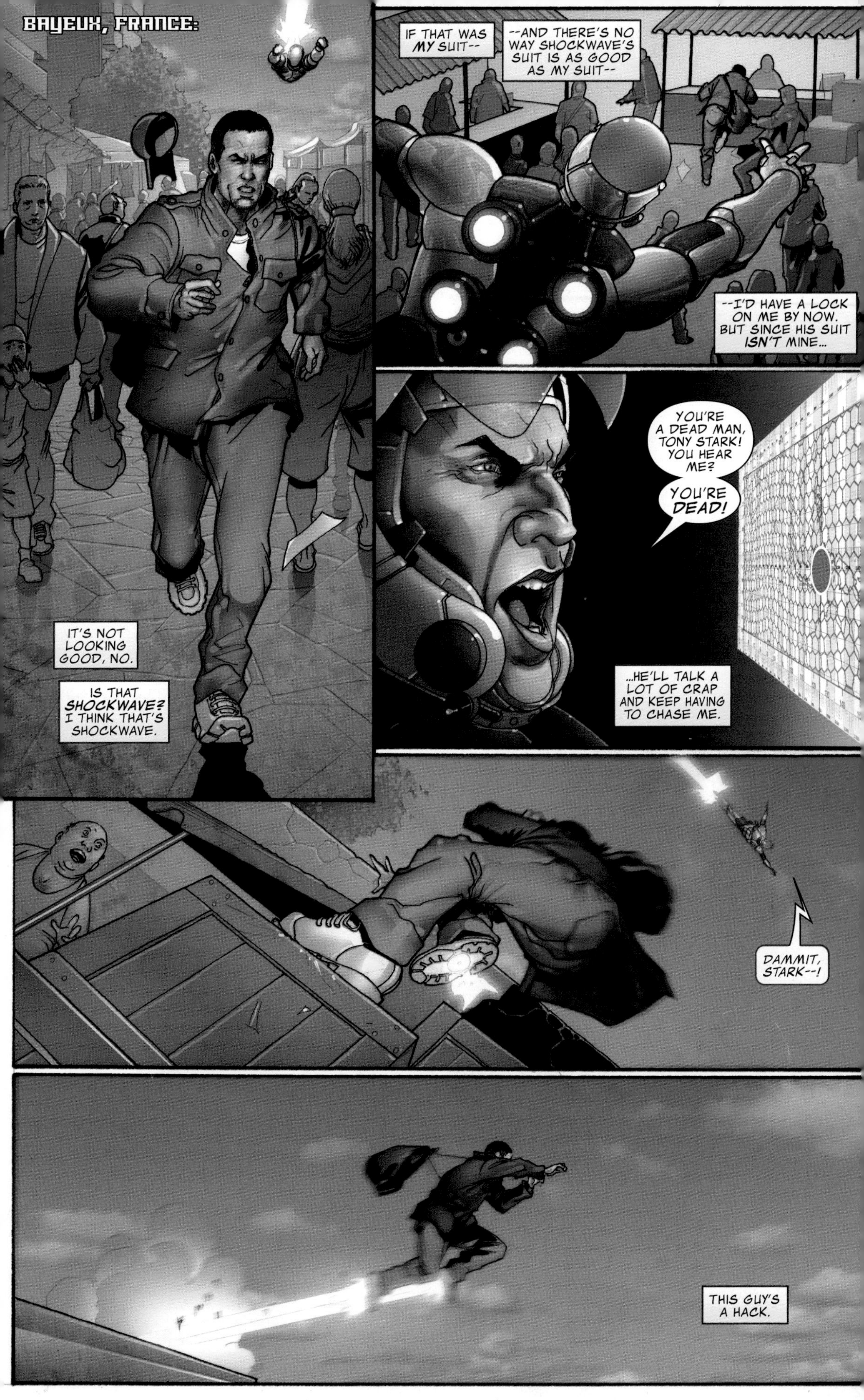
BAYEUX, FRANCE:
IT'S NOT LOOKING GOOD, NO.
IS THAT SHOCKWAVE? I THINK THAT'S SHOCKWAVE.
IF THAT WAS MY SUIT--
--AND THERE'S NO WAY SHOCKWAVE'S SUIT IS AS GOOD AS MY SUIT--
--I'D HAVE A LOCK ON ME BY NOW. BUT SINCE HIS SUIT ISN'T MINE...
YOU'RE A DEAD MAN, TONY STARK! YOU HEAR ME?
YOU'RE DEAD!
...HE'LL TALK A LOT OF CRAP AND KEEP HAVING TO CHASE ME.
DAMMIT, STARK--!
THIS GUY'S A HACK.

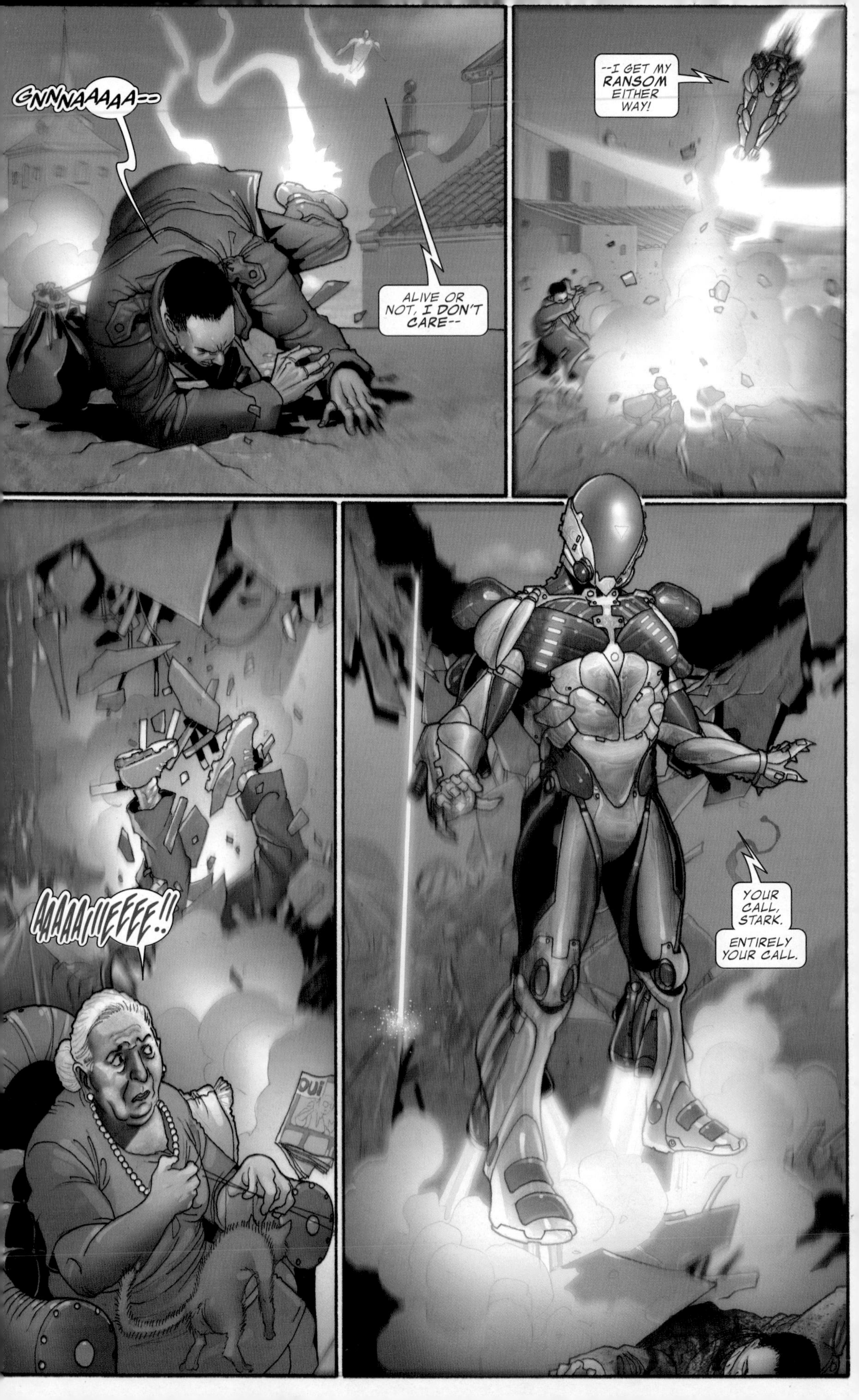
GNNNAAAAA--
ALIVE OR NOT, I DON'T CARE--
--I GET MY RANSOM EITHER WAY!
AAAAIIIEEEEE!!
YOUR CALL, STARK.
ENTIRELY YOUR CALL.

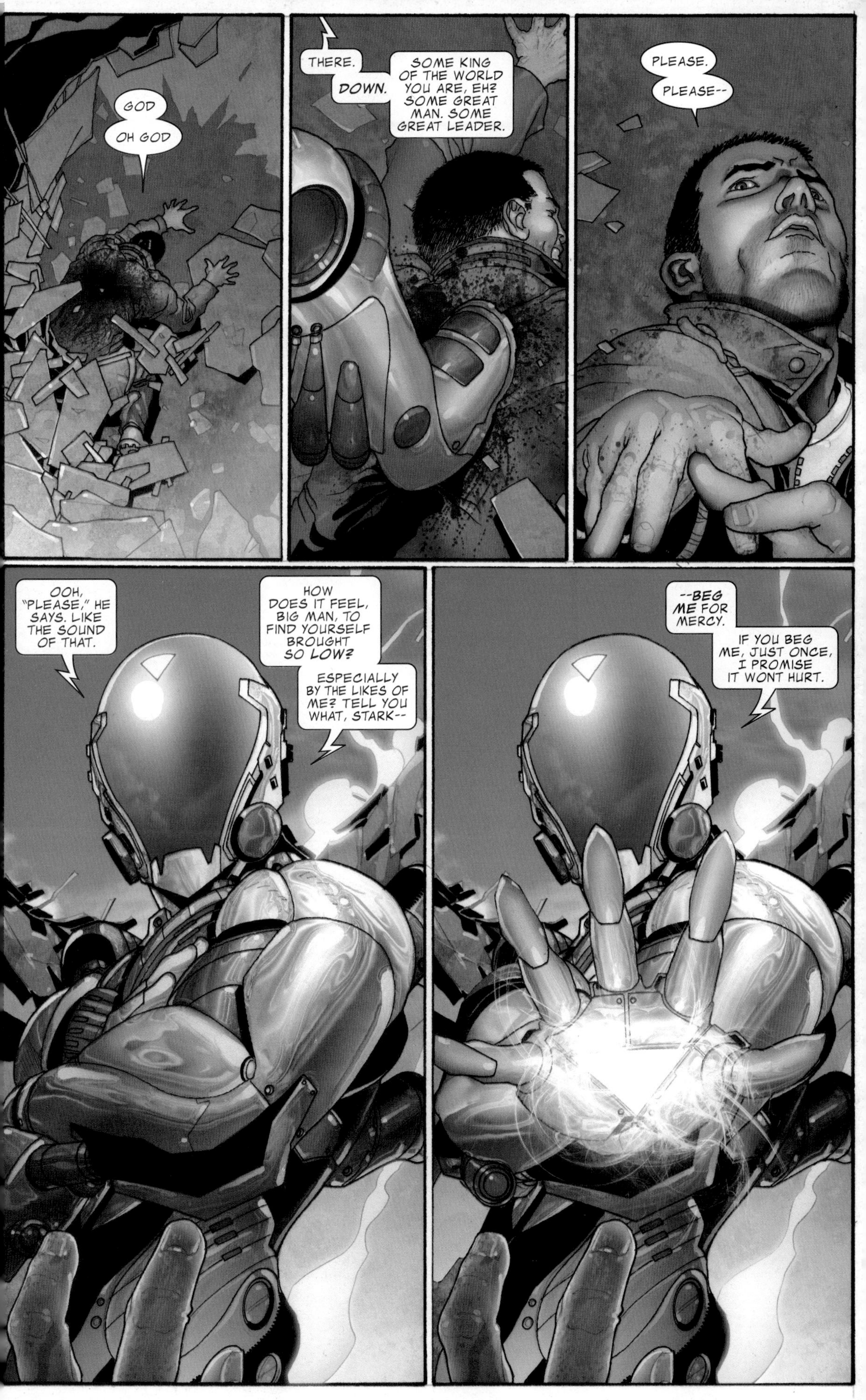
GOD
OH GOD
THERE.
DOWN.
SOME KING OF THE WORLD YOU ARE, EH? SOME GREAT MAN. SOME GREAT LEADER.
PLEASE.
PLEASE--
OOH, "PLEASE," HE SAYS. LIKE THE SOUND OF THAT.
HOW DOES IT FEEL, BIG MAN, TO FIND YOURSELF BROUGHT SO LOW?
ESPECIALLY BY THE LIKES OF ME? TELL YOU WHAT, STARK--
--BEG ME FOR MERCY.
IF YOU BEG ME, JUST ONCE, I PROMISE IT WONT HURT.

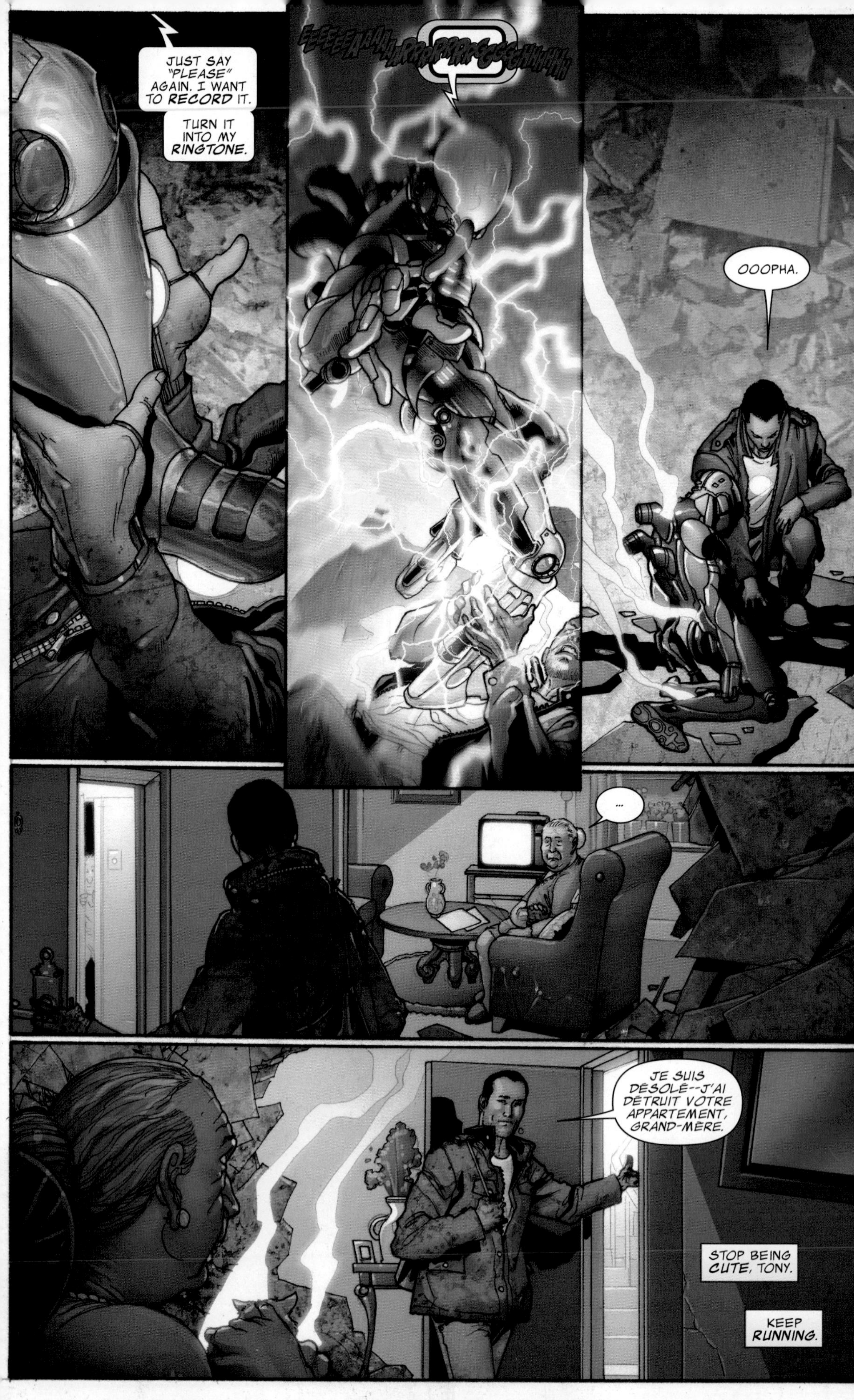

JUST SAY "PLEASE" AGAIN. I WANT TO RECORD IT.
TURN IT INTO MY RINGTONE.
OOOPHA.
...
JE SUIS DÉSOLÉ--J'AI DÉTRUIT VOTRE APPARTEMENT, GRAND-MÈRE.
STOP BEING CUTE, TONY.
KEEP RUNNING.

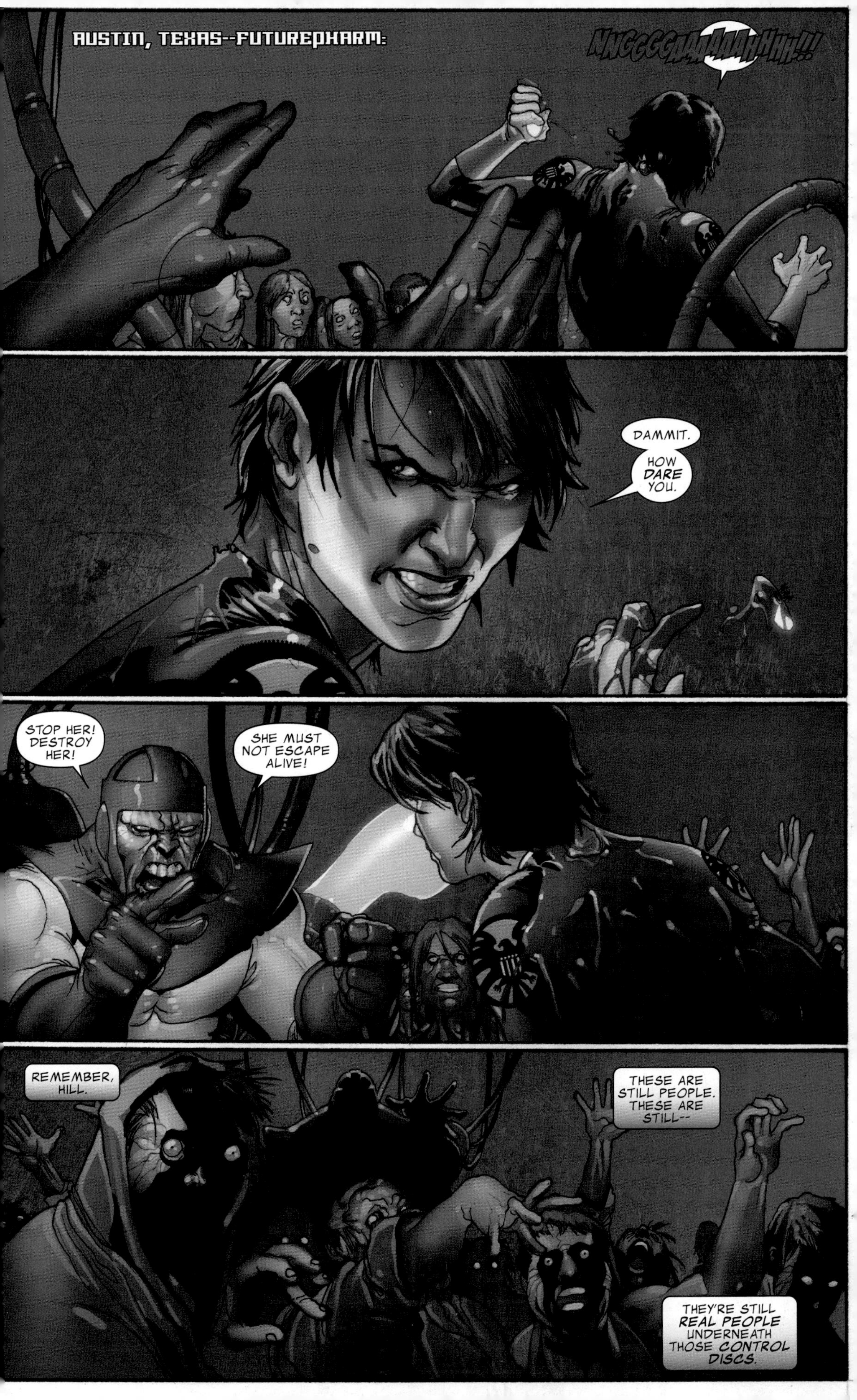
AUSTIN, TEXAS--FUTUREPHARM:
NNGGGGAAAAAARHHH!!!
DAMMIT.
HOW DARE YOU.
STOP HER! DESTROY HER!
SHE MUST NOT ESCAPE ALIVE!
REMEMBER, HILL.
THESE ARE STILL PEOPLE. THESE ARE STILL--
THEY'RE STILL REAL PEOPLE UNDERNEATH THOSE CONTROL DISCS.

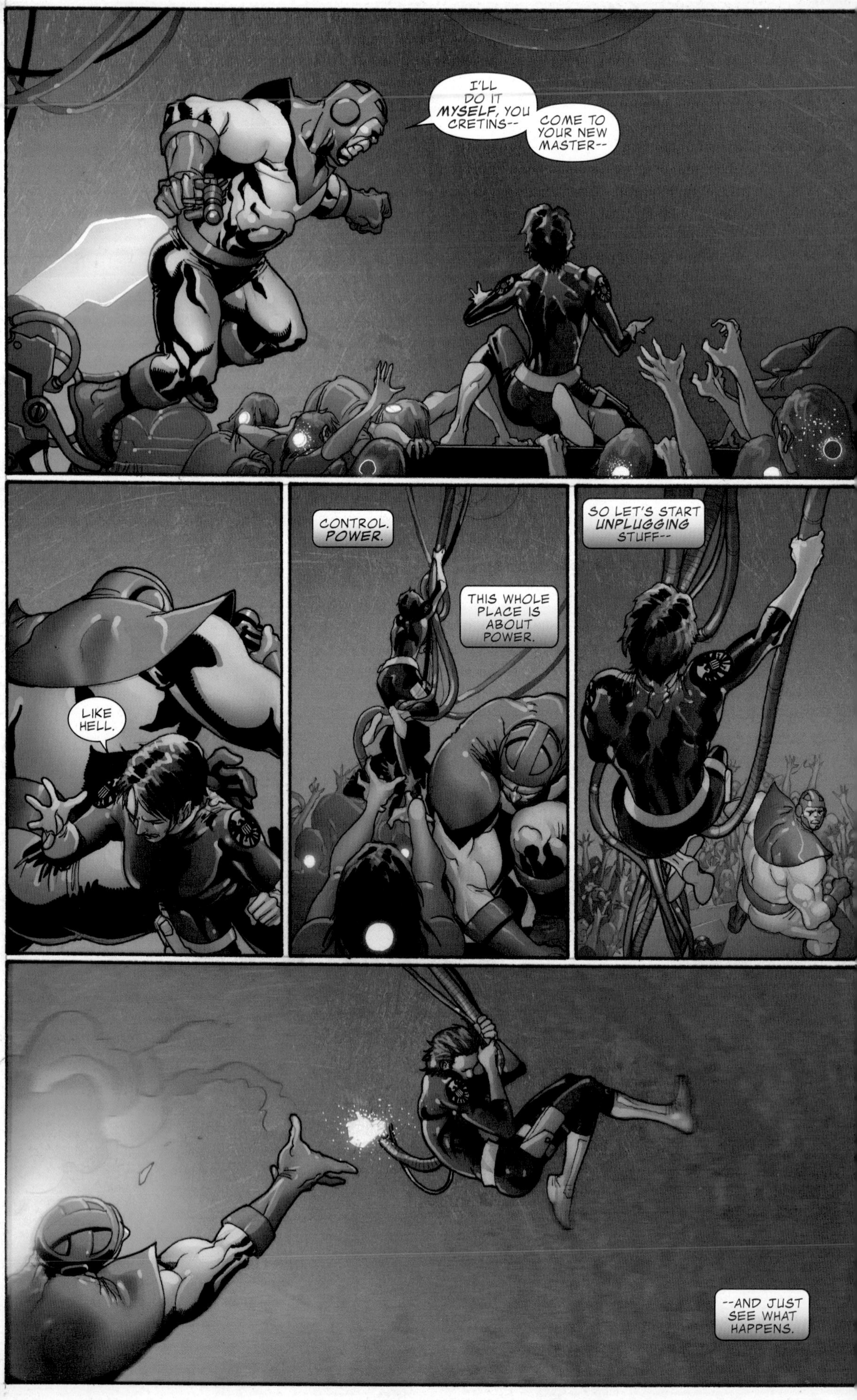
I'LL DO IT MYSELF, YOU CRETINS--
COME TO YOUR NEW MASTER--
LIKE HELL.
CONTROL. POWER.
THIS WHOLE PLACE IS ABOUT POWER.
SO LET'S START UNPLUGGING STUFF--
--AND JUST SEE WHAT HAPPENS.

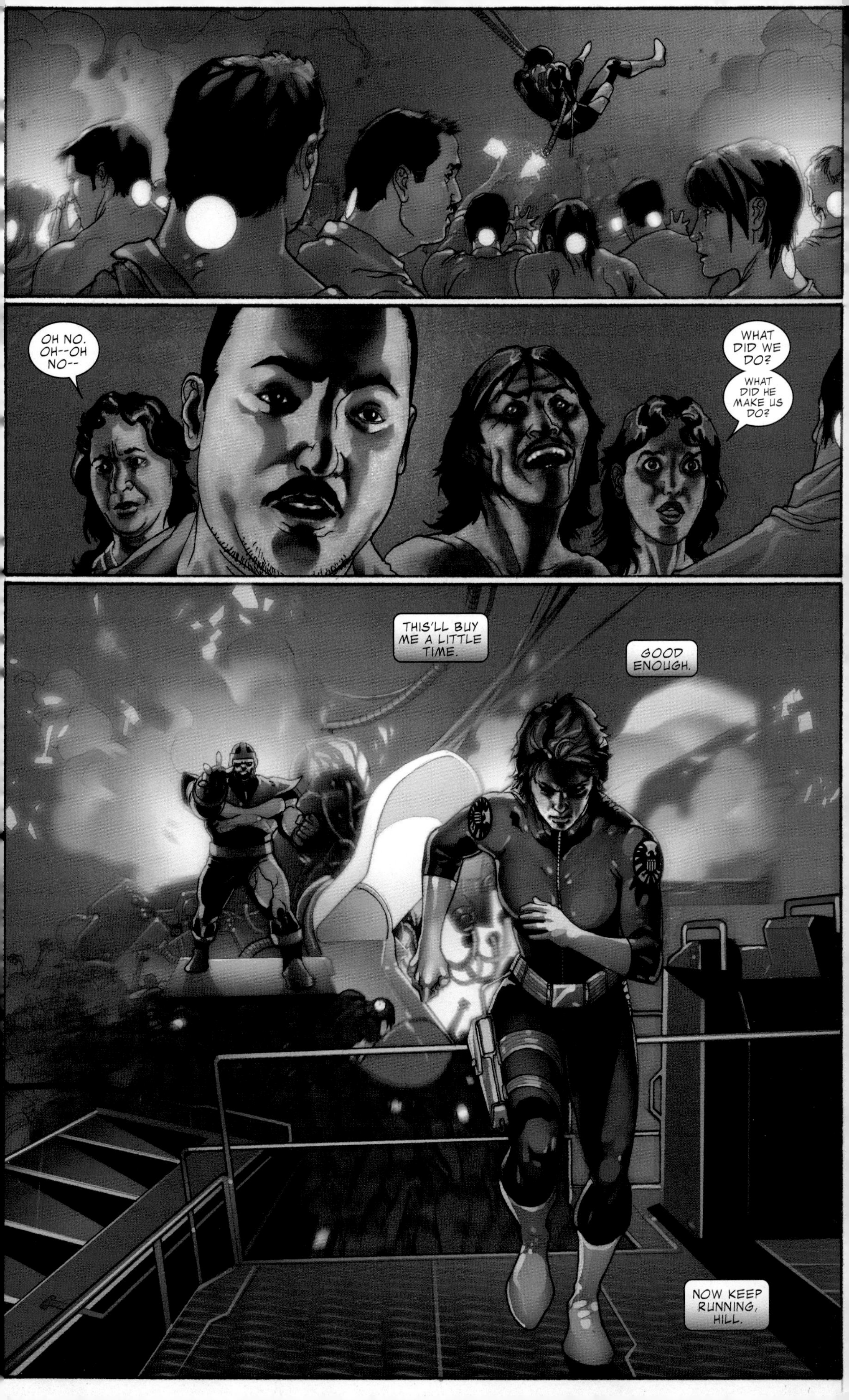
OH NO. OH--OH NO--
WHAT DID WE DO?
WHAT DID HE MAKE US DO?
THIS'LL BUY ME A LITTLE TIME.
GOOD ENOUGH.
NOW KEEP RUNNING, HILL.

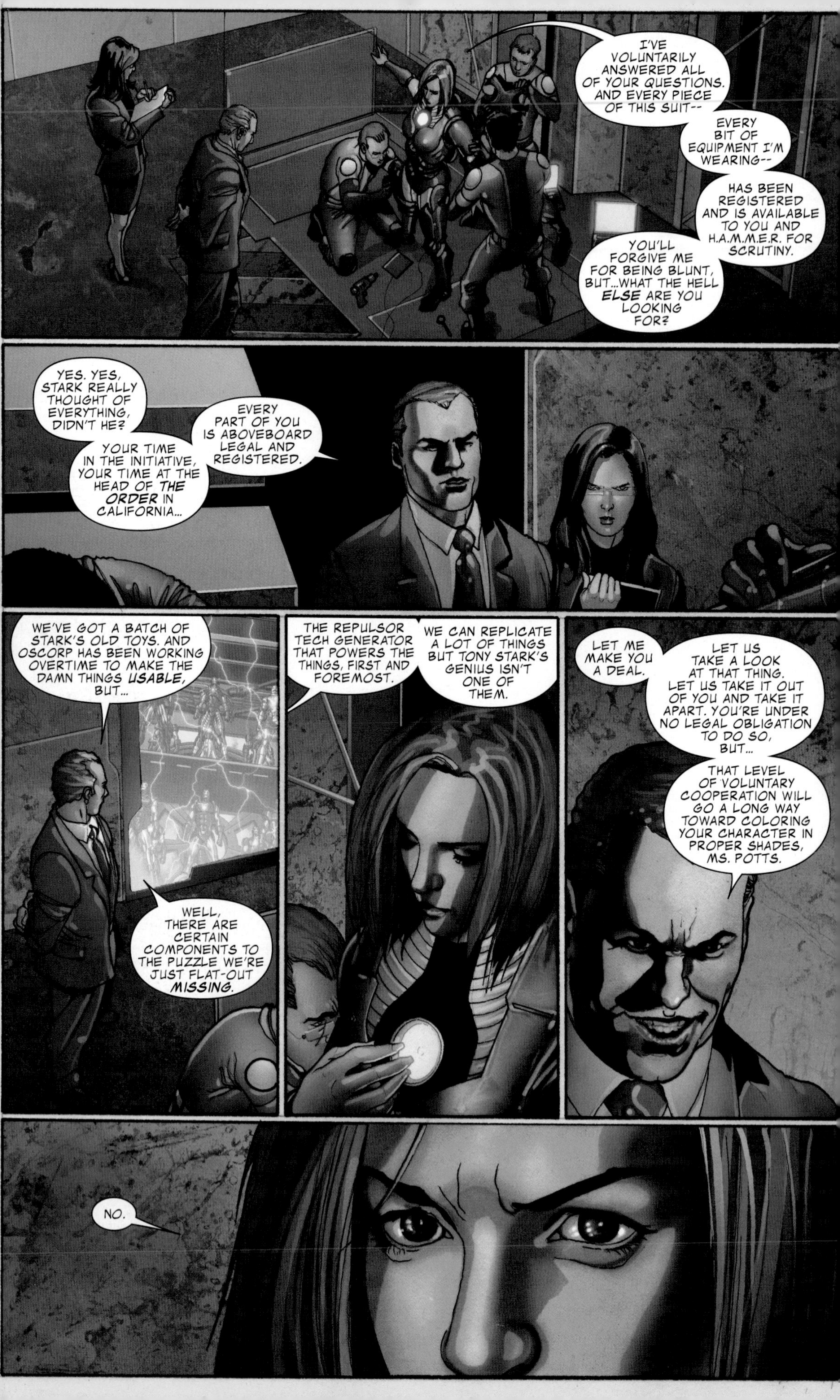
I'VE VOLUNTARILY ANSWERED ALL OF YOUR QUESTIONS. AND EVERY PIECE OF THIS SUIT--
EVERY BIT OF EQUIPMENT I'M WEARING--
HAS BEEN REGISTERED AND IS AVAILABLE TO YOU AND H.A.M.M.E.R. FOR SCRUTINY.
YOU'LL FORGIVE ME FOR BEING BLUNT, BUT...WHAT THE HELL ELSE ARE YOU LOOKING FOR?
YES. YES, STARK REALLY THOUGHT OF EVERYTHING, DIDN'T HE?
YOUR TIME IN THE INITIATIVE, YOUR TIME AT THE HEAD OF THE ORDER IN CALIFORNIA...
EVERY PART OF YOU IS ABOVEBOARD LEGAL AND REGISTERED.
WE'VE GOT A BATCH OF STARK'S OLD TOYS. AND OSCORP HAS BEEN WORKING OVERTIME TO MAKE THE DAMN THINGS USABLE, BUT...
WELL, THERE ARE CERTAIN COMPONENTS TO THE PUZZLE WE'RE JUST FLAT-OUT MISSING.
THE REPULSOR TECH GENERATOR THAT POWERS THE THINGS, FIRST AND FOREMOST.
WE CAN REPLICATE A LOT OF THINGS BUT TONY STARK'S GENIUS ISN'T ONE OF THEM.
LET ME MAKE YOU A DEAL.
LET US TAKE A LOOK AT THAT THING. LET US TAKE IT OUT OF YOU AND TAKE IT APART. YOU'RE UNDER NO LEGAL OBLIGATION TO DO SO, BUT...
THAT LEVEL OF VOLUNTARY COOPERATION WILL GO A LONG WAY TOWARD COLORING YOUR CHARACTER IN PROPER SHADES, MS. POTTS.
NO.

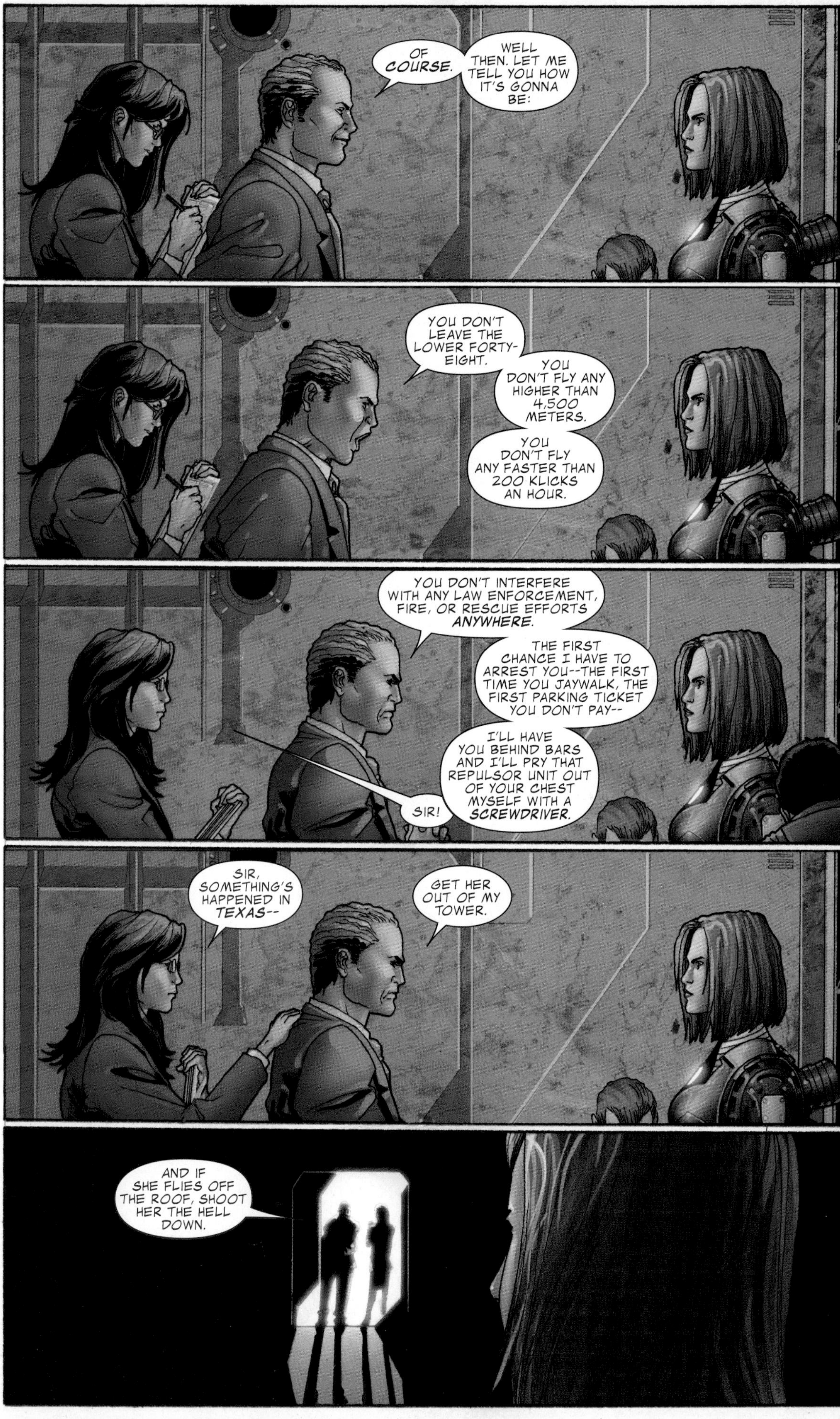
OF COURSE.
WELL THEN. LET ME TELL YOU HOW IT'S GONNA BE:
YOU DON'T LEAVE THE LOWER FORTY-EIGHT.
YOU DON'T FLY ANY HIGHER THAN 4,500 METERS.
YOU DON'T FLY ANY FASTER THAN 200 KLICKS AN HOUR.
YOU DON'T INTERFERE WITH ANY LAW ENFORCEMENT, FIRE, OR RESCUE EFFORTS ANYWHERE.
THE FIRST CHANCE I HAVE TO ARREST YOU--THE FIRST TIME YOU JAYWALK, THE FIRST PARKING TICKET YOU DON'T PAY--
I'LL HAVE YOU BEHIND BARS AND I'LL PRY THAT REPULSOR UNIT OUT OF YOUR CHEST MYSELF WITH A SCREWDRIVER.
SIR!
SIR, SOMETHING'S HAPPENED IN TEXAS--
GET HER OUT OF MY TOWER.
AND IF SHE FLIES OFF THE ROOF, SHOOT HER THE HELL DOWN.

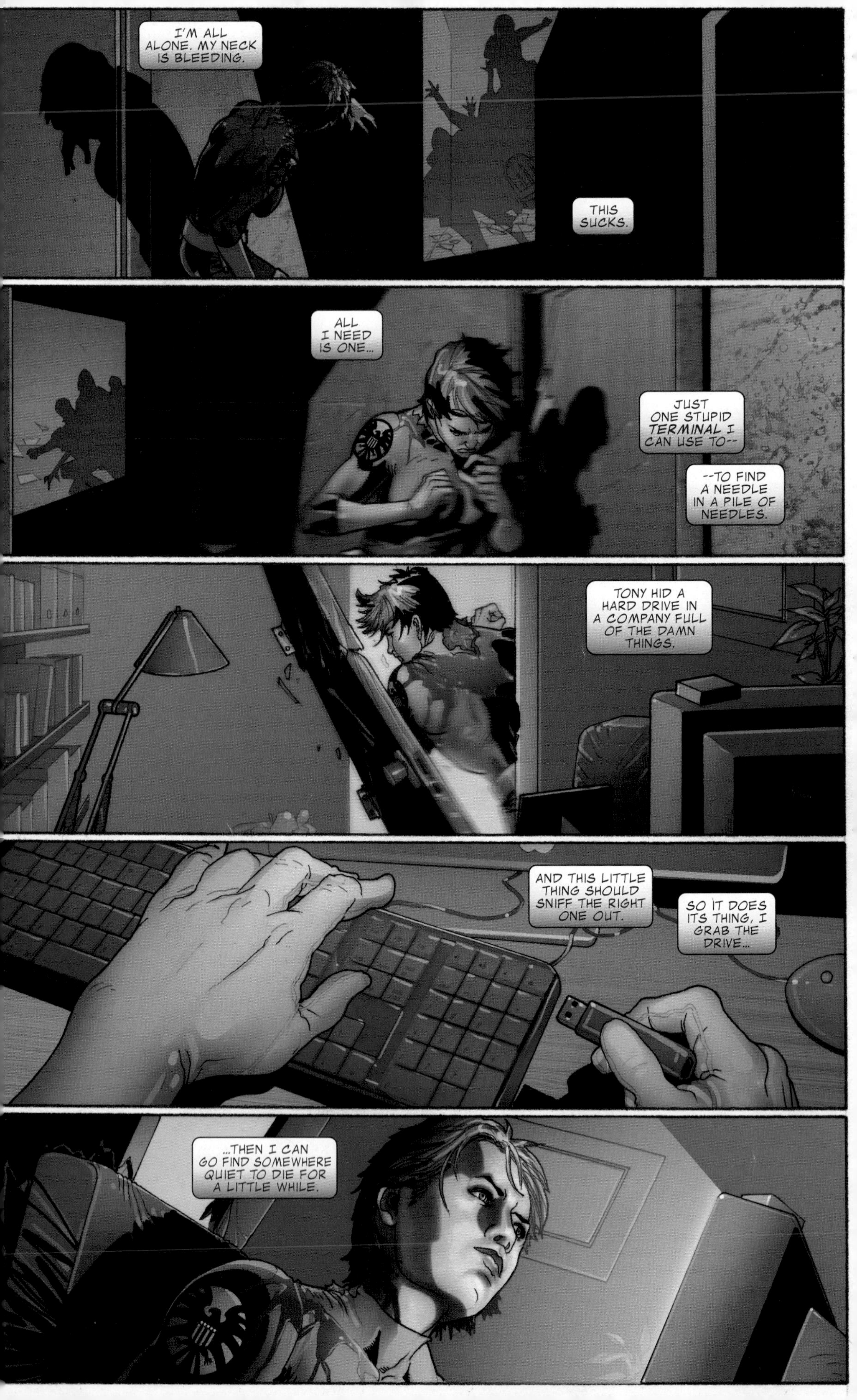
I'M ALL ALONE. MY NECK IS BLEEDING.
THIS SUCKS.
ALL I NEED IS ONE...
JUST ONE STUPID *TERMINAL* I CAN USE TO--
--TO FIND A NEEDLE IN A PILE OF NEEDLES.
TONY HID A HARD DRIVE IN A COMPANY FULL OF THE DAMN THINGS.
AND THIS LITTLE THING SHOULD SNIFF THE RIGHT ONE OUT.
SO IT DOES ITS THING, I GRAB THE DRIVE...
...THEN I CAN GO FIND SOMEWHERE QUIET TO DIE FOR A LITTLE WHILE.

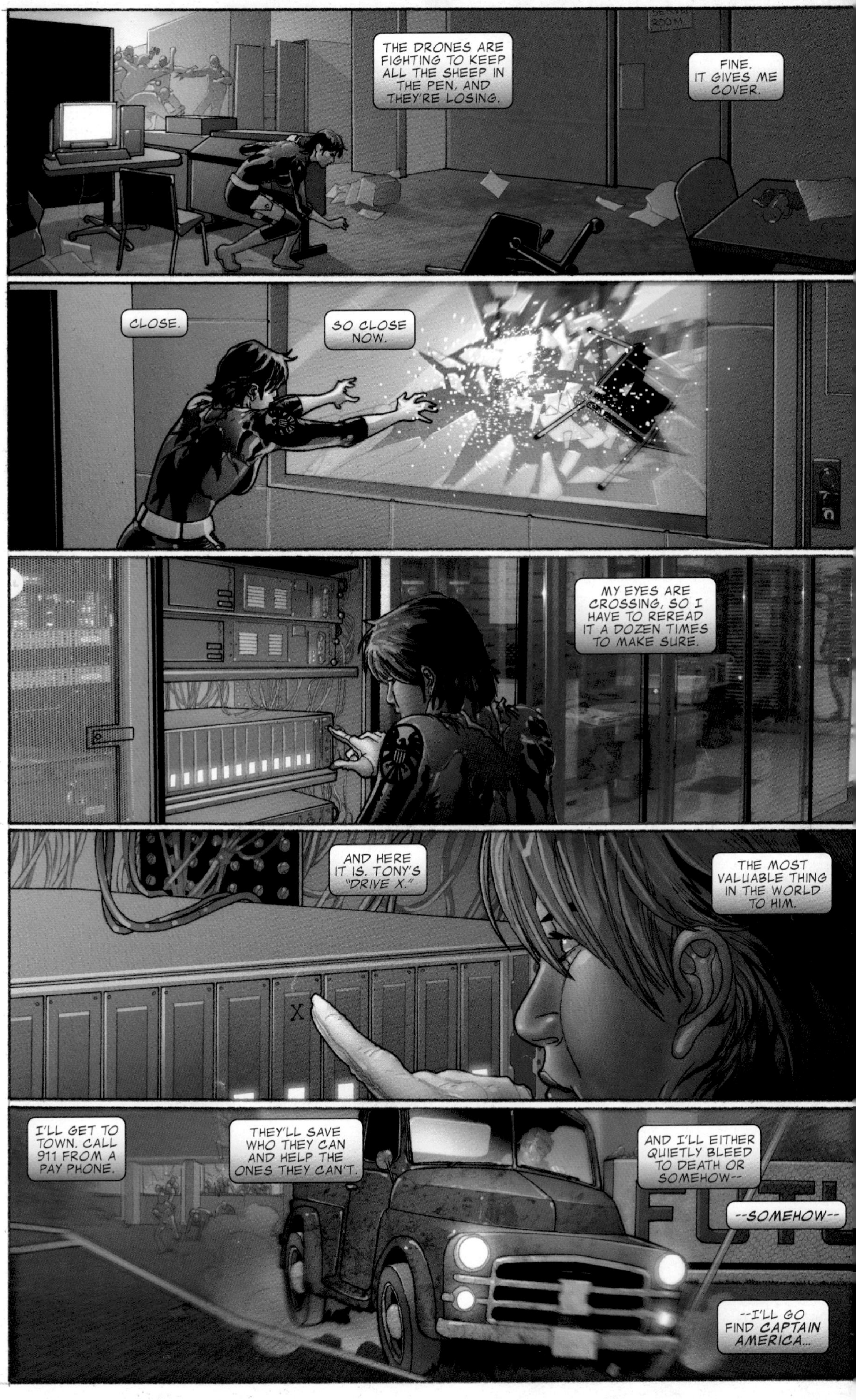
THE DRONES ARE FIGHTING TO KEEP ALL THE SHEEP IN THE PEN, AND THEY'RE LOSING.
FINE. IT GIVES ME COVER.
CLOSE.
SO CLOSE NOW.
MY EYES ARE CROSSING, SO I HAVE TO REREAD IT A DOZEN TIMES TO MAKE SURE.
AND HERE IT IS. TONY'S "DRIVE X."
THE MOST VALUABLE THING IN THE WORLD TO HIM.
X
I'LL GET TO TOWN. CALL 911 FROM A PAY PHONE.
THEY'LL SAVE WHO THEY CAN AND HELP THE ONES THEY CAN'T.
AND I'LL EITHER QUIETLY BLEED TO DEATH OR SOMEHOW--
--SOMEHOW--
--I'LL GO FIND CAPTAIN AMERICA...

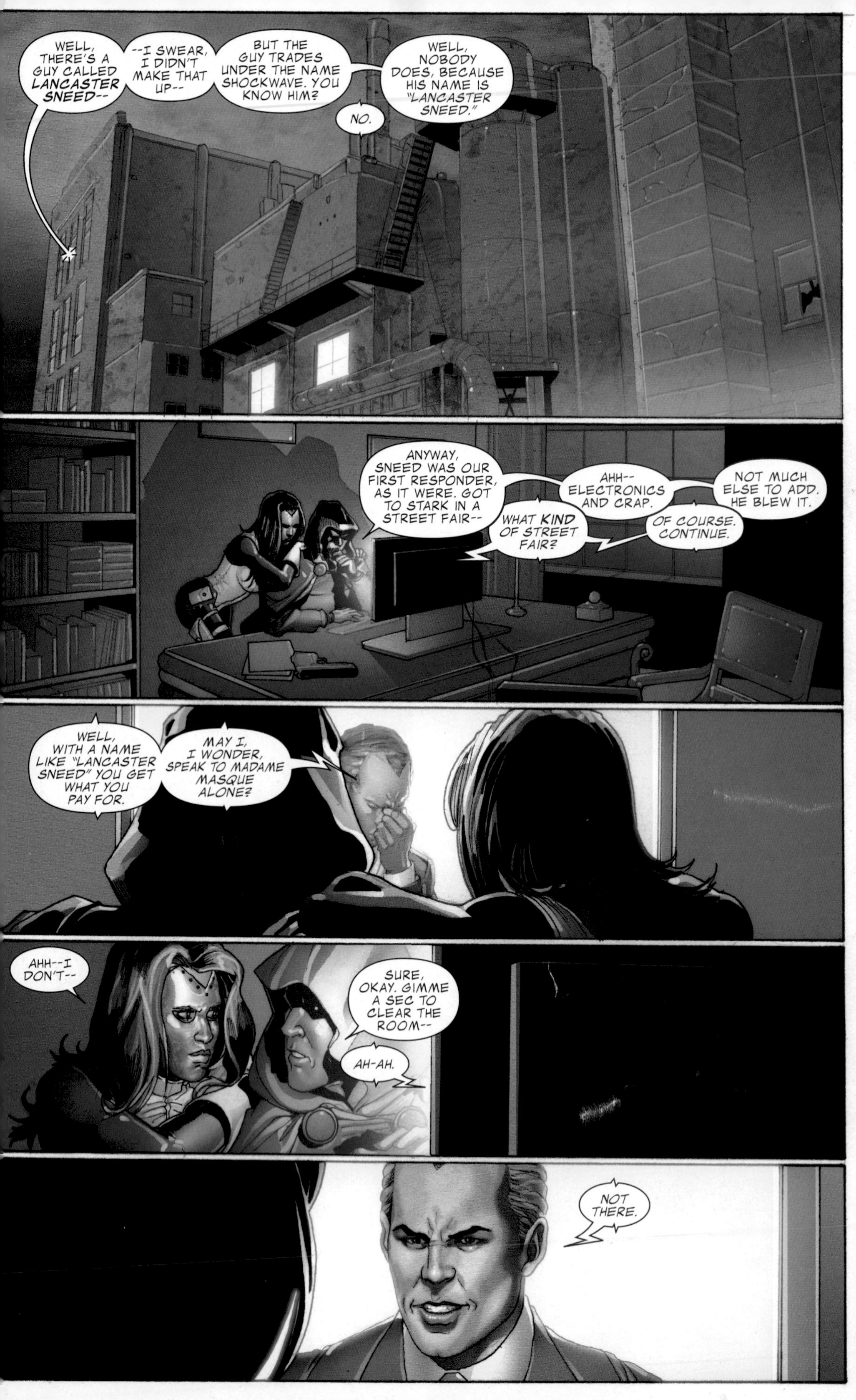

WELL, THERE'S A GUY CALLED LANCASTER SNEED--
--I SWEAR, I DIDN'T MAKE THAT UP--
BUT THE GUY TRADES UNDER THE NAME SHOCKWAVE. YOU KNOW HIM?
NO.
WELL, NOBODY DOES, BECAUSE HIS NAME IS "LANCASTER SNEED."
ANYWAY, SNEED WAS OUR FIRST RESPONDER, AS IT WERE. GOT TO STARK IN A STREET FAIR--
WHAT KIND OF STREET FAIR?
AHH-- ELECTRONICS AND CRAP.
OF COURSE. CONTINUE.
NOT MUCH ELSE TO ADD. HE BLEW IT.
WELL, WITH A NAME LIKE "LANCASTER SNEED" YOU GET WHAT YOU PAY FOR.
MAY I, I WONDER, SPEAK TO MADAME MASQUE ALONE?
AHH--I DON'T--
SURE, OKAY. GIMME A SEC TO CLEAR THE ROOM--
AH-AH.
NOT THERE.

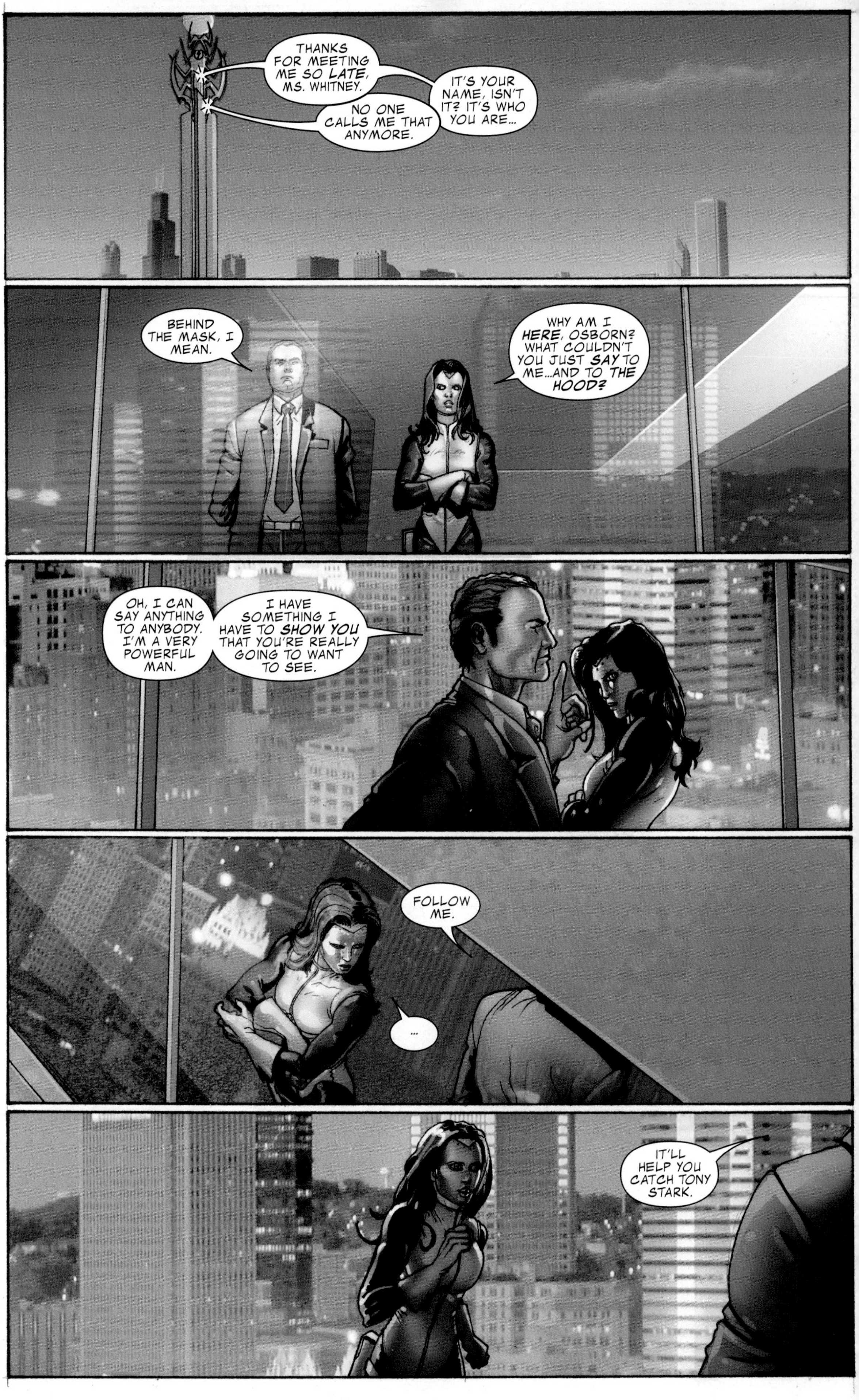
THANKS FOR MEETING ME SO LATE, MS. WHITNEY.
IT'S YOUR NAME, ISN'T IT? IT'S WHO YOU ARE...
NO ONE CALLS ME THAT ANYMORE.
BEHIND THE MASK, I MEAN.
WHY AM I HERE, OSBORN? WHAT COULDN'T YOU JUST SAY TO ME...AND TO THE HOOD?
OH, I CAN SAY ANYTHING TO ANYBODY. I'M A VERY POWERFUL MAN.
I HAVE SOMETHING I HAVE TO SHOW YOU THAT YOU'RE REALLY GOING TO WANT TO SEE.
FOLLOW ME.
...
IT'LL HELP YOU CATCH TONY STARK.

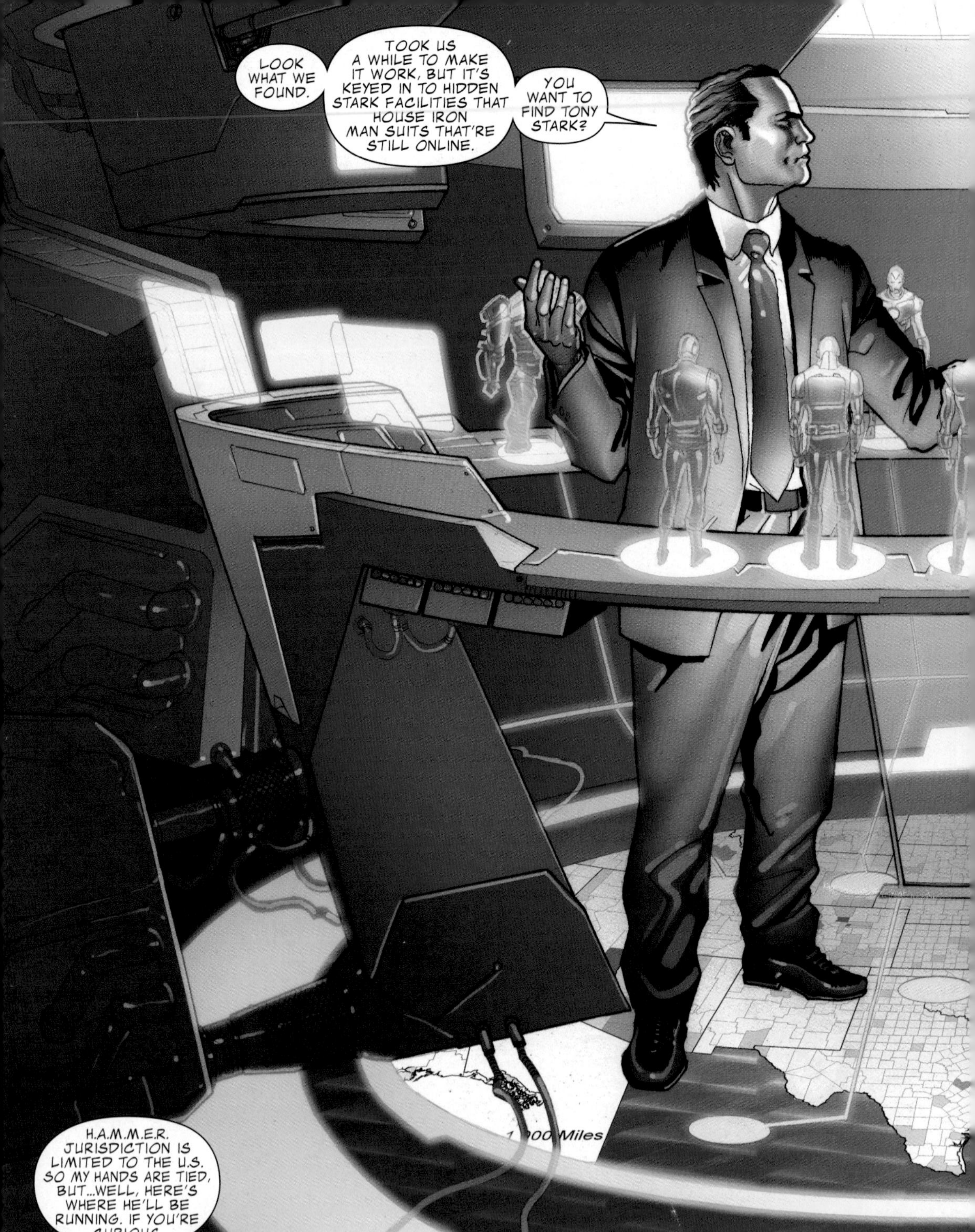
LOOK WHAT WE FOUND.
TOOK US A WHILE TO MAKE IT WORK, BUT IT'S KEYED IN TO HIDDEN STARK FACILITIES THAT HOUSE IRON MAN SUITS THAT'RE STILL ONLINE.
YOU WANT TO FIND TONY STARK?
H.A.M.M.E.R. JURISDICTION IS LIMITED TO THE U.S. SO MY HANDS ARE TIED, BUT...WELL, HERE'S WHERE HE'LL BE RUNNING. IF YOU'RE CURIOUS.

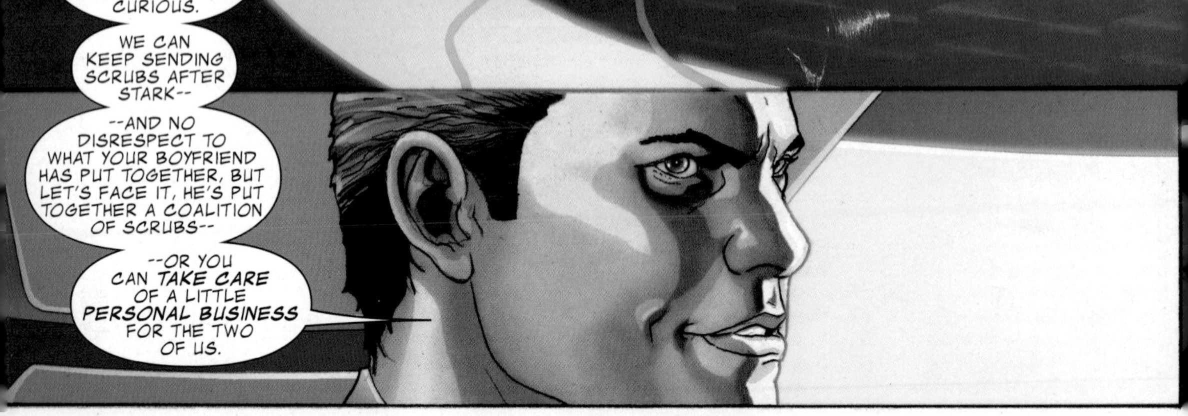
WE CAN KEEP SENDING SCRUBS AFTER STARK--
--AND NO DISRESPECT TO WHAT YOUR BOYFRIEND HAS PUT TOGETHER, BUT LET'S FACE IT, HE'S PUT TOGETHER A COALITION OF SCRUBS--
--OR YOU CAN *TAKE CARE* OF A LITTLE ***PERSONAL BUSINESS*** FOR THE TWO OF US.

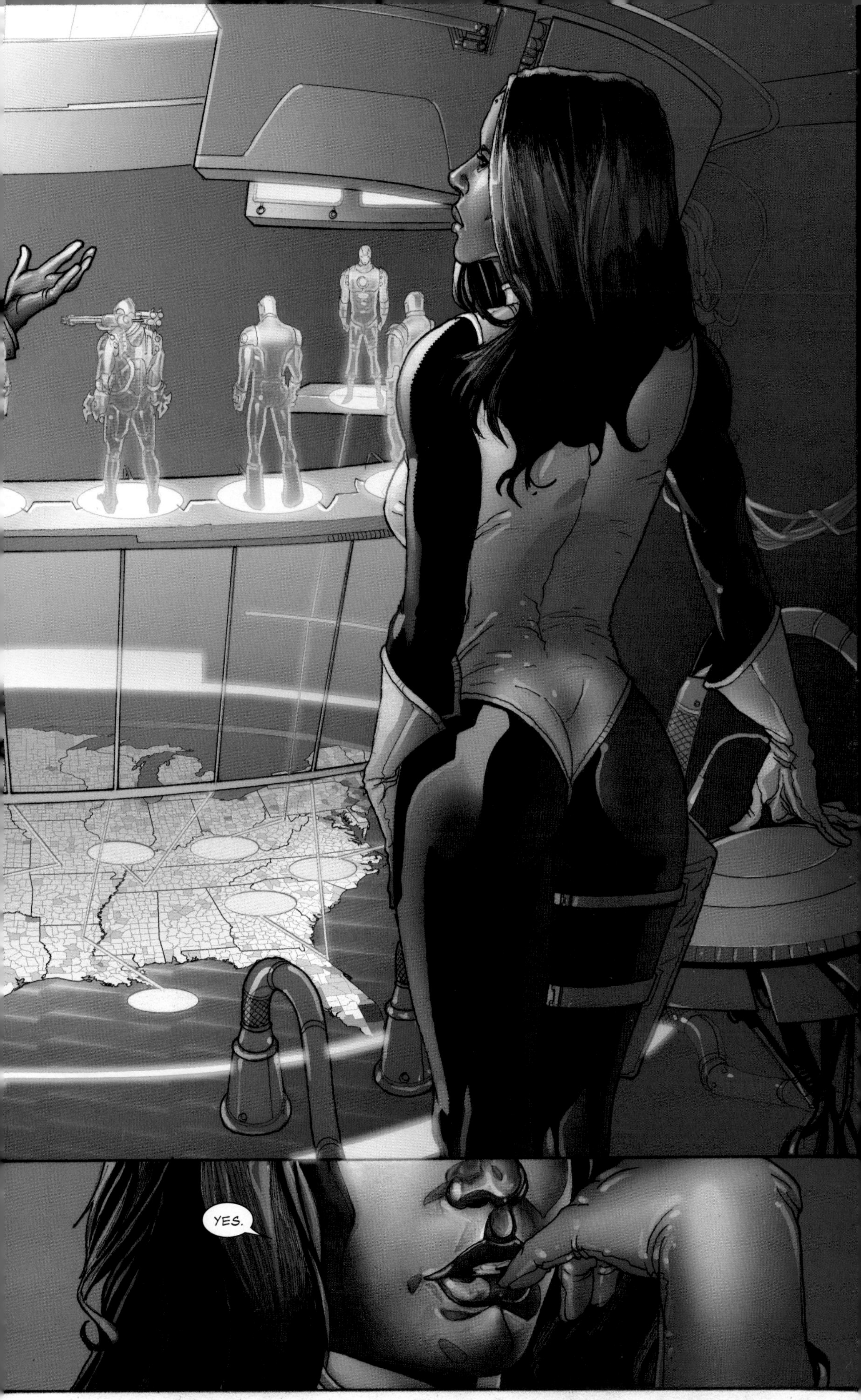
YES.

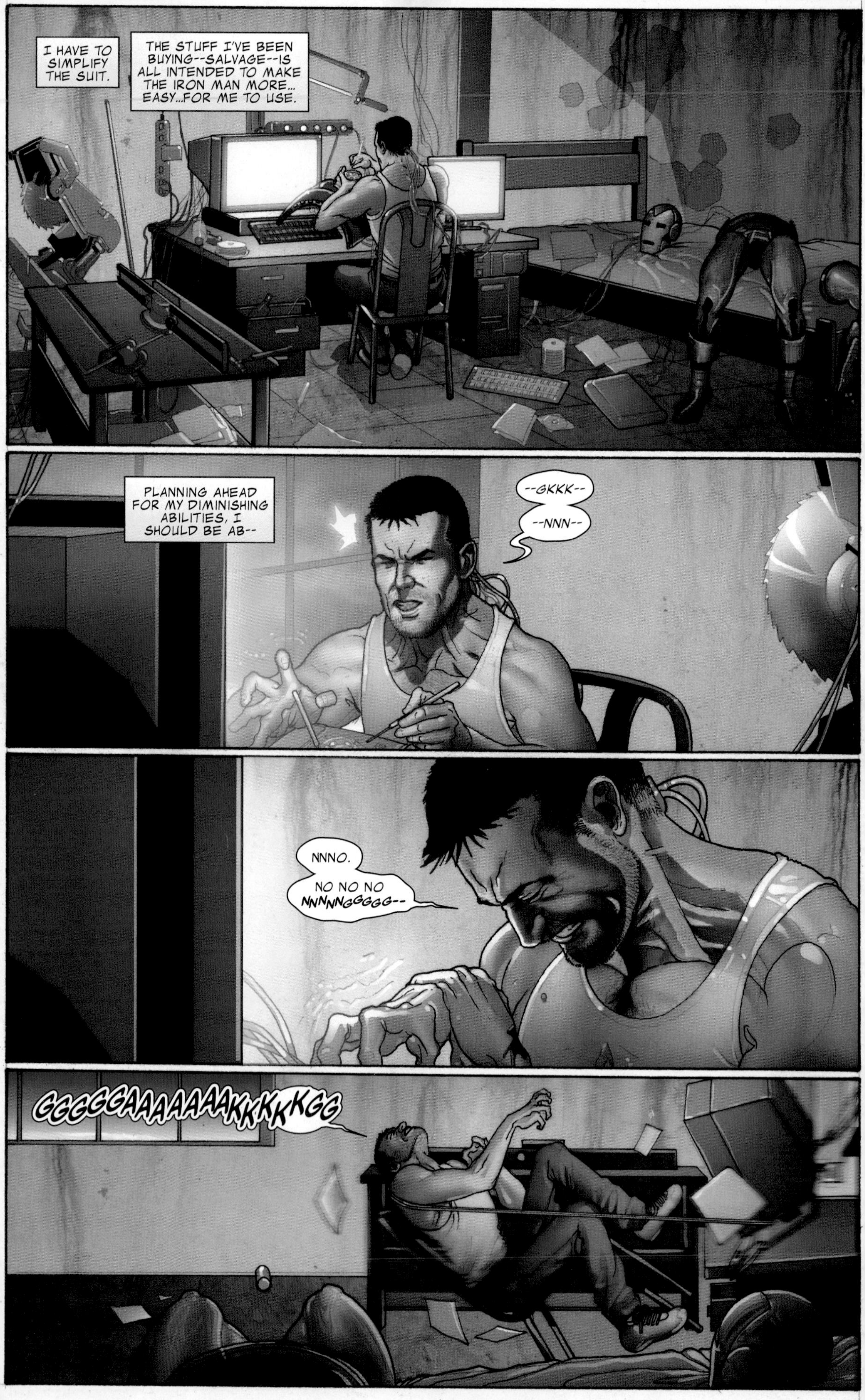
I HAVE TO SIMPLIFY THE SUIT.
THE STUFF I'VE BEEN BUYING--SALVAGE--IS ALL INTENDED TO MAKE THE IRON MAN MORE... EASY...FOR ME TO USE.
PLANNING AHEAD FOR MY DIMINISHING ABILITIES, I SHOULD BE AB--
--GKKK--
--NNN--
NNNO.
NO NO NO NNNNNGGGGG--
GGGGGAAAAAAKKKKKGG

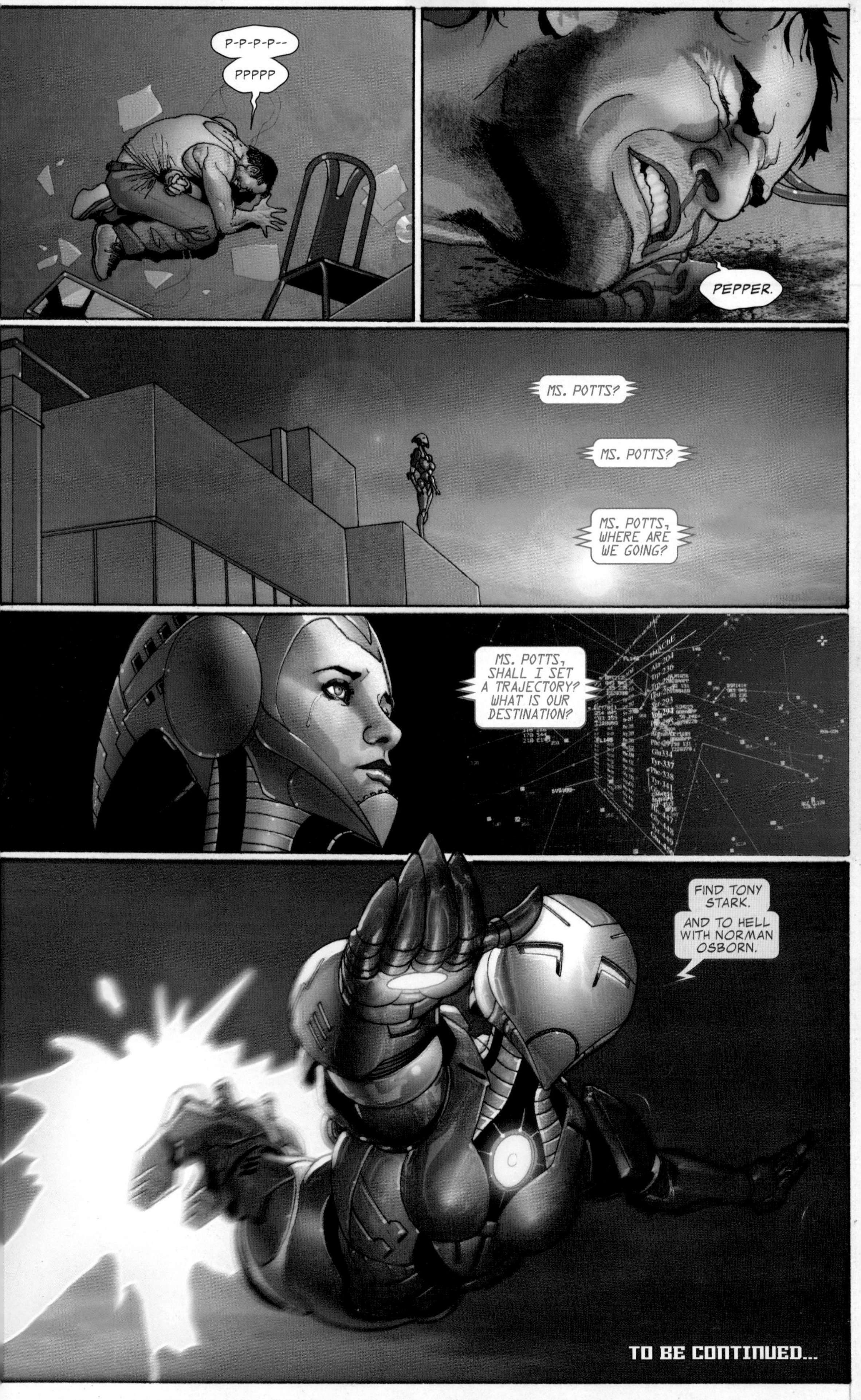
P-P-P-P--
PPPPP
PEPPER.
MS. POTTS?
MS. POTTS?
MS. POTTS, WHERE ARE WE GOING?
MS. POTTS, SHALL I SET A TRAJECTORY? WHAT IS OUR DESTINATION?
FIND TONY STARK.
AND TO HELL WITH NORMAN OSBORN.
TO BE CONTINUED...

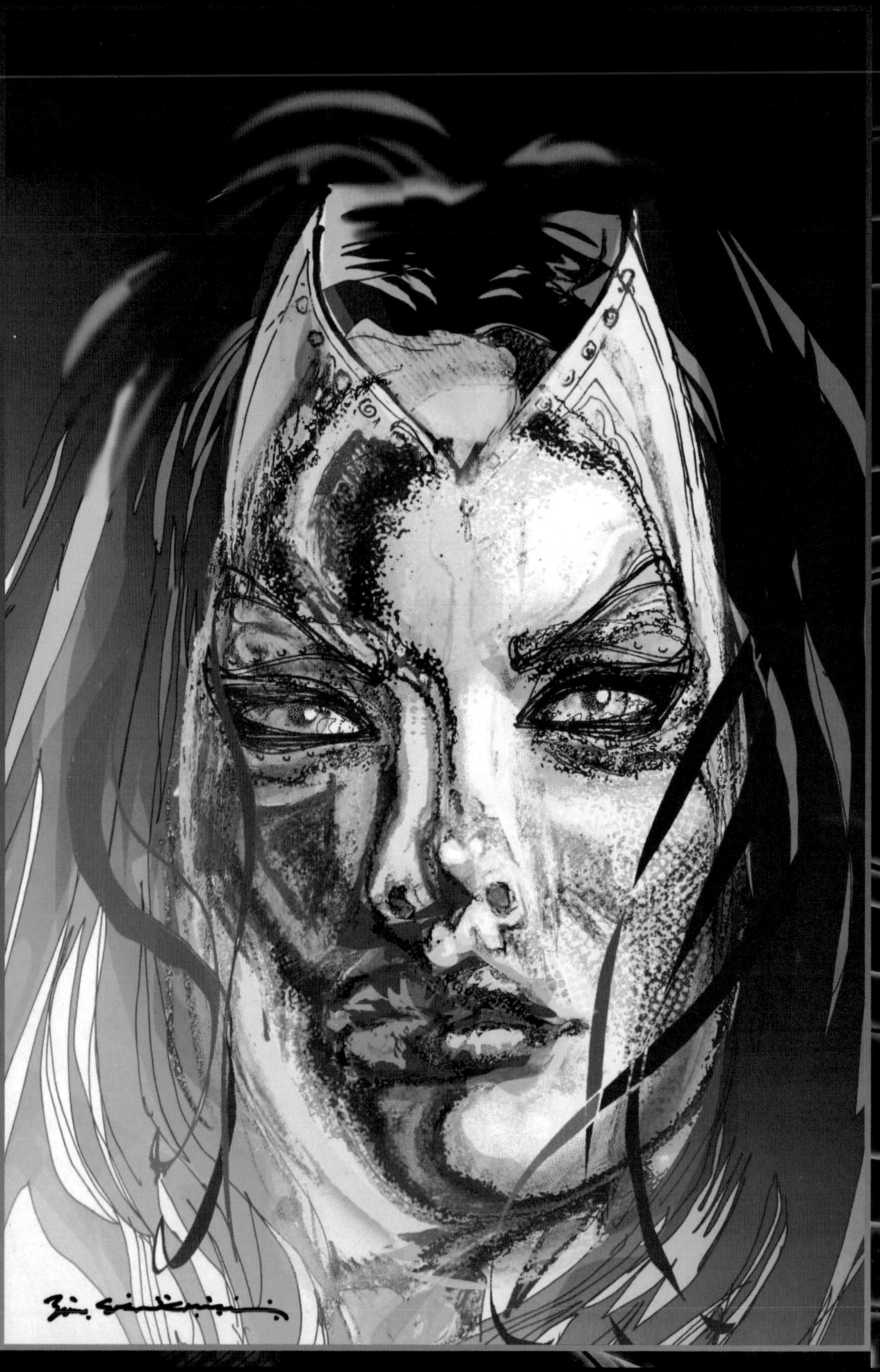

#8 VILLAIN VARIANT BY DAVID AJA
& BILL SIENKIEWICZ

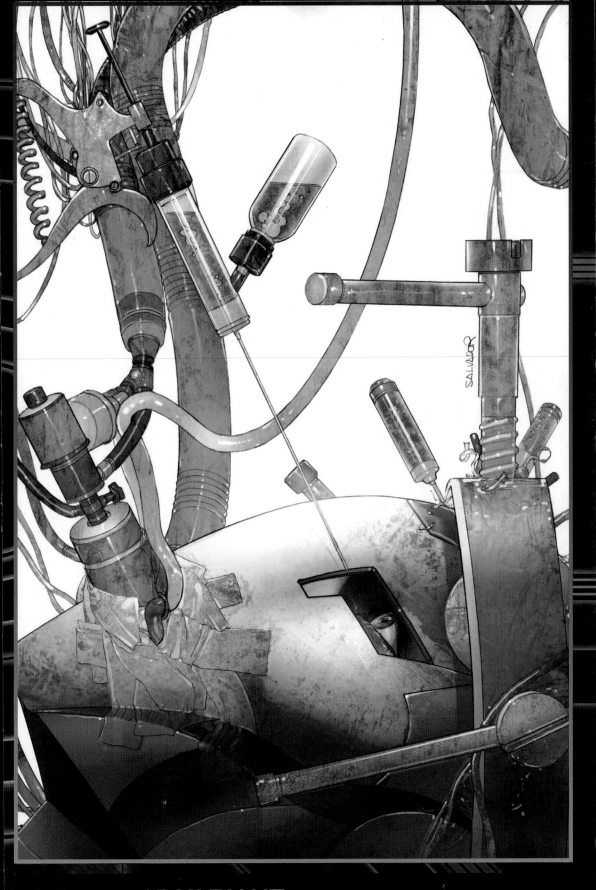

#10 VARIANT BY SALVADOR LARROCA

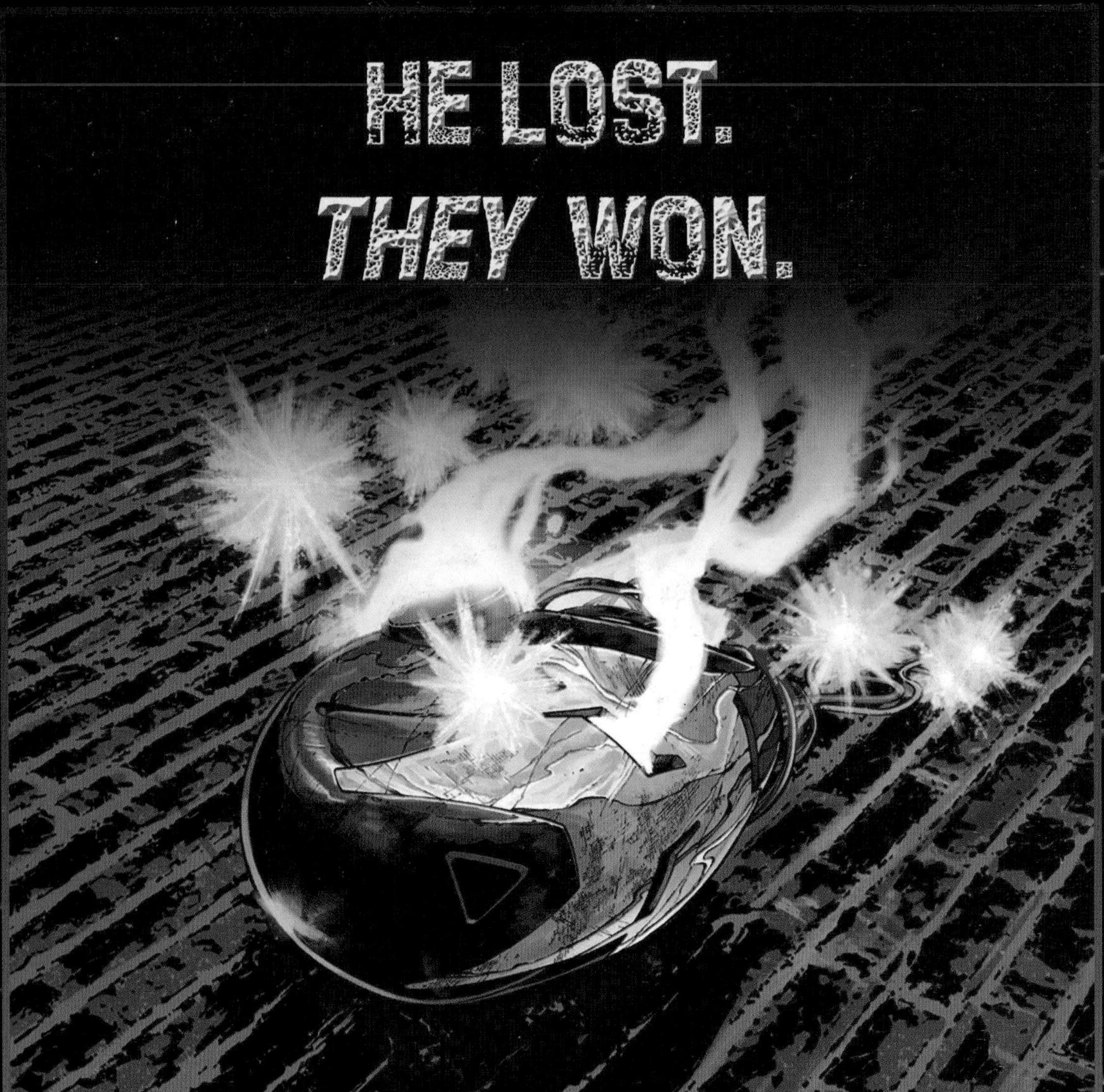
HE LOST.
THEY WON.
ACCEPT CHANGE
DARK REIGN
HAS BEGUN
MARVEL
TM & © 2008 Marvel Characters, Inc. All rights reserved.

DARK REIGN HOUSE AD BY JOE QUESADA

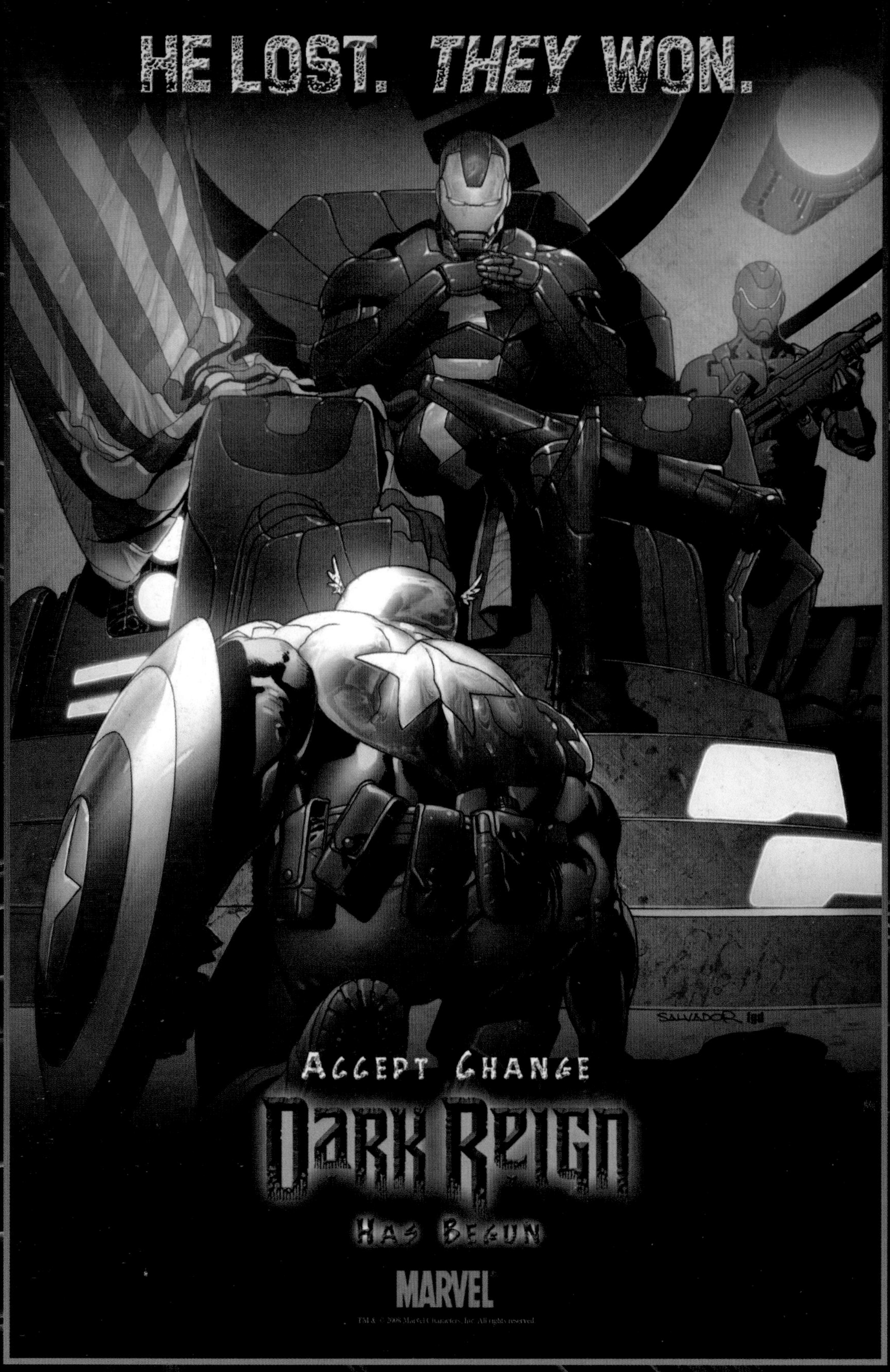

HE LOST. THEY WON.
SALVADOR
ACCEPT CHANGE
DARK REIGN
HAS BEGUN
MARVEL

DARK REIGN HOUSE AD BY SALVADOR LARROCA

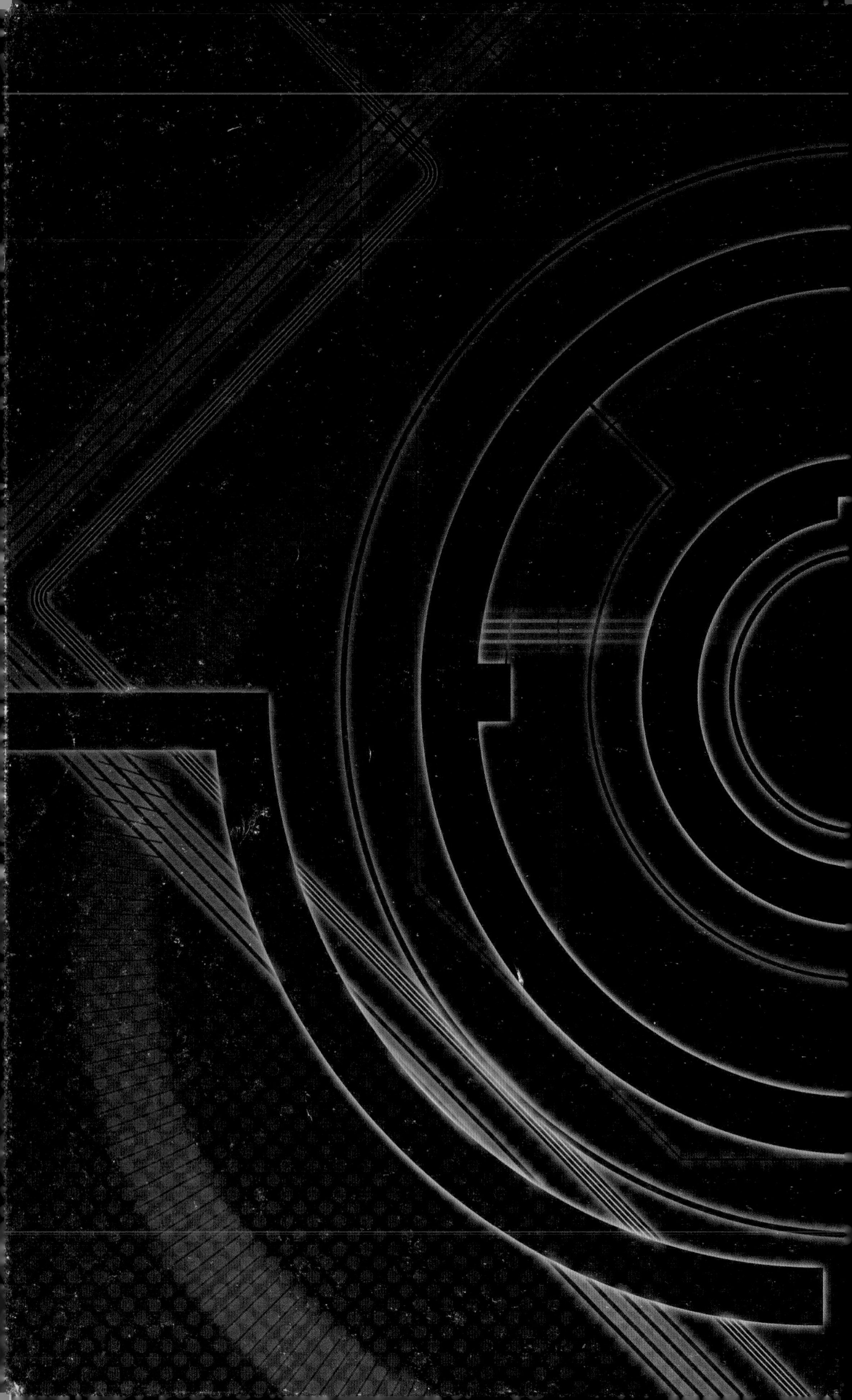